# THE NEW INSURGENCIES

**A Foreign Policy Research Institute Book**

This book is part of a series of works sponsored by the
Foreign Policy Research Institute in Philadelphia.
Founded in 1955, the institute is an independent, nonprofit
organization devoted to research on issues affecting
the interests of the United States.

# THE NEW INSURGENCIES

## Anticommunist Guerrillas in the Third World

### Michael Radu

*With contributions by*
Anthony Arnold, Paul Henze, Justus van der Kroef,
and Jack Wheeler

Transaction Publishers
New Brunswick (U.S.A.) and London (U.K.)

Copyright © 1990 by Michael Radu

All rights reserved under International and Pan-American Copyright Conventions. No part of this book may be reproduced or transmitted in any form or by any means, electronic or mechanical, including photocopy, recording, of any information storage and retrieval system, without prior permission in writing from the publisher. All inquiries should be addressed to Transaction Publishers, Rutgers-The State University, New Brunswick, New Jersey 08903

Library of Congress Catalog Number: 89-35249
ISBN: 0-88738-307-6
Printed in the United States of America

**Library of Congress Cataloging-in-Publication Data**

The New insurgencies : anti-communist guerrillas in the Third World / [edited by] Michael Radu ; with contributions by Anthony Arnold . . . [et al.].
    p.    cm.
    "A Foreign Policy Research Institute book"—Prelim. p.
    Includes bibliographical references.
    ISBN 0-88738-307-6
    1. Anti-communist movements—Developing countries.  2. Guerrillas--Developing countries—History—20th century.  3. Developing countries—Politics and government.  I. Radu, Michael.  II. Arnold, Anthony.
D883.N49    1989
303.6′4—dc20
                                                                                              89-35249
                                                                                               CIP

# Contents

| | | |
|---|---|---|
| Introduction<br>*Michael Radu* | | 1 |
| 1 | ERITREA<br>*Paul B. Henze* | 95 |
| 2 | ANGOLA<br>*Michael Radu* | 127 |
| 3 | MOZAMBIQUE<br>*Jack Wheeler* | 161 |
| 4 | CAMBODIA<br>*Justus van der Kroef* | 197 |
| 5 | AFGHANISTAN<br>*Anthony Arnold* | 233 |
| 6 | NICARAGUA<br>*Michael Radu* | 259 |
| Selected Bibliography | | 289 |
| About the Contributors | | 297 |
| Index | | 299 |

# Introduction

*Michael Radu*

**The Nature of the Phenomenon**

*The Century of the Guerrilla*

Irregular warfare has become the dominant form of war. Unlike conventional wars of this and past centuries, which generally had clear starting and ending points, guerrilla wars seldom begin or end on a specific date. Insurgencies continue for many years, even when the chances of victory are remote or nonexistent. In fact, the very meaning of victory in such wars is drastically different from victory in conventional conflicts: for the governments under attack by insurgents, victory often means the containment rather than the eradication of the guerrillas.

Thus, the British won the Malaya campaign of the 1950s when the Communist party of Malaya (CPM) ceased operating in large areas of the peninsula; Communist guerrillas, however, still operate sporadically in peninsular Malaysia today, almost two decades after the "end" of the conflict. The case of the Omani, British, and Iranian victory over the Dhofar insurgents was far more clearcut, but peculiar circumstances and an unusual terrain played a unique role in that conflict.[1] In Colombia, where the first Communist insurgency started sometime in the late 1950s, the government still faces a continuing challenge from a number of Marxist-Leninist guerrilla groups. None of these groups has ever threatened the existence of the Colombian government, but the government has not been able to eradicate them and completely pacify the countryside, either. This pattern of an insurgency never deadly but never quite dead has plagued the governments of Burma since the 1950s, Guatemala since 1962, Thailand since the 1950s, South Africa (in Namibia and to some extent at home) and Ethiopia since the 1960s, and Nicaragua since 1961.

The Philippines is still the only place in which US military advice and force can claim a decisive share in a victory over a Communist insurgency, over the Huks of the 1950s and early 1960s. However, the first supreme commander of the new and still highly successful New People's Army (NPA), Bernabé Buscayno ("Commander Dante"), now a "legitimate politician," was once a Huk leader.[2]

There are more examples of such indecisive campaigns: Cambodia, Morocco, Chad, Angola, and Mozambique all are countries experiencing more than fifteen years of internal irregular warfare. Insurgencies in El Salvador, Peru, Uganda, Indonesia, Afghanistan, and other countries are at least ten years old. It has become increasingly clear that the twentieth century, which invented the concept of "total war," has also seen permanent internal war develop into a universal phenomenon. Indeed, a growing number of countries, almost all in the Third World, have by now experienced a state of internal war for at least a generation. Cases on three continents, including Colombia, Uganda, the Philippines, Israel, South Africa, Namibia, and Angola, confirm both the geographic and cultural scope of the phenomenon. Finally, in political and legal terms, although the permanent wars phenomenon is a highly unorthodox form of conflict in that none of them has resulted in a formal declaration of war, the concept itself seems to be at least selectively accepted as legitimate by such international sources of public opinion as the International Court of Justice and, particularly, the General Assembly of the United Nations. The implication is that guerrilla wars are acceptable, even legitimate, as long as they have a degree of moral acceptance; the problem is that the criteria of acceptance and ultimately the moral values justifying them are decided by governments whose values and political mores have little in common with those of the West.

In contemporary global political discourse, Japan, New Zealand, Australia, Israel, Western Europe, the United States, and Canada (and sometimes even South Africa, Taiwan, Singapore, and Hong Kong), are all considered "Western." The implicit distinction is between such advanced and essentially politically tolerant countries and the overwhelming majority of states. However, neither language nor political tradition justifies lumping together such diverse countries.

Dismissing the UN or world opinion as misguided or irrelevant, a constant temptation for Western conservatives, raises more questions than it answers, however, especially at a time when a strong Western stance supporting democracy and morality, and the will to enforce it, are increasingly lacking.

The persistence of terrorism, which in itself could be seen as a form of irregular warfare and is always part of guerrilla wars, complicates the picture even further.[3] Terrorism is not simply an adjunct of insurgency; it often takes on a life of its own and becomes a goal rather than a means, especially when used in democratic or relatively democratic countries. Terrorism for its own sake has sporadically plagued the United States (mostly, but not exclusively in regard to Puerto Rico), France, the United Kingdom, West Germany, the Netherlands, and Italy for at least the past fifteen years. However, outside Western Europe, the United States, South Africa, and the Southern Cone of South America, terrorism has seldom flourished for long. In other words, it is primarily in heavily urbanized, industrialized, and most often democratic countries that terrorism, as represented by Action Directe in France, the Red Army Faction in West Germany, the Communist Combatant Cells in Belgium, or the SLA and Weathermen in the United States, has played the most significant role.

It is clearly no accident that all the Western terrorist groups, whether openly Marxist-Leninist and internationalist or separatist, are actively and often rabidly pro-Third World. Without going into the motivations and social or psychological characteristics of such groups, it suffices to say that they all have one major aim in common—the rejection of the moral values, economic principles, and political beliefs central to Western civilization, which are alien and hence inimical to the Third World's own traditions.

While terrorism is the preferred form of action for alienated and marginal groups in developed societies and in traditional Communist societies, guerrilla warfare is the dominant form of action in the Third World and its often rural, always poorly administered and integrated societies. These are also the countries least prepared militarily, technically, and ideologically for the insurgent onslaught. Dubious nationalist credentials, estranged elites, ineffective administration, and urban-biased economic priorities all provide fertile ground for insurgencies. Nevertheless, despite prevailing myths in the West, there is no satisfactory explanation for the appearance, development, or chances of success of any guerrilla group in any Third World country. They may appear, grow, and flourish at a time of renewed hopes for democracy, as Sendero Luminoso did in Peru beginning in 1980; conversely, they may lose the war against decidedly undemocratic regimes, as in Guatemala in the early 1970s and again in 1983–1985; they may also persist or even expand under demagogic or populist regimes (Garcia's Peru, Isabel Perón's Argentina, Corazon Aquino's Philippines) or against democratic ones (as in Colombia and Uruguay before 1973).

The guerrillas' origins thus often have less to do with the "objective" realities in a given country than with the internal dynamics of marginal and alienated groups. Rejection of Western ideas and values is the most important common motivation of such groups, whether "Third Worldist" European or North American terrorists, Islamic fundamentalists in the Middle East, Maoists in Peru and the Philippines, or assorted other Marxist-Leninist sects in southern Africa and Latin America. One may reasonably argue, for example, that the Arabs see Israel as an enemy less for reasons of land, justice, or the Palestinians' right to self-determination than because of the Jewish state's Western, hence alien orientation. Similarly, the Africanization of post-colonial African states did not simply involve the promotion of natives to positions of power. It also involved the rejection of the symbols and bearers of non-African culture, by replacing English with Swahili as the official language in Tanzania, shedding parliamentary democracy as alien, and forcing the mass emigration of millions of Algerian *pied noirs*, Angolan and Mozambican whites, and various other "settlers" across the continent. Even in Latin America, the trend seems to be toward a nostalgia for the pre-Colombian past. The Mexicans' love affair with the Aztecs and their sentimental preference for Cuauhtémoc over Cortés is a symbolic reminder of this trend; the obsession of white, middle-class, educated young Uruguayans, Peruvians, and Argentines' with Túpac Amaru, a defeated Indian chief of eighteenth-century Peru, is another; and Sendero Luminoso's profoundly reactionary politico-economic program is centered on a return to the pre-Colombian "golden age" of the Tehuantinsuyo, the Inca Empire.

*Changing Winds*

For a long time Marxism-Leninism, or more precisely the adaptation of certain basic Marxist ideas to underdeveloped societies as articulated by Lenin, Stalin, and Mao, has served as a useful vehicle for Third World nativists, allowing them to hide a deeply reactionary mentality behind the mantle of Marxist-Leninist ideas of progress. Indeed, while one may have serious doubts that Karl Marx, the German disciple of Hegel and admirer of United States and British cultures, would recognize Abimael Guzmán, Pol Pot, Mengistu Haile Mariam, or Najibullah as his heirs, Lenin, and particularly Stalin and Mao, would.[4] The latter is still perceived as the archetypical Third World interpreter of Marxism-Leninism, even by those groups and regimes that, for pragmatic reasons having to do with their dependence upon Moscow for survival or success, refuse to admit that fact in public. From its inception, in fact, communism as a politico-economic system has been attractive to underdeveloped societies. Lenin's Russia was a decidedly primitive society, politically, economically, and socially, not only by European standards but also in some respects even by comparison with the neighboring central Asian states of Bukhara,

Samarkand, or Khiva. Without exception, Communist regimes have come in power on their own only in relatively underdeveloped countries: China, Yugoslavia, Albania, Vietnam, Cuba, Nicaragua, and Grenada. Everywhere else, they have had to be imposed by force of arms from the outside (East Germany, Hungary, Poland, Czechoslovakia, and even Bulgaria and Romania).

The growing rejection of Westernism in the Third World, Leninism's appeal for African, Asian, or Latin American potentates bent upon conquering and maintaining power, the decline of US power and interest in the Third World after Vietnam, and the opportunistic Soviet involvement in the area after 1975 all led to the emergence of a growing number of hybrid or "pidgin" Marxist-Leninist regimes in Africa, Asia, and Latin America.[5]

The rise of such regimes and their dependence upon foreign — essentially Soviet bloc — support for survival, however, brought about a collusion between communism and Third World traditions. What initially made Marxism-Leninism attractive to Third World elites — its profoundly antidemocratic and anticapitalist nature — increasingly came to be countered by its own Marxist and "Western" inputs: its antireligious, bureaucratic, and antinationalist nature. Marxism-Leninism succeeded as a counter to Westernization, but its inherent totalitarianism provoked increased resistance in the Third World. Socially, Third World Marxism-Leninism appeals principally to alienated elite elements (the intelligentsia, students, and so forth) and lumpenproletarian, marginal urban groups, but it remains alien and threatening to the largely rural population. Third World peasants have little or no experience with government intrusion into their daily lives except for taxation; in other words, they have for centuries lived in what Gunnar Myrdal called *soft states*. According to Myrdal, "The term 'soft state' is understood to comprise all the various types of social indiscipline which manifest themselves by: deficiencies in legislation and particular law observance and enforcement, [and] a widespread disobedience by public officials on various levels to rules and directives handed down to them."[6]

The concept of the soft state helps to account for the growing number of contemporary anticommunist Third World insurgencies, since the soft state is by definition incompatible with Marxism-Leninism. As a revolutionary project, communism is openly hostile to established traditions, as was demonstrated when a handful of well-educated, young Kabul students spread through the Afghan countryside in 1978–1979, carrying the red flag of the "Saur Revolution," killing tribal elders, confiscating land, and forcing girls into schools.[7] This pattern has been repeated from Cambodia to Ethiopia, from Angola to Mozambique, and from Nicaragua to the Peruvian highlands. The government, once a remote and widely distrusted master with whom one could negotiate the price of being largely left alone, suddenly became an overbearing, brutal, threatening, and all—intrusive alien force. In addition, the new authorities, almost universally coming from among minority, usually privileged groups, have only the scantiest knowledge of the realities of their own countries (and often of Marx and Engels as well)[8] but a highly inflated view of their own superiority over the uncouth masses.

In most instances (Nicaragua and Cambodia are prominent exceptions, Eritrea perhaps another), the new Marxist-Leninist regimes did not initially face specifically nationalist resistance to their inherently internationalist outlook. Religion, however, as well as regional and ethnic or racial differences were important from the start. By its very nature Marxism-Leninism seeks to marginalize, discredit, and ultimately eliminate any alternative sources of collective loyalty. The new revolutionary governments, however, were perceived as alien to the majority by the population, and this impression was reinforced by massive numbers of foreigners brought in to support the new governments. In many of these cases, that intrusive alien presence also inflamed historic hatreds—Khmers vs. Vietnamese, Eritrean—Ethiopians vs. Arabs, Afghans vs. Russians—or racial conflicts—blacks vs. whites and *mestiçoes* or Indians in Africa, Indians and Creoles vs. "Spaniards" on Nicaragua's Atlantic coast.

It is in this context that the growing number of insurgencies directed against Marxist-Leninist Third World regimes should be seen. The combination of hostility to Western cultural and political imports, increasingly including Marxism-Leninism in its modernizing and revolutionary forms, and the peasants' reflexive hostility toward an intrusive, internationalist, elitist, urban-based, antireligious, and foreign-supported government explains the motives behind those insurgencies far better than the idea that they stem from a thirst for democracy. Neither history nor political culture, practice, and traditions provide credibility to Cambodian, Afghan, Eritrean, Mozambican, Laotian, or Angolan claims of allegiance to Jefferson's political ideas or Adam Smith's economics.

*A New Development?*

Guerrilla warfare directed against Marxist-Leninist governments is far from new: it started almost at the time the first Communist government was established by the Bolshevik coup of 1917. Indeed, the new Soviet authorities had to deal with periods of endemic ethnic violence in central Asia—the *basmachi* insurgency—until the late 1920s; a strong insurgent movement developed in Tambov in central European Russia in the 1920s;[9]

sporadic "bandit" activities took place in the Ukraine during the collectivization campaign of the 1930s; massive guerrilla activities developed in the Ukraine and Lithuania after World War II, requiring serious efforts and a number of years for the Red Army to eliminate them. In Eastern Europe a large-scale insurgency (Armiya Krajowa) developed in Poland at the same time,[10] and a more limited one (*partizanii*) persisted in Romania until 1956–1957. In the aftermath of Mao's 1949 conquest of power in China, elements of the former nationalist army (KMT) on the southwestern border areas turned to semi-guerrilla tactics against the new regime in Beijing. Finally, in the early 1960s, following Castro's open shift toward Marxism-Leninism and his alliance with the Soviets, a violent insurgency flared in the Sierra de Escambray for a few years.[11]

The long history of insurgency against Marxist-Leninist regimes took on new dimensions on a global scale during the late 1970s and the 1980s, although the contemporary insurgencies in some ways resemble their older precursors. The most significant elements of similarity or continuity are the following:

(1) In many instances, both the old and the new insurgents had to fight against regimes that had themselves come into power through guerrilla warfare—in China and Cuba in the past, and in Nicaragua, Mozambique, Angola, Ethiopia, Cambodia, and Afghanistan today.
(2) In all past and present cases, the insurgents fought against newly established regimes going through a period of consolidation of power. In most instances the regimes in power were recently established; in those of Lithuania, the Ukraine, and Eritrea, the guerrillas fought against the absorption of their countries by the new government.
(3) An important motivation of the insurgents in the past and at present has been the perception that Marxism-Leninism is alien and hostile to local traditions, values, beliefs, national independence, and ethnic/regional self-determination.
(4) In all instances the bulk of the guerrillas' followers and supporters were peasants.

In a philosophical sense, then, what has always served as a catalyst for anticommunist insurgency has been a widespread sense of resistance to forced change as imposed by self-proclaimed revolutionaries of any persuasion. Nationalism as such played a decisive role in the older insurgencies, but, with the exception of Eritrea and post-1978–1979 Cambodia and Nicaragua, played a smaller role, initially, in less developed, more typically Third World societies. From Central Asia in the 1920s[12] to Angola and Mozambique since the late 1970s and Afghanistan in the 1980s, such societies have lacked a national consciousness; instead, popular loyalties, and hence the roots of anticommunist violence, lay in ethnic or even tribal traditions, sometimes supplemented by religion.

The role of Islam in insurgencies in central Asia, Afghanistan, and Eritrea is far more important than the role played by Catholicism in Poland, Lithuania, and Nicaragua, or the Coptic Church in Ethiopia. As an all-inclusive set of religious, moral, legal, and political values and standards, Islam is far more likely to be infringed upon by the totalitarian approach of Marxism-Leninism. Moslems are far less willing to compromise with an all-intrusive, rival set of values and beliefs, to "give to Caesar what is Caesar's," because there can be no Caesar outside the frame of Islam's world view. Moslems cannot easily concede the economic, legal, and political realms to a secular authority and relinquish respect for strictly religious values as easily as Christians have. The Eastern Orthodox form of Christianity, for example, has a long tradition of obedience to the state, which in the Soviet Union and Romania (and now probably Ethiopia as well) has even included clergymen doubling as secret police officers. Marxism has also made inroads into Catholicism under the guise of "liberation theology." As for countries like Angola and Mozambique, where Christianity is limited to a minority of the population, the dominant animism lacks the institutional infrastructure and cohesion necessary to serve as an effective counter to "scientific socialism."

On the other hand, the totalitarian nature of Marxism-Leninism has tended to create instant but sometimes lasting coalitions of individualists rejecting state interference and their opposite: tightly knit ethnic, tribal, religious, or regional groups that resent what they perceive as threatening and alien interference with their old traditions, religion, or group identity. Protracted warfare against a culturally, religiously, and more often than not ethno-racially alien enemy tends to erase or at least minimize old regionalistic, tribal, religious, or other rivalries, and frequently leads to the creation of genuine nationalism, even where none existed before. Nowhere is this process more obvious than in Afghanistan and Angola.[13] In the former instance the almost universally noticed trend toward cooperation between the guerrilla organizations inside the country, though not necessarily among the varying Peshawar politicians, has resulted in uniting Tajiks, Pashtoons, and Turkic-speakers around effective and charismatic commanders, a feat unheard of prior to the 27 April 1978 Communist coup. In Angola, UNITA has attracted not only Ovimbundus, or the related Chokwe and Ganguela ethnics, but also Owambos and recently, and even more important, growing numbers of Bakongos and even Mbundus. The insurgencies in both cases seem to have been catalysts for a new sense of nationhood that has succeeded where traditional anticolonialism and "progressive" proclamatory nationalism had failed.[14] Even in Mozambique, a far more chaotic ethnic and cultural environment, the presence of Soviet bloc military personnel and of Zimbabwean and Tanzanian troops appears to have led to an increasing Mozambican consciousness associated with RENAMO or on the way to doing so.

In a very general sense, anticommunist insurgencies, old as well as new, were the result of a natural rejection of the forced modernization, regimentation, "internationalism," and antinational policies of Marxism-Leninism itself. From Tibet to Croatia, the former Baltic States to Macedonia to Uzbekistan and Georgia or Armenia, the Nicaraguan Zelaya to Eritrea, Marxism-Leninism has consistently and accurately been perceived as a deadly enemy of particularism, whether in the form of cultural traditions, nationalism, or regionalism. Ever since the time of Lenin, Marxism-Leninism of all hues and at all times has proved incapable of resolving what its ideologues from Marx to Stalin euphemistically defined as "the national issue." In fact, that very "national issue" haunts even the Warsaw Pact today, as is demonstrated by the unusual public remonstrances flowing between Budapest and Bucharest over the treatment of the ethnic Hungarians in Romania.

The strongly separatist character of certain contemporary anticommunist insurgencies, then, should come as no surprise. The point is not that Marxist-Leninist regimes are any more prone to secessionist challenges than noncommunist ones, but that they have proved to be as unprepared and ineffective as any other in dealing with them.

A related element is the insurgents' rejection of a strong modernizing government. This has much to do with the nature and origins of both old and new Marxist-Leninist regimes, most of which, as previously mentioned, have been established in politically, culturally, and economically backward countries. In such cases, the state is *soft* in the sense that it does not have the means and skills to control the national territory effectively, but it has an ideological urge to act forcefully. As a result, especially in the consolidation phase, there is an ever-growing and decisive dependence upon "proletarian internationalism" which, in plain terms, means Soviet bloc military and security support. This in turn sharpens the conflict between the regime and the national, ethnic, religious, and regional interests it tries to suppress, resulting in higher levels of resistance requiring even greater dependence upon foreign support. Simply put, since no Third World, Marxist-Leninist regime can come to power and retain it on its own, dependence upon external support is essential. In certain instances, generally involving small countries, that external support may be provided by a neighboring regime of similar orientation, as in the case of the São Tomé and Principe regime of President Manuel Pinto da Costa, whose 100,000 subjects are kept in line by some 600 Angolan troops. More often, however, and in larger countries, external support means large numbers of foreign troops speaking alien languages and exhibiting a drastically different cultural orientation.

As previously mentioned, contemporary Third World anticommunist insurgencies share certain features with older examples of resistance to Communist expansion. The question remains why some peoples did not react violently in the late 1940s, while others did in the 1970s and 1980s, and why those who did fight four decades ago lost, while those fighting today survive and even seem to succeed.

The historic examples of earlier European anticommunist insurgencies aside, organized anticommunist violence has historically been concentrated in Third World areas. Mentality, opportunity, and tradition all play a decisive role in explaining why the Czechs, for instance, accepted totalitarian occupation twice in thirty years without any active opposition or why the Polish Solidarnosc movement did not evolve into a guerrilla or at least urban terrorist organization, while the Afghans took arms against the Communist regime almost instantly.

To begin with, the role of the intelligentsia, susceptible to Marxist influences or prepared to argue and negotiate, is minimal in most of the countries now experiencing anticommunist insurgencies, largely because that social group is both numerically insignificant and essentially removed from any influence over the bulk of the population. Second, the settled, urbanized, and urban societies of Europe have lived under strongly bureaucratic and efficient governments for centuries. Most important, however, is the political culture of so many Third World societies, in which violence is an accepted and perennial instrument of political discourse.

In Angola, Mozambique, Ethiopia, Afghanistan, Laos, Nicaragua (although not in Cambodia), as well as in many other "developing" countries, internal warfare, coups, and other forms of political violence are an endemic and accepted means of political change. The ensuing mentality tends to guarantee that violence is among the first options considered and employed. Specifically, for example, the latest continuous bout of political violence began in Angola in 1961, about the same time as in Eritrea; political violence has been a way of life in Afghanistan for centuries; civil wars have been perennial in Nicaraguan politics since the last century; and internal warfare in Mozambique was only temporarily interrupted by Portuguese rule and has taken on new forms and a new virulence since the mid-1960s.

The majority of the population in Eritrea, Angola, Mozambique, and Cambodia are young enough to have experienced continuous political violence throughout their lives. As an observer of the Eritrean insurgency noted, "I saw only enthusiastic support for EPLF fighters, many younger than the war itself; from birth to combat they have known nothing but struggle against Ethiopia."[15] Afghan toddlers of 1978 are by now experienced guerrilla fighters, and a very significant number of Nicaraguan insurgent field commanders were born between 1958 and 1960, just a few years before the FSLN began its guerrilla campaign against the Somozas.

A culture in which warfare is a central element, having nothing to do with such old-fashioned, paternalistic concepts as *warlike peoples* but based on an acceptance of violence and adaptation to it, is quite incomprehensible to most Westerners, which explains the US fiasco in Lebanon, for instance. And if Western governments have not found a way to deal with this phenomenon, Communist governments are often equally baffled and unable to respond appropriately.

The location of ongoing anticommunist insurgencies, while not a decisive factor in their existence or degree of success, is nevertheless essential for any understanding of their activities and distinguishes them from their older predecessors. All of the six major ongoing insurgencies directed against a Marxist-Leninist government are in countries contiguous to non-Marxist governments; in fact, all are in countries neighboring at least one openly anticommunist state: Honduras for the Nicaraguan RN; South Africa, Zaire, and Malawi for the Angolan UNITA and Mozambican RENAMO, respectively; Sudan and Saudi Arabia for the Eritrean/Tigrean insurgents; Pakistan and Iran for the Afghans; and Thailand for the Cambodians. This is in sharp contrast with the geographical isolation of the Lithuanian and Ukrainian guerrillas during the 1940s (not to mention the Tambov insurgents, isolated in the middle of European Russia). Similarly, socialist Burma was an uncertain sanctuary for the KMT insurgents, and the Escambray's peasants operated in isolated pockets within Cuba.

In addition, contemporary anticommunist insurgents have some of the most forbidding terrain in the world on their side. The dry and often barren Eritrean highlands of Denden and Wanja Mountains and their hot lowlands, Angola's "land at the end of the earth," Mozambique's poorly inhabited Gorongosa massif and the Nyassa, Tete, and Cabo Delgado provinces, Cambodia's Cardamom Mountains and jungle-covered Thai border regions, the Afghan Hindukush, and the inhospitable eastern half of Nicaragua all provide opportunities for the guerrillas and obstacles for their enemies that did not exist in Eastern Europe in the 1940s or in Cuba in the early 1960s.

Finally, with the exception of Afghanistan, the insurgents operate in regions far removed from the Soviet Union. Despite modern logistics, communications, weapons, and transportation, this fact is in favor of the insurgents. Politically, logistically, and ultimately in practical terms, the Soviets can only do so much in support of their beleaguered satellites. Clearly, neither the Soviets nor their protégés, primarily because of distance, logistical difficulties, and personnel constraints, can employ the same primitive but effective counterinsurgency methods that they used in eastern Poland, the western Ukraine, Lithuania, Romania, or Cuba—sheer saturation of the field with troops and sealing off the borders.

What was once a principal advantage for the Communist insurgencies, and set them apart from older anticommunist ones—friendly and immune havens—has been lost in many instances for Communist anti-insurgent forces. The costs of sustained and massive Vietnamese attacks against Thailand, or Soviet attacks against Pakistan, Iran, or China, and so forth, is simply prohibitive. On the other hand, control of borders is essential in any attempt to contain, let alone eliminate an insurgency. Alternatives may be devised, but they cannot be as effective as geographical isolation. The days of fighting against brave but isolated nationalist Lithuanians or Ukrainians, or Tambov peasants are decidedly over. Moreover, in a time of global communications, and despite the limitations the Western media impose on itself, "quiet" genocide as an effective counterinsurgency strategy is increasingly difficult, as are the massive shootings of peasant insurgents and their families as in Sierra de Escambray or the Ukraine.

*Ideology*

The new anticommunist insurgencies, unlike the older ones, lack a uniform ideology. Some are anticommunist only insofar as they fight against established Marxist-Leninist regimes, but not in terms of their own ideological inclinations. Thus, the largest and most effective group in the Cambodian insurgency continues to be the Khmer Rouge, themselves committed Maoists and one of the most radical, bloody, and extreme sects of Maoism at that; at least one of the major Eritrean guerrilla forces (the EPLF), as well as the Tigray National Liberation Front in Ethiopia are also self-proclaimed Marxist-Leninists. At least in the case of the Eritrean guerrillas, the roots of the leadership's ideological inclinations are a result of the following influences: a dominant Third World elite perception of "imperialism and neo-colonialism" as a strictly Western characteristic; educating insurgent leaders in European and North American universities dominated by left-wing faculty; and a search for simple solutions to the problems of underdevelopment. In addition, *proletarian internationalism*—manifested by past Cuban and Soviet military, financial, and training support—has shaped insurgent ideologies. Indeed, until the Soviet Union and Cuba decided that internationalism and geo-political interests could justify support for the Addis Ababa regime in 1977, the EPLF was one of Havana's and, indirectly, Moscow's favorites. As time went by, however, Eritrean nationalism developed as a result of the war, and the previous "internationalist solidarity" of the Soviet bloc and Cuba with the Eritrean "freedom fighters" gave way to pro-Ethiopian, anti-secessionist policies. Pressures from below, frustration, a sense of betrayal, and practical considerations requiring an adjustment to the interests of the Saudis, Kuwaitis, and other conservative Arab sources of funds and arms resulted in the Eritrean leadership's downplaying Marxism-Leninism. The original leaders did not change their beliefs (Marxist-Leninists seldom do), but they were increasingly faced with factional challenges, forced into compromises, and threatened with splits within the organization that ultimately led to their being replaced with more opportunistic leaders.

As for the Khmer Rouge, while there should be no illusions about their proclaimed conversion to political pluralism or economic free enterprise, the very fact that they have made public statements to that effect indicates their understanding of the nature of their struggle. The same applies to the Khmer Rouge's main supporter, China, which publicly admits that anticommunism, nationalism, rather than a sectarian intra-Communist fight, is the best image to present to the outside world. It thus appears that for opportunistic and pragmatic reasons, rather than ideological conversion, committed, hard-line Cambodian Communists are prepared to pay lip service to Western values, including democracy and free enterprise, because in the opinion of their Chinese sponsors that is the only alternative to political oblivion.

Almost inevitably, the long record of successes by pro-Communist guerrillas and their tactics had a strong impact on anticommunist insurgents. All of them, to some extent, have learned from and imitated Communist insurgency methods, another indication of the latter's theoretical and practical attractiveness. In fact, even the Nicaraguan insurgents, by history and attitude the least inclined towards Marxism-Leninism, are increasingly making use of traditional leftist guerrilla tactics.[16] Indeed, significant elements of the Nicaraguan resistance were and some still are socialist-inclined, although not Marxist, and some, like Edén Pastora, have openly espoused admiration for Ernesto "Che" Guevara.

None of the well-established tactics of Communist guerrillas is new for Jonas Savimbi of UNITA, who has himself claimed to be pro-Chinese, as has Holden Roberto of the FNLA. Some of the founding leaders of RENAMO were former members of the self-proclaimed Marxist-Leninist (and initially pro-Chinese) FRELIMO. These examples are indications of the deep appeal of Leninism, particularly in its Third World incarnations (Maoism and Guevarism); more important, however, they also suggest that while its methods are recognized as useful and effective, they could be employed in support of anticommunist goals. It is indeed ironic to witness UNITA being far more successful in its indoctrination and politicization of the Angolan masses than its orthodox Communist foes in Luanda.

Some of the most successful anticommunist insurgents today have been influenced by Communist guerrilla strategies. Jonas Savimbi met Mao Zedong and he admires and still follows Mao's basic politico-military precepts; Ahmad Shah Massoud's Panjshir Valley organization in Afghanistan is to no small extent the result of Massoud's studying Mao's strategy and tactics;[17] and the Nicaraguan resistance commander Enrique Bermudez is also well-versed in Mao's theories on irregular warfare. In fact, all successful insurgents of the twentieth century have been students of Mao, Fidel Castro and Vo Nguyen Giap, rather than George Washington, in both ideological and tactical terms.

The paradox of Communist methods being used against Communist regimes by anticommunist insurgents raises a number of methodological as well as practical questions, the most important of which relates to the definition of an anticommunist insurgency. Are the Khmer Rouge or the EPLF "anticommunist" when they continue to see themselves as Marxist-Leninists? The answer to this question is twofold: ideologically, such insurgent groups are clearly not anticommunist; but in terms of the target of their activities — a self-proclaimed Marxist-Leninist regime — they clearly are. In Leninist parlance they are "objectively" anticommunists; similarly, in geopolitical terms they are also "anticommunists."

This distinction between ideological and functional anticommunist guerrillas is crucial and has been taken into consideration throughout this study. Clearly, the Khmer Rouge, the TPLF and the EPLF are extremely effective insurgent forces — far more so than their respective non-Marxist allies, and that very fact raises practical as well as moral and political questions for the United States. Indeed, if the US goal in various parts of the world, such as Cambodia and Ethiopia is the establishment of independent instead of pro-Soviet regimes, support for groups such as the EPLF or the Khmer Rouge makes practical sense. On the other hand, if the aim is the establishment of noncommunist regimes in such countries, the only means available for reaching it is arming the weak and ineffective noncommunist groups and preparing for a three-way war: between the ruling Communist regime, the noncommunist and the Communist guerrillas. That is precisely the quandary facing Washington in Cambodia, where neither the continuous presence of the Vietnamese occupation troops nor a victory of the anti-Vietnamese coalition as presently constituted (i.e. militarily dominated by the Khmer Rouge) seems acceptable. The main solution offered, that of Congressman Stephen Solarz, involves US arming the Sihanoukists and the forces of Son Sann against both the Khmer Rouge and the Phnom Penh regime. Not surprisingly, Solarz' approach faced heavy congressional and executive resistance, since it implied US micromanagement of a remote guerrilla war in Indochina — a place Congress and the White House alike would like to avoid — and on the side of the weakest elements.

Their formal ideological commitments aside, the recruitment, mobilization, command and control, propaganda, and training patterns of *functional* anticommunists (such as the Khmer Rouge) often differ sharply from those of the *ideological* anticommunist insurgents (such as the Nicaraguans, RENAMO and UNITA). The former are far more likely to employ coercion to recruit followers or to use civilians than the latter; conversely, the latter are far more vulnerable to outside pressures in the name of human rights and democratic freedoms, even when those are weakening their military effectiveness.

Despite the often confused and confusing proclamations of various anticommunist insurgent groups, certain patterns are discernible in their general ideological orientation. Leaving aside the Marxist-Leninist Khmer Rouge and EPLF and some of the minor and more incoherent Nicaraguan groups claiming a socialist orientation, the fundamental thrust of anticommunist insurgent movements is directed toward cultural and political self-determination rather than either nationalism or "democracy." Certainly, the KPNLF and MOULINACA (Mouvement de Libération Nationale du Cambodge, composed of the followers of Prince Norodom Sihanouk) in Cambodia are primarily nationalists whose aim is to preserve the Cambodian people and culture, which were threatened with extinction by the Khmer Rouge until 1978 and by the massive Vietnamization which followed it. The Eritreans and Tigreans, their leaders' Marxism-Leninism aside, pursue fundamentally separatist goals on behalf of a growing national consciousness in those regions. For UNITA and, in a less articulate manner for RENAMO in Mozambique and for the Afghans, the main motivation is the rejection of an alien ideology and system of government propped up by foreign troops. In neither case could this combination of motives be defined as nationalism, but the trend seems to be toward an incipient and increasingly articulate national consciousness.

Only in Nicaragua is the fundamental goal of the insurgents accurately defined by Western standards of nationalism as a democratic expression.

Convenient rhetoric aside, nowhere else is democracy the genuine goal of the insurgents. Jonas Savimbi, Afonso Dlakhama, Gulbuddin Hekmatyar and Yunis Khales, Prince Norodom Sihanouk, and Son Sann are certainly not Jeffersonians at heart, and they are all aware of the incompatibility between democracy and their countries' traditional political culture. They are all, at least in part, products of their native political culture and, regardless of their real or alleged personal beliefs, they continue to represent their followers' inchoate, but hardly democratic, political beliefs.

As expressions of societies in an uneasy transition between pre-modern and contemporary patterns of societal development, the anticommunist insurgencies are seldom in a position to formulate clear, articulate, or coherent *programs*. The West, more familiar with the articulate and detailed programs presented by even the most insignificant Marxist-Leninist organizations, more often than not led and created by university graduates, has great difficulty in accepting the fact that the peasants of Afghanistan, Angola, Mozambique, Eritrea and Tigray, Cambodia, and Nicaragua are less articulate than the rulers of the regimes they fight against. Nowhere is this problem more acute than in the case of Mozambique, where RENAMO's inability to produce sleek propaganda pamphlets is widely interpreted as an indication that the insurgents are nothing but "bandits." In fact, RENAMO is simply the least sophisticated but arguably one of the most popularly rooted contemporary insurgencies, whose military leaders are simple men lacking the sophistication of a Jonas Savimbi (who has a Ph.D. from Lausanne), the American-trained Calero and Bermudez, French- or even Sorbonne-educated Saloth Sar (a.k.a. Pol Pot), Son San, and Norodom Sihanouk, the West-European-trained Eritrean leaders, or the Islamic scholars leading the political fronts of the Afghan resistance.

To a large degree RENAMO represents the purest Third World rejection of Marxism-Leninism and Western political ideas in general; perhaps for this very reason it remains the most alien and therefore the least palatable of the anticommunist insurgent groups, even for such consistently anticommunist Western leaders as Margaret Thatcher, Ronald Reagan, and Aníbal Cavaco da Silva of Portugal. RENAMO's rejection of Westernism is shared to some degree by all anticommunist insurgent movements but, unlike RENAMO, few of the others lack totally the well-educated and articulate spokesperson who could make such groups more acceptable to Western conservatives. In other words, RENAMO lacks the basic and vital public relations capabilities of most other contemporary insurgent groups on both the left and the right.

The functional and ideological types of anticommunist insurgency share some of the same theoretical and practical principles, as well as classic insurgency and counterinsurgency theories. In strictly military terms, Marxist strategic and tactical theories may be the most important factor to consider in examining the performance of many anticommunist insurgencies and their government adversaries, and they can perhaps best be understood as a paradoxical result of the decades-long Western neglect and ignorance of the true nature of guerrilla warfare.

*The Reversibility of Warfare Posture*

It is often said by counterinsurgency professionals that the best anti-insurgency tactic is to imitate the methods of the insurgents themselves, and in fact some of the most successful counterinsurgency campaigns of this century have been based upon this principle. The success of the Guatemalan military in eradicating most of the Marxist-Leninist guerrillas in the late 1960s and again in the mid-1980s was in large part due to the role played by the *Kaibiles*, special troops trained to operate like guerrillas in small, self-sufficient, and self-sustaining units. Similarly, the Rhodesian Selous Scouts, by far the most effective element in the Rhodesian counterinsurgency effort, operated exactly like their insurgent opponents;[18] the most effective US units in Vietnam were special forces and long-range reconnaissance units that copied their opponents' techniques; and the similarly trained Portuguese *flechas* (arrows) and *trupas especiais paraqaidistas* were equally successful in Mozambique and Angola.[19] These units, however, although trained to mimic the tactics of guerrilla warfare, do not really illustrate the phenomenon of reversibility I analyze here, which only became a recognizable pattern after the chain of Communist guerrilla successes inaugurated by the Chinese under Mao.

The new pattern of reversal of roles affects both sides of the conflict. On the one hand, in such countries as Nicaragua, regular anti-insurgency elite troops have became insurgents themselves. On the other hand, guerrillas have been retrained in the tactics of regular warfare.[20] RENAMO guerrillas like Afonso Dlakhama and the organization's founder, André Matsangaisse, were retrained as regulars by Hungarian, Soviet, and Cuban instructors only to return to irregular warfare as dissidents; after a decade of guerrilla warfare, UNITA experienced a brief and unsuccessful period as a regular force in 1975-1976, only to return to the bush afterwards; the Khmer Rouge guerrillas conquered power and trained as regulars under Chinese supervision for a brief time, but they returned to unconventional warfare less than three years afterwards,[21] and Nicaraguan anti-Somoza insurgents, retrained as regulars by the Soviets, Cubans, or East Europeans, are now back in the hills as guerrillas.

In all of these instances the present guerrillas have at least some experience as regular soldiers; only in Ethiopia and perhaps Afghanistan have the insurgents had little or no experience in regular warfare and counterinsurgency.[22] For the most part, then, anticommunist insurgents may well be the best-trained and most experienced and effective irregular forces in the world today.

Their opponents, however, in Nicaragua, Afghanistan, Mozambique, Angola, and Cambodia have had little or no anti-insurgency combat experience, or, as in the cases of Mozambique, Angola, and to some extent Nicaragua, were retrained for conventional warfare due to misguided and ideologically based threat perceptions. Thus, Nicaragua's enormous army has been armed and trained to resist a US invasion and to deter its neighbors from reacting to Managua's subversion of their societies, rather than to fight the *contras*; the Angolan and Mozambican armies were retrained and rearmed to meet anticipated South African (or Rhodesian) conventional attacks, with no thought of counterinsurgency—after all, "the people" are not supposed to rebel, let alone organize and arm themselves against the government of a "people's republic." The situation was different in Afghanistan, although even there the invading Soviet army expected some type of conventional challenge and therefore included air-defense units among its troops. In Cambodia, where the guerrillas are still largely the Khmer Rouge, a semi-regular force by 1978, the occupying Vietnamese troops had a more reasonable motivation for being conventionally armed.

At present, efforts by Marxist-Leninist regimes against their internal insurgent opponents seem to demonstrate that it is far more difficult for former guerrillas to become an effective counterinsurgency force than for former counterinsurgency forces or guerrillas either to be effective or to increase the level of their effectiveness. This is amply demonstrated by the relatively poor performance of the Vietnamese army in Cambodia and by the even less impressive performance of the Angolan and Mozambican armed forces (FAPLA and FPLM, respectively), both of which were retrained in conventional warfare tactics by Soviet bloc officers.

It is in light of all these complex patterns of role reversal and their implications that the performance of the anticommunist insurgents should be examined, as well as their intelligence, logistical, communications, and equipment capabilities. Furthermore, you should keep in mind that these are guerrilla groups, and therefore cannot be judged by the criteria applicable to regular forces.

## Performance

The criteria for successful guerrilla warfare are resiliency and survivability, adaptability and growth, low casualty ratios, and an expanding area of operations. Judged by these criteria, a number of the contemporary anticommunist insurgencies are performing extremely well.

Resiliency and survivability characterize all six insurgencies considered in this study. The Eritrean insurgency started in September 1961 against the former Ethiopian empire and has continued unabated ever since; UNITA, established in 1966, started its war against the MPLA even before the latter became the recognized government of Angola in November 1975; RENAMO's activities began in 1978, as did those of the largest of the Afghan mujahedeen organizations; the Khmer Rouge were active from the moment they were pushed out of Phnom Penh by the invading Vietnamese, and the KPNLF and Sihanoukhists began fighting by 1980; the Nicaraguan insurgency started in 1981. The Eritreans, UNITA, and the Khmer Rouge all now have many fighters and even low-level field commanders who were born after the beginning of the insurgency.

All insurgent organizations have also recovered from apparently decisive defeats: the Eritreans in 1978–1979, UNITA in 1976–1977, the Khmer Rouge in 1979, RENAMO in 1980, the Afghans in 1984–1985, and the Nicaraguans in 1985. All fight against well-armed and often very large forces, including seasoned foreign troops, but they have succeeded, nevertheless, in steadily increasing their numbers and expanding their appeal to the population. If, as Mao Zedong put it in 1937, "the first law of war is to preserve ourselves and to destroy the enemy," a law still not understood by many US congressmen, all anticommunist insurgencies have at least succeeded in meeting the first condition.

## Adaptability and Growth

If the ability to survive over time in the field is the basic criterion for assessing a guerrilla organization's performance, its ability to adapt to changing military and political circumstances and to expand are good indications of its chances for success. In terms of the ability to make the transition from a completely irregular force engaged in hit-and-run operations against relatively small targets to a semi-regular force capable of taking or defending static positions against large enemy forces, UNITA is clearly the most successful. Its defeat of some 10,000 FAPLA troops in head-on clashes along the Lomba River in November 1987 is only the most recent conventional battle fought and won by Savimbi's forces. The

Eritrean insurgents have long proved adept at a largely positional, "Verdun"-type (mass assault, World War I massive casualty attack) trench warfare, at least in the mountains,[23] and they have also successfully resisted conventional attacks against major positions, such as Nacfa. The KPNLF and the Khmer Rouge, during the 1985 "war of the camps" successfully slowed down the advancing Vietnamese and evacuated their forces and the civilian population in order; the Nicaraguans demonstrated in 1987 that they can attack, if not defend significant installations like Siuna and Rosita in Northern Zelaya. As for RENAMO, it appears capable of taking small- or medium-sized localities in Mozambique, and has repeatedly done so, but it does not have the means to retain or protect them, particularly against air attacks. In terms of Mao's definition of the stages of guerrilla warfare—preparation and indoctrination; sabotage, terrorism and hit-and-run tactics (or progressive expansion); and decision or destruction of the enemy—UNITA, RENAMO, and the mujahedeen are in varying degrees well into the third stage.[24] The Eritreans temporarily reached that stage in 1977, while the Cambodians and Nicaraguans have reached the second. The small anticommunist insurgencies still in progress in Laos and Vietnam are still in the early period of the first stage.

Mao's prescriptions for the establishment and evolution of a guerrilla organization, however, have not been followed to the letter by the six major anticommunist insurgencies. Mao's theoretical premise, reinforced by his own experience, is that an insurgency begins at the political level and translates political support and popular acceptability into military strength as it goes along. That was clearly the path followed by UNITA and the Khmer Rouge (as well as the other two Cambodian insurgent forces), and by the Eritreans and RENAMO. In the case of Afghanistan, however, there was little need for political work among a population thoroughly alienated by the post-April 1978 regime and already armed (or at least experienced with weapons). The mujahedeen, simply skipped Mao's first stage, while the Nicaraguan insurgents began as a military force of ex-professionals, either former guardsmen or ex-Sandinista revolutionaries, and went back to Mao's first stage in order to reach the second stage in a far stronger position.

How guerrillas adapt to changing circumstances is particularly relevant in the case of the anticommunist insurgents. Indeed, drastic counterinsurgency strategies are not normally to be expected from noncommunist regimes in response to leftist guerrilla pressures, except as a result of the change from a democratic to a military regime, and leftist guerrillas have a rather poor record in adapting to such changes. As demonstrated by the followers of Carlos Marighella in Brazil in the 1960s, the Tupamaros in

Uruguay, and the Montoneros and ERP (Ejercito Revolucionario del Pueblo) in Argentina in the early 1970s, radical changes in counterinsurgency tactics often result in the extirpation of "progressive" insurgent groups. Anticommunist insurgents, however, have proved more adaptable. The Eritreans successfully withstood Mengistu Haile Mariam's ruthless mass attacks; UNITA thrives today, even in the face of attacks by a Cuban-backed and Soviet-trained FAPLA; and the Nicaraguans and RENAMO have successfully shifted from counterinsurgency to insurgency and from one type of insurgency to another, which indicates a high degree of flexibility and adaptability. The Khmer Rouge seem to have been born to be guerrillas, and they may have actually welcomed the return to irregular warfare imposed upon them by the Vietnamese in December 1978. KPNLF officers trained in conventional and COIN (counterinsurgency) warfare by the United States and France and marginally active against the Khmer Rouge before 1979 have also proved themselves adept at irregular warfare.

Contemporary counterinsurgency is a far cry from what it was as late as the Malayan and even Dhofar campaigns; and Communist counterinsurgency has always differed from that of British, French, or American campaigns. High technology, HIND helicopter gunships, jet-fighter ground support, heavy use of armor, and sophisticated and ruthless intelligence collecting are the rule for Communist COIN. As a result, the guerrillas had to adapt their largely peasant force to the demands of contemporary warfare. Contrary to many accepted Western notions, there seems to be no relationship between the technological sophistication of a country, as defined by such criteria as literacy, number of radios, TV sets, and computers, and the insurgent forces' ability to master modern weapons. What mujahedeen leader Abdul Haq claimed regarding his own people and the use of the stinger ground-to-air missile may be equally applicable to other Third World guerrillas, of both Marxist-Leninist and anticommunist persuasions: "Most Afghans have a natural understanding of weapons. It may take several months to train an American soldier to use the stinger. I am sure some of my mujahedeen can use the stinger with only a few hours of training."[25]

It is interesting to note that UNITA's rate of success with the stinger by 1987 was about 80 percent while the mujahedeens' was only 60 percent. Perhaps the reason is that UNITA's fighters, trained in Morocco and South Africa, were more familiar with modern weapons than the Afghans, who had to graduate from 1898 Lee Enfields to stingers in only one year. One fact is clear and disproves narrowly racist views about adaptability: black Ovimbundus and "Aryan" Pashtoons, facing the same challenge, succeed according to prior experience and training, not because of race, culture, or literacy levels. It is a lesson that the Soviets in Afghanistan, with their contempt for the "uncouth savages" of the Hindukush, or in Angola, where they have consistently treated UNITA (as well as their own MPLA allies, for that matter) as inferior, have never really understood.

Difficult though it may be for a Westerner to accept, it is far easier for an Afghan, Angolan, or Mozambican to learn how to use a sophisticated missile than to learn to read and write in his own language. Statistics support the claim of rapid adaptation to the use of modern weapons: after only one year of using stingers, the mujahedeen came close to having identical kill ratios with UNITA.

*Casualty Ratios*

Successful COIN results in a high casualty rate for insurgents. For instance, the South African Defense Force (SADF) in Namibia has consistently reached a 10:1 or even 20:1 casualty ratio against the SWAPO insurgents over the past two decades,[26] and the Rhodesians maintained a ratio of well over 10:1 against the Patriotic Front guerrillas between 1973 and 1978.[27] No Communist counterinsurgency operation during the past decade has resulted in such advantageous kill ratios. In Angola and Mozambique, government forces and their assorted allies may in fact have suffered higher casualties than UNITA and RENAMO, at least over the past five years. In Nicaragua the EPS has perhaps reached a 2:1 ratio, probably more than the Kabul/Soviet forces in Afghanistan and perhaps the same as the Vietnamese in Cambodia. Likewise, at least until the shift from mass attacks to more conventional counterinsurgency tactics in the early 1980s, the Addis Ababa regime has suffered far more casualties than the Eritrean and Tigrean insurgents.

The very size of the insurgent forces in most instances makes it impossible for government forces to reach the 10:1 numerical advantage required by orthodox COIN doctrine.[28] Even by the most conservative estimates available, in Angola the regime's forces of 100,000, supplemented by about 65,000 assorted foreign troops, face over 40,000 guerrillas; the almost 400,000 Ethiopian forces (of which 169,000 are militiamen) face some 34,000 guerrillas; in Mozambique, 25,000 regulars and militias, plus as many as 10,000 allies (mostly Zimbabweans), face a 15,000-strong RENAMO; the 77,000 regulars and territorial militias of the Kabul regime and their 115,000 Soviet allies faced as many as 200,000 mujahedeen by mid-1988; the 160,000 Vietnamese regulars and 35,000 Phnom Penh forces faced some 60,000 guerrillas at the end of 1988; and in Nicaragua the approximately 100,000 EPS regulars and militiamen confronted more than 20,000 insurgents at the height of hostilities in 1987.[29] In other words, only in Ethiopia is the "ideal" numerical ratio a reality, a fact that until recently had a great deal to do with Addis Ababa's ability to contain the insurgents.

*Expanding Area of Operations*

Over the past few years, all anticommunist insurgencies have succeeded in steadily expanding their areas of operations. The apparent exception of Ethiopia until the first few months of 1988 was due to the peculiar nature of the insurgencies in that country, which have only been able to operate in ethnically and linguistically congenial regions. In March and April 1988, however, the insurgents in both Eritrea and Tigray suddenly broke out of their traditional defensive positions and inflicted the heaviest casualties on Addis Ababa's forces since the beginning of their civil wars.[30] In Nicaragua at the time of the shaky cease-fire signed in Sapoá in March 1988, the insurgents were operating in two-thirds of the country, and the Afghan insurgents are active in all areas of the country except for the poorly inhabited northern regions along the Soviet border. The three Cambodian organizations have struck as far east as the Vietnamese border, the Khmer Rouge have established a quasi-permanent presence along the Tonlé Sap in the central part of the country and have occasionally moved into the environs of Phnom Penh itself. UNITA is active in all but the three least populous provinces of Angola (Namibe, Cunene, and Benguela), while RENAMO is inactive only in Mozambique's northeastern corner in parts of the Cabo Delgado province.

The very fact that the insurgents have expanded their operational theaters not only demonstrates that the governments they fight against have failed to find effective countermeasures but also that new opportunities and challenges face the guerrillas. Most of these are related to the need to expand and strengthen propaganda, recruitment, and political indoctrination over ever-increasing areas and among growing numbers of people.

*Propaganda*

Contemporary propaganda activities in the Third World, whether conducted by governments or guerrillas, have had to consider two important factors: the increased sophistication of the equipment and skills required and levels of illiteracy — 80 percent or higher in countries like Afghanistan and Mozambique. Illiteracy and the availability of cheap radios favor propaganda via radio broadcasts, which in turn requires skilled personnel and safe locations. Those with broadcasting skills were immediately available only in Nicaragua, where a lively anti-government media had existed before 1979. Experienced newsmen like Pedro Joaquín Chamorro Barrios, and radio station owners like Manuel Jirón were available to the resistance, as was US equipment. The result was that the Nicaraguan resistance's two radio stations, Radio 15 de Septiembre and Radio Liberación, have established themselves as technically superior, more interesting, and more credible than the government's Radio Sandino.

In Angola, UNITA's Voice of the Black Cockerel is seen by the population as infinitely more trustworthy than Radio Luanda, and this perception is supported by the fact that the station's and UNITA's casualty reports in general are by far the most reliable ones. The Cambodians (particularly the Khmer Rouge), the Afghans, and RENAMO all have their own broadcasts, almost always transmitted from neighboring countries. UNITA and RENAMO broadcasts cover the entire country, as do the Nicaraguan broadcasts; Afghan broadcasts from Pakistan are heavily jammed by the Soviets, particularly in the northern areas, while China relays Cambodian resistance broadcasts all over Vietnam.

All resistance movements engage in other forms of propaganda, including pamphlets and graffiti, and in all six cases the target is the urban population. UNITA and the mujahedeen (or their supporters) also produce publications in the West, while RENAMO and the mujahedeen are known to have succeeded in painting slogans on or even attacking government buildings in Maputo and Kabul respectively.

One of the major differences between anticommunist and Communist insurgent groups is their use of legal or semi-legal internal political fronts. Even under the most maligned anticommunist governments, groups sympathetic to the insurgents or outright fronts operate legally or semi-legally, if not freely, and are able to contact the foreign press and to present their views; but the very nature of Marxist-Leninist regimes denies such opportunities to anticommunist guerrillas.[31] The result is that the guerrillas have to make use of other, less effective means of indoctrination and political action.

Anticommunist insurgents face the same problem in their external political activities. Whereas Communist insurgent groups often succeed in developing massive support networks in foreign countries, especially in the United States and Western Europe, and do so with massive support from the Soviet bloc's worldwide propaganda machine, nothing comparable is available to anticommunist forces. Their foreign operations therefore are for the most part limited to diplomacy and formal contacts with policy-makers, and informal links with sympathetic private individuals.

Furthermore, Communist and anticommunist insurgents differ in yet another important way, in that the latter are denied an essential political weapon: legal or semi-legal organizations, all banned in a Communist-ruled state. The FMLN in El Salvador, the Sandinistas before 1979, FRELIMO, MPLA, and the Algerian FLN have all usually achieved success in discouraging their opponents or their foreign backers to continue the war. None of those means is available to those fighting the Soviet Union or Cuba or attempting to replace regimes of the type ruling in Managua, Hanoi, Maputo, Luanda, or Addis Ababa. Despite such major handicaps, anticommunist insurgents are engaged in active diplomatic efforts in a growing number of countries, with some success.

*Guerrilla Diplomacy*

World opinion often has a great deal to do with the success or failure of insurgency. As the French learned in Algeria, the United States in Vietnam, the Portuguese in Africa, and the Israelis in their conflict with the PLO, successful counterinsurgency is to little or no avail as long as the insurgents are widely perceived as a legitimate force fighting a just cause. Overused as it might be, the argument that an insurgency's success is decided in the political and diplomatic arena far more often than in the field is certainly a valid one and is pertinent to any analysis of contemporary anticommunist insurgencies. Governments react to international acceptance of an insurgent group as much as they do to that group's military prowess. When, as in the case of Cambodia, a majority in the United Nations recognizes the insurgents as the legitimate government, moral and material support are far easier for the insurgents to obtain than would be the case otherwise. Similarly, when significant Third World governments decide, for one reason or another, to support an insurgent group, its chances of receiving aid are far better than when a Western power alone does so. Thus, the Afghan mujahedeen are publicly, if only implicitly, supported by the Islamic Conference states, which in turn encourages the continuation of Pakistan's policy of open aid to the insurgents and Saudi Arabia's financing of the resistance. Once added to this type of Third World support, Western military aid to the mujahedeen did not become an international issue. Conversely, because the United States publicly supports the Nicaraguan insurgents without Third World support, Washington has come under sustained criticism from many countries. And when small states like the Comoros or Malawi discreetly helped a group like RENAMO, or a pariah state like South Africa did the same, the indignant noise of international public opinion was often deafening.

Since public opinion can change, however, an insurgent group's persistence, political skill, and record of success in the field can make a great difference over time. The best example remains UNITA, which has gone from being recognized by the Organization of African Unity as a legitimate "liberation movement" in 1974–1975, to being maligned as a "South African puppet," to being implicitly recognized as a legitimate contender for power by some fourteen of the OAU's fifty-one members, including such prominent ones such as Nigeria, Egypt, Ivory Coast, Zaire, and Morocco.

In terms of diplomatic and public relations skills, the dubious distinction of being the most inept and ineffective anticommunist guerrilla organization can only be assigned to RENAMO. That group has never managed to avoid an embarrassing factionalism and inefficiency in its foreign propaganda and public relations activities, and has failed to maintain even a minimal façade of coherence, organization, and legitimacy abroad. RENAMO has never successfully challenged the patently absurd claim of its foes that it is simply a South African creation. Indeed, even such hostile publications as *Africa Confidential* admit that RENAMO has massive Shona support, "between 10,000 to 22,000 fighters under its control," and a coherent military structure, largely under the command of ex-FRELIMO fighters.[32] RENAMO is known to have painted graffiti on the presidential palace in Maputo, to have mined heavily protected beaches in the capital (blowing up a few Soviet advisers in the bargain), and generally has the reputation of being a militarily successful anticommunist organization. That no country, including South Africa, could afford to arm, sustain, and pay 22,000 "mercenaries" should be self-evident, as should be the fact that "bandit gangs," a term still used not only by FRELIMO but by the US State Department as well, do not operate in such a well-organized manner and in such numbers. To decry liberal bias or the State Department's misguided beliefs, a favorite conservative tactic, only confuses the issue. The fact is that RENAMO has not yet learned even the essentials of diplomacy and public relations, and for this reality the barely literate Afonso Dlakhama is directly responsible with his mistrust of nonmilitary, educated cadres abroad, his reluctance to delegate responsibility, poor communications, and sheer incompetence. RENAMO's mistakes include toleration of personal infighting between spokesmen in Washington, Lisbon, and West Germany, which sometimes takes on unpleasant racial undertones, uncertainty as to who actually speaks for Dlakhama, lack of financial support for the group's missions abroad, and incoherent and often purely defensive public statements.[33]

RENAMO's opposite is UNITA, whose North American and West European, as well as African public relations operations are as sophisticated as they are successful. Unlike RENAMO, UNITA maintains a political presence in many African and West European capitals, as well as in Washington. The consistency of Savimbi's message succeeded in turning the principal liberal argument in favor of Marxist-Leninist insurgencies into support of UNITA's role as a progressive, nationalist group trying to improve its country's situation. If Marxist-Leninist groups claim they have to accept Soviet bloc support in the absence of Western aid, UNITA uses the same argument to justify its relationship with South Africa. It took some years, but by 1987 UNITA had managed to attract the support of significant sectors of the United States' black leadership, finally tired of seeing black Angolans being killed by the thousands by Cubans, Soviets, and East Germans on the battlefields of Cuando Cubango, Bié, Huambo, and Huila. In addition, certain African governments have come to reject reflexive slogans about "Boer aggression" against Angola in the face of the grim reality of an international, mostly non-African expeditionary force killing Africans in the name of Marxist-Leninist internationalism.

The mujahedeen, themselves no experts at public relations or diplomacy, do have an effective and committed network of Western and Islamic supporters. As a result, although most Americans know very little about the nature, aims, and membership of the mujahedeen groups, a combination of anticommunism and an instinctive sympathy for underdogs in conflict with a superpower resulted in at least some popular support for the aid the administration and Congress decided to provide to the resistance. In Western Europe the same is true, with the mujahedeen (despite being far better known and understood there than in the United States) gaining sympathy as the underdogs. Arab and Islamic support for the Afghan insurgents also presents a unique instance of the West and Islam acting in accord. In addition, West European and US aid to the Afghans entails no immediate threat of Soviet retaliation and supports their claims of being tough on communism.

The Nicaraguans, on the other hand, are the victims and sometimes the dubious beneficiaries of a polarized American public opinion made up of committed supporters and all-out enemies in both parties. They aren't effective spokesmen for their own cause and depended far too heavily on the often unrealistic and changing attitudes of the Reagan administration. For many West European and Latin American governments, support for the contras would be seen as support for Washington, an undesirable image at home, and one they avoid by stressing "nonintervention" and support for self-determination. The Nicaraguan resistance's inability to cope successfully with such perceptions is one indication that total reliance upon any single source of external diplomatic and material support, particularly if it is the United States, is suicidal for an anticommunist insurgency today. The fact that the most successful insurgent groups have more than one major external supporter only strengthens the argument that no anticommunist insurgency can hope to win as long as it is dependent upon a single source of supplies and diplomatic and political support. Furthermore, if that single source is the United States, the chances of success are lessened even further, a problem the Nicaraguans have either not recognized or not found a remedy for. Like RENAMO, with its previous unduly close relationship to Pretoria, and the Eritreans, with their reliance on notoriously unreliable (and unstable) Arab regimes (Iraq, Syria, and, most recently, Saudi Arabia and the Gulf states), the Nicaraguans have to realize the need for multiple sources of support, even if in the short term their supplies and thus operational capability were reduced.

The Eritreans and Tigreans have almost no Western support, largely due to their Marxist-Leninist and secessionist goals. By their own choice they continue to be isolated. MOULINAKA and KPNLF may be victims of the American desire to forget Indochina, while the Khmer Rouge will remain a pariah to Western politicians, regardless of their ideological feelings; but both ASEAN and China are bound to keep the Khmer Rouge in the forefront of international recognition and serve as aid channels for strictly practical military reasons: the Khmer Rouge, whether one likes them or not are by far the most effective military instrument pushing Hanoi out of Cambodia.

Another primary goal for any insurgency is to obtain reliable intelligence, and their ability to do so is also a good, although not decisive, indication of how much popular support they have gained.

*Intelligence and Infiltration Capabilities*

Of the anticommunist insurgent groups, the most successful at infiltrating enemy ranks are the mujahedeen and RENAMO. In Afghanistan there have been repeated instances of guerrilla attacks being coordinated with mutinies by Kabul's army. Among the Afghan groups, the best known intelligence network belongs to the Jamiat-e-Islami, particularly Massoud's Panjshir organization.[34] Intelligence and counterintelligence efforts are well coordinated and data is promptly processed. As a result, practically no Kabul-regime or Soviet operation against a significant mujahedeen concentration in Afghanistan has achieved tactical surprise. The guerrillas learned of enemy plans and acted accordingly. Similarly, UNITA has been aware of details of enemy offensives, as have RENAMO and, especially, the Nicaraguan guerrillas. In all but one instance (Ethiopia), the guerrillas' tactical intelligence is supplemented with data collected by their foreign supporters (the United States, China, or South Africa) through aerial reconnaissance, radio interceptions, or satellite photography.

The field intelligence of the insurgent forces indicates how much popular support they enjoy. Without such support many of the most spectacular attacks, particularly in urban areas, would have been impossible. Indeed, were UNITA no more than an Ovimbundu ethnic organization, its destruction of the Luanda oil refinery in November 1981 would be inexplicable,[35] as would the mujahedeen's regular attacks in Kabul, Herat, or Kandahar, and RENAMO's in or near Maputo.

Another significant indication of a guerrilla organization's capabilities, strength, and level of organization is its ability to mobilize, establish long-term control over, and motivate the civilian population—in other words, their ability to establish areas of permanent control, or in revolutionary parlance *liberated zones*. In some instances, such zones are in effect mini *counter-states*, providing an administrative, military, and ideological alternative to the ruling Marxist-Leninist regimes.

*Counter-States*

Although a guerrilla force usually cannot hope to prevent the army from penetrating any given area, at least before the final stage of the war, it can make the cost of doing so high. In all significant insurgencies going on today, whether leftist or anticommunist, there are liberated areas under the quasi-permanent control of the insurgents. Examples range from Morazán in El Salvador, to Bicol in the Philippines, Angola's *terra ao fim do mundo*, Afghanistan's Panjshir Valley, and northern Eritrea. In addition, an insurgent group may gain control over areas in a country neighboring its own, as in the cases of the ANC in Zambia, SWAPO in Angola, POLISARIO in Algeria, the contras in Honduras, and the Cambodian resistance groups in Thailand. Control of such areas, however, is usually interpreted as less important than the establishment of liberated zones in their own country.

A liberated zone may be no more than an area of guerrilla control located in a remote and relatively unpopulated region (as in Colombia, Mozambique, Guatemala), protected largely by distance and harsh terrain. Such areas are therefore of only limited value for the insurgent movement, since both recruits and food are scarce and the same distance that protects the zone minimizes the guerrillas' ability to threaten government targets.[36] A liberated zone close to a major city, or even the capital, on the other hand, poses a clear threat to the regime in power. In either case, what really counts for long-term success is the ability of the insurgents to establish a functioning administration, a *counter-state* as an alternative to the government.

Of the six insurgencies under discussion here, UNITA has been most successful in establishing an effective state-within-a-state. Jamba, Savimbi's headquarters in a remote area in southeastern Angola, was built in the late 1970s, and although it has some of the characteristics of a Potemkin village, it is a functioning town. In addition to Jamba, UNITA has also succeeded in establishing an administration throughout most of Cuando-Cubango and in parts of Moxico, Huambo, and Bié, including towns and many villages. They provide schools with a centralized curriculum, medical facilities, food production and distributions, and an incipient commercial and trade network that enables UNITA to export such items as timber, ivory, and diamonds.

The population under direct UNITA influence, if not permanent control, is large enough to enable the organization to recruit more new fighters than the Luanda regime. UNITA is not self-sufficient, but, according to most reports, the zone under its control seems quieter, better administered, and better able to provide basic food staples than the rest of Angola. UNITA cadres, including administrators, teachers, political commissars, and military personnel, have free access to the entire zone, which by the end of 1987 encompassed some 30 percent of Angola's territory and covered most of the Namibian, Zambian, and Zairean borders.

In Mozambique, large swaths of territory in the central provinces of Gaza and Manica, particularly in and around the Gorongosa mountain range, as well as in Nyassa, Zambezia, Inhambane, Sofala, and Tete, have been outside government control for five years or more. These zones expand or contract according to the vagaries of war and the role of foreign (Zimbabwean) troops, but an extensive core region remains consistently untouched by the government administration. This area is largely self-sufficient in terms of food production and hence is not seriously affected by the famine in Maputo-controlled areas. The region is large enough to ensure that RENAMO's supply of recruits and food will not be seriously threatened in the foreseeable future. Since few Western journalists have access to RENAMO areas, all that is known for certain is that the motorcycle is the main "military" transportation and that Afonso Dlakhama is seen as at least a minor deity by his followers.[37]

In Afghanistan the best-known liberated area is the Panjshir Valley organization of Jamiat-e-Islami commander Ahmed Shah "Massoud," because it is the only such zone to have been seriously examined in a scholarly article.[38] Once again, the guerrillas' aim is to create an alternative to official propaganda, "education," and intelligence.[39] Kandahar,

Herat, and Nuristan area leaders have apparently succeeded in similar enterprises.

The emerging political culture of the refugee camps on the Thailand-Cambodia, Ethiopia-Sudan, Honduras-El Salvador, and Honduras-Nicaragua borders reflects years of guerrilla control over education, food, and medical supplies and the impact of relatives fighting and dying across the border in guerrilla ranks. While some of the refugees hope for emigration to distant countries, most have lost such hope and are now resigned to their fate. They often join the guerrilla organizations, and the supplies they receive, whether food, money, or medicines, are often immediately channeled to the fighters. Whether within Cambodia or close by in Thailand, present and former MOULINAKA, Khmer Rouge, or KPNLF camps like Dong Rek, Ampil, Nuong Samet, and Nong Chan serve as indoctrination, supply, and recruiting areas for the insurgents, and the same is true in northern Eritrea, as well as in Eritrean refugee areas just north of the border in Sudan. Most of the children in such refugee camps have grown up with guns, see war as the only possible type of life for themselves and are totally commited to the insurgent cause.

As the liberated areas expand, more of the population are exposed to a different way of life than that imposed by the ruling regimes, and more often than not, they prefer the alternative to the "progressive" solutions offered at gunpoint by Luanda, Maputo, Kabul, Phnom Penh, Addis Ababa, or Managua. Such choices in themselves may have little if any impact on the conflicts at stake. In combination with other factors, however, such as the guerrillas' vitality and their increasing capabilities, as well as the widening scope of the insurgencies, these choices may have an important impact on international politics.

*Cumulative Impact*

Ties among anticommunist insurgencies are greatly hampered by ideological, ethnic, racial, cultural, and practical differences. Attempts to bring insurgents together have been few and far between, largely limited to occasional meetings that are more symbolic than substantive. A number of meetings involving Afghan, Laotian, Cambodian, Nicaraguan, and Angolan representatives have taken place, most frequently in the United States.[40]

All the insurgencies I am studying here have their own programs and their own deeply felt motivations and cultural aspirations that their followers accept as worth fighting and dying for, but differences among the groups often make them incompatible. It is hard indeed to see what, other than having the same enemy in common, would bring together

Nicaraguan democrats trained in the United States, Cambodian Maoists, and Islamic fighters in Afghanistan.

Furthermore, even if there were some attempt at strategic cooperation between UNITA and the Nicaraguan RN, KPNLF, and the mujahedeen, geographic conditions would pose serious obstacles. The "time of the guerrilla," the rainy season when air attacks are impossible and the terrain impassable for heavy vehicles, occurs from November to May in Angola and Mozambique and from May to October in Nicaragua; the insurgencies in the northern hemisphere have to cope with the long Afghan winters, the rains of Indochina and Central America, or the perennial droughts of Eritrea and Tigray. Tactical coordination is thus impossible, and political and ideological cooperation is still unlikely to go beyond occasional meetings.

The cumulative impact of the anticommunist insurgencies on the Soviet bloc's global influence and status, however, has not been given the attention it deserves.

First, the cost of fighting insurgents has been high. Since 1977 the Soviet Union has provided Ethiopia with over $3 billion in military hardware. At least the same amount has gone to Angola since 1975, and close to $2 billion was sent to Nicaragua after 1979. The cost of Soviet activities in Afghanistan and support for the Kabul regime reached millions of dollars per day by 1980,[41] and Mozambique has been the recipient of over $500 million in Soviet bloc weaponry since 1976. Soviet subsidies to Vietnam and Cuba, amounting to some $5 billion a year, enable Hanoi to sustain its counterinsurgency efforts in Cambodia and reward Havana for its massive involvement in similar operations in Angola, Ethiopia, and, to a lesser extent, Nicaragua and Mozambique. With the partial exceptions of Angola and Afghanistan, the recipients of Soviet military aid are in no position to repay their debts.

The total number of casualties suffered by the Soviet bloc, its allies, and its protégés in COIN operations is difficult to assess, but their order of magnitude can be estimated from existing information. Some 10,000 Cubans were wounded, killed, or missing in Angola by the end of 1987;[42] the Soviet Army lost perhaps twice that many in Afghanistan, and a similar number of Vietnamese have probably been incapacitated or have died in Cambodia. A few thousand Cubans have also been killed or otherwise put out of action in Eritrea, Ogaden, Mozambique, and Nicaragua, and a few hundred East Europeans suffered the same fate in the same countries. All together, since 1975 the Soviet bloc has been directly involved in counterinsurgency for some 20,000 days, twice as long as the United States was in Indochina. Even at a rate of three casualties per day, a highly conservative calculation considering the fact that, unlike the

Cubans in Angola, the Soviet and Vietnamese armies bear the brunt of the fighting in Afghanistan and Cambodia, the lowest possible number of casualties suffered in those countries must have reached at least 60,000 by the end of 1987.

The most conservative assessment of the casualty rate for the Angolan, Nicaraguan, Ethiopian, Afghan, and Mozambican forces compared to their Soviet, Vietnamese, or Cuban allies is 10:1, judging by the available data from Angola, Ethiopia and Nicaragua, and far higher for Mozambique and Afghanistan.[43] This means that between the beginning of the second civil war in Angola in 1975 and the end of 1987, some 700,000 Communist troops have become casualties of the anticommunist insurgents. Such figures give a clear picture of the cost insurgents exacted for the spread of Soviet influence and Marxist-Leninist ideology in the Third World. On the other hand, at least 1.5 million insurgents have been killed or maimed in combat on three continents, and many times that number of civilians have suffered the same fate or, more often still, have died as a result of the concomitants of Communist counterinsurgency—famine, disease, and exhaustion on the way to refugee camps across borders.

These figures alone clearly indicate the scope and impact of anticommunist insurgencies over huge areas of the Third World, but these insurgencies also have a direct impact on neighboring states, which means that a total of twenty-two Third World countries on three continents are directly involved. Of these, Thailand, Pakistan, Iran, South Africa, Zimbabwe, Zambia, Tanzania, Somalia, the Sudan, Zaire, Honduras, and El Salvador, or 10 percent of the Third World countries, are involved militarily—either in support of the anticommunist insurgents or as a result of military pressure from the insurgents' foes, or both. As a consequence, these countries have had to add to their military forces, divert scarce resources toward supporting millions of displaced persons and refugees, and have become involved in border clashes with Communist forces claiming "hot pursuit" rights or, alternatively, with insurgents trying to establish bases along their borders. In some cases they have also intervened in the fighting, both within and across their own borders.

The very scope and geographical spread of contemporary anticommunist insurgencies makes them a global phenomenon, with an enormous and immediate impact on the present and future stability of many countries and on the global balance of forces. The West, particularly the United States, has failed to see the overall picture and act accordingly for reasons that I will discuss below; it also appears, however, that the Soviet bloc has so far been only partially successful in developing a coherent response to this phenomenon, as demonstrated by its reactions to conflicts in various areas.

## The Reaction of the Enemy

The Soviet Union became a superpower following its victory in the battlefields of Europe in World War II and has established and expanded its Third World empire since then through skillful manipulation or cooptation of "national liberation movements," especially during the 1960s and 1970s. Not since the early 1920s has Soviet power been challenged in Russia proper, and until the mid-1970s the Soviets acted behind the scenes and were not targets of Third World guerrilla warfare. Furthermore, as sponsors and supporters of "wars of national liberation," the Soviets have consistently used proxies, rather than their own forces, largely limiting their support to propaganda, material, and funds. The end result has been that the Soviet military has developed no coherent theory of counterinsurgency, and political planners have been limited by the incorrect assumption that "wars of national liberation" can only be directed against "imperialists" and their protégés. These ideological blinders have made a realistic assessment of Soviet history and experience impossible. As a result, from Nicaragua to Angola to Afghanistan, the Communist counterinsurgency efforts have suffered.

*The Soviet Record in Counterinsurgency*

There is no question that the Red Army today is the most formidable conventional force history has ever seen. In terms of all types of conventional weapons, the Soviets have a spectacular quantitative advantage over Western and Chinese armed forces. In qualitative terms, they enjoy superiority in attack helicopters and artillery and are catching up in aircraft; only in naval terms does the West maintain a numerical and qualitative advantage, but that is the least significant element in counterinsurgency. Furthermore, the Red Army has enjoyed many of these advantages, as well as numerical superiority, since the final years of World War II.

Despite all this, the Soviet army and the Warsaw Treaty Organization, as well as Vietnam and Cuba, have an unimpressive counterinsurgency record,[44] even compared to Western, particularly British and French forces, which are often less effective than such Third World counterinsurgency forces as those of South Africa, Guatemala, Argentina, Indonesia, and Colombia. This reality raises a number of intriguing and potentially far-reaching questions, and an overview of Soviet bloc counterinsurgency is edifying in terms of assessing Soviet capabilities.

The Red Army began its COIN experience with the Tambov revolt of the early 1920s. It took almost a year to put it down, despite drastic economic and social policy changes in Moscow, represented by Lenin's NEP, that actively undermined the revolt's political roots. Indeed, since the entire affair was largely the result of the excesses of "war communism," including forced requisitions, once NEP was in place the main reason for the revolt was gone. NEP, however, was not decided or conceived in Moscow as a reaction to the Tambov revolt, but as a policy change intended to benefit the majority of the Soviet population, the peasantry. It just happened that the Tambov rebels were peasants and fell under the spell of the promises of NEP. The Tambov events were important enough to warrant sending the prominent general, Tuchachevsky, to put it down, although cordoning off of the region with large numbers of troops and saturating it with police were sufficient in themselves.

The second and far more extensive Red Army experience with guerrillas was during the *basmachi* campaign in central Asia, from 1917 to 1931. This was a rather confused and confusing affair, involving at various points Pan-Turkic sentiments against Bolshevik-style internationalism, Turanic pseudo-nationalism, and Islamic religious reactions against official Soviet atheism, as well as a racial rejection of Russian Slavic imperialism, mixed with banditry and a tribalism opposed to central control by aliens. The basmachis were also a very disorganized and poorly led, armed, and organized lot, with no outside support worth mentioning or safe havens across friendly borders.[45] Nevertheless, it took the Red Army, by then victorious in the civil and anti-interventionist wars, fourteen years to eliminate the basmachis.

Following World War II and the Soviets' forcible "integration" of the Baltic states of Lithuania, Estonia, and Latvia, as well as the submission of Eastern Europe, a new wave of challenges faced the Red Army and its newly established branches in Poland and Romania. Both of these countries are relatively large (the largest and second largest Warsaw Pact states after the Soviet Union itself) and have a long tradition of anti-Russian sentiment, as Czechoslovakia and Bulgaria did not. Polish hopes for Western aid and Romanian hopes for Yugoslav support also encouraged resistance.

It took the Red Army, the largest and most ruthless of the anti-Nazi victors, some twelve years to defeat the hopelessly isolated Ukrainian Peoples' Army (UPA) and the Lithuanian guerrillas. The Polish puppet regime installed by Stalin in 1944 took six years, even with the direct and massive involvement of the Red Army, to defeat the Polish guerrillas. Even in the case of Romania, whose people are not known for their history of protracted, violent resistance against alien invaders, the local Communist regime only succeeded in eliminating the last insurgents in the mountainous areas bordering Yugoslavia in 1956–1957, and then only after the Bucharest-Belgrade rapprochement led to Tito's cutting off aid to the insurgents.

Castro's experience with counterinsurgency began soon after his victory as a guerrilla leader. The Sierra de Escambray guerrillas, almost all of local peasant origin, were labeled "bandits" and CIA agents; "batallions to fight the bandits" (Batallones de Lucha contra los Bandidos or BLBs) were established to operate against the some 3,500 insurgents.[46] The operation, led by Raúl Menéndez Tomassevich, now a senior Cuban general and active in the early days of the Angola campaign, was conducted in the traditional Soviet manner perfected in the Ukraine, Lithuania, the Romanian Carpathian Mountains, and eastern Poland. The region was cordoned off, massive sweeps of the countryside were relentlessly pursued, and civilians were herded into concentration camps. Soviet helicopters and East German dogs played major roles, and rebels were shot on the spot.[47] Casualties were high on both sides, perhaps higher on the government side, but the guerrillas were physically eliminated.

In none of these campaigns were orthodox COIN tactics used. No small-unit tactical approach was employed, no significant "hearts and minds" strategy denied civilian support to the insurgents, no political compromises were offered or made, and seldom was amnesty for the leaders decreed and implemented. Only in central Asia during the 1920s did the Soviets promise respect for Islam, bribe or threaten a number of mullahs into cooperation, talk about improving the economic situation of the rural population,[48] and consistently pursue a "divide and conquer" policy among the various central Asian peoples. It should, however, be pointed out that of all early anticommunist insurgencies the *basmachis* alone had a chance of receiving foreign support and an area of operation bordering potentially friendly countries, which may explain the slightly different and more sophisticated approach adopted by the Red Army in that case.

Except in part for the basmachi experience, Communist counterinsurgency has consistently been directed toward the physical elimination of the guerrillas. Similar means have been used consistently, whether in Lithuania, the Ukraine, Eastern Europe, or Cuba, and have centered on the government's principal advantage: total conventional and overwhelming numerical superiority. Air power, artillery, armor, and large regular formations have been used since the anti-*basmachi* campaign, with no regard for civilian casualties.

The only orthodox COIN method sometimes used by Soviet or Soviet-style regimes has been the forcible, often massive resettlement of surviving civilians. The Soviets themselves used it against the central Asians, as did the Chinese against the Tibetans, but not until the beginning of the new insurgencies in the mid-1970s has it became a more or less consistent approach.

*Contemporary Counterinsurgency, Soviet-Style*

With such a tradition of counterinsurgency as the one described above, particularly in light of its successes in the past and the inertia of military institutions in general and Communist ones in particular, even the limited level of flexibility and adaptation demonstrated by Soviet-type forces in recent COIN operations is surprising.

One of the most striking characteristics of contemporary Soviet-style counterinsurgency is its relative uniformity, from the Indochinese jungles to the mountains of Afghanistan, and from the arid regions of Ethiopia and Angola to the Mozambican bush. This phenomenon is clearly related to the weapons and equipment used (all Soviet-bloc-made and principally intended for use in large-scale conventional warfare), to training in the Soviet Union, Eastern Europe, and Cuba, and to a reliance on Soviet doctrine ideology and political outlook. These factors favor uniformity of approach, and have consistently overridden the potentially useful specific experience of some Third World counterinsurgent forces, despite the previously mentioned phenomenon of reversibility of warfare in places like Mozambique, Indochina, Angola, and Nicaragua. A number of aspects of Soviet-style COIN must be examined with these characteristics in mind.

*Technology.* The Soviets believe that high technology is a shortcut to victory. Whether this is the result of an emerging Soviet COIN doctrine or just the persistence of long habit and past experience is unclear; what is clear is that the use of relatively sophisticated equipment is the rule from Cambodia to Nicaragua and Angola to Eritrea, with Mozambique the only current exception. Similarly, the frequent use of combined armor and air operations in Angola, Afghanistan, Cambodia, and Ethiopia is a clear demonstration of Soviet bias in favor of conventional strategies developed since World War II and originally intended for European conditions. The most recent (late 1988) example is the deployment of long-range SCUD missiles in Afghanistan and the use of strategic bombers against the mujahedeen. While a case could be made that these weapons were introduced with a strictly political goal in mind, their use also follows a long-standing, and long-discredited pattern.

The massive yearly offensives against the Panjshir Valley in Afghanistan, Jamba and Mavinga in Angola, the camps along the Thai-Cambodian border, and guerrilla concentrations along the Asmara, Assab, and Massawa roads in Eritrea all involve a heavy use of tanks, APCs, and aircraft. All such offensives have failed, usually because the insurgents have refused to be involved in pitched battles. More recently in Afghanistan, Angola, and to a lesser extent in Nicaragua, the insurgents have made use of effective antitank and antiaircraft weapons. In the first two cases, US-made TOWs and stingers, while not necessarily altering the outcome of the war, have imposed the need for a painful reassessment of the Soviet-inspired strategy. The stingers, in particular, have seriously impaired Soviet or allied ability to conduct combined-arms operations in Afghanistan; worse still, in Angola the presence of the South African Air Force has limited the use of helicopter gunships, alone or in support of armored and motorized ground assaults, anywhere within the range of Namibia-based South African jets. Furthermore, amazing as it may seem, it often appears that Vietnamese commanders in Cambodia, Soviets in Afghanistan, and Soviets and Cubans in Angola have not yet realized that African, Afghan and Indochinese roads are not similar to those of central Europe. When the rains come (or the snows in Afghanistan), even the few existing transportation arteries become impassable and the cloud cover precludes air operations. That the Soviets, who throughout their history have relied on Russia's poor transportation network and harsh climate to defeat better-led and better-equipped enemies, seem unable to cope with such factors themselves suggests that there are serious limitations on their ability to adapt to an unfamiliar type of warfare.

When it finally occurred to Soviet commanders in Afghanistan that large combined-arms operations were not effective in counterinsurgency, they took a small step toward adapting to the new reality. In 1985 the Combined-Arms Reinforced Battalions (CARBs) were established.[49] Yet, the result was only that the overwhelming Soviet numerical and firepower advantage over the mujahedeen was largely lost, especially after the 1986 introduction of the stingers. Vietnamese armored and air attacks on the Khmer Rouge, KPNLF, and ANS (Armée Nationale Sihanoukiste, MOULINAKA's armed branch) border camps remain limited to the dry season and have become increasingly predictable and avoidable. In Ethiopia, government troops, using armor and MIG jets, can always reopen the main transportation arteries to the Eritrean coast, usually at heavy cost to themselves and the civilian population; what they have consistently been unable to do is to keep them open. As a result, by the spring of 1988 even emergency food supplies through Tigray and Eritrea have stopped, and the insurgents are on the offensive again.[50] Ethiopian MIGs have indeed bombed most Eritrean towns in the interior out of existence, but the insurgent counterstate has simply moved underground and continues its operations at night and during the rare rainy periods.

The collapsing Mozambique regime is the only one that does not employ the combined-arms attacks that characterize contemporary Soviet-style counterinsurgency. The reason for this, at least until 1983, however, was simply a lack of means. With only an obsolete and unreliable air and armor force, an incompetent officer corps, and a vulnerable geographic position, the recently retrained FPLM had little opportunity to employ Soviet-type counterinsurgency, particularly after it suffered massive personnel and equipment losses as a result of Rhodesian attacks and ill-conceived assaults on guerrilla strongholds in the central provinces. FRELIMO's Zimbabwean supporters lack the strength to engage in counterinsurgency throughout Mozambique and limit themselves to often futile attempts to retain control over their own vital outlet to the sea, the Beira Corridor.

While doctrine and tradition largely explain the above-mentioned Soviet-style COIN, the nature of the training received by officers and troops helps explain the difficulty Marxist-Leninist forces have in adapting them to new situations.

*Training.* At the rank-and-file level, there are consistent reports from Angola, Afghanistan, Ethiopia, Nicaragua, and Mozambique that recruits receive only a few weeks of largely conventional training before being sent into combat. The Soviets alone seem to have tried to improve the quality of the training of their conscripts, for instance by expanding the percentage of those trained in night warfare from 30 to 50 percent and increasing the number of troops trained in mountain warfare in Bulgaria.[51] Nevertheless, the ordinary conscript, whether Soviet, Vietnamese, Nicaraguan, Angolan, or Ethiopian, is still seen as cannon fodder, a fact demonstrated by the disproportionately high number of conscripts involved in static defenses and mass offensives, both of which entail high casualties. Morale is therefore low, and is lowered even further when local forces are used. Heng Samrin or Najibullah's troops are widely and accurately seen as unreliable, poorly motivated, and ineffective; the FPLM is despised even by its Zimbabwean allies, while the Angolan FAPLA harbors strong resentment against both its Cuban and Soviet allies and the war as a whole. In Angola, Eritrea, and Mozambique, government regulars are not familiar with the terrain of the combat regions. Illiteracy, ignorance of even the simplest modern technology, and cultural or racial differences raise further obstacles to Soviet or allied attempts to forge effective COIN forces out of the limited number of supporters of the Marxist-Leninist regimes in Africa, Cambodia, or Afghanistan.

One peculiarity of the Soviet COIN doctrine seems to be the reliance on yearly, massive offensives against major insurgent defensive positions.

Such offensives have become larger and larger in scale, but apparently less and less successful. For example, the Soviets have been obsessed with the Panjshir Valley in Afghanistan, against which they have staged seven major attacks between 1979 and 1984. All ended inconclusively. The April 1984 operation was described as the largest military engagement in Afghanistan since the Soviet invasion, involving some 15,000 Soviet and 2,000 Afghan troops, and 400–600 tanks and APCs.[52] The 1987 offensive to relieve the besieged garrison of Khost also involved thousands of troops. By far the largest such COIN mass attacks, however, have taken place in Ethiopia, with Soviet involvement and, very likely, Soviet planning. The October 1985 Operation Red Sea was said to have involved 90,000 Ethiopian troops, a paratrooper regiment, armor and helicopters, and to have resulted in some 43,000 Ethiopian casualties, of which 15,000 were lost in the fighting around Nacfa alone.[53] Following the March 1988 fighting in Eritrea and Tigray, the EPLF claimed to have killed or captured some 18,000 Ethiopian troops and three Soviet advisers.[54]

The major Vietnamese offensives against Khmer Rouge and KPNLF bases close to the Thai border in 1984 and 1985 were major conventional operations. As for Angola, the annual offensives of the 1983–1988 period have all failed, at growing cost. The latest, against Mavinga in November 1987, resulted in the loss of between 1,500 and 3,000 Communist troops (vs. 1,000 UNITA combatants and twenty-two South Africans), and the value of the equipment lost, including thirty-five T55 tanks, seven MIG 21 and 23 jets, and 400 vehicles, was estimated at $300 million.[55] Mozambique clearly does not have the means to pursue such massive operations, and the Nicaraguans have purposely avoided such massive, usually futile operations, with the notable exception of cross-border raids into Honduras, two of which, in March 1986 and March 1988, involved up to 3,000 EPS troops.

Such insistence on massive conventional attacks against well-entrenched insurgents, particularly after it has become clear that they have not succeeded in eliminating the guerrillas, raises important questions regarding the ability of the Soviet military to adjust their thinking to the realities of contemporary counterinsurgency. A partial answer to these questions may lie in the ideological and political outlook that colors Communist perceptions of an armed, large, and motivated internal enemy.

## Perceptions and Attitudes

Soviet perceptions of anticommunist guerrillas seem to have changed only marginally since the time of the Tambov and *basmachi* rebellions. Publicly, and often as a result of deeply held ideological convictions, the insurgents are described as simple criminals, bandits, or mercenaries. Invariably, the insurgents are also described as foreign puppets and alien to the "people," who are allegedly represented by the ruling "vanguard parties." In most instances the guerrillas are also described as remnants of what was or is supposed to have been an oppressive former regime: "genocidal followers of Pol Pot" in Cambodia, "Somocistas" in Nicaragua, "Boer puppets" (*fantoches*) in Angola and Mozambique, and Sino-Pakistani-American criminals in Afghanistan. In line with such perceptions, Marxist-Leninist regimes treat captured insurgents like common criminals or traitors in the pay of a foreign power.

Alone among target regimes, Nicaragua claims to have no provision for capital punishment. In all other instances, the death penalty is seen as a fitting punishment for captured guerrillas. In Mozambique, captured RENAMO personnel have been "tried" in front of proregime mobs and, under the direct incitement of high-ranking officials, including Politburo members, have been sentenced to death and lynched. The luckier ones have been publicly flogged. UNITA saboteurs have been shot after summary trials in Luanda, Huambo, and Benguela; in December 1978, sixteen "bandits belonging to the puppet groups" were sentenced to death in a "people's trial" and shot in Huambo.[56] Many of the Afghan mujahedeen arrested or captured have been killed in Kabul's Pul-i-Sharki prison. Unlike most noncommunist governments faced with Marxist-Leninist insurgent threats, which do not have the death penalty and where the justice system is often used by captured insurgents to their advantage, Communist "justice" is swift and brutal, although often discreet.[57] Few specific data are available of the number of guerrillas tried and shot in Angola, Mozambique, Ethiopia, Cambodia, and Afghanistan, but a number of reliable sources indicate that even the numbers that are known, large as they are, are far from indicative of actual deaths among those captured. Indeed, many captured insurgents in these countries are shot without the benefit of any trial. As for the apparently odd case of Nicaragua, captured contras and ex-guardsmen were killed, and on a rather massive scale, a fact in part admitted by Interior Minister Tomás Borge Martínez himself.

In most cases, the judicial approach to captured "enemies of the people," "bandits," or "traitors" is different from that applied to common criminals. The public trials in Mozambique mentioned above involved not only bloodthirsty mobs, but also "judges" ("people's representatives") with no legal training whatsoever, as did the People's Anti-Somocista Tribunals in Nicaragua between 1980 and 1988. At least in the case of Ethiopia in 1977, the aim of government reprisals against urban (Marxist) insurgents was clearly defined by the official name of the campaign: Red Terror. Official counterterror is, however, clearly the goal of the government's judiciary in all six cases I am examining, although more discreetly so in Nicaragua. The most powerful and ubiquitous instrument of such official terror as part of the counterinsurgency strategy is, in all instances, the political police.

*The Role of the Secret Police*

The political or secret police invariably play an essential role in the period of consolidation of any Communist regime. The creation of such an institution was relatively simple in countries like Russia or the Soviet-occupied areas of postwar Germany and Eastern Europe, where powerful police organizations existed long before the Communist takeover. Powerful Western liberal myths to the contrary, repressive anticommunist Third World regimes do not usually have an effective police organization to draw from after they take power. The Portuguese in Africa, imperial Ethiopia, Somoza's Nicaragua, and pre-1978 Afghanistan all lacked the large, ruthless, and effective political police organization needed to cope with their opponents. As a result, when Marxist-Leninist regimes came into power in those countries, they had few potential recruits for their local KGB-type organizations. This deficiency was particularly glaring since the new regimes had little or no popular support, weak military forces, and significant internal opposition. The solution, in all instances, was to import a working secret police system from the Soviet bloc.

Unlike the police organizations in noncommunist countries, Marxist-Leninist secret police organizations are all-inclusive, prevention-oriented institutions. They have the power to investigate, arrest, interrogate, and detain actual and potential opponents of the regime, run concentration camps and prisons, combine propaganda, intelligence, and counterintelligence capabilities at home and abroad, and are in charge of internal political, common, and "economic" crimes. Such institutions are often legally independent of the judicial and government authorities and controlled by the top party leadership. Finally, the secret police control their own military forces—interior ministry troops and border troops as a rule—which at least in Afghanistan actually outnumber the official military forces.[58]

The Nicaraguan DGSE, Mozambican SNASP, Afghan KHAD, and their Vietnamese, Ethiopian, and Angolan counterparts are in the forefront of COIN operations in their respective countries. At least in Afghanistan, the 40,000-strong police forces of KHAD are more effective than the Kabul regime's dwindling army; in fact, by almost all accounts they provide the only effective local support for the Soviet forces.[59]

These secret police forces are alike in their training, methods, and role.

To begin with, all have been established by Soviet-bloc experts, more often than not East Germans.⁶⁰ In Angola, Ethiopia, and Mozambique, the East Germans have actually created the secret police and intelligence-counterintelligence services; in Nicaragua they (and the Bulgarians and Soviets) play a significant role, although a less important one than that of Cuba's DGI.⁶¹ The result is that the operational methods of these police forces tend to be strikingly similar and include a massive role in counter-insurgency. The secret police is present in every COIN operation, by virtue of both its direct responsibilities and its control over the political commissar network operating in all Marxist-Leninist regular forces. It is directly involved in urban and rural COIN operations, in intelligence and external operations, and in instances when regime and opposition or rulers and subjects meet directly. The political police, then, is essential and also usually the most or only local effective force available to the regime.

*Special Operations or Short Cuts?*

All COIN forces in modern history have used special forces against the guerrillas and in cross-border operations. The United States employed special forces in Cambodia and Laos; the French did so in Tunisia and Morocco; the Rhodesians and South Africans did so against Angola, Zambia, and Mozambique; the Portuguese did so against Guinea, and so forth. In this respect, at least, contemporary Communist COIN tactics are similar to well-established methods that have been applied by anti-revolutionary forces for a long time, and they explain Soviet air attacks against Pakistan, Vietnamese incursions into Thailand, and Nicaraguan forays into Honduras. The goals are to intimidate the border country's government, to make border areas unsafe for the insurgents, and to eliminate as many guerrillas as possible before they can enter into action at home.

Interestingly, however, Communist forces involved in cross-border, hot-pursuit operations have not succeeded in inflicting casualties on the insurgents on a scale comparable to the damage done by the United States against Vietcong sanctuaries in Cambodia, the Rhodesians in Mozambique, or the South Africans in Angola. In light of the large and poorly defended guerrilla refugee camps in Pakistan, Sudan, Honduras, and Thailand and the means available to Communist forces, the reason for this is clearly political rather than military. Posing as the supporters of regimes widely known as weak, the Soviets, Cubans and Vietnamese could hardly inflict devastating cross-border damage while at the same time claiming to be present on behalf of a "defenseless" regime.

Whereas direct Communist cross-border attacks are limited in both scope and duration, the same is clearly not the case with sabotage, terrorism, and subversion. Communist terrorist attacks on neighboring countries are neither a new development nor are they limited to states where insurgents receive safe havens, help, or protection. The scope and duration of such terrorist and subversive activities, which are deniable and only indirectly controlled by the KGB or its sister organizations in Cuba, Vietnam, and East Germany, clearly surpasses anything the Portuguese in Africa, the French in Algeria, or even the South Africans in southern Africa since 1976 have either intended or implemented.

The Afghan KHAD, involving hundreds or even thousands of Soviet citizens of central Asian origin,[62] as well as hundreds of East-German-trained members of the Iranian Communist party (Tudeh), are heavily involved in a terrorist and disinformation campaign in Pakistan and Afghanistan. In the first instance the means are often indiscriminate bombings of civilians in Pakistan, penetration of resistance groups in Peshawar, and support for anti-government opposition inside Pakistan. In the second instance, Iranian Communists have been quite successful in dividing the Hazara resistance in central Afghanistan (particularly the Bamian province), and in taking advantage of the Hazaras' Shia Muslim religion and historical mistrust of the dominant Sunni Pashtuns and Tajiks.

In Nicaragua, the newly established Sandinista secret services managed by 1980 to kidnap and kill the primary candidate for a renewal of the military resistance and to assassinate Anastasio Somoza. Efficient counterintelligence in South Africa and Thailand prevented similar exploits against those countries, while the disjointed, acephalous Sudanese regimes made Ethiopian attempts to do the same largely irrelevant.

The idea of fighting insurgency with insurgency was not discovered by Communist forces, as demonstrated by the Rhodesians' role in helping RENAMO against FRELIMO and the Israelis' aid to dissident Lebanese groups fighting the PLO and/or the Syrians. But the Communists have brought counterinsurgency to a new level of efficiency and predictability. Certain Communist forces have made such efficiency a rule of counterinsurgency. Mozambican and Angolan support for the ANC, Angola's for SWAPO,[63] Nicaragua's massive aid to the FMLN in El Salvador and its consistent efforts to create a "national liberation" organization in Honduras, Vietnam's taking over the moribund Thai and Malaysian Communist insurgencies deserted by China, Kabul's (i.e., Moscow's) discreet encouragement to Baluchi separatists in Pakistan, and Ethiopia's massive support for southern Sudanese and Somali separatists and dissidents are all following the same predictable pattern. In some cases this pattern is a combination of COIN strategy and ordinary "proletarian internationalism" (as in El Salvador, Sudan, Namibia, and South Africa), inasmuch as it results in aid to already existing leftist insurgent groups; in other instances (Honduras and Somalia, for example), it means working to create such groups.

*Special Forces*

The use of special forces has become a permanent feature of modern counterinsurgency; the difference is in the nature of such forces, of their methods of operation, and of their background.

In "normal" counterinsurgency, as it has evolved from Guatemala's Kaibiles, Rhodesia's Selous Scouts, South Africa's Thirty-second Battalion and paratroopers, the British SAS in Malaya, and the US Special Forces in Indochina, elite forces are supposed to be technically superior and better equipped than the insurgents, but also able to fight them on their own terrain.

Judging by these criteria, the Soviets are not well-suited to special-force COIN operations in the Third World. Not only do they have a well-established image as racist, arrogant, or aloof, but they also refuse to integrate their operations with the local forces. The Cubans in Angola, despite the heavy use of black troops, are little better, and the same is true of the Zimbabweans in Mozambique and the Vietnamese in Cambodia. Captured documents indicate that Nicaraguan-trained Salvadoran leftists expected to operate in Honduras did not know the local dialect. The result is that, as insurgent counterintelligence capabilities improve, intelligence and infiltration become increasingly difficult, if not impossible.

Despite these drawbacks, Communist special-force operations remain highly effective and have inflicted significant damage on the resistance in their respective countries. Sandinista Special Operations Forces, trained by East Germans and operating in Matagalpa and Jinotega, disguised as insurgents and succeeded in convincing the Western, particularly US media that the contras were guilty of atrocities against the civilian population.[64] In a number of instances, Sandinista special units allowed Westerners, including American citizens sympathetic to the "revolution," to be kidnapped or even killed in action by the insurgents, inspiring predictably pro-Managua reactions.

Whether the Soviets' Spetsnaz in Afghanistan, Nicaragua's BLIs (Batallones de Lucha Irregular),[65] or the far less known Mozambican Clean Brigade, it is one of the main aims of Communist special COIN forces to create confusion and to discredit the insurgents. By definition, such forces are generally relatively small, although wherever they exist they play a disproportionately large role in the actual combat. For instance, the Soviet Spetsnaz in Afghanistan are said to number no more than 20,000 but have been in the forefront of combat since about 1983.[66]

In line with the peculiar nature of the Communist use of special forces, particularly mountain and airborne special units, they appear to be dependent upon air domination, a paradoxical approach in light of the skills expected from such units. Thus, in spite of the growing alarm in the West about the capabilities of Spetsnaz, it is clear that in Afghanistan they were simply used as heliborne commandos; once the introduction of stingers made helicopter operations exceedingly risky, the offensive use of elite units declined dramatically. Between 1984 and late 1986, Spetsnaz groups were landed above resistance-controlled valleys, thus denying the mujahedeen the advantage of altitude necessary for the maximal use of their weapons. The advent of the stingers resulted in a cessation of such tactics by 1987.

On Cambodia's border or in Khmer-Rouges-infested areas, the Vietnamese army uses elite divisions or regiments, rather than smaller special-force units, and the accent seems to be on heavy use of firepower rather than any particular counterinsurgency skills. The same, by and large, applies to Ethiopia, at least since the 1977–1978 attempt to use mass attacks (involving poorly armed and motivated, largely Amhara peasant militias) against the Eritreans. The best Ethiopian army regular divisions, rather than special forces, are used as the spearhead of offensive operations both in Eritrea and Tigray. In Mozambique, the FPLM lack elite regular units and have few special forces, and it is the elite Zimbabwean units that bear the brunt of anti-RENAMO operations. Trained by the North Koreans, such units, particularly the Fifth Brigade, have a very poor record, and even the newly retrained FPLM and Zimbabwean units have yet to demonstrate satisfactory results. In Angola, there are practically no FAPLA special forces, but elite regular units are used to spearhead attacks on UNITA strongholds. Finally, in Nicaragua, the pattern is quite different, as practically all the units active in counterinsurgency are BLIs or Interior Ministry units. The regulars are largely used for static defense and semi-conventional operations requiring large numbers and massive firepower. BLI personnel are largely volunteers or known Sandinista sympathizers, and are well motivated and generally well-trained in the use of the weapons. Their counterinsurgency skills, however, are limited, and the preference for large-unit operations is evident.

What characterizes all Communist special-force operations in a COIN mode is their avoidance of long-range reconnaissance patrols or operations, excessive reliance on rapid air and often armor support, and generally their blitzkrieg approach. Even the Nicaraguan EPS, when attacking insurgent camps in Honduras, relies heavily on heliborne reinforcements and supplies, at the expense of surprise and at the risk of US, Honduran, or insurgent defensive action. In March 1986 and again in March 1988, the Sandinistas engaged in similar tactics, with similarly marginal results in military terms and heavy political damage. In all instances, the fundamentally intrusive and alien nature of Communist COIN forces explains the absence of self-sufficient, low-technology, and locally adapted small-unit operations. In addition, such small-unit operations, at platoon or smaller strength, are in direct contradiction to the usually centralized and tightly organized command-and-control pattern of operations of Communist forces everywhere.

*Militias and Population Control*

Anticommunist COIN forces have defeated Marxist-Leninist insurgents only after heavily involving the civilian population in the war by arming selected but relatively large numbers of the rural population and organizing them into paramilitary, militia-type organizations. Occasionally such organizations were established in order to prevent the establishment of a leftist insurgent infrastructure in the first place, as was the case with the Salvadoran ORDEN (Organización Democratica Nacionalista) in the late 1960s. More often, however, they were established in response to an ongoing insurgency, usually with the encouragement of the government or the military. In Guatemala in the late 1960s and again since 1983, in El Salvador during the late 1960s and early 1980s (first as ORDEN and then as "death squads"), in the Philippines in the 1950s, and in Dhofar, armed and organized civilians have played a major role in containing or defeating leftist insurgents.

In light of the well-established political and military value of using armed civilians in counterinsurgency, it is interesting to note that few Communist regimes have relied to any significant extent on arming civilians against anticommunist insurgents. True, almost all Communist regimes now under attack by insurgents claim to have the support of the "people" and to arm them against the "bandits." In at least one case, that of Nicaragua, that claim is often echoed by leftist or uninformed observers, who allege that the very existence of Sandinista militias is proof that the regime is not afraid to arm "the people," and hence that it enjoys their support.

The reality is quite different in all instances. In Nicaragua it is clear that the militias are FSLN activists and ordinary citizens shanghaied or threatened into joining by the ubiquitous CDSs. Their performance in defending certain installations—the essential military purpose of such organizations to begin with—is unimpressive at best. Their higher casualty rates, compared with those of the regulars and elite COIN forces, are to be expected, given their light weapons and rudimentary training. Such organizations have also been infiltrated by the insurgents, which lessens their effectiveness even further.

In Afghanistan the Soviets have taken a more sophisticated and well-proven approach to using civilians in COIN operations by simply bribing local leaders and mujahedeen field commanders. The problem with this is that, to paraphrase an old saying, you can rent an Afghan warlord, but you cannot own him.[67]

The use of Khmer militias against Cambodian resistance forces was never seriously attempted by the Vietnamese for the simple reason that those Khmers prepared to serve against the Khmer Rouge, and even they are a declining number, are clearly not prepared to do so against Sihanouk or Son Sann.

In Ethiopia, the Addis Ababa regime's massive use of Amhara peasants against the Eritreans in the late 1970s involved a combination of poorly trained recruits and land-hungry peasants—hardly a militia. At any rate, the attempt was a dismal failure, with huge casualties for the government side and few for the guerrillas.

In the general vein of mimicking what they think is an orthodox "scientific socialist" approach to social mobilization, the Angolan and Mozambican regimes established "militias" even before they had to face any significant insurgent threat. The Angolan "People's Defense Organization" (ODP) and the Mozambican militias have both been characterized by a dismal military record, lack of discipline, including massacres of civilians,[68] and, in the case of the ODP, which was pro-Nito Alves in 1977, political unreliability as well.

*Urban COIN Tactics*

While Soviet or other Communist counterinsurgency experience has been limited, experience in urban counterinsurgency simply did not exist until a little over a decade ago. Before then, whether in the forests of Poland, Lithuania, and the Ukraine, the mountains of Cuba, or the deserts of central Asia, Communist armies usually faced rural insurgents.

To a large extent the absence of urban insurgencies was the result of the efficiency of the secret police organization and its huge network of informers; it is their effective police organization that allows the Sandinistas to maintain their grip over the urbanized Pacific coast of Nicaragua. Nicaragua aside, however, urban guerrilla warfare has increasingly become a reality in Angola and has existed from the beginning in Afghanistan. In fact, the first major assault on the newly established Communist regime in that country took place in March 1979 in Herat, the second largest city.⁶⁹ Kabul itself is still not pacified, as demonstrated by the November 1987 mujahedeen mortar and rocket attack on the presidential palace at the time of Najibullah's swearing-in ceremony.

The very nature of many Third World cities is drastically different from that of Western or Communist states. In Europe (including most of the Soviet Union) the cities are the economic and social centers of the country, while the countryside plays a subsidiary role. By contrast, in Mozambique, Afghanistan, Eritrea, and Angola, the cities are simply islands in a rural sea. As a rule, communications and transportation are poor or nonexistent, and the city population itself is still largely nonurban due to the presence of recent arrivals from the countryside who retain at least some of their old habits, allegiances and contacts. The result of these peculiarities is that control over cities in a counterinsurgency environment is both more difficult and less significant than one would expect. Similar considerations also apply to the special case of Soviet air bases in Afghanistan, such as Bagram and Shindand.⁷⁰

The best and one of the lesser known methods used by Communist forces operating in an urban environment is the *quadrillage* technique, perfected by the French in Algiers and now used by the Soviet army in Afghanistan. There, in the Kandahar area, the Soviets built a road network within the city for the use of their tanks and armored cars, and by intensive patrolling of the areas thus delimited tried to eliminate the resistance.⁷¹ They were largely successful, principally because the desert terrain there is flat and thus easy to control once the few wells are taken or destroyed. Similar methods were used in Kabul, but the presence of foreign embassies and of more than three million refugees, as well as the availability of refuge areas controlled by the resistance, particularly Panjshir, prevented the same level of success.

In Angola it is by now quite clear that UNITA has a viable and well-established underground acting in the country's second largest city, Huambo, in most towns along the Benguela Railway, and to a certain extent, in Luanda proper. RENAMO's presence in Maputo, and particularly in Beira, Chimoio, and Nampula, is well documented. In the three largest cities of Eritrea (Asmara, Assab, and Massawa), the suffocating Ethiopian military presence and population transfers have clearly driven the insurgent infrastructure deeply underground and largely limited its usefulness to intelligence collecting. Cambodia is another peculiar case, since the Khmer Rouge regime between 1975 and 1978 practically destroyed its cities, particularly Phnom Penh. As a result, the insurgents, whether the Khmer Rouge, APN, or KPNLF, have as hard a time establishing a network in the newly created cities of post-1978 Cambodia as the invaders and their local puppets have in attempting to prevent their doing so.

In Nicaragua, the peasant insurgency has not become national in scope because of the resistance's inability to operate in the populous urban regions of the Pacific coast. The main reason for this, confidentially admitted by both the armed and legal political opposition to the Sandinistas, is the effectiveness of the DGSE and of Tomás Borge's Interior Ministry (MININT). With everyone under surveillance by the huge informant network, known as the Sandinista Defense Committees, and the regime's use of paid lumpenproletarians in the cities as a violent (and officially sanctioned) counter to opposition demonstrations and strikes, the opposition is bound to be intimidated.

Nicaragua however, is an exception to the general rule precisely because it has a large, fragmented, and timid urban middle class. Everyone knows everyone else, which facilitates DGSE control over the cities. Nowhere else is that the case, and nowhere else is the secret police's job as easy. Race, ethnicity, and tribal allegiances make this level of effectiveness difficult elsewhere, and dubious over the long term in Nicaragua as well.

All-out destruction of cities, quadrillage, permanent street patrols, and secret police saturation are of dubious value, and they also tend to limit, diminish, or constrain the scope of rural COIN operations, which are by far the most important, at least over the long term. On the other hand, the rural COIN methods pursued in Afghanistan, Mozambique, Nicaragua, and Ethiopia have paradoxically created additional problems as the displaced rural populations have moved into the swelling capital cities.

*Rural COIN*

By and large, the Communist counterinsurgency approach in the countryside has remained essentially unchanged since the Lithuanian, Ukrainian, and Polish campaigns of the late 1940s. Essentially, the approach centers on two basic goals, both related to population control: concentration and resettlement. The accent falls on resettlement in Ethiopia, Mozambique, Nicaragua, and Angola, and on concentration in Afghanistan and Cambodia, but a combination of the two approaches is the most common pattern.

As in other aspects of the counterinsurgency, the FRELIMO regime in Mozambique has proved to be the most inept, vacillating, and ineffective in dealing with the rural insurgency. Mozambique also provides the clearest indication of the reasoning behind such tactics, with its combination of ideological dogmatism, totalitarian instincts, and brutality. By the late

1970s it became clear that FRELIMO's policies were directed toward the drastic reduction of the urban population, especially in Maputo. The unemployed, the poor, and those recently arrived from the countryside were forcibly relocated to rural areas. It was a policy reminiscent of the Khmer Rouge's depopulation of Phnom Penh in 1975, albeit lacking the KR's ferocious and deadly efficiency. The rural population was forced into collective farms modeled after those Stalin established in the 1930s. Ironically, the old Portuguese *aldeamentos*, strategic villages established as a counter to FRELIMO's activities north of the Zambesi, became the new collective villages.

One FRELIMO innovation was the establishment of *mental decolonization* camps,[72] mostly in Nyassa and Cabo Delgado, which were little different from the post-1975 Vietnamese "reeducation" camps in South Vietnam. These were concentration camps for "social misfits" relocated from Maputo (prostitutes, beggars, and the unskilled), disaffected former FRELIMO guerrillas,[73] ethnic dissidents like the Makondes, families of the former Portuguese army and administration personnel, and so forth. The impossible living conditions and poor security in the camps proved to be FRELIMO's undoing, since many of the mental decolonization camps were liberated by RENAMO, mass escapes were frequent, and insurgent recruiting highly successful.

RENAMO's increasing strength made maintaining the poorly defended concentration camps in remote areas too risky, and at the same time, the "collective farms" established by FRELIMO in the old Portuguese *aldeamentos* collapsed under the weight of a combination of economic inefficiency, neglect, the dissolution of the nationalized distribution system, and lack of the means to control them. The result was that by the early 1980s, and certainly by 1983, the Mozambican rural population scattered again, but this time without the cohesion that had been provided by local chiefs and witch doctors, most of whom had been eliminated by FRELIMO. The resulting vacuum was immediately filled by RENAMO, the only real alternative to the government.

The *collective village* approach is not necessarily associated with antiinsurgency operations. It has been used by Communist regimes throughout the world, regardless of the presence or absence of an insurgent force, largely as a result of Stalinist influences. The theory was that collective agricultural production under state guidance and control would result in higher productivity and better social and health services, and provide incentives for the peasants. These unrealistic expectations were never realized, and the collectivist approach failed in country after country.

It continued to be applied, however, for reasons that have nothing to do with production, efficiency, or equality, but everything to do with population control. Whether the inhabitants of collective villages starve, produce little, or subsist, they are easy to control, and, by virtue of their size, collective villages become miniature cities, which means that saturation with informants becomes the rule. Although collectivization of the rural population failed, resettlement tactics did not.

While collectivization is theoretically an expression of Communist ideology, resettlement is clearly a response to an insurgent threat. Whether it takes the form of the Nicaraguan resettlement of unruly peasants from Nueva Guinea and Jinotega to keep them from supporting the insurgents, or the Soviets' purposeful depopulation of Afghanistan, or the Ethiopian regime's "famine related" resettlement of hundreds of thousands of Eritrean and Tigrean peasants, the goal is the same. If, in Maoist terms, the guerrilla is the fish swimming in a sea of sympathetic peasants, the antiguerrilla forces are trying to empty that sea by denying the insurgents contact with the population.[74]

In Afghanistan, the strategy of emptying the countryside took on genocidal proportions and resulted in the wanton destruction of villages in order to force the population out and to deny the resistance a source of local recruiting, supply, and indoctrination. In Nicaragua, resettlement in *asentamientos*, newly established large villages under EPS and CDS control, resulted in as many as 250,000 peasants being "relocated" from Nueva Guinea and Jinotega—some 10 percent of the country's total population. In Angola, the pattern is less clear, since the MPLA regime has only limited means for resettling the rural population in conflict areas, most of which remain under the control of Ovimbundu and other central or southeastern ethnic elements sympathetic to UNITA. Resettlement as a basic counterinsurgency method is also clearly a part of the Vietnamese decision to encourage the Khmer population displaced by the Khmer Rouge to return to the cities. More ominously still, from the point of view of the survival of the Khmers as a nation, is the massive settlement of hundreds of thousands of Vietnamese peasants in eastern Cambodia.

Collectivization and resettlement tend to attract the attention of the Western media, are expensive, and, most important, have repeatedly proved to be counterproductive for the short term. Thus, the massive migration of the Afghan population, internally to Kabul and externally to Pakistan's Northeastern Frontier, resulted in less, rather than more, security in Kabul, and the three million displaced persons on the border have become a source of recruiting and indoctrination for the mujahedeen. Similarly, although on a smaller scale, Cambodian refugees camps in Thailand and Nicaraguan camps in Honduras served to create guerrilla strongholds rather than to deny support for the insurgents as intended. In

Nicaragua, peasants forcibly resettled from Nueva Guinea became even more hostile to the Managua regime and threatened to "infect" their new neighbors.

These realities, the clear inability of most of the military institutions of the regimes under guerrilla attack to deal with them, as well as the logistical problems of fighting irregular wars in distant corners of the globe, have required that the Soviet Union and its closest allies and proxies seek more effective and less expensive solutions to the problems posed by the guerrillas. In general, however, such options as the use of special forces, chemical warfare, and cross-border terrorism are beyond the means of the local Marxist-Leninist regimes and their poorly motivated armed forces, and have to be undertaken either by the Soviets themselves or by their older satellites and friends, such as Cuba, Vietnam, North Korea, and the East Europeans.

*Public Relations and the Media*

The unorthodox and ruthless COIN methods of Communist regimes and their natural obsession with secrecy combine to explain their consistent hostility toward independent media presence on the battlefields. In Afghanistan, the Soviets and their Kabul protégés actually went so far as to offer rewards for the capture or murder of Western journalists traveling with the mujahedeen, while the Luanda regime has consistently warned journalists against visiting UNITA areas, permitting only its own "guided tours." There is virtually no media access to either the Vietnamese/PRK or the Khmer Rouge side of the Cambodia war, and very little to the Ethiopian conflict.

When foreign media representatives are not banned and journalists caught with the guerrillas are not killed or tried for "espionage," every attempt is made to manipulate them. The process of manipulation and disinformation is greatly facilitated by the fact that, in the absence of proinsurgent legal or semi-legal organizations in government-controlled areas, there is no immediately available alternative source of information. Most foreign journalists allowed inside government-controlled areas, moreover, are far from objective to begin with; in fact, their friendly view of the government is usually the condition for their presence in the first place. The result of these limitations on the media is successful propaganda for the Communist regimes.

Of all such regimes facing insurgent challenges today, the Sandinistas are by far the most skilled in manipulating the Western media. Not only do they enjoy sympathetic treatment from the US and European media, but the massive pro-Sandinista support network in the United States and

Western Europe is always ready and often capable of manufacturing news stories favoring the regime. Western fellow travelers in Nicaragua also work on behalf of the FSLN. Finally, the very raison d'être of groups like the US-based Witnesses for Peace is to create propaganda (i.e., media opportunities) for the Sandinistas, more often than not by (usually falsely) accusing the insurgents of atrocities, abuses, and crimes.[75]

I should point out that the Sandinistas' propaganda successes are unique among contemporary Communist regimes under insurgent attack, in no way equaled by the Vietnamese, Soviets, Ethiopians, or Angolans. Only the Mozambican regime, which has succeeded in acquiring the support of the State Department against RENAMO, has demonstrated skills that even approach those of the Sandinistas. Nevertheless, the relatively successful media blackout imposed by Communist regimes has resulted in persistent distortions and misperceptions of the goals, nature, and strength of the insurgents. Moreover, in the United States, and also in West European countries like France, West Germany, and Britain, the media's treatment of the wars in remote countries has led to massive public ignorance of and indifference to the importance of the anticommunist insurgencies that continue to play such an important role in the contemporary history of the Third World. It is that ignorance and indifference that often explain the West's responses to the anticommunist insurgencies as a phenomenon, particularly with regard to the United States.

## Western Responses and the *Reagan Doctrine*

*Can There Be a Reagan Doctrine? Perceptions and Constraints*

By most of the standards of orthodox COIN practice and theory, Communist regimes have performed less than impressively in the past, and their contemporary performance in the Third World has declined over time. With the exception of Nicaragua, the chance for a successful Communist COIN campaign today is fairly remote, while the possibility of Communist defeats in Angola, Ethiopia, Afghanistan, and Mozambique remain quite real. No Communist "hearts and minds" campaign has either been successful or, more important, has ever been conducted on a national basis during the almost seventy years since the Tambov campaign. Nevertheless, until the mid-1970s, Communist regimes invariably defeated insurgents, whether in Lenin's Russia, in the East European "people's democracies" of Poland and Romania, in China (Tibet), or in Cuba's Sierra de Escambray.

The paradoxical phenomenon, which appears to contradict contemporary Western counterinsurgency and geo-strategic wisdom, of Communist regimes being able to defeat insurgents at the height of the Cold War but largely unable to do so in a period of détente (whether Nixon- or Reagan-style), also raises some important historical and political questions regarding the West in general and the United States in particular.

The most obvious question is posed by the notion that the Cold War, whether defined by the revisionist Left or the conventional historians in the West, was a period of all-out enmity between communism and the democratic West. For the demonologists of the revisionist Left, the West, or specifically the United States, tried to overthrow the "progressive" Soviet and East European regimes between 1919 and 1950, using means fair and foul. That clearly does not square with the almost total absence of Western support for Lithuanian, Ukrainian, Polish, or Romanian insurgents against the newly established Communist authorities. Alternatively, conservative complaints that détente, whether in the Nixon-Ford, pre-1979 Carter version or in the post-1985 Reagan variant, has undermined anticommunist insurgencies also raise at least some problems: most of those insurgencies started, grew, or (as in Afghanistan) seem to have succeeded precisely at those times. At the very least this fact seems to suggest that Soviet-American détente, however it is defined, does not have a clear impact on the performance or existence of such insurgencies. In fact, all indications are that the West's, and particularly the United States's role in and impact on those insurgencies has far more to do with domestic politics dynamics and perceptions than with the state of formal relations with Moscow. As a result, it is largely a moot question whether the "new détente" defined by Ronald Reagan's summits and understandings with Mikhail Gorbachev will result in victory for the mujahedeen, UNITA, or the Cambodian resistance. After all, it is the American elites and public's perceptions and our policy-making processes that seem to determine Washington's policies on such issues.

That does not mean that what Moscow does, avoids doing, or states has no impact on the outcome of anticommunist insurgencies (most obviously, as in Afghanistan and to a limited extent in Angola, it does have a major impact). But the impact of such Soviet actions is best understood and most effective only as it is filtered through the shifting sands of American perceptions and domestic politics. And shifting sands they are, puzzling America's Western allies and confusing Third World friends and foes alike, including anticommunist insurgent leaders.

There may be no completely satisfactory solution to this puzzle, but a combination of factors tends to indicate that the key to it has as much to do with the waning Western ideological and geo-political challenge to communism as it does with the peculiarly American and Western failure to understand either the Third World in its post-decolonization phase or the nature of the kind of warfare that is actually waged in such countries.

Regarding the first issue, decolonization, it is and always was Washington's opinion that colonialism, which in practice meant Western (French, British, and Portuguese) colonialism, is evil, and that decolonization is an unmitigated blessing. So strong was that perception that almost three decades of African post-decolonization realities, including growing poverty and brutally undemocratic rule, are still not enough to force Washington into a more nuanced approach to the issue. A related, and even stronger myth, equally shared by conservatives and liberals, is that "democracy," defined as political pluralism and free elections, is not only an ideal goal to pursue in the Third World for moral reasons, but also a practical one, as it is supposed to guarantee stability and progress. Thus, in an October 1988 interview, then Assistant Secretary of State for Inter-American Affairs Elliott Abrams bluntly stated that Latin American "democratization" is always good for the United States on the grounds that "it's easier for us to have a closer relationship with a government that shares our values than with one that represses its people or engages in human rights abuses."[76] Abrams also claimed, in support of his opinion, that in some countries, "especially Uruguay, Argentina, and Brazil" the fear that a return to democracy would mean greater leftist gains did not materialize.[77]

In fact, with the possible exception of Uruguay, that was precisely what happened. In Argentina, the demagogic populist, anticapitalist and anti-American nationalism of Peronism has come back to power with Carlos Menem. In Brazil, the equally demagogic, anticapitalist and anti-American Leftist sects of the Workers' party of Luis Inácio da Silva ("Lula") and of the Democratic Labor party of Leonel Brizola, are two of the most serious competitors for the presidency in 1989. None of them, or the equally democratically elected Alan García regime in Peru, could seriously be described as sharing American values or of being compatible with US interests. More importantly, none could seriously be seen as guaranteeing stability; on the contrary, all seem to open the way for either the totalitarian Left or the military. More generally, democratically elected regimes in the Third World, whether in the Philippines, Peru, El Salvador, Brazil or Argentina, tend to be at least as vulnerable to attacks from the terrorist Left as their authoritarian predecessors, and probably more so. Thus the general perception of American voters and politicians of the relationship between democracy, capitalism, stability, and pro-Western policies has little to do with empirical evidence.[78] It is, however, a glaring example of the unrealistic transfer of the unique American historic experience to Third World societies that we don't understand. The same mentality made former President Ronald Reagan compare the Nicaraguan insurgents to the American "founding fathers," thereby producing excessive and unrealistic expectations. That myth-based approach, unrealistic as it was by itself, was further compounded by the historic American reflexive distaste for "dirty" undeclared wars — which is to say, for most contemporary Third World civil conflicts.

Indeed, the ongoing and very bloody conflicts in the Third World are all "irregular" in nature, while the ordinary American voter (and usually his congressman) sees war as an unfortunate, formalized, and thus *legal* military clash between nations who could not "find a diplomatic solution" to their differences. One of the more perversely self-defeating approaches to the issue is embodied in the claim that US support for challengers to Communist rule in the Third World may bring about "another Vietnam" or even a nuclear exchange.[79] As has been demonstrated over the years, however, Moscow is no more prepared to engage in a nuclear exchange over Angola or Nicaragua than the United States was over Indochina. Third World conflicts are seen by both superpowers as well below the threshold for World War III, although this fact is not recognized by many leaders of the Democratic party or by many of the groups influencing it, all of whom pretend to believe that conflicts over Angola, Afghanistan, Mozambique, or Nicaragua may bring about a nuclear winter.

The problem goes far beyond a simple misperception of present conflicts by ordinary voters. For the late senator and vice-president Hubert Humphrey, for example, Africa was a collection of savage tribes of no import to the United States; before her election, Senator Barbara Mikulski could not name the prime minister of Israel or the leader of UNITA (she was against the latter, nevertheless); and the Republican governor of Nebraska in 1988 did not know who Adolfo Calero, then the main Nicaraguan insurgent leader, was. This is not really surprising in a country in which a majority of Texas high school students do not know what country borders the United States to the south. The (usually) less than five minutes averaged by the networks in presenting foreign news on prime time television, not to mention the bias often manifest during those few minutes, does not improve the American public's knowledge, understanding, or ability to reach an informed opinion on developments in such hard-to-pronounce and impossible-to-locate places as Cambodia, Mozambique, Ethiopia, or Nicaragua.[80] The result is that the American public continues to respond to simplistic, emotional slogans about "a new

Vietnam," or "noninterference in other people's affairs," to which the Carter administration succeeded in adding the counterproductive and dangerously vague idea of human rights.

In such circumstances it is very difficult for even the most committed, clear-headed, and articulate political leader to gain coherent and steady popular support for anticommunist guerrillas, let alone to win consistent congressional support for them. Despite the claims of both his detractors and admirers, even Ronald Reagan, "the great communicator," was unable to do so. In fact, Reagan's first real attempt to obtain support for the contras of Nicaragua was delayed until more than two years into his presidency.[81] In addition, the Reagan administration's inconsistency including the opening of a new era of détente, its supine accommodation to liberal demands regarding South Africa and the constraints imposed on aid to Nicaragua, the often unclear signals regarding Afghanistan and Angola, and the outright support for FRELIMO raised serious questions over the nature, depth, and seriousness of the so-called Reagan Doctrine. Liberals and conservatives alike, however, projected their own idea of what a clear policy regarding the Third World and anticommunist insurgencies should be on a Reagan administration—the former by attributing it a dangerously dogmatic recklessness it never had, the latter by labelling spasmodic gestures as a *doctrine*.

For a long time, in disregard of elementary realities familiar to the most illiterate Ovimbundu follower of UNITA or Jamiat-i-Islami mujahedeen peasant fighting "vanguard parties" and their Soviet tanks, the Western Left has declared the Cold War over, anticommunism a dangerously obsolete conservative fixation, and containment irrelevant. George McGovern, whose philosophy has clearly become dominant in the Democratic party's leadership, put it most openly by stating that "so clearly is communism neither the wave of the future nor the major challenge to American security that our anticommunist orientation has become irrelevant and obsolete."[82] To further confuse the picture, the end of the Reagan years also witnessed similar statements from such "cold warriors" as the president himself and most West European leaders, including Prime Minister Margaret Thatcher.

For conservatives, who often interpret the Cold War as a conflict between Communist Darkness and democratic Light, the problem is to explain why the United States, the unchallenged champion of the West and all it then stood for, failed to help East European, Tibetan, or Cuban insurgents against their Communist foes. Furthermore, in light of that failure, and of the fact that the military balance of power has clearly shifted toward parity and even possible Soviet superiority, why should a revised US containment policy fare any better now than it did three or four decades ago? Perhaps the best conservative answer is inspired by a comment by Alvin Bernstein: "In confronting the global expansion of Soviet strategic capability, the US seems to have ruled out direct use of its forces in major Third World conflicts, and regional allies seem to lack either the strength or the will to intervene. The Reagan Doctrine offers only limited gains for limited costs, but what other courses are left?"[83]

What McGovern and Bernstein have in common, although they would both deny it, is a certain pessimism regarding US influence in the Third World. They reflect the unspoken but largely accurate opinion that the United States is steadily losing the capability, will, interest, and means to intervene in Third World conflicts, and that an action like the one in Grenada was really irrelevant in the global context of declining US power.

One sign of this is that US foreign policy has come to be dominated by questions of international law. In the United States the Democratic leadership, from former House Speaker Wright to 1988 presidential candidate Michael Dukakis, is in favor of entrusting American national interests and security to such international bodies as the United Nations, the Organization of American States and the World Court, or even to informal, *ad hoc* groups like the Contadora governments (Mexico, Panama, Colombia, and Venezuela). That process reached its height with the consistent and exclusive support offered by Democratic leaders to the "peace plan" for Central America proposed in August 1987 by President Oscar Arias of Costa Rica. The Democrats' public explanation for such a blatantly isolationist stand was well defined by the slogan "give peace a chance," a transparent way of accusing the Reagan administration of warmongering. Perhaps more significant still is that slogan's implication that peace *per se* is more important than liberal democracy or safeguarding the United States's strategic interests in Central America.

From this point of view, *any* unilateral political and military action by Washington in the Third World, whether in Grenada or against Libya, is worse than dangerous: it is blatantly "illegal." The Sandinistas, among others, have quickly capitalized on this attitude, and have gone so far as to sue the US government in US courts, as has the PLO. Furthermore, the Sandinistas have also successfully sued the United States at the International Court of Justice — with most of their lawyers being American leftists.[84]

The growing legalistic approach to foreign policy, at least in the Third World, is not primarily the result of the intensified propensity of Americans to solve disputes of any kind in courts, although a case could plausibly be made that such trends are relevant. Far more important is the moral factor, the overall perception of American and Western elites of their own societies' values. Those who believe that the United States and the Soviet Union are equally guilty of moral trespassing also tend, for emotional or pragmatic political reasons, to rely on "international law," the role of "international public opinion," and the United Nations, in complete disregard of historic experience and the present impunity with which outlaw states like Libya, Iran, Syria, and North Korea act in the present international system.

Liberals in the United States and most of the democratic parties of the Left in Europe (the French Socialists are a notable exception) exhibit a strong dislike of unilateralism, particularly when it is engaged in by Washington. The most recent and blatant example of this was the attempt on the part of the leading congressional Democrats to hide behind President Oscar Arias of Costa Rica and "the Central American presidents" on the subject of US policies in Central America, which left the question of how to contain a Marxist-Leninist regime like the Sandinistas' in the hands of the pacifist president of a small, disarmed country. Absurd as such an approach is, it was logical for those who wished above all to avoid the use or even threat of force at any cost, and whose main fear, in Central America at least, was the possibility of a unilateral action on the part of the Reagan administration, rather than the proven and well-documented aggression of the Sandinistas. The same trend was most recently demonstrated during the 1988 presidential campaign, particularly by Democratic candidate Michael Dukakis. Quite openly, and repeatedly, Dukakis claimed that Third World conflicts were a matter of "the people" fighting for "justice," and that any US interference in such conflicts should be strictly multilateral within the most narrow bounds of "international law." Thus, Dukakis had doubts about the international legality, and thus the legitimacy of the 1983 US intervention in Grenada;[85] he opposed any aid to UNITA and particularly the "contras"; and he clearly conditioned any US involvement in Third World conflicts on multilateral, internationally legal arrangements.[86]

In fact, judging by their public statements, present and recent Democratic congressional leaders, from Speakers Tip O'Neill and Jim Wright to House Whip Tony Coelho, often seem angry when Sandinista actions threaten their efforts to appease Managua, instead of being concerned by the implications of Sandinista actions for the stability of Central America and the interests of the United States. Tip O'Neill, for instance, fumed when Daniel Ortega's visit to Moscow in 1986, just after the speaker had succeeded in killing contra aid, led Congress to renew it; and then Speaker Wright complained that the Sandinistas were "snatching defeat from the jaws of victory" when it appeared that Managua would not comply with even the minimal and unenforceable requests of the Arias Plan at the end of 1987.[87]

In addition to the element of partisan politics, one must also take into account the impact of the organized Left in the United States and other Western nations, as well as the role of such institutions as certain religious groups and the media.

Despite the much-vaunted separation of church and state in the United States, parishioners are often influenced by the attitudes of their ministers, rabbis, and priests.[88] Former House Democratic Speaker Tip O'Neill demonstrated the extent of such influence when he admitted that his information on Central America, particularly Nicaragua, was "reliable" because it came from the Maryknoll brothers and sisters. What the speaker did not mention, and probably did not realize, was that Maryknoll is a Catholic order that has been working on behalf of Marxist-Leninist guerrilla and terrorist groups in Latin America for over two decades. Most of the national leadership of the Lutheran, Presbyterian, Episcopalian, and Methodist churches, the American Friends Service Committee and a few prominent Catholic bishops and organizations, not to mention the entire National (and World) Council of Churches, have taken a decidedly negative attitude toward support for anticommunist groups in the Third World, and have fervently expressed their views from the pulpit.[89]

Washington's policies toward anticommunist insurgencies are also affected by the efforts of the old Left, including the CPUSA's decisive role in establishing the Committee in Support of the People of El Salvador (CISPES), the main support organization providing propaganda for the Communist FMLN in that country.[90] Trotskyite and Maoist groups on university campuses also play a significant role, as do some of the Communist Left's old friends, some of whom are now important members of Congress. The now rather elderly New Left uses its positions of control in such organizations as the Latin American Studies Association, the Institute for Policy Studies, Transafrica, the North American Council on Latin America, the Latin American and Africa sections of such human rights groups as Amnesty International and Americas' Watch, to promote distorted and ideologically biased images of events in Latin America and southern Africa.[91] All those images inevitably find their way into the Congressional Record and staff papers directed to liberal or simply ignorant or negligent members of Congress. A similarly large-scale campaign is clearly developing in regard to the Philippines, which is at least implicitly and often explicitly supportive of the Communist party of the Philippines and its New People's Army (NPA).

Despite such blatant examples of partisanship, most of these groups and organizations, their grass roots representatives, and associated academic experts tend to concentrate openly on attacking US involvement in the Third World, rather than actually supporting Communist advances. Opposing containment in any form rather than advocating Marxism-Leninism is their strategic aim; opposition to anticommunist insurgencies is a less immediate and less visible tactical goal.

The disproportionate impact of such groups on America's Central American and southern African policies is the direct result of public ignorance and indifference. When the ordinary voter has problems locating Mozambique, Nicaragua, or El Salvador on the map, it should come as no surprise that "public" debate in Washington is dominated and controlled by motivated, "informed" special interests. The American public has long forfeited its right to play an active role in the formulation of US policy in Central America as is demonstrated by the repeated polls indicating that Americans are opposed to communism in Central America in just the same proportion that they oppose indirect US attempts to counter its expansion (i.e., through support for the Nicaraguan insurgents). Furthermore, when large segments of the Democratic party support Jesse Jackson and his claims that the Sandinistas are a legitimate government, while the Salvadoran or Guatemalan anticommunist counterinsurgencies amount to "war against the people," they only underscore the moral and political confusion dominating America's heartland regarding practically all of today's Third World conflicts.

In all six instances examined in this book, the immediate target of the guerrillas are local regimes claiming to be independent and "popular."[92] With the exception of Heng Samrin's People's Republic of Cambodia, these regimes are recognized under international law and by the United Nations.[93] As a result, they all claim to be defending themselves against *bandits*, to the limited extent that they even admit the existence of such adversaries. However, they also unanimously claim that their domestic foes are the tools of outside powers, instruments of "imperialism" or at best ignorant masses manipulated by reactionary politicians. In other words, the Communist regimes fighting insurgents officially and publicly see themselves as victims of an *ideological* and *external* attack, whether from "imperialists" or "revisionists." Such an approach, fancifully unrealistic as it is, implies that the issues involved in any US support for anticommunist insurgents are a matter of international law and morality, rather than ideology or national interest. It is a matter of international law inasmuch as bandits are supported from outside against the principle of noninterference in internal affairs of other states, enshrined in the UN Charter, and it is a matter of morality inasmuch as "innocent victims" are killed by Washington's dollars given to the bandits. On both counts the claims of the Angolan, Afghan, Nicaraguan, and Cambodian regimes are compatible with the claims of Western liberal politicians: help for insurgents is immoral since it results in the death of innocents, and it is illegal since (with the exceptions of Angola and Cambodia) it is done against governments recognized by the United States.

American conservatives[94] and liberals alike[95] accused the Reagan administration of taking an ideological, rather than a nationalist or pragmatic approach to anticommunist insurgencies. However, it seemed fairly clear that the administration was following the Wilsonian missionary utopian tradition, stressing Third World "democracy" just as assiduously as the Carter administration had stressed "human rights." By 1988 the Reagan administration was proudly boasting of having chased Ferdinand Marcos and Jean-Claude Duvalier from power, and of trying the same tactics against the Noriega regime, seemingly unaware that in doing so it created dangerous political vacuums in its search for an elusive "democracy" in the Philippines, Haiti, and Panama. Actually, it appears that US-type democracy is as alien in such countries as Leninism, and trying to impose the former may well result in strengthening the appeal of the latter, as seems to be the case in Panama. The recent history of the Third World in general, and of Latin America in particular, has repeatedly and abundantly demonstrated that Jeffersonian democracy and stability are more often than not incompatible. The much trumpeted Latin American (and Philippino, South Korean, or Tunisian) trend toward democracy claimed by the Reagan administration is hardly compatible with stability. Indeed, in countries like Peru, El Salvador, Honduras, the Philippines, and South Korea, democratically elected civilian regimes seem to face stronger, rather than weaker, challenges from the totalitarian Left, whether they are legal and peaceful or illegal and violent.

This very same tendency to misread the nature and goals of Third World societies also extends to US perceptions of anticommunist insurgencies[96] — hence, unrealistic and counterproductive claims like former President Reagan's that the Nicaraguan insurgents are the "moral equivalent of the Founding Fathers" and the simplistic conservative view of them as "freedom fighters." While the former claim could and should be seen simply as rhetorical overkill, the latter label is far more complicated than it seems. Indeed, while the anticommunist insurgents are indeed freedom fighters, their notion of freedom often has little to do with the American view of the concept, since it has little if anything to do with freedom of the individual, the right of property, equality under law, and political pluralism. It does, however, have everything to do with freedom from foreign domination, foreign forms of political organization, and alien political and cultural values. In other words, and with the benefit of hindsight, anticommunist "freedom fighters" today are just another form of anticolonialism, this time against domination by the Communist "Second World" rather than the older West European "First World."

The misunderstanding regarding the nature and goals of anticommunist insurgents is as much a political, moral, and ideological one as the result of partisan interests. For the ordinary American and the US Congress, there is no real distinction between freedom and democracy. Certain aspects of the US view of freedom are puzzling even for our West European allies, but its essence is completely alien to Jonas Savimbi, the mujahedeen, KPNLF, and RENAMO; it is only congenial (in part at least) to the Nicaraguan insurgents, the least politically successful of all anticommunist insurgent groups.

American democracy is centered on individual freedoms under law; as Michael Ledeen has pointed out recently, "Our elected officials do not swear an oath to defend the national interests; they swear to uphold the Constitution, which in turn defines the rights of individual citizens. Elsewhere, leaders swear to defend the interests of the nation."[97] Individualism, the bedrock of American democracy, however, is simply not a factor in most Third World societies, where the values and interests of the group take precedence, whether that group is defined in terms of the family (Latin America), the tribe and ethnic group (Africa), or the ethno-religious community (Cambodia or Afghanistan).

The mujahedeen do not die for the sake of checks and balances or the right to privacy or "equal worth" pay; nor do they die for the right of one man to one vote or representative government. They fight and die for "Islam," a concept only vaguely understood in the West that stresses the right to live according to traditional customs, to select their own local leaders, to be left alone to pursue their own old feuds, and even to be exploited by their traditional leaders.

No one who has met UNITA's people could seriously believe that they fight for democracy. They fight for the right to be themselves and to protect their ethnic, cultural, and collective identity against the regimentation imposed by Marxism-Leninism. The same is true of the Nicaraguan peasants who make up the bulk of the contras, and perhaps even more so of the Miskitu, Rama, and Sumo Indians or the Black Creoles of the Atlantic coast. There is not a Jeffersonian among them, except at the level of the American-trained, Westernized leadership. In fact, it is the ability to shed an acquired Western veneer and to appeal to old traditions like nationalism and Catholicism that makes a Bermudez or Calero popular among the rank and file. It is their inability to do so that limits the appeal of some of the political representatives of the Nicaraguan resistance.

Similarly, it is far more likely that former King Norodom Sihanouk and Prince Son Sann derive their authority and ensure the loyalty of their followers on the basis of the historic Khmer allegiance to Mahayana Budhism and a national consciousness dominated by hatred for the Vietnamese than from any Western political ideas, including democracy. Even the genocidal Khmer Rouge can attract popular support; genocidal they may be, but they are also Khmers with a long and excellent record of fighting the Vietnamese intruders. It is typical of the moral and practical difficulties facing Western (and particularly American) diplomats that the 1988/1989 negotiations on Cambodia were centered less on the future of that country in general, following the promised Vietnamese withdrawal, than on how to keep the strongest insurgent movement, the Khmer Rouge, out of power. At no time was the real issue addressed: the reason that the Khmer Rouge are the strongest and largest anti-Vietnamese force, despite their genocidal past. The reason is unpleasantly clear: to ask such question would demand an answer to the comfortable equation of anticommunist insurgents = freedom fighters. The Khmer Rouge expanded and improved their forces because many Cambodians, particularly the youth, saw them as the most effective nationalist enemies of the Vietnamese intruders. That democracy, respect for human rights, and pluralism played a minor role at best for Khmer Rouge recruits is unsettling enough for most Westerners; that a far larger number of Cambodians, more than a decade after the Pol Pot genocide, still prefer totalitarian discipline under Pol Pot to loyalty to pro-Western groups like those led by Sihanouk and Son Sann is more unpleasant still. Unpleasantness aside, however, the Khmer Rouge's case vividly demonstrates that Third World anticommunist insurgents are often motivated by anything but Western-defined notions of democracy, that they are anything but conventional "freedom fighters."

In Eritrea, as in Cambodia and Nicaragua, national, rather than religious or ethnic consciousness (as in Afghanistan, Angola, and Mozambique) fuels the resistance and also helps to explain the growing cooperation between Moslems and Christians. In the context of the multinational Ethiopian Empire, the Eritreans played a role similar to that of the Jews in the Tsarist empire or the Palestinians in the Arab world today—they are a better-educated, culturally distinct, and discriminated against minority. Unlike those groups, however, the Eritreans have a well-defined territorial base. They were attracted by the siren songs of the Left when the oppressor was the decrepit, feudal empire of Haile Selassie, and then have had difficulty adjusting to the new and "progressive" regime of

Mengistu Haile Mariam's "Democratic Ethiopia." Since 1977, however, there has been a slow (but steady and observable) shedding of Marxism-Leninism, at least in their public rhetoric, by EPLF leaders, who had been led to believe that Marxist-Leninist "progress," supported by Soviet and radical Arab weaponry, was the natural answer to an Amhara imperialism supported by the United States.

RENAMO is perhaps the quintessential example of an anticommunist group that is almost incomprehensible to Westerners. The few educated Mozambican elites have chosen Leninism or been killed or driven into exile, so that the leadership of the resistance cannot seriously be expected to come from sophisticated cadres, simply because there are none left.[98] Samora Machel himself, the first leader of independent Mozambique, was a male nurse with only four years of schooling. Afonso Dhlakhama, poorly educated as he is, is no less educated than Samora Machel was, and he is clearly more representative of the general level of the Mozambican public than is university-educated President Joaquim Chissano. Nevertheless, the West in general and the United States media in particular expect a certain level of political sophistication, and they have no faith in RENAMO because they see it as lacking a clearly articulated political program. Of course, RENAMO does have a political program, simple though it may be, as is demonstrated by Jack Wheeler's essay in this volume, and to accuse the resistance in what may well be one of the most primitive and poorest countries on the planet of lacking political articulation and sophistication is unrealistic at best. RENAMO's program is a positive one involving respect for traditional authorities and economic decentralization and denationalization. The problem however, is that advocating a return to traditional authorities, whether village chiefs or councils of elders is not progressive, modern, or intellectually exciting. American politicians and the media, however, expect a statement of intentions, no matter how fraudulent, rather than a description of the ordinary, simple aims of the ordinary, simple people of a country like Mozambique. Marxist-Leninists, whether in the government or opposing it, are adept at articulating their programs; ordinary Africans, however, are not.

In the United States, conservatives and liberals are equally guilty of trying to avoid the unpleasant realities of Third World conflicts. The conservatives choose to describe anticommunist insurgents as "freedom fighters," implying that they are fighting for democracy. Convenient utterances by Savimbi, Massoud, Sihanouk, and Dhlakhama are quoted to prove this point, and Reagan himself, in a frequently quoted statement, claimed that Enrique Bermudez and Adolfo Calero are the "equivalent of the Founding Fathers." The liberals' dilemma is different in nature but not in essence. They have used statements about "international law" and "nonintervention" when opposing Reagan's half-hearted attempts to change the nature of the Managua regime, but they are also proud of their anti-Somoza, anti-Marcos, anti-Botha, and anti-Duvalier record; and Jesse Helms and Jesse Jackson happily joined forces against a Noriega. Liberals for the most part oppose foreign intervention and invasion anywhere, but their "strong support" for the remote mujahedeen in Afghanistan and the ANS and KPNLF in Cambodia has helped to counter Republican accusations of being "soft on communism." Since for many years neither the Afghans nor the Khmers seemed to have a real chance of military success, supporting them has also fit into the Democratic leadership's obsession with "diplomatic solutions" in which the Congress they control is expected to play a major role.

A charismatic black like Jonas Savimbi, who does not fit into familiar patterns, poses a special set of problems for liberals. Savimbi's color makes it difficult to dismiss him as a "fascist," so the refuge is in emotional arguments. A typical example is MIT Africanist and *Christian Science Monitor* columnist Robert Rotberg, in his reaction to the Reagan administration's intention to provide stinger missiles to UNITA. According to Professor Rotberg, helping Savimbi in any way would align the United States with South Africa—a very bad idea in his opinion, regardless of the circumstances. Equally bad, strengthening UNITA would only encourage the Cubans and Soviets to give even more aid to the Luanda regime, which would even give them "credibility" at a time they were supposedly losing it.[99] What Professor Rotberg conveniently forgets to say is that many African governments also support Savimbi, even if they do so discreetly, and that an even larger number of such governments also have open ties with Pretoria as well. Furthermore, the liberals themselves have consistently dismissed conservative suspicions regarding the Marxist Leninist nature of such "liberation movements" as SWAPO, the ANC or the pre-1979 Sandinistas, on the grounds that such groups' ties to the Soviet bloc were based on necessity and convenience rather than ideological kinship.

It is true and at the same time disingenuous to claim, as many liberals do, that supporting Third World insurgents or actually engaging in helping counterinsurgent forces is incompatible with the American democratic principles and moral values. The liberal response to the CIA manual for the Nicaraguan insurgents is typical in this respect. The manual, an American version of the quintessential Maoist, Guevarist, and ultimately the common-sensical ideas on guerrilla warfare, became a lightning rod for all those who, for legitimate "democratic" and less than legitimate prototalitarian reasons, wanted to get the United States out of the insurgency business in the Third World — whether in support of anticommunist guerrillas or of anticommunist government forces. Aryeh Neier put it in the clearest terms:

> The CIA manual, *Psychological Operations in Guerrilla Warfare*, promotes violations of U.S. law and international law. It makes the United States member of the company of outlaw nations that sponsor international terrorism. It also raises questions about our pursuit of foreign policy by means that would not withstand democratic scrutiny and debate.[100]

The inhabitants of Hamburg and Dresden burned alive by US and British aircraft during World War II, as well as the Kurds gassed in 1988 by the Iraqi government enjoying implicit US support, or the millions of Afghan civilians killed by the Soviet army would hardly take comfort from such remarks. On the other hand, Neier may well be representative of the general American attitude toward "dirty wars" — and insurgency or counterinsurgency are "dirty" by definition.[101]

Such perceptual and conceptual limitations in assessing the meaning and importance of anticommunist insurgencies are not limited to fringe elements of the Democratic party, leftist academics, and professional "human rights" activists. Nor can they be explained as the result of the activities of organized fronts for the Sandinistas, for the FMLN, et cetera. They are reflected in congressional politics and have become the underlying rationale for one side of the ongoing foreign policy debate in the United States.

One result of that debate is the so-called Reagan Doctrine on communism in the Third World. Since its target is an ideologically motivated phenomenon, a strong anticommunist consensus, or at least a large, informed, and consistent anticommunist majority in the body politic, the media, and Congress is required for the doctrine to succeed. But there is no real anticommunist consensus among elites in the United States. If anything the remnants of the old one of the 1950s and early 1960s, already almost eliminated by Vietnam, is today being buried by Mikhail Gorbachev's public relations offensive. Politicians who made frequent statements in favor of the Sandinistas, Castro, or the ANC, not to mention Gorbachev, are common, ran for president in 1988, dominate the Democratic party, and are not absent in the Republican party. Academics with past favorable opinions of Ayatollah Khomeini, the FSLN, the Salvadoran FMLN or even Pol Pot are accepted as experts, and their views are included in official US publications. Anticommunism has fallen into disgrace as a legitimate concept in "elite" company in the United States. The results of this situation are most apparent in the debate over US support to the Nicaraguan insurgents. In fact, it was the debate over the issue of aid to the contras that best defined the conflicting trends within the US body politic over the entire issue of anticommunist insurgencies.

From the beginning of the debate a majority of the Democrats claimed that their main concern over the thrust of the Reagan administration's policy was that it would lead to direct US military involvement in Nicaragua. The administration and its supporters, on the other hand, denied any intention of committing US forces — as recently as March 1988 when former Secretary of State Shultz made a public statement reiterating the administration's position. Furthermore, Ronald Reagan and other contra supporters outside the administration consistently claimed that support for the Nicaraguan insurgents was the best way to prevent the involvement of US forces in Central America. In other words, at least publicly, from 1981 to 1988 the Democratic leadership and the administration both claimed to agree on one fundamental issue — that the United States should not become involved militarily. Nevertheless, the Democrats continued to oppose US support for the Nicaraguan insurgents, and, since the summer of 1987, they have consistently argued in favor of the "Arias Plan," despite its toothless enforcement provisions, fundamentally pacifist thrust, and disregard for the ideological, political, and geopolitical realities of Central America.

Thus, from the beginning, both sides have taken for granted the proposition that US military force should not be used in Central America, an implicitly isolationist premise. For the Democrats, the majority party of Congress since 1987, it took little time to take the next logical step of favoring any solution to the Nicaraguan conflict other than the use or even the threat of force. While the Reagan administration gradually went from one half-baked articulation of hostility toward the Sandinistas to another, the Democrats' path from isolationism to appeasement was far more direct and rapid. There is a clear continuity between Walter Mondale's 1984 all-out opposition to aid to the Nicaraguan insurgents, coupled with the threat of a blockade of Nicaragua if Soviet strategic weapons were deployed there, and Michael Dukakis's 1988 admission that he would be prepared to live with a Soviet satellite in Managua — provided that there were no Soviet strategic weapons on Nicaraguan soil.

Both Mondale and Dukakis were in effect telling Daniel Ortega that the United States is prepared to live with another Cuba in Central America under the same conditions that Kennedy accepted in 1962. Yet Nicaragua is a country with one-third of Cuba's population. It is an unconsolidated Marxist-Leninist regime still facing a viable popular insurgency and legal political opposition, and it lacks even the shaky commitment Moscow had made to Castro by 1962. In fact, as Elliott Abrams put it, the Democratic critics of contra aid "have felt compelled not to criticize Nicaragua for fear of helping Reagan. . . . such people run the risk of becoming apologists for the Sandinistas."[102] Quite clearly the Democratic party as a whole has not learned from the Cuban experience;[103] on the contrary, they choose to ignore the very idea that Marxist-Leninist, pro-Soviet regimes or insurgent groups pose a threat to US interests or values. Soviet strategic hardware placed embarrassingly close to US shores may still raise some eyebrows, but the inherent isolationism and pacifism now dominating the party makes even that gesture look less than convincing.

While the goal of avoiding US military involvement in Central America became a major aspect of the administration's defense against its critics, for the Democrats it was the primary goal from the beginning. Naturally, a policy predicated on the avoidance of military conflict cannot but fail against a motivated and aggressive enemy like the Sandinistas. By publicly accepting the notion that the avoidance of US direct intervention is a major goal of its Nicaragua policy, the Reagan administration lost its most potent instrument.[104] Similarly, by shifting its publicly stated objectives in supporting the contras from "preventing" Nicaraguan aid to the Salvadoran guerrillas, to "democratizing" the Sandinistas, to have them "cry uncle" as Ronald Reagan put it, the Reagan administration only confused its friends at home and abroad and provided gratuitous ammunition to its domestic foes.[105]

Finally, in a startling demonstration of the complete collapse of bipartisanship between White House Republicans and Democrats on Capitol Hill, Elliott Abrams, expressing directly what most Republicans say in private, simply accused then Speaker Wright of being a Sandinista fellow-traveler: "Wright bet all his money on the Sandinistas and, ultimately, painted himself into a corner where it became critical for him to defend their behavior."[106] Abrams might have been correct in his assessment of the former House speaker, but his surprise was misplaced. Individual opinions, even those of such influential players in the policy-making process, are less important than the more general circumstances making such politicians as Wright or Senators Harkin, Kerry and Dodd important in the first place and their opinions representative for a majority of the House and a blocking minority of the Senate. It may well be that the most important reason Ronald Reagan's Nicaragua policy (to the extent one was consistently articulated) failed was his administration's misunderstanding of both the strength and motivations of the congressional opposition and the lack of public interest, knowledge, and understanding of the issues at stake.

Indeed, when Reagan came into office, the number of conservative experts on the Third World was insignificant—hence, for example, Chester Crocker had to be accepted as the only prominent non-liberal or leftist Africanist in the country with any connections in Washington. Toward the end of Reagan's tenure, and as a result of the changes he brought about, the pool of conservative Third World experts had expanded rapidly, although African studies remains a left-dominated field. Most of these experts, however, remained outside the administration and became increasingly disenchanted with its policies. As a result, and despite the efforts of a few institutions like Hoover, the American Enterprise Institute, the Institute for Foreign Policy Analysis, and a few others, as well as the lobbying efforts of the Heritage Foundation and the work of a few independent analysts and courageous academics, the conservative side of Third World studies remains largely unknown to the public at large, to the Congress and the media, and was unknown to the Reagan administration itself. That administration also relied on State Department, CIA, and DIA analysts, all of them, despite their professionalism, career bureaucrats with decisive incentives to avoid *ideological* (i.e., principled and conceptual) assessments of Third World realities. The result has been a confusion of habits and bureaucratic or career interests with national interests.

Somewhat paradoxically, another problem raising often insuperable obstacles for any consistent anticommunist policy in the Third World is a very old American political disease: missionary zeal in the service of democracy. The worst, but by no means only serious outbreaks of this epidemic occurred during Democratic administrations of this century: Wilson's, FDR's, and Carter's. But Republicans are also susceptible, and Ronald Reagan succumbed to the disease, although exhibiting different symptoms from his predecessor. Jimmy Carter believed that "human rights," as commonly understood in the United States, are of universal applicability, and Walter Mondale clearly stated that "human rights transcend ideology. We believe all nations, regardless of political systems, must respect those rights."[107] Such an opinion was clearly based upon the conviction that political systems and ideological differences are not really very important to begin with. While visiting Poland in 1977, President Carter proclaimed that "old ideological labels have lost their meaning," while his ambassador to the United Nations, Andrew Young, sought to "break the sterile impasse between 'capitalism' and 'Socialism.'"[108] Such statements and others, like Jimmy Carter's rejection of "our inordinate fear of communism," were both the logical continuation of a trend started in the Democratic party with George McGovern's 1972 presidential campaign and the immediate root of Ronald Reagan's problems with the Democratic-controlled House of Representatives. Indeed, it was the House rather than the more conservative—and between 1981 and 1987, Republican-controlled—Senate that effectively opposed the Reagan "doctrine" from the beginning. This is not only because many of the younger and most dynamic Democratic members of the House were elected during the post-Vietnam and post-Watergate era, but also because most of the leadership was and still is clearly to the left of center. Former Speaker Jim Wright was involved in leftist politics in his youth and was a consistent supporter of the Sandinistas beginning in 1979, while most leaders of other relevant sub-committees of the House's foreign relations committee are also decidedly on the left of the political spectrum. For instance, the chairmen of the Western Hemisphere, Africa, and East Asia sub-committees, reps. George Crocket, Harold Wolpe, and Stephen Solarz, respectively, are all among the most liberal members of the House. In such circumstances it was no surprise that the anti-Reagan opposition, centered in the Democratic party but far from being limited to it, took on a decidedly anticommunist posture. By itself, such a fundamental disagreement over the very principles of the United States's foreign policy in general, and attitudes toward anticommunist insurgencies in particular, would have made any bipartisan consensus an illusory goal, but the Reagan administration's own lack of consistency and clarity of purpose further hindered its own stated goals.

Reagan came into power in 1981 as a polarizing candidate — the most charismatic and popularly liked president in recent memory, while at the same time the one provoking the most passionate hostility and hatred. Nevertheless, by the time he left office eight years later, Ronald Reagan's foreign policy received high marks of appreciation from the very groups in the Democratic party that consistently opposed the "Reagan Doctrine." The two main reasons for that apparent paradox were the new detente with Moscow and the successful role of the administration in removing from power a number of staunchly anticommunist, Third World dictators, such as Ferdinand Marcos in the Philippines and Jean-Claude Duvalier in Haiti, and of nudging pro-American authoritarian regimes in Chile and South Korea toward political democracy. On both counts the interests of the liberal Democrats were served because, ironically, Ronald Reagan succeeded where Jimmy Carter largely failed. On the other hand, however, Reagan's own goal, to expand democracy throughout the Third World in general, and in Marxist-Leninist-ruled countries in particular, was only partially reached. Indeed, with the possible, but not probable exception of Afghanistan, and the clearer one of Grenada, democracy is nowhere closer to implementation in Communist-ruled Third World countries than it was in 1980. On the contrary, it appears that the Reagan administration, in its final days, might have paved the way for yet another Marxist-Leninist regime in Namibia. It thus appears that the remnants of a bipartisan consensus on Third World policy in Washington have largely resulted in successfuly removing anticommunist dictators from power, more often than not at the expense of both short-term stability and the long-term institutionalization of democracy.[110] It did not extend to self-proclaimed Marxist-Leninist regimes, the Afghanistan case remaining an exception, but on the contrary it rapidly broke down in the case of Nicaragua. The reason was both clear and unspoken: ideology.

The immediate reasons for the two sides, the administration and the House, cooperating in the overthrow of Duvalier and Marcos and of trying to do the same with Pinochet, Stroessner, Botha, or others are quite different. Nevertheless, on a deeper level there is a truly non-partisan and all-American shared belief in the myth that democracy is always the best solution and that it is exportable or applicable in most instances. The idea that Jeffersonian democracy in places like Haiti, South Africa, Lebanon, or the Philippines might not be applicable or desirable is perceived as a "far Right," "fascist," and un-American view. Unfortunately or not, American political culture is centered on a strictly narcissistic view of the world: if democracy is good for us, it therefore has to be good for the natives, even if they do not realize it.

Sharing this belief makes it possible for the two major isolationist schools of thought in the United States to meet in practical terms. Those who think that we are too good for the corrupt outside world meet those who believe that the world is too good for us corrupt Yankees. In all respects, then, the deepest aspects American political convictions work against even an articulate presentation of a Reagan Doctrine, let alone its consistent application.

*Was There a Reagan Doctrine?*

It is often said that nothing concentrates minds as much as success. The Soviet withdrawal of troops from Afghanistan by February 15, 1989 clearly provided all those supporting the Reagan Doctrine with a very good reason to cheer — correctly, but misleadingly and, most importantly, *ex post facto*. Indeed, one major politico-military defeat for Moscow, and for Afghanistan, was the first such defeat ever, despite Soviet attempts at obfuscation. But this does not make a successful strategic doctrine for rolling back Soviet influence in the Third World. The facts that the victory of the *mujahedeen* came at almost the same time that the contras were effectively declared dead by the central American presidents meeting in El Salvador, and that the prospects for anticommunist victories in Angola and Cambodia are cloudy at best, only underscores the tentative nature of any objective assessment of the impact and ultimate success or failure of the Reagan Doctrine. The difficulty of assessing its impact and success, however, are only some of the important questions we must ask about.

Because of its woolly conceptual structure, the Reagan Doctrine is extremely difficult to define, and there are serious problems as to the degree to which it is either Reagan's or a doctrine. To begin with, little in Reagan's own political career suggests any degree of strong conceptual and theoretical geo-political interests. Certainly, a visceral anticommunism and support for democracy are long-standing features of Ronald Reagan's political outlook. Nevertheless, neither the president nor his closest advisers displayed or pursued clear geo-political aims.

The so-called Reagan Doctrine, briefly defined, is a statement of principle to the effect that it is the policy of the United States to support local forces opposing existing Marxism-Leninist regimes. Its scope was never described in detail by any member of the Reagan administration, including the president himself,[111] although the general inference from presidential and other official statements was that it was limited to post-Vietnam, Third World additions to the Soviet ideological, political, and strategic camp. Equally important, even the most dedicated admirers of the Reagan Doctrine admitted that it started taking shape only in 1985.[112] Before that the term was only used by the *New York Times* and the *Washington Post* as a label for what they considered to be Ronald Reagan's conservative foreign policy in the Third World. After the 1984 presidential elections and Reagan's landslide victory, the president himself, key members of his cabinet including Secretary of State George Shultz, and a plethora of conservative groups, spokespersons, and personalities all made their own contributions to defining the still hazy concept.

The president's State of the Union Message of 5 February 1985 included a reference to "freedom fighters," and his weekly radio address of 16 February 1985 mentioned the Afghan, Ethiopian, Angolan, and Cambodian freedom fighters' aiming to "undo the infamous Brezhnev Doctrine."[113] A week before the 1985 State of the Union Address, Secretary Shultz claimed that: "experience shows that we cannot *deter or undo* Soviet geopolitical encroachments except by helping, in one way or another, those resisting directly on the ground."[114] The same month, Secretary Shultz delivered an address to the Commonwealth Club of San Francisco that remains the most extensive and elaborate official description of the Reagan Doctrine.

The secretary of state claimed that it is an American "moral responsibility" to accept the role of supporters of Third World peoples prepared to fight for the survival of their "cultures and freedoms," not exclusively because of the American tradition of support for "democracy and freedom" but also for reasons of national interest. Furthermore, the Soviets have found a low-cost and highly successful instrument for destabilizing foreign governments via their support for "national liberation movements" and have consolidated those successes through the Brezhnev Doctrine. Hence, the *implied* US response should be to use similar means in support of democracy and freedom.[115] The three reasons for supporting anticommunist insurgencies given by George Shultz were thus morality, the national interest, and cost effectiveness. The question of morality is perhaps the crux of the problem, since it provided arguments for both supporters and critics of the administration's approach.

Critics claim that support of insurgents against established governments is illegal under international law since it threatens world order and stability and encourages bloodshed.[116] It is doubtful that US aid to insurgents in Cambodia or Afghanistan threatens world order in a way comparable to the occupation of those countries by Vietnam and the Soviet Union. Furthermore, the Nicaraguan, Mozambican, Angolan, and Ethiopian regimes have been heavily involved in destabilizing their neighbors and forcing them to concentrate their attention on staying in power and dealing with internal attacks, which may actually have increased regional stability. Indeed, Angola, Nicaragua, and Mozambique have all become far less active in their regional destabilization efforts (although none has stopped them) or are at least on the defensive. As for the argument that US support for insurgencies encourages bloodshed, one may simply reply that civil strife and bloodshed have always characterized Third World politics, independent of Washington's actions; furthermore, the absence of US support did not lessen the bloodshed in Ethiopia or Mozambique, and, inasmuch as US weapons made the mujahedeen better able to defend themselves, it actually decreased the number of casualties in Afghanistan.

A related "morality" issue, and in the cases of Angola, Mozambique, Cambodia a central one,[117] is that of implicit US cooperation with or support for groups or regimes that are themselves undemocratic. Thus, the main "argument" of the Black Caucus in the US House of Representatives against renewing US aid to UNITA was that "Any such assistance, whether military or so-called humanitarian aid, whether covert or overt, would definitely ally the United States with South Africa's minority regime."[118] That argument has also been used against US aid to RENAMO, and has been mentioned by the few members of Congress opposing aid to the Cambodian insurgents because of the Khmer Rouge's participation in the insurgent alliance. The Cambodia case was solved by simply limiting US assistance to the non-Marxist elements of the anti-Vietnamese coalition (KPNLF and MOULINACA). The Angolan case is more complicated, since there are many congressmen, particularly Democrats, who seriously argue that apartheid is such an absolute evil that any connection with it irredeemably taints the United States. That, however, is an emotional and ideological reaction rather than a rational argument. Indeed, few people (other than Bishop Desmond Tutu) would exhibit such ignorance of history and reality as to claim that the limited overlapping of US and South African interests in Angola "taints" the US more than the open World War II alliance with Joseph Stalin's regime, nor would they accept the (ludicrous) premise that apartheid is the contemporary equivalent of Nazism.[119] One may also argue that in supporting anticommunist insurgents, the United States is perforce associated with less than perfectly democratic regimes, whether in Pakistan, Thailand, Zaire, Honduras, and, in the cases of Afghanistan and Cambodia with the Chinese. Such considerations also demonstrate the degree to which morality and geopolitical interests are difficult to reconcile.

If, as some commentators have argued, the Reagan Doctrine took shape only after the 1984 presidential elections, when Ronald Reagan won one of the most decisive victories in US political history, one may ask why it fared so badly. One would expect that such an extremely popular president, with such an overwhelming popular mandate, would have been able to prevail on a foreign policy issue of such importance. Conservatives would argue that the Republicans' loss of the Senate in 1986 is one reason for Reagan's failure, but that begs the question of why so little was accomplished between 1984 and 1987. The real answer lies in the administration's failure to present a coherent policy to the American public and Congress.

The administration never successfully resolved the question of whether the United States should support any insurgency as long as it was directed against a pro-Soviet regime, even if its leadership was Communist or antidemocratic. The Reagan administration chose to avoid the Khmer Rouge and the EPLF, on the grounds that they were both totalitarian in nature, a proven fact in the case of the former, but far less so in that of the latter. Nevertheless, such considerations, decent and morally correct as they are, made the "doctrine" less than global and less than coherent. After all, Washington did provide substantial aid to Tito during the late 1940s, although he was no less totalitarian than the Soviets, on the ground that he was anti-Moscow; it established relations with and still cooperates with the Communist regime in Beijing over Afghanistan and Cambodia, as well as elsewhere, for similar reasons; and until 1988, under three administrations (Ford, Carter, and Reagan), it pampered the openly Stalinist regime of Nicolae Ceausescu in Romania. It is thus clear that the Marxist-Leninist nature of a regime has not been a decisive obstacle for lending US support. Admittedly the Khmer Rouge are in a league by themselves as the most murderous Communist regime in history, but the same cannot be said about the others.

The choice between supporting an insurgent group because its adversary is Communist—that is, negative support—and assistance to a noncommunist organization is a real issue for any democratic government, despite the above-mentioned fact that the most effective noncommunist anti-Leninist insurgents today, UNITA and the mujahedeen, are far from being Jeffersonian democrats themselves. Nevertheless, it raises an important, perhaps crucial question regarding US strategy and global interests: Is the enemy communism as such, or is it the Soviet Union as a rival superpower, regardless of ideology?

In response to such questions, the Reagan administration gave the most confusing signals of all American governments since World War II. On the one hand, the president himself at one point declared the Soviet Union an "evil empire" by virtue of its ideology; on the other hand, the administration engaged in what can only be described as a second round of détente, and the president himself gave Mikhail Gorbachev the benefit of the doubt on Afghanistan by stating that he had simply "inherited" the problem. Perhaps far more important was the notion, increasingly dominant in the State and Commerce departments, that Communist regimes in general, and Third World ones in particular can be "weaned" away from Marxism-Leninism through economic and political means.

The best example of incoherence and conflicting goals is the response to the FRELIMO regime in Mozambique. Because the regime was forced, threatened, or blackmailed by South Africa into avoiding becoming a full-fledged Soviet satellite, and because it refused to support the Soviet and Vietnamese occupations of Afghanistan and Cambodia respectively, the Reagan administration decided that the People's Republic of Mozambique should be aided against RENAMO, arguably the most successful anticommunist insurgent movement in the world today. The spectacle of Washington, London, and somewhat more circumspectly Lisbon, under their most conservative leaders in decades, helping FRELIMO against RENAMO should be an object lesson for would-be or actual anticommunist Third World guerrillas. As Jack Wheeler enthusiastically argues in this volume, RENAMO is no different in nature from the mujahedeen, UNITA, or the Nicaraguan insurgents, except for its consistently demonstrated incompetence in the public relations realm.

The case of RENAMO is only the most obvious example of the type of inconsistency that has plagued American policies toward anticommunist insurgencies in the Third World. Of the seven such insurgencies in progress today, the United States provides no assistance whatsoever to three (in Mozambique, Laos, and Ethiopia) and only marginal support to the Cambodian insurgents.[121] It only started a modest assistance program to UNITA in Angola in 1986, and aid to the Nicaraguan insurgents, despite the administration's unusual rhetorical consistency, can only be characterized as sporadic, unreliable, and insufficient. Afghanistan is the sole exception, an instance when consistency of policy and purpose allowed for the provision of significant and adequate assistance. But aid to the mujahedeen alone does not constitute a doctrine.

If the lack of a coherent conceptual framework and consistency have disqualified the Reagan administration's approach to Third World anticommunist insurgencies as a doctrine, its inability to articulate clear goals and define the necessary means resulted in a weak set of disparate regional policies generally lacking public support.

What the goals of the administration have been in any Third World region with ongoing anticommunist insurgencies remained unclear. In Nicaragua the publicly defined goals of a policy of assistance to the insurgents shifted with the congressional mood. Those goals were first described as interdiction of Sandinista military supplies to the Salvadoran Marxist-Leninist forces, a very implausible goal indeed, and one consistently and publicly contradicted by the insurgent leaders. Later the goal was "redefined" as the democratization of Nicaragua's regime and pressuring the Sandinistas to negotiate with the opposition.

In Angola, after Secretary of State Shultz unsuccessfully tried to prevent aid to UNITA in 1985, State Department officials, led by Assistant Secretary for African Affairs Chester Crocker, continued to talk with the Luanda regime as if no change had taken place. On the one hand the United States affirmed that UNITA was a legitimate force in Angolan politics and that the Cuban military presence in that country was a destabilizing factor; on the other, it seemed to expect the MPLA to commit political suicide by having the Cubans leave following US-sponsored negotiations. Only in Afghanistan and Cambodia was the administration's public goal—the withdrawal of the foreign occupation troops—consistently articulated from the beginning.

The lack of clarity in Washington policy vis-à-vis Third World anticommunist insurgents was often underscored by its pursuit of bilateral negotiations with the insurgents' enemies. In May-June 1984, the United States and Nicaragua were engaged in protracted talks in Manzanillo, Mexico, at the same time that Washington continued publicly to support the insurgents; Assistant Secretary Crocker was practically commuting between Luanda and Washington before and after the Congress forced the administration to provide assistance to UNITA. This dual-track policy may have been intended as an incentive for the Communist regimes under attack to save face and make concessions, although in no instance have they seriously done so. But it also sent conflicting signals and raised doubts in the minds of the insurgents as to the reliability of US support. More important still, it created confusion at home. How was the ordinary American voter to understand why his/her government supported insurgent forces against governments it recognized, talked to, and maintained diplomatic relations with, as in the cases of Nicaragua and Afghanistan? With only one exception in 1983, there was no public call for an anticommunist victory anywhere in the Third World by any important figure in the executive branch of the Reagan administration.[122]

To further add to the confusion, there was a persistent gap between the aid requested by the Reagan administration for support to one insurgent group or another and the resources actually required to deal with the threat. If the Sandinistas were indeed a threat to the security of the entire region from Panama to the Rio Grande, as alleged by the administration's spokespersons, the assistance provided for the anti-Sandinista forces was always patently inadequate, amounting to less than $200 million between 1981–1988, less than the Soviet annual average expenditure on military aid to the Sandinistas. The $5 million annually allotted to the two Cambodian anticommunist groups was at best a token; and if it were not for the inclusion of stingers and TOWs, the $15 million given Jonas Savimbi since 1986 would also have been little more than symbolic. While it is true that military assistance to insurgents is far more cost effective than aid to governments involved in counterinsurgency (a $50,000 stinger can destroy a $10 million aircraft), symbolic assistance is simply inadequate. The administration could not always blame Congress for this: in the case of Cambodia at least, and probably Afghanistan as well, Congress actually increased the amount of insurgent support requested by the president.

The Reagan administration's policy vis-à-vis anticommunist insurgents, then, was never well understood, led to no consistent policy, and was never accepted by a majority of the American people and Congress. In fact, one may safely state that there never really was a "Reagan Doctrine," despite the paranoid fears of liberal critics and the wishful thinking of many conservatives.[123]

A late, but highly significant indication that the "Reagan Doctrine's" has very shallow roots indeed, even in the Republican Party, was the behavior of the Bush Administration vis-à-vis anticommunist insurgents worldwide. Without exception, the Bush people tried to reach "political solutions" to anticommunist insurgencies in Afghanistan, Cambodia, Angola, Nicaragua and Mozambique, and encouraged former president Jimmy Carter to play a role in a similar approach to Eritrea.

Regardless of the practicality of such an approach, the very notion of treating ideologically rooted insurgencies as subjects of diplomacy is a clear rejection of whatever was the ideological and moral content of Ronald Reagan's scattered utterances on a US "freedom crusade" in the Third World. In many respects the Bush Administration treats the insurgencies in Nicaragua, Angola, and Cambodia as geopolitical and diplomatic pawns to be exchanged for the sake of "political solutions." Afghanistan is only slightly different, insofar as the Bush Administration has no solution to the civil war after the Soviets' withdrawal, while Mozambique and Eritrea remain, as they were under Reagan, uncomfortable oddities to stay away from.

Despite all evidence that there isn't, and cannot be a "bipartisan consensus" on anticommunism as long as the Marxist Leninist challenge is close to home and active in the US, as demonstrated by the history of US aid to the Nicaraguan resistance, the Bush Administration bet on a deal with the Democratic-controlled Congress. The result, naturally enough, was the revival of the specter of South Vietnam in 1975—the perception, and to some extent the reality, of the United States once again deserting a naive but committed ally shedding blood for a cause supposedly shared by Washington.

In an era of *glasnost* and exaggerated expectations of Soviet retreat from the Third World, whatever was left of the "Reagan Doctrine" is by now obsolete; the Bush Administration treats it as an embarrassing inheritance and nothing more.

*Should There Have Been a Reagan Doctrine?*

From the preceding analysis it is clear that neither the American public nor political elites in the United States were ideologically, morally, or strategically prepared or willing to pay the political and perhaps the financial costs of a global strategy of active containment of Soviet Third World expansionism. In only one instance, in Afghanistan, was a strong bipartisan consensus reached in support of an anticommunist insurgent force. Zbigniew Brzezinski managed to convince the outgoing Carter administration to provide aid to the mujahedeen, and afterward the only arguments on the issue were over the amounts of aid, never over its continuation. In the case of Cambodia, Congress supported and even upped the administration's request for aid to the KPNLF and ANS, but its goal was not to provide the wherewithal for victory or even short-term military success—hence the paltry sums provided, which placed the United States behind Singapore as a supporter of the anti-Vietnamese guerrillas. In Angola's case, the public and congressional support for aiding

UNITA has always been fickle, and the amounts involved only barely larger than those given to the Cambodians.

In certain instances, however, the United States can make a real contribution in areas where Communist regimes are under pressure, if it is secondary to a strong leading role on the part of regional powers. Indeed, for the mujahedeen victory against the Soviet invaders and their local puppets, future historians will have to give the lion's share of the credit, as far as outside actors are concerned, to President Zia of Pakistan rather than to George Shultz or Ronald Reagan. At huge risks to his regime and country, Zia pursued a steady, shrewd, and tough policy vis-à-vis Kabul, and forced an often reluctant United States to support it. The policy and politics of the Cambodian insurgency are defined in Beijing and Bangkok rather than in Washington; and the main external anticommunist actor in Angola is not the United States but South Africa. One may argue that in material terms Morocco and Saudi Arabia have also contributed more to Savimbi's success than has the United States.

*The Little Matter of Safe Havens*

Both Western and Communist observers have increasingly been forced to reconsider their previous assessment of the role of safe havens for irregular forces. Liberal Western observers have consistently dismissed the role of neighboring countries in supporting Marxist-Leninist or other leftist insurgent forces. From the liberal point of view, a revolutionary group engaged in guerrilla warfare is the natural or "inevitable" result of "injustice," "inequality," poverty, and so forth. Not surprisingly, Communist observers have made identical claims and in regard to the same cases. In both cases assumptions about the roots of the insurgent movement led to a decisive underestimation of the role of external support in general and of that of the neighboring states in particular.

In fact, no insurgency could conceivably win or even reach significant strength without massive support from neighboring states. Ideology as such has nothing to do with this simple reality, as demonstrated by the fact that both Marxist-Leninist and successful anticommunist insurgent movements have always depended heavily on safe havens across national borders. In this regard, guerrilla wars of any type are more a matter of international politics than a question of domestic politics. Indeed, contrary to Marxist or liberal determinism, the creation of guerrilla and terrorist organizations is a matter of will; their chance of success, however, is a question of capabilities. In this respect Guevara's belief that a handful of professional revolutionaries could create the conditions required for a successful revolution were completely out of step with the reality, and reality caught up with him at Quebrada de Yuro in 1967. The total dependence of guerrillas on friendly neighbors and external support is a relatively new phenomenon, although foreign help to insurgent forces in neighboring countries is not. Such dependence is also closely related to the drastic changes in the ideological, technological, and political context of guerrilla warfare in the twentieth century.

In numerous instances, pre-World War II guerrilla movements were supported by foreign powers: the British helped royalist insurgents in the Vendée during the French Revolution and the Arab guerrillas against the Ottomans during World War I, and the Germans sent weapons to the diehard Boer guerrillas at the end of the Anglo-Boer War. The Serbian state provided extensive support to Slavic terrorists attacking Austro-Hungarian authorities in Bosnia, Herzegovina, Montenegro, and Croatia in the wake of World War I, and the Allies provided massive support to partisan movements throughout German-occupied Europe.

What changed in the post-World War II period was the political, legal, and technological relationship between foreign governments and guerrillas. The almost universal pattern before then was the state's support of guerrillas fighting a foreign government when the state was at war with that government: Britain with revolutionary France and Turkey and the Allies with Germany. Serbia ended up at war with Austria-Hungary precisely because of Belgrade's help to anti-Austrian terrorists. Support for insurgents was almost universally seen as another instrument to be used in defeating an enemy army in what remained essentially a conventional conflict. Even so, governments were often of two minds about supporting hard-to-control foreign irregulars, even when doing so made good military sense. Nazi Germany only briefly flirted with the idea of aiding anti-Soviet guerrillas in the Baltic countries and the Ukraine, finally deciding to attempt to disarm them, thus turning some of them against the Wehrmacht.

The dramatic shift that occurred during the late 1940s was the result of the dramatically expanded international role of Communist states and the equally dramatic increase in their numbers. Probably the first instance of a government supporting insurgent forces operating against what was technically still an allied foreign government was Stalin's aid to the Greek Communist guerrillas during the late 1940s. At the same time the Soviets and Chinese dramatically increased support for the Vietminh in then French Indochina. For perhaps the first time in history a government technically at peace or even "allied" with another provided material and political support to irregular forces trying to replace that regime. Waging unofficial warfare rather than declaring war proved to be far more congenial in our era than the old, "gentlemanly" ways of engaging in warfare. In the West, what was once a rare and quite peculiar exception—helping others defeat an enemy government with whom one is technically and legally on peaceful terms—became the rule. War itself, whether between regular forces, by proxy, or by supporting foreign insurgents, has also become surreptitious. Legally, war has not been declared by any state since 1939, but in actual fact warfare has become more deadly than ever, if judged by the number of casualties. Wars are probably more frequent than ever as well.

One of the major implications of this pattern of engaging in undeclared warfare on a consistent and even, in the case of the Soviet Union, permanent basis is that the international atmosphere thus created allows small powers to do what used to be the privilege only of big powers—to engage in *secondary* warfare themselves with fewer than usual fears of retribution on the part of their targets or those targets' foreign sponsors. When the big powers change the rules of the game, the smaller ones are naturally inclined to do the same and to take advantage of any loophole in the new rules.

This is not to say that the change of rules was not the joint responsibility of the United States and the Soviet Union. After all, it was the latter that engaged in supporting Greek Communist partisans against the legitimate Athens government. The United States soon afterwards engaged in actual-but-not-formal warfare in Korea and later in Vietnam. Thus was the new pattern established and sanctioned by the United Nations. Naturally, the UN's Afro-Asian-Latin American majority intended its formal endorsement of "liberation movements" to apply only to favorite sons of the left-wing persuasion. What actually happened, and what so many Western conservatives still fail to take advantage of, is that the United Nations' support for "national liberation movements" begged the question of the definition of such a movement.

While the West in general is as busy if not busier wrestling with its conscience as it is with assessing the nature and importance of the threat, Third World regional powers are operating under different assumptions. Thailand and South Africa may well be limited or unsatisfactory democracies, and Pakistan is not democratic at all by American standards, but they all have a clear understanding of the threat represented by Communist regimes on their borders. They are aware of the fact that the issue is not democracy or the lack of it, but national survival, and that perception concentrates their minds, resources, and will. The Thai way of life is threatened by the Cambodia war. The same is true for Pakistan, an artificial entity caught between the Soviets and their Indian friends. The South Africans see the Angolan war as one link in a chain that may well end in Pretoria. In other words, the perception of the stakes involved separates Washington from Bangkok, Islamabad, and Pretoria — and perhaps, in a more subtle way, from Khartoum, Tegucigalpa, and Lilongwe as well.

The Democratic House leadership is openly prepared to concede the representation of US interests in Central America to the politically and militarily impotent President Oscar Arias of Costa Rica and his muddled Peace Plan. The same approach could be used with far better results and long-term global implications by those who believe in containing Soviet military, political, and ideological expansion in Africa, Asia, and Latin America. In other words, if Jim Wright could hide his appeasement behind Arias, conservatives could also hide their anticommunism behind the Thais or Pakistanis.

American power in the Third World has been discredited over too long a period and for too many reasons to be rebuilt for many years. Nevertheless, we have essential interests in common with key regional powers and could provide essential diplomatic backing and sophisticated weapons that could make an important difference. Even more important, it is perfectly feasible, in a period of growing American economic chauvinism and xenophobia, to win support for countering the Soviet attempts to shift the cost of empire from themselves to the West.

Contrary to what conservatives and liberals believe, Soviet domestic and foreign policies are not primarily economically motivated or sustained. We may believe that Gorbachev's reforms and restructuring are economically based and represent an attempt to devise a more efficient economic policy, as many Western analysts do; we may even believe that economic difficulties would usher in a period of Soviet global contraction, as both conservatives and liberals tend to do. We may even claim, as the "orthodox" Left and cynical anti-Marxists do, that Marxism is, after all, economics. But to do so ignores the impact of Leninism and of the Russian (perhaps even Soviet) peoples' infinite ability to absorb, cope with, or accept economic misery. For the Third World outposts of the Soviet Union, however, the situation is different.

The MPLA in Angola, FRELIMO in Mozambique, and the Mengistu regime in Ethiopia were all inclined to follow Lenin's NEP policies and have the capitalists pay for the economic revival of the country. A Communist regime, whether in Eastern Europe or Africa, has to destroy the entrepreneurial class via currency "reform" and nationalizations. That destroys the economy, at least as most people understand it; hence the need to "encourage" a new group of entrepreneurs controlled by the state and vulnerable to political pressures. Hence islands of Western investment are encouraged and invited (in Cabinda, Maputo, Managua), but only as sources of capital, technology, and know-how. This "pragmatism" uses Chevron Oil, through its Gulf subsidiary, to pay for the 50,000 Cuban troops in Angola, and Western-subsidized "humanitarian" programs to support Mengistu's claims that he is "helping the people."

One feasible way to force containment on the Soviets would therefore be a decision by Washington to renounce trying to wean Communists in Mozambique, Angola, Ethiopia, or elsewhere from Marxism-Leninism at the American taxpayers' expense. Such regimes should be forced to choose, and the results of such choices could easily prove to be more favorable to US interests in the Third World than the results of recent vacillating and incoherent policies.

## Notes

1. For an analysis of the Dhofar campaign, see Ian F. W. Beckett and John Pimlott, *Armed Forces and Modern Counterinsurgency* (New York: St. Martin's Press, 1985), pp. 16–45.
2. See Peter Samuel, "The Evolving Character of the Philippines Insurgency," *Global Affairs*, Winter 1988, pp. 94–104.
3. For the relationship between insurgency and terrorism in the specific case of Latin America, see Michael Radu, "Terror, terrorism and insurgency in Latin America," *Orbis*, Spring 1984, pp. 27–46.
4. For an unintentionally but devastatingly pertinent analysis of Stalinism's ties to the spiritual world of the Third World, see Isaac Deutscher, "Marxism and Primitive Logic," in *The Stalinist Legacy*, ed. Tariq Ali (Harmondsworth: Penguin Books, 1984), pp. 106–117.
5. As of the end of 1987, the following countries were ruled by regimes claiming some sort of allegiance to basic Marxist-Leninist principles and retaining power by using a combination of Soviet-bloc security support (including weapons and often troops or security personnel as well), statist and collectivist economics, single-party rule, omnipotent secret police, and militarization of the society:

- In Africa: Algeria, Libya, Ethiopia, Seychelles, Mozambique, Madagascar, Angola, São Tomé, Congo, Benin, Ghana, Burkina Faso, Guinea Bissau, Cape Verde, and the pseudo-state of the Sahrawi Arab Democratic Republic.
- In Asia: People's Democratic Republic of Yemen, Syria, and Iraq.
- In Latin America: the Cooperative Republic of Guyana and Nicaragua.

The point here is not that these states are Soviet puppets—a few (Syria, Algeria, Libya, and Iraq) are essentially self-sustaining, and a number of the others are clearly not able to survive without massive Western economic support. What they do have in common, however, is a basic incompatibility with democracy and capitalism, and an outlook analogous to that of established communist states.

6. Gunnar Myrdal, *The Challenge of World Poverty* (New York: Vintage Books, 1970), p. 208.

7. See Nancy Peabody Newell and Richard S. Newell, *The Struggle for Afghanistan* (Ithaca and London: Cornell University Press, 1981), pp. 76-80.
8. The case studies in this volume provide a clear idea as to the nature of the leadership of the six governments targeted by the major anticommunist insurgencies today. In addition, one may consult *Violence and the Latin American revolutionaries*, ed. Michael Radu (New Brunswick, N.J.: Transaction Books, 1988), for an analysis of Latin American revolutionary elites, which can largely be applied to African and Asian revolutionary elites as well. The fact that Pol Pot and his inner circle were all Sorbonne graduates or dropouts, that Babrak Karmal, Taraki, Hafizullah Amin (a Columbia University graduate), Agostinho Neto and Lucio Lara in Angola, Marcelino dos Santos in Mozambique, Mengistu and many of his Dergue colleagues in Ethiopia, and most Sandinista leaders seldom had to work for a living, were highly educated, and often traveled abroad, only partly explains why their policies had so little to do with national realities. Marxism-Leninism's inherently dogmatic character plays an equally important role.
9. One of the few analyses of the Tambov events of 1920 and the Red Army's earliest counterinsurgency campaign is David R. Jones, "Lessons of the Tambov Campaign of 1920," paper presented at the Conference on Soviet counterinsurgency experience, University of New Brunswick, Fredericton, NB, October 3-4, 1987.
10. For Lithuania, see K. V. Tauras, *Guerrilla Warfare on the Amber Coast* (New York: Voyage Press, 1962); for both the Ukraine and Lithuania, see Frederic Smith, "The War in Lithuania and the Ukraine against Soviet Power," in *Combat in Communist Territory*, ed. Charles Moser (Lake Bluff, Ill.: Regnery Gateway, 1985), pp. 2-21; and Alexander Shtromas, "The Baltic States," in *The Last Empire. Nationality and the Soviet Future*, ed. Robert Conquest (Stanford: Hoover Institution Press, 1986), pp. 183-197.
11. For a discussion of the anti-Castro insurgents, including those of Sierra de Escambray, see Carlos Alberto Montaner, *Secret Report on the Cuban Revolution*, trans. by Eduardo Zayas-Bazán (New Brunswick, N.J.: Transaction Books, 1982), pp. 193-204.
12. The best analysis of the "basmachi" insurgency of Turkestan, the first Soviet experience with a Third World, Moslem insurgency, and one still having a certain impact on the Soviet Army's approach to the Afghan insurgency, is to be found in Glenda Fraser's two-part study in *Central Asian Survey*, vol. 6, nos. 1-2 (1987).
13. Chad, under decades-long Libyan threat, appears to be undergoing a similar process.
14. Veteran "national liberation movement" observer Gérard Chaliand noted in 1982 that "in Afghanistan as elsewhere, foreign domination in this era may prepare fertile ground for the seeds of modern nationalism." *Report from Afghanistan* (New York: Viking Press, 1982), p. 61.
15. Anthony Suau, "Region in Rebellion: Eritrea," *National Geographic*, September 1985, p. 388.
16. James LeMoyne, "Teaching the Contras Leftist Rebel Methods," *The New York Times*, 8 March 1987.
17. Far and away the best analysis of Massoud's administrative, organizational, and military accomplishments is the little-known study by Rahimullah Yusufzai, "Resistance in Afghanistan: the Panjshir Model," *Regional Stud-*

*ies, Quarterly Journal of the Institute of Regional Studies* (Islamabad), vol. 3, no. 3 (Summer 1985), pp. 83–131.
18. See, for instance, Reid Daly and Peter Stiff, *Selous Scouts. Top Secret War* (Alberton, South Africa: Galago Publishing, 1982), *passim*; for a more critical analysis, see J. K. Cilliers, *Counterinsurgency in Rhodesia* (London: Croom Helm, 1985), chap. 5.
19. See Beckett and Pimlott, *Armed Forces and Modern Counterinsurgency*, pp. 136–62.
20. Cambodia is another example. Thach Reng, special-forces commander under the Khmer Republic, joined the KPNLF in August 1982. See Timothy Carney, "The Heng Samrin Armed Forces and the Military Balance in Cambodia," in *The Cambodian Agony*, eds. David A. Abling and Marlowe Hood (Armonk and London: M. E. Sharpe Inc., 1987), p. 198.
21. Nayan Chandra, *Brother Enemy* (New York: Harcourt Brace Jovanovitch, 1986).
22. Even in Afghanistan there are cadres, including at least one former general, Safi, who were trained in anti-insurgency by the British in Malaya, by the United States, *and* by the Soviets. They now train mujahedeen elements in guerrilla tactics in Pakistan.
23. See *Soldier of Fortune*, February 1987.
24. *Mao Tse-Tung on Guerrilla Warfare*, trans. and with an introduction by Samuel B. Griffith (New York: Praeger, 1961), pp. 20–22.
25. *Janes' Defence Weekly*, 12 March 1988, p. 471.
26. See Francis Toase, "The South African Army: The Campaign in South West Africa/Namibia since 1966," in Beckett and Pimlot, *Armed Forces and Modern Counterinsurgency*, pp. 190–221.
27. Cilliers, *Counterinsurgency in Rhodesia*, p. 242. These figures do not include the thousands of insurgents killed in Zambia, Mozambique, and Angola.
28. The 10 : 1 ratio should not be taken too seriously, since it is based on Western military establishments with their disproportionate number of noncombat and rear troops. It does not take into consideration such important variables as terrain, the overall size of a country, new technology, etc. Nevertheless, it is useful in that it points to the fact that, by its very nature as a defense-and-offense-oriented force, the counterinsurgent establishment needs a decisive numerical advantage over its largely offense-oriented foes.
29. *The Military Balance 1985-1986* (London, IISS 1986). The IISS figures consistently underestimate guerrilla strength and the number of Cubans in Angola.
30. So heavy were the losses of the demoralized Ethiopians that Mengistu Haile Mariam himself referred to the engagements as "grim battles." Credible but unproven reports mentioned as many as 18,000 Ethiopians dead in the first months of 1988. See the *New York Times*, April 7 and April 11, 1988.
31. The only limited and recent exception is Nicaragua, which does allow the political opposition certain very limited and marginal political rights. Those do not, legally, include open support for the contras, and when a group of politicians met insurgent political leaders in Guatemala in January 1988, they were promptly arrested.
32. *Africa Confidential*, 4 March 1988, pp. 5–6.

33. For instance, I was briefed by RENAMO representatives about the alleged Homoine massacre of 1987; for reasons that are still mysterious, their articulate, plausible, in fact common-sensical arguments never made their way into the Western media.
34. Rahimullah Yusufzai, "Resistance in Afghanistan," p. 101. Details of Massoud's tactical intelligence capabilities are also provided in *Insight*, 25 January 1988, pp. 13–15.
35. Fred Bridgland, *Jonas Savimbi. A Key to Africa* (New York: Paragon House, 1986), p. 346.
36. Typical in this respect are the EPLF zones in northern Eritrea, particularly those around Orotta and Nacfa. For a first-hand description of life in such regions, see Suau, "Region in Rebellion."
37. The much maligned *Soldier of Fortune* staff is one remarkable exception and provides the only serious (although openly biased) source of information from inside RENAMO's "liberated zones," except perhaps for Jack Wheeler.
38. See Yusufzai, "Resistance in Afghanistan," *passim*.
39. It is important to note in this respect that Massoud's operations have expanded to include large numbers of non-Tajiks, particularly Turkic-speakers and also Pashtuns.
40. The most active US groups organizing such meetings are the American Security Council and the World Anticommunist League.
41. Since the introduction of the stingers in Afghanistan in the summer of 1986, the Soviets have lost an average of one aircraft a day, each costing a few million dollars.
42. *General del Pino Speaks* (Washington, D.C.: The Cuban American Foundation, 1987), p. 15.
43. The Phnom Penh regime army is too small and irrelevant to be considered.
44. It is unclear how an experienced observer like Rod Paschal can claim, in an otherwise important article, that "the ruling governments of [the USSR, Cuba, and Vietnam] are actually quite experienced in the methods of counterinsurgency." Rod Paschal, "Marxist Counterinsurgencies," *Parameters*, vol. 16, no. 2 (1986), p. 5.
45. Under the idealistic but totally incompetent leadership of Enver Pasha, an ex-Turkish general with a long history of failure, the basmachis actually tried to win a conventional victory over the Bolsheviks, with predictably disastrous results. They were far more successful as guerrillas, under native leaders like Ibrahim Bek.
46. *Granma*, 25 May 1970, quoted in Montaner, *Secret Report on the Cuban Revolution*, p. 200.
47. Ibid., pp. 201–202.
48. See Glenda Fraser, "Basmachi-II," *Central Asian Survey*, vol. 6, no. 2 (1987), pp. 17–19.
49. Yossef Bodansky, "Soviet Military Involvement in Afghanistan," in *Afghanistan. The Great Game Revisited*, ed. Rosanne Klass (New York: Freedom House, 1987), p. 251.
50. *Time*, 28 March 1988, pp. 41–42. This article estimates that 80 and 85 percent of the two provinces have been lost to the government.
51. But "they are still very bad at night," according to mujahedeen field commander Abdul Haq. *Janes' Defence Weekly*, 12 March 1988, p. 471.

**Introduction** 89

52. Yusufzai, "Resistance in Afghanistan," pp. 83, 112–13.
53. The Eritreans claimed to have captured fifteen T-54/55 tanks, howitzers, and 4,000 Kalashnikov rifles. John Edwin Smith, "Eritrea," *Soldier of Fortune*, February 1987, p. 87.
54. *New York Times*, 1 April 1988.
55. *InformAfrica*, 12 December 1987, p. 16. The usually well-informed Al J. Venter claimed that between $1 and $2 billion worth of Soviet equipment was lost in the offensive late in 1987 and in the fighting around Cuito Cuanavale early in 1988. ("Siege at Cuito Cuanavale," *Soldier of Fortune*, May 1988, p. 42.)
56. *Africa Contemporary Record, 1977–1978* (London: 1978), p. B487.
57. For a particularly sharp attack on the Peruvian justice system's inability to cope with the terrorism of Sendero Luminoso, see "La Justicia de Pilatos," *Caretas*, 8 February 1988, pp. 37–39.
58. Paschal, "Marxist Counterinsurgencies," p. 10.
59. Even Bodansky, the only Western analyst who seems to believe that the Afghan regime's army is improving, admits KHAD's dominant role.
60. The Soviets themselves had to ask for East German counter-intelligence experts to aid in Afghanistan. See Bodansky, "Soviet Military Involvement in Afghanistan," p. 251.
61. For details see the testimony of ex-DGSE agent Alvaro Baldizon, in *Inside the Sandinista Regime: A Special Investigator's Perspective,* (Washington, D.C.: US Department of State, February 1986).
62. See, for instance, Bodansky, "Soviet Military Involvement in Afghanistan"; Paschal, "Marxist Counterinsurgencies"; as well as the daily Pakistani press in the relevant series of the Foreign Broadcasting Information Service (*FBIS*).
63. Mozambique's late president, Samora Machel, was shown to have plotted the overthrow of Malawi's president and is known to have openly threatened him with long-range missile attacks. In the case of both Angola and Mozambique, support for anti-South African insurgents, whether SWAPO, the ANC or both, proved to be more of a liability than an asset, as it provoked South Africa or—depending on one's viewpoint—provided Pretoria with a plausible pretext for helping their enemies.
64. See L. Bouchey, M. Waller, and S. Baldwin, *The Real Secret War* (Washington, D.C.: Council for Inter-American Security, 1987), pp. 36–37.
65. For details on the BLIs activities and tactics, see *Janes' Defence Weekly*, 11 April 1987, pp. 636–37.
66. *Time*, 22 February 1988, p. 40.
67. Once again, Bodansky provides useful data but greatly exaggerates its importance. Indeed, ex-mujahedeen defectors could do real damage, as he points out; on the other hand, most of the defectors were paid in cash as well as weapons, with the result that many, perhaps even a majority, used their new riches to assert their local independence, rather than follow Kabul's orders, or simply "changed their minds" and reverted to insurgency with their shiny new weapons. "Soviet Military Involvement in Afghanistan," p. 261.
68. The famous Homoine "massacre" of 1987, skillfully but unconvincingly pinned by FRELIMO on RENAMO, seems to have been yet another example of undisciplined, hungry militias taking the law in their own hands and

being forcibly suppressed by the regulars of the FPLM. One also has to keep in mind that FRELIMO has an excellent track record of fabricating nonexistent "massacres" by its foes, going back to the fake Wiryamu massacre of the pre-independence period.
69. See Thomas T. Hammond, *Red Flag over Afghanistan* (Boulder, Colo.: Westview Press, 1984), p. 74.
70. This is a point that is completely missed by, among others, Yossef Bodansky. He claims that "the chief purpose of those Soviet forces dedicated to confronting the Resistance has been to deny it access to Soviet strategic assets. . . . As of this writing the Resistance has been unable to hit any major Soviet installations." "Soviet Military Involvement in Afghanistan," p. 249. Not only is the basic argument factually inaccurate, as demonstrated by mujahedeen mortar attacks on Bagram and Shindand, constant threats to the Salang Tunnel, and the destruction of aircraft at Bagram by Afghan army sympathizers of the Resistance, but even if they were accurate it would indicate a strictly defensive Soviet approach, a clear and well-proven recipe for defeat in a counterinsurgency campaign.
71. Robert Kaplan, "The View from Baluchistan," *American Spectator*, March 1988, p. 23.
72. Thomas Henriksen, "The People's Republic of Mozambique," in Dennis L. Bark, ed., *The Red Orchestra. The case of Africa* (Stanford: Hoover Institution Press, 1988), p. 168.
73. Andre Matsangaisse, RENAMO's founder, escaped from such a camp.
74. For a devastating analysis of the resettlement and "villagization" programmes of the Ethiopian regime, and their genocidal intent and results, see Robert D. Kaplan, *Surrender or Starve. The Wars behind the famine* (Boulder, Colo.: Westview Press, 1988).
75. For details on the Sandinista support network in the United States and its enormous impact, see *The Real Secret War. Sandinista Political Warfare and its Effects on Congress*, ed. by L. Francis Bouchey, J. Michael Waller, and Steve Baldwin (Washington, D.C.: Council for Inter-American Security, 1987).
76. "Foggy Bottom Freedom Fighter. Elliott Abrams talks candidly about Reagan Policy in Latin America," *Policy Review*, Winter 1989, p. 2. A more detailed exposition of the same over optimism and misunderstanding of Latin American democratic traditions is to be found in Gregory A. Fossedal, *The Democratic Imperative. Exporting the American Revolution* (New York: Basic Books, 1989).
77. Ibid.
78. In Peru, the Philippines, and El Salvador, to mention just a few examples, the insurgent Left actually increased its strength and activities following the establishment of democratically elected governments.
79. Mining the fear of "another Vietnam"—i.e., another American defeat in the Third World—has long been a favorite tactic of the Sandinistas. Recently, drug-trafficking peddlers like Panama's Noriega have also taken to using the same tactics against US attempts to force them out.
80. According to opinion polls, for example, as late as 1988 a majority of the American public did not know which side the United States was on in the Nicaraguan and Salvadoran civil wars.

81. Indeed, it was not until the end of April 1983 that President Reagan personally made his first public statement in support of the Nicaraguan resistance.
82. George McGovern, "The 1988 election: US policy at a watershed," *Foreign Affairs. America and the World*, 1987/1988, p. 614.
83. Alvin H. Bernstein, "Insurgents against Moscow," *Policy Review*, Summer 1987, p. 29. Bernstein is clearly wrong regarding the will of local Third World powers to intervene on behalf of anticommunist insurgents, as demonstrated most clearly by the actions of Thailand, South Africa, and Pakistan, but his is an accurate reflection of domestic US conservative perceptions.
84. For a thorough analysis of the legal issues involved in the US-Nicaragua conflict, see Robert F. Turner, *Nicaragua v. United States: A Look at the Facts*, Institute for Foreign Policy Analysis, Pergamon-Brassey's, Washington, D.C., 1987, *passim*.
85. The clearest legalistic analysis, and rejection of the Grenada intervention, and the main theoretical basis for the Dukakis campaign's similar approach, is Robert A. Pastor, "The invasion of Grenada: a pre- and post-mortem," in Scott B. MacDonald et al., eds., *The Caribbean after Grenada. Revolution, Conflict, and Democracy* (New York: Praeger, 1988), pp. 87-108.
86. Dukakis's legalistic position should sometimes be seen in contrast to Jesse Jackson's ideological one. Nevertheless, for campaign purposes, Dukakis did go far beyond legal bounds, at least as they were defined by the always cautious State Department bureaucracy, in agreeing to define South Africa as a "terrorist state," on strictly "moral" rather than legal grounds.
87. By that slip of tongue the speaker admitted that the "Arias Plan" and the Guatemala and Esquipulas agreements were in fact victories for Managua — a fact known from the start by most Central Americans, including some of those who signed the agreements, and by close observers of the region.
88. The 1988 campaigns of such figures as Jesse Jackson and Pat Robertson are, of course another indication of the political agendas of their respective religious networks.
89. Many laypersons, however, are openly opposed to the leftward drift of their churches, and a steadily declining membership is in itself is an indication of disenchantment with the hierarchy's attitudes.
90. For detailed documentation in this respect, see Uri Ra'anan et al., *Hydra of Carnage* (Lexington, Ma.: Lexington Books, 1985), pp. 350-359.
91. Amnesty International's senior staff member for Latin America, Michael McClintock, became the author of a blatantly Marxist-Leninist apologia on Central America, *The American Connection* (London: Zed Books, 1985) and two volumes supporting the FMLN and URNG (the Guatemalan Communist umbrella organization).
92. In the old terminology of Stalinism, Angola and Mozambique are "people's republics," Afghanistan, Cambodia, and Ethiopia are "democratic republics," while in Nicaragua the army, which is simply the armed branch of the FSLN, is itself "popular."
93. The Luanda regime is not officially recognized by the United States, but it is recognized by virtually all other countries.
94. See, e.g., William R. Hawkins, "Reagan Rebellion or National Renewal," *The World & I*, April 1988, pp. 555-567.

95. Kenneth Sharpe, "The Real Cause of Irangate," and Viron Vaky, "Positive Containment in Nicaragua," both in *Foreign Policy*, Fall 1987.
96. It is relevant to note that conservative discussions of anticommunist insurgencies are marked by misspellings, inaccuracies, and elementary mistakes of interpretation; by contrast, the Left and liberal analysts know their facts, names, and places, but misinterpret their data.
97. Michael A. Ledeen, "Secrets," *The National Interest*, no. 10 (Winter 1987), p. 49.
98. Mozambique may well be the only African country to have more of its highly skilled physicians in the United States than at home.
99. Robert I. Rotberg, "Angolan Sting," *Christian Science Monitor*, 16 April 1986.
100. Aryeh Neier, "The Legal Implications of the CIA's Nicaragua Manual," in *Psychological Operations in Guerrilla Warfare* (New York: Vintage Books, 1985), p. 101.
101. Ironically, it may well be the case that the mujahedeen have pursued the most vicious tactics of all contemporary anticommunist insurgents, while the contras are the "cleanest." The almost complete lack of firsthand mainstream Western media access to the former and the accessibility of the latter virtually ensured that the media depiction of the two groups was exactly the reverse of the actual situation.
102. "Foggy Bottom Freedom Fighter," *Policy Review*, p. 2
103. There has always been a significant, but steadily declining minority of Democrats, mostly but not only southerners, who have not agreed with the party's slide toward consistent appeasement of Marxism-Leninism almost everywhere in the world. Nevertheless, few of those have any significant impact on the party's congressional leadership.
104. For a detailed conservative critique of the Reagan administration's Central America policies, see International Security Council, *Central America: A political strategic assessment: 1988* (New York, 1988).
105. Elliott Abrams admitted as much, as well as the mistake of starting aid to the contras as a covert operation, and he also admitted that an outright invasion of Nicaragua immediately after Grenada would have been the ideal solution. "Foggy Bottom Freedom Fighter," *Policy Review*, p. 3.
106. Ibid.
107. Quoted in Joshua Muravchik, *The Uncertain Crusade. Jimmy Carter and the Dilemmas of Human Rights Policy* (Washington, D.C.: American Enterprise Institute, 1988), p. 57.
108. Ibid.
109. As has been abundantly demonstrated by the voting record of such Republican senators as Weicker of Connecticut, Stafford of Vermont (both now retired or defeated), Hatfield and Packwood of Oregon, Specter of Pennsylvania, and congressmen like Leach of Iowa, Green of New York, and Conte of Massachusetts.
110. Indeed, the removal of Duvalier in Haiti resulted not in democracy but in a free for all political chaos, dominated by a weak, corrupt, and undisciplined military; democracy in South Korea has so far proved to be a bonus for antidemocratic, violent, and irrational students rather than encouragement for meaningful political participation; and the Aquino regime in the Philippines appears to be as ineffective and corrupt as Marcos's was, with the additional

result that irresponsible anti-American demagogues and the fronts of the Communist insurgents have a field day.
111. In fact, one of the most articulate proponents of the "Reagan Doctrine," sometimes mistakenly described as the author of the term itself, is Charles Krauthammer, a democrat and senior editor of *The New Republic*, where he published his "Guerrilla Warfare. Morality and the Reagan Doctrine" (6 September 1986, pp. 17-24).
112. William R. Bode, "The Reagan Doctrine in Outline," in *Central America and the Reagan Doctrine*, ed. Walter H. Hahn (Lanham, Md.: University Press of America, 1987), pp. 248-49.
113. Text in *Weekly Compilation of Presidential Documents*, vol. 21, no.8 (25 February 1985), p. 186.
114. Emphasis added. See Bode, "The Reagan Doctrine in Outline," p. 248.
115. Text of the February 22 address in U.S. State Department Current Policy, no. 659.
116. An excellent rebuttal of these criticisms could be found in Krauthammer, "Guerrilla Warfare."
117. Leftists like Alexander Cockburn in *The Nation* have tried to raise the "morality issue" in the case of Afghanistan as well, describing the mujahedeen as bloodthirsty savages unworthy of US support on moral grounds.
118. See *The New York Times*, 29 October 1985.
119. Ridiculous as this approach appears to any serious observer of the international scene, influential Democratic politicians like Jesse Jackson openly claim that Pretoria is untouchable, while Gorbachev's Moscow is, or should be a "partner."
120. These arguments are presented in the State Department's *Fundamentals of US Foreign Policy* (Washington, D.C.: Department of State, Bureau of Public Affairs, 1988), pp. 78-79.
121. One may argue that the hundreds of millions of dollars provided to the Ethiopian regime in food aid during the last four years amounted to indirect support for the regime. It allowed the regime to continue and increase its military operations against the various insurgent groups, instead of diverting resources toward famine relief. Moreover, in the midst of massive famine, whose consequences were only limited by Western aid, Addis Ababa engaged in a massive resettlement of population in guerrilla regions, a clear counterinsurgency tactic. See Jason W. Clay and Bonnie K. Holcomb, *Politics and the Ethiopian Famine 1984-1985* (Cambridge, Mass.: Cultural Survival, Inc., 1986).
122. The under secretary for defense for policy at the time, Fred Iklé, in a speech on 12 September 1983, said that "We do not seek military defeat for our friends. We do not seek a military stalemate. We seek a victory for democracy." Quoted in Curtin Winsor, "From Reagan Doctrine to Detente," *Global Affairs*, Winter 1988, p. 78.
123. A good sample of these fears is to be found in Kenneth E. Sharpe, "The Real Cause of Irangate," *Foreign Policy*, Fall 1987, pp. 19-41. Sharpe claims that the "doctrine" goes beyond containment and aims at "rolling back" Soviet advances in the Third World by "undermining and overthrowing Third World revolutionary governments."

# 1

# Eritrea

*Paul B. Henze*

**Introduction and Summary**

Marxism has never been a *causative* factor in the long rebellion in Eritrea, Ethiopia's northernmost province, where one of the modern world's oldest little wars continues to be fought. Local particularism, regional rivalries, and great power politics are the intermingling currents that have combined in different ways at different times to determine the course of developments. Dissidence in the region was raised in the late 1960s to the level of insurgency by support, for reasons of great power politics, from radical Arab and distant Marxist governments for groups of predominantly conservative separatists. An avowedly Marxist faction coalesced only when the initial phase of the insurgency produced new leaders. The rebellion suffered a serious setback when the Communist Chinese withdrew their support in 1971, and the Sudanese and Ethiopian governments agreed to cease abetting insurgents operating against each other's countries.

Marxist Eritreans expanded their political influence during the early 1970s, a period of military stalemate which contributed to the ferment weakening Haile Selassie's government. It culminated in the assumption of power in Addis Ababa of a makeshift military junta (the *Derg*) in the summer of 1974.[1] Soviet-leaning Derg officers who found it necessary to present themselves as ultra-nationalists to justify and consolidate their hold on Ethiopia could find no common ground with separatist Marxist Eritreans. The fact that both were insecure and had to operate in highly factionalized political contexts propelled them away from compromising. Both competed to become Soviet-chosen instruments for achieving hegemony in the Horn of Africa while conflicts on the ground in Eritrea reached unprecedented levels of intensity in the years 1975-1977.

The Soviets avoided choosing between the two sides until they were forced by the Somali attack on Ethiopia in 1977 to give massive military aid and full political backing to the Derg. Considerations of great power politics led them to abandon the Eritrean Marxists. Nevertheless, during this very period the Eritrean Marxists had decisively strengthened their position within the insurgency. Regional rivalries prompted conservative Arab states to replace much of the arms and money from communist and radical Arab sources that had previously sustained the Eritrean insurgency.

For the past ten years neither the Derg nor the insurgents has been able to gain the upper hand in the guerrilla war in Eritrea. Eritrea thus offers the seemingly incongruous spectacle of a Marxist anti-Marxist insurgency. It has become increasingly apparent that both the Derg's Marxism and that of the EPLF are irrelevant to the actual problems of Eritrea. These, ironically, are primarily economic and social, but Marxism, despite its pretensions to economic determinism, has no constructive solutions to offer.

## The Geographic Background

As a geopolitical concept Eritrea is barely a century old, "an artificial creation of European imperialism," like so many other African territories.[2] It does not constitute a natural geographic region, for its terrain is extremely varied: a long, barren seacoast; a narrow, hot coastal desert; a rugged escarpment; a high plateau with temperate climate but uncertain rainfall; and northern and western lowlands that for the most part belong to the Nile basin. Linguistic and ethnic unity are lacking. At least a dozen different ethnic entities are distinguishable. There are even more languages, for four non-indigenous languages are in use: Amharic, English, Italian, and Arabic. Religious distinctions are many and do not always match ethnic divisions. There are no majorities in Eritrea either in terms of religion or ethnicity. It is a region where minorities acutely conscious of distinctions that set them off from others have guarded their interests for millennia.[3]

There are great variations in patterns of life, ranging from pastoral nomadism in arid areas to village-centered agriculture in the highlands where complex societies based on farming and trade had already reached a high level of civilization before the Christian era. Massawa has inherited a coastal tradition of urban life based on seaborne trade dating back to ancient times. Asmara, an attractive Afro-Mediterranean city barely a hundred years old, is a focal point for government, industry, commerce, and education. With a population approaching half a million, it is home to almost 20 percent of Eritrea's population. Several subprovincial capitals—Keren, Adi Ugri, Tessenei, Barentu—serve as trade and communications centers.

Compared to neighboring areas, Eritrea has good basic infrastructure: roads, power lines, communications facilities. Italians made substantial investments in Eritrea during their fifty years of colonial rule. They saw Eritrea primarily as a base for the conquest of the rest of Ethiopia, but some came to settle permanently and to develop agriculture and industry. After British Commonwealth forces defeated the Italians in 1941, Eritrea became an important World War II support and communications hub for Allied Forces in the Middle East and prospered as a result. Even today, Eritrea accounts for one-third of Ethiopia's entire industrial base and provides its only direct links to the sea via the ports of Assab and Massawa.[4]

## The Historical Background

Historically Eritrea is a classic crossroads region. Ancient Egyptians passed here on their way to the Land of Punt. Greek and Roman traders made regular calls at Eritrean ports. The region was an avenue between the civilization of ancient South Arabia and the Ethiopian highlands. Christianity reached Ethiopia via Eritrea in the fourth century AD, and, three centuries later followers of the Prophet Mohammed, fleeing Mecca, took refuge here. All these historic forces have left their mark on the region. Highland Eritrea was an integral part of the Axumite Empire, the first Ethiopian state. When the Ottomans advanced into the Red Sea in the sixteenth century and captured Massawa and its hinterland, they called the province *Al Habasha*, the traditional Arab name for Ethiopia, which Europeans turned into "Abyssinia." By this time Islam had spread widely in the lowlands, while the highlands remained part of Ethiopian Orthodox Christian civilization.

To Ethiopian rulers Eritrea was simply the northern part of their age-old inheritance and important, *inter alia*, because it provided access to the sea. They never abandoned their claim to it even when it was firmly held by the Turks. As Ottoman power waned and was eventually reasserted by Egypt, Ethiopian rulers from the time of Emperor Tewodros aspired to regain full control of the coastal region. Tewodros came to grief when the famous British Napier Expedition landed in 1868 near the old Axumite port of Zula (Adulis)[5] and proceeded up into the highlands to defeat his forces at the great fortress of Magdala. But instead of capitalizing on their victory by establishing a protectorate over Ethiopia, the British withdrew and left the country to sort itself out. The energetic Tigrean Emperor Yohannes IV might well have succeeded in regaining control of the coast but he had both internal rivals and the Sudanese Mahdists to contend with and was killed in 1889 in battle against the latter.

Meanwhile a private Italian company had set up a trading station at Assab in 1869. The Italian government, belatedly joining in the scramble for Africa, took it over in 1882 and three years later moved into Massawa, where the British had conveniently removed the Egyptian garrison a year earlier. Italian ambitions grew rapidly, and in early 1887 they dispatched an expeditionary force to the highlands. It was almost annihilated by Ras Alula, the ruler of Hamasien (the region around Asmara), at Dogali, in the coastal plain.[6] This was only a temporary setback. By 1890 through a combination of force, diplomacy, and intrigue Italy had succeeded in gaining control of the entire territory between the coast and the Mareb River and proclaimed it *Colonia Eritrea* — the Red Sea Colony. Thus the name first came onto the map.

The already mature and battle-hardened King of Shoa, Menelik II, who had followed Yohannes IV to the imperial throne, proved to be a formidable opponent of Italian imperial ambitions. When he frustrated their efforts to reduce Ethiopia to the status of a protectorate, the Italians prepared for conquest. The crushing defeat Menelik inflicted on General Baratieri's armies near the Tigrean town of Adowa in March 1896 forced Italy to postpone its conquest of Ethiopia for nearly forty years.

The Battle of Adowa resulted in European acceptance of Ethiopian independence, hitherto always in doubt, and participation by Ethiopia along with several European powers in dividing up unoccupied territory in the Horn of Africa. As a Shoan, Menelik's highest priority was to expand Ethiopian power in the south and west. Biding their time, imperial-minded Italians still regarded Eritrea as a staging area for the eventual conquest of Ethiopia. Ethiopians, on the other hand, were not reconciled to the permanent loss of the region. Religious and cultural links remained close.

Mussolini prepared systematically for the invasion of Ethiopia from the late 1920s onward. Conquest proved costlier than he had anticipated and generated a good deal of hostile international reaction, though with no effective countermoves. The Italian East African Empire, proclaimed in 1936, was short-lived. Partisans, called "Patriots," retained control of several parts of Ethiopia and played a role in its liberation in 1940–1941. Haile Selassie, advancing with British forces from the Sudan, returned to

Addis Ababa on 5 May 1941, exactly five years from the day he had fled from the Italians, and reestablished his government.

In Eritrea, British forces set up a military administration. British military rule being mild, Eritreans enjoyed both prosperity and relative personal freedom. Italian colonial policy had not envisioned Eritrean independence or self-rule. The British, though military occupiers, took a more liberal approach.

British military administrators, in fact, encouraged the politicization of Eritrean society, although no single British plan for the future of the colony was developed. Some Britons favored amalgamating all or part of Eritrea with Sudan; others envisioned a closer association between Eritrea and the neighboring Ethiopian province of Tigre. In terms of history, religion, and ethnic composition, the Eritrean highlands are an extension of Tigre. Italy formally surrendered all claim to Eritrea in the 1947 peace treaty. Its future was to be decided according to the wishes of its inhabitants with the United Nations supervising the process. No Eritrean nationalism developed during the period of British military administration. Instead political opinion became polarized for and against unification with Ethiopia. Haile Selassie strongly favored unification, for he wished to succeed where his illustrious predecessor had to compromise and bring all historic Ethiopian territory back into the empire.

## The Political Background

Had the Eritrean question come onto the international agenda a decade later than it did, the province would probably have been granted independence, as occurred with almost every other separately administered African political entity during the 1960s. Eritrean nationalists thus have some entitlement to feel cheated by history: why should Bangui and Bujumbura become capitals with foreign embassies, let alone Ouagadougou, Kigali, and Nouakchott, while cosmopolitan Asmara remains a provincial backwater? Why shouldn't educated Eritreans become ministers and ambassadors and go to the United Nations and take part in international meetings? These are retrospective resentments, however, for such heady prospects were not on the horizon at the time of the Eritrean settlement. The difficult process of resolving the Eritrean question took five years. No majority opinion could be found. Conflicting views became more marked and more parochial as the province experienced an economic slump during the late 1940s. Britain was too preoccupied with the process of imperial dismantlement to accept a commitment to any scheme for major territorial realignment.[7] Ethiopia, which had invested substantial resources in supporting the Unionist party in Eritrea, gravitated toward the United States, especially after the Korean War broke out in 1950. This war underscored the importance of Eritrean military facilities at Kagnew Station in Asmara, which the United States inherited from Britain in the 1940s. Thus the United States, which had never had a policy toward the Horn of Africa before, became a major participant in the Eritrean settlement and favored amalgamation of the territory with Ethiopia. The solution, crafted under UN auspices, was federation, which came into effect on 15 September 1952.

Like most federations devised to deal with awkward political problems, this one was bound to fall short of expectations. Nevertheless, it lasted for ten years, longer than any other similar post-World War II arrangement in the Third World. Problems which arose from the disparities in size of the two "partners" were minor compared with contrasts in internal political structure and public attitudes.

While Eritrea had gone through a process of intense politicization during the decade 1942-1952, Ethiopia had been in effect depoliticized during the same period.[8] Eritrea was given a framework for representative government, including a popularly elected assembly in which several political parties held seats.[9] There were labor unions, a lively press, and independent institutions and associations of many kinds. A substantial proportion of the population had some degree of modern education. Wartime economic expansion had aroused Eritreans' expectations of rapid economic development. Ethiopia, on the other hand, was an authoritarian monarchy where the emperor himself was more committed to modernization than the majority of his subjects who were content to fall back into traditional patterns following the ejection of the Italians. The country had barely begun to develop a framework for modern economic and political life.

The history of the ten years of the Ethiopian-Eritrean federation is the story of failure to live up to the complete, complex federal structure ideally envisioned in 1952. This decade also witnessed the gradual erosion of Eritrea's separate institutions and imposition of direct rule from Addis Ababa.[10] Haile Selassie never regarded the federation as more than a "temporary obstacle on the road to full reunification,"[11] but he was always mindful of the requirements of international respectability and might have maintained the fiction longer if it had not been for the tension Nasserist revolutionary fervor was causing in the entire region.

The writings of Eritrean separatists and their enthusiasts in the United States and Europe present a mythological picture of unified Eritrean nationalist sentiment welling up during the period of the federation and provoked by its dissolution into armed struggle for independence. The great majority of Eritreans made the best of the numerous opportunities federation that Ethiopia offered them. With advantage in education, technical experience, and exposure to more modern conditions of life, Eritreans were eagerly sought for positions in government, industry, and the professions throughout the country. They rose to high positions in the army and the civil service. They played a major role in new institutions such as Ethiopian Airlines, the telecommunications authority, and the university in Addis Ababa. They found opportunities for private practice as lawyers, doctors, and accountants in the capital and in provincial towns. Many became active in business in various parts of the country. At a lower professional level, Eritreans found ready employment as teachers as the country's educational system expanded.

Ethiopia needed Eritrea's industry and the produce of its agriculture. Italian entrepreneurs were encouraged to stay or return and invest. The 1950s and 1960s were a period of slow but steady economic expansion in Eritrea with greater employment opportunities for a growing population. Eritrea benefitted from American, European and Israeli economic development assistance. US military installations employed a sizable local labor force and US military personnel, who numbered in the thousands, contributed several million dollars a year to the Eritrean economy. Plans for accelerated development of the agro-industry to serve European markets were brought to an abrupt halt by the closure of the Suez Canal in 1967, and Eritrea went into economic recession. This was one of many factors which contributed to growth of dissidence and spread of insurgency.

The United States, Italy, and Israel were the most active foreign countries in Eritrea in the 1960s. They were also the most popular. The presence of US military installations provoked no local resentment. Even after insurgent movements began receiving substantial support from Soviet-surrogate, Chinese communist, and radical Arab sources in the late 1960s, they avoided attacking or even propagandizing against US military installations, knowing that such actions would not win approval of the local population.

### Origins of the Insurgency

A small number of Eritreans strongly opposed to federation with Ethiopia fled abroad during the 1950s. When Nasser took power in Egypt and sought influence throughout Africa and the Middle East, some found welcome in Cairo. One, Wolde-Ab Wolde-Mariam, a Protestant trade union leader, began broadcasting over Radio Cairo. Nasser stopped these broadcasts when Haile Selassie came to his support during the Suez crisis of 1956. Wolde-Ab and others nevertheless persisted in opposition and established the Eritrean Liberation Movement (ELM) in 1959. Christians in Eritrea did not respond to its calls for rebellion.

A broader group called the Eritrean Liberation Front aimed to unite Christians and Muslims and superseded the earlier ELM in 1961. It was dominated by Muslims of the interior Beni Amer tribe. One of them, a native of Tessenei, mounted an attack on an Ethiopian military position on 1 September 1961. This episode has subsequently been glorified as the beginning of the armed struggle in Eritrea.

During the next six years, the ELF, whose exile leaders were established in Beirut, Damascus, Cairo, and Baghdad, profited from the rising tide of Arab nationalism. They attracted material support from several Arab governments. These exiles formed a Supreme Council in Khartoum and divided Eritrea into five regional commands patterned after those of Algerian rebels. The commands had considerable autonomy which reduced the effect of the factionalism that divided Muslims even more than Christians. Efforts to accommodate Christian rebels were complicated by pressure from the ELF's Arab backers, who saw Eritrea as Arab territory. Muslim fighters were trained in Syria, while young Christians were trained separately in camps in Sudan. Both were expected to speak Arabic, a demand that became a source of contention. Periodic hit-and-run operations were carried out in various parts of Eritrea but their military effect was negligible. Despite claims of 2,000 fighters inside Eritrea by 1967, active insurgent strength probably numbered no more than a few hundred.

At this point ELF activities were no more than mildly worrisome to Haile Selassie's government. In fact, it saw the rebels primarily as a manifestation of age-old Muslim-Arab enmity toward Christian Ethiopia. Ethiopia's close relationship with Israel influenced this judgment. Until the latter half of the 1960s the rebellion had no significant East-West dimension. The ELF was predominantly conservative, traditional, and by no means irrevocably separatist in orientation. Socialism did not interest anyone. Muslim Eritreans felt little affinity with African anticolonialist liberation movements. Haile Selassie's skillful diplomacy in the United Nations and in the Organization of African Unity (OAU) preempted their efforts to gain international recognition both then and later.

The situation changed decisively during 1967. Arab defeat during the Six Day War resulted in a surge of radicalism which the Soviets were quick to exploit. Since 1966, Cuba, with Moscow's blessing, had been expanding its Third World operations. Soviet-Chinese competition for influence over revolutionary movements of all kinds was intensifying.

The incipient Eritrean insurgency looked inviting to all these forces eager to challenge the status quo. Dissident and rebellious Eritreans were ready to accept support from any quarter with little concern for its ultimate implications. Blockage of Suez nipped in the bud a promising period of economic expansion in Eritrea and swelled the ranks of idle young men.

## Expansion of the Insurgency, 1967–1971

Benefitting from an accelerated inflow of funds and steadier supplies of arms, and with opportunities for more extensive guerrilla training in Cuba, China, and in PLO camps in the Middle East, the ELF expanded its operations on the ground. The movement received a boost when Tedla Bairu, originally a supporter of union with Ethiopia and first chief executive under the federation, joined it in 1967. Hit-and-run operations in Eritrean cities, attacks on military vehicles, and hijackings of Ethiopian Airlines flights gave the Eritrean separatist movement continual publicity but did not really challenge Ethiopian civil and military control of the province.

Greater activity brought two disadvantages: tension and disagreements between guerrilla fighters and exile leaders abroad and rivalry among guerrilla commanders in the five insurgent regions. Tribal and religious differences were never far beneath the surface. The Ethiopian government infiltrated some guerrilla bands and persuaded sizable numbers of Christians to accept amnesty. ELF factions accused each other of double-dealing with the Ethiopians. All these strains, including resentment of Supreme Council direction, resulted in a split in the movement inside Eritrea in September 1968. This was accompanied, in turn, by increased competitiveness among exile leaders. It would be tedious to recapitulate all these shifts and maneuvers. Suffice it to observe that a tendency common in exile and guerrilla movements was clearly discernible by 1969: those advocating the most extreme and uncompromising positions gained influence.

Osman Salih Sabbe, an energetic Muslim from the coastal town of Arkiko (and thus a natural rival of the Beni Amer leaders of the interior), was one of the few Eritrean insurgent leaders who spoke native Arabic. First functioning as secretary general of the ELF, he gained the backing of radical Arab governments and the PLO to establish a new leadership for the Eritrean movement. Tedla Bairu contributed Christian support to this movement which proclaimed itself the Popular Liberation Forces (PLF) in June 1970. It dominated operations in the coastal and adjacent highland regions, strategically the most important sectors of Eritrea.

Dissension among exile leaders and fighters on the ground did not inhibit expansion of the insurgency. In fact, it encouraged it, for groups competed to mount operations to assert their preeminence over rivals, publicize themselves, and do Ethiopian government forces maximum harm. Their zeal would not have carried them far, however, if foreign benefactors had not been increasingly generous with arms and supplies to all groups.[12]

Eritrean insurgents were direct and immediate beneficiaries of Nimeiry's seizure of power in Khartoum in May 1969. Nimeiry welcomed Soviet military assistance, and it began to arrive in large quantities. He used it to step up the fight against the southern Sudanese rebellion, but there was plenty left over for the Eritreans. Qaddafy, who also seized power in 1969, was eager to support the Eritreans. Syria, Iraq, and newly independent South Yemen all served as channels for arms and funds, often originally of Communist origin.

To prevent the Soviets from gaining the upper hand through their surrogates, the Chinese stepped up their support from 1968 onward and utilized both Yemens as channels for getting it to Eritrea. The Soviets, who maintained proper relations with Haile Selassie's government, observed the principle of "plausible denial," trained no Eritreans themselves, used surrogates to channel assistance, and let Cuba conduct propaganda operations attacking Haile Selassie and championing the Eritrean cause.

By the end of 1969 Eritrea was becoming a worrisome military problem for Addis Ababa. Insurgents were getting heavier weapons and vehicles across the Sudan border. During 1970 they became bolder in carrying out assassinations, urban infiltrations, and attacks against rail and road communications. Militarily they were now able to challenge Ethiopian forces for control of territory. By the end of that year they had established a firm hold on areas near Keren and in the northern Sahel and repulsed repeated Ethiopian army attacks. They were also able to harass traffic on most main roads, forcing use of convoys, and had gained sufficient strength to intimidate the rural population into avoiding cooperation with the government.

Haile Selassie's government sought help from its American and Israeli military advisory missions. The US gave advice but avoided active involvement in counterinsurgency operations. Israeli advisers worked directly with Ethiopian military units. The PLF exploited this fact to publicize the Eritrean insurgency as an aspect of the Arabs' anti-Zionist and anti-imperialist struggle spearheaded by the PLO, which was doubtless pleasing to the Kremlin. As tension heightened, especially after the insurgents succeeded in ambushing and killing the senior Ethiopian army general in Eritrea in November 1970, Ethiopians who argued for flexibility and political sophistication in coping with the insurgency were overruled by advocates of tough tactics including reprisals against civilians suspected of siding with the guerrillas. Ras Asrate Kassa, a high-ranking Amhara noble, was replaced as governor in Asmara by a senior general. Serious as the insurgency appeared at this time, as the Ethiopian government appeared to commit itself to an uncompromising military solution, it is important to see it in perspective, especially for the sake of comparison with the situation the Derg has faced since 1974.

Retrospective claims to the contrary, total insurgent strength in 1971 was probably not much more than 2,000.[13] The Ethiopian armed forces, primarily dependent on US military aid averaging $12 million a year during this period,[14] totaled slightly over 40,000. No more than half this manpower was ever deployed in Eritrea. Best evidence indicated that the bulk of the Eritrean population, though resentful of Addis Ababa's paternalism, had not become irretrievably alienated from Ethiopia and lacked confidence that the guerrilla movement could prevail or bring prosperity to the territory if it did. Despite the economic slump caused by the prolonged closure of the Suez Canal, economic development in Eritrea continued and several new public-works projects were completed. An impressive national exhibition, EXPO-72, opened in Asmara in the spring of 1972. By this time unexpected international developments had a serious negative impact on the insurgents' struggle.

In the early 1970s the Lion of Judah, approaching eighty, was still capable of statesmanship of a kind not seen in the Horn of Africa since. Informed by President Nixon of the advancing US rapprochement with Mao's China,[15] he hurried off to Peking in October and concluded an agreement with Mao and Chou. In return for establishment of formal diplomatic relations and acceptance of Chinese aid, China agreed to cease all support for the Eritrean insurgency. Returning to Addis Ababa, Haile Selassie successfully mediated the conflict between the southern Sudanese insurgency and President Nimeiry with whom Ethiopia established warm relations. Nimeiry, disillusioned with close Soviet ties after the Sudanese Communist party had attempted to oust him a few months before, promised to curtail Eritrean activities from Sudanese territory.

While Nimeiry was never able to stop all Eritrean activity—and probably never intended to because of his desire to preserve his status as an Arab leader—he forced a significant reduction of it. The Chinese rapidly implemented a complete reversal of their previous policy toward Ethiopia.[16] The result was a severe but not fatal setback for the Eritrean separatist movement.

## The Insurgency Deadlocked, 1972–1974

The insurgents lost Chinese and Sudanese aid at a time when factionalism, which had intensified during 1971 and 1972, was beginning to have a detrimental effect on guerrilla momentum. It lead to situations where rival groups devoted more time to sparring and even fighting with each other than to harassing the Ethiopians. The ELF went through a complex process of internal strain, exacerbated by competition with the PLF, culminating in the establishment of the Revolutionary Council (RC) at the end of 1971. Henceforth the organization became known as the ELF-RC, claiming to be the only valid representative of Eritrean nationalism. Meanwhile other former ELF elements moved toward merger with the PLF and announced formation of the Eritrean Popular Liberation Forces (EPLF) in February 1972. Wolde-Ab Wolde-Mariam and Osman Salih Sabbe emerged as president and general secretary, respectively, of this new increasingly Marxist-oriented and PLO-favored grouping.

On the ground in Eritrea contention persisted. A field commander who sought compromise with the ELF-RC was found poisoned and several small groups went their own way. The guerrilla struggle was severely affected:

> The establishment of the ELF-RC and . . . did not end the period of organizational fluidity in the Eritrean movement. The two organizations were merely amalgams of different groups and were far from internally stable; moreover, the rivalry and enmity between them grew constantly. . . . The gap between the organizations, as well as the endless internal rivalries, arose from the pluralist nature of Eritrea. . . . The situation was made even more complex by the network of personal rivalries and religious, ethnic and other differences.[17]

The Imperial Ethiopian Government (IEG) proved incapable of exploiting the favorable situation its diplomacy and insurgent divisiveness had brought about. Ethiopian military domination of civil government in Eritrea inhibited political creativity. IEG initiative for restoration of some form of regional self-government would not have risked a great deal, could have tested the mood of the population, and might have shifted their expectations for the future onto Addis Ababa initiatives rather than those of the insurgents.

By the fall of 1973 when the Yom Kippur War opened the way for early resumption of traffic through the Suez Canal, with positive impact on Eritrea's economy, it was too late. Ethiopia fell victim to the ensuing petroleum price war. The old emperor's break in relations with Israel, although it had no concrete immediate impact, cost him the confidence of many of his closest supporters. The situation in Eritrea remained deadlocked and provoked restiveness in the Ethiopian armed forces.

How did Moscow regard all these developments? Direct evidence remains scanty. In spite of continued support for Eritrean separatism by so many of their surrogates and proxies (Syria, Iraq, Libya, South Yemen, Cuba, and the PLO), the Russians remained comfortably in the background. They avoided direct relations with Eritrean exile leaders although many of these, according to subsequent admissions, assumed Soviet benevolence toward their cause. Russian expectations for rapid gains in Ethiopia remained low until the mid-1970s. Their program for gaining predominance in the Horn of Africa was long-range and centered on Somali president Siad Barre[18] who saw Moscow's objectives as identical with his own. The Soviet Union's first response to the Ethiopian Revolution was to sign a Treaty of Friendship and Cooperation with Somalia in July 1974 and step up military assistance.

The Soviets saw the Eritrean insurgency as serving their purposes on a much slower track. How much guidance or advice Moscow gave to the EPLF is unknown, but even if they made no direct input, CPSU strategists had to be pleased with this group. EPLF leaders sacrificed immediate gains to build a strong and disciplined movement with a solid social and ideological base—no easy task among Eritreans:

> The early EPLF represented a coalition between the more educated eastern Muslims who initially formed a majority of the membership, and Christian highlanders. The EPLF leadership still reflects this original composition. The EPLF's program of social transformation and their secular nationalism proved attractive to the younger generation of Christian students at high schools, college and universities, who, after 1973, joined the EPLF in large numbers and now form the dominant element of the middle ranks. . . . The EPLF's stress on the need for social revolution to accompany the military struggle . . . challenged the ELF, who in turn modified their own political program. But this remained a largely paper exercise.[19]

Eritrean factionalism and the setbacks the movement had suffered as a result of loss of Chinese and Sudanese support gave the Soviets little reason to expect that a major investment would pay early dividends. It was better to bide time and experiment with a group that offered promise of evolving into a Marxist-Leninist Vanguard party (MLVP) amenable to Soviet direction.[20] This kind of calculation is typical of many the Soviets made during this period.

## The Eritrean Insurgency and the Ethiopian Revolution

When mutinies broke out in February 1974 among Ethiopian forces in Eritrea and troops arrested their officers, IEG officials came from Addis Ababa to mediate. The soldiers made demands for higher pay and better service conditions. There was initially little evidence of military sympathy with the insurgents, but locally recruited police and commando units influenced the newly created Coordinating Committee of the Armed Forces of the North to propose legalizing the ELF-RC. By this time both insurgent groups were more interested in jockeying for position against each other than they were either in fighting or negotiating with Ethiopian forces. No accommodation occurred.

Ferment spread throughout Ethiopia and in June a national Armed Forces Coordinating Committee, which quickly became known as the Derg, was formed in Addis Ababa. On 3 July 1974, the Derg persuaded Haile Selassie to appoint General Aman Andom, an Eritrean, chief of staff. When a new government was formed at the end of July, Aman became minister of defense. He flew to Eritrea and made public appearances throughout the province. Hopes for an Eritrean settlement rose. Aman

> admitted that Ethiopian hard-liners, by resorting exclusively to military power, had encouraged Eritrean separatism; but at the same time, he emphasized that "Eritrea had been historically an integral part of Ethiopia . . . that the problem of Eritrea is the problem of the entire Ethiopia . . . [and that] we are jealous of our unity.[21]

On September 9, back in the capital, Aman submitted a nineteen-point plan for dealing with Eritrea. Hopes rose further on September 12 when the Derg deposed Haile Selassie and declared Aman its chairman and acting head of state. It appeared that the Derg was committed to settling the Eritrean problem.

Aman appointed Christian Eritrean's governor-general and chief of police of the province. He passed word to EPLF leaders through Nimeiry in Khartoum that he was ready to negotiate restoration of Eritrean autonomy. They rejected his overtures. Their priorities were to defeat the ELF-RC and insist on independence. In early October ELF-RC and EPLF forces clashed in a pitched battle lasting several days near a village north of Asmara. Six hundred fighters were killed. The fighting came to an end only when 30,000 Asmarans marched en masse to the battlefield and effected a reconciliation among the warring rebels. A rally followed which gave the impression that the people of Eritrea were forming a spontaneous mass movement to take matters into their own hands. This alarmed the new military commander in Eritrea, General Teferi Banti, an Oromo from the south. Aman flew again to Asmara to dissuade Teferi from dispatching troops against the insurgents and at a mass meeting in the Asmara central stadium vowed to achieve peace through compromise. Both rebel factions responded with a call for all-out war against Ethiopia. The situation was deadlocked.

In the Derg in Addis Ababa, Eritrea provoked intense contention. This junta was still a loosely organized body where no one was sure of his power and none of the major contenders for predominance could risk being accused of softness on the issue of Ethiopian unity. Foremost among these was Major Mengistu Haile-Mariam. Under circumstances that remain obscure, Aman was besieged and killed at his house in the capital on 23 November 1974 and that night fifty-nine imprisoned IEG officials were summarily shot.[22] General Teferi was called back from Eritrea to replace Aman as Derg chairman and acting head of state. The Ethiopian Revolution until this point had been bloodless. Henceforth it became ever more violent and Eritrean policy was more often than not a major cause of divisiveness in the Derg. Hardliners on both sides — in the Derg and among the insurgents — blocked all moves toward compromise.

The November 1974 events in the capital had rapid repercussions in Eritrea. Bands of insurgents infiltrated Asmara in late December and attacked Ethiopian military and government facilities. A Derg mission arrived and met with hundreds of Eritrean dignitaries, including leading churchmen, who insisted on a negotiated settlement. In early January the police commissioner appointed by General Aman defected to the insurgents and many of his men followed. Hundreds of young men left Asmara and Massawa to join insurgent bands. Popular pressure forced ELF-RC and EPLF leaders to meet at Coazien on the last day of January 1975 and effect a reconciliation. They followed it with a major assault on Asmara which lasted through most of February, resulting in hundreds of casualties on all sides, but failed to dislodge the Ethiopian forces. An attack on Keren also failed. The two insurgent groups claimed to have more than 10,000 fighters between them by this time. They probably had at least half that number.[23]

The Derg launched a major offensive in Eritrea in 1975, and, still dependent on the United States for military support, pressed for increased aid. During the next three years US military assistance totaled $90 million, almost triple the yearly average during the period preceding the Revolution. In addition, the Derg bought $100 million worth of US military supplies with funds it inherited from Haile Selassie's well-managed treasury. The 1975 offensive nevertheless failed. Both insurgent factions gained ground and new recruits. Although the Coazien reconciliation was not followed by political agreement and the leadership abroad remained competitive and often hostile, there was a substantial cooperation in the field. During this same period the Tigre Popular Liberation Front, an offshoot of the EPLF, took control of much of the area immediately south of Eritrea.[24]

The year 1975 ended with more Ethiopian military manpower in Eritrea than in Haile Selassie's time and less territory under Addis Ababa's control. Derg leaders developed a plan for a decisive end to the Eritrean rebellion. A massive peasant militia recruited in the south would march into Eritrea and eradicate resistance which was described to southern Christian peasants as being primarily Muslim. If necessary, the entire Eritrean population would be driven out or killed and southerners would resettle their land.[25]

Word of this genocidal scheme reached the United States through Ethiopian diplomats abroad. The Ford administration reacted sharply. Henry Kissinger had just approved delivery of a squadron of the latest US fighter-bomber, the Northrop F5-E, which had been promised to Haile Selassie in 1973. He sent a message to the Derg threatening a cut-off of military aid, and the genocidal offensive was dramatically scaled back.[26] The 1976 operations in Eritrea left even less of the province under Addis Ababa's control and drove most of the population into active support of the insurgents, now claiming 30,000–45,000 fighters. They were carrying out large-scale conventional military operations. Derg control of much of the rest of northern Ethiopia was being challenged by half a dozen dissident and separatist groups.

### Reversal of Alliance

As subsequent developments were to demonstrate, the greatest threat to the country was from Somalia. With armed forces equipped and trained by the Russians, the Somalis were systematically preparing to seize the entire southeastern third of Ethiopia. They had gradually infiltrated the Ogaden, from which most Ethiopian troops had been withdrawn to fight insurgents in Eritrea, Tigre, and elsewhere in the north. In Ogaden border regions they preempted civil authority and Somali currency was more widely used than Ethiopian. Relations with Sudan had deteriorated, and Sudan was actively aiding the ELF-RC as well as the Ethiopian Democratic Union (EDU) which was strong in Gondar province.

Not surprisingly, multiple rebellions and threats from across the country's borders provoked intense strain leading to bloodshed in the Derg itself. Things came to a head in early February 1977 when General Teferi and eight other Derg members were killed and Mengistu emerged as chairman. The Soviet ambassador rushed to congratulate him, but the Russians were still hedging their bets, supplying arms to both the Somalis and the Eritreans. Meanwhile Ethiopia, promised Soviet military support in December 1976, was recruiting thousands of additional soldiers to form a new army to bring Eritrea to heel.

In Eritrea the two insurgent organizations, intermittently cooperating and going their own way, were steadily gaining new victories. Together they brought Keren under siege in October 1976. In January 1977, the EPLF captured its first town, Carora in the north, and later seized the Sahel subprovincial capital, Nacfa, in March. During the same period the ELF-RC took Om Hager and Tessenei in the western lowlands. In July the EPLF captured Decamere, a short distance southeast of Asmara, and Keren was lost after a long battle in which Ethiopian casualties numbered in the thousands. By September 1977 of major Eritrean towns only Asmara, Massawa, Barentu, Adi Caieh, and Assab remained under Derg control. The Derg's new recruits made headway against the TPLF and the EDU at the beginning of the summer, but the Derg's attention was no longer centered on Eritrea.

Soviet assurances notwithstanding, Somali forces moved into the Ogaden in July and rapidly approached the edge of the highlands. Jijiga fell on 12 September 1977, the third anniversary of the Revolution, and Harar came under siege. Having broken off the US military relationship in April 1977, Mengistu was still waiting for large shipments of Soviet arms. A South Yemeni brigade helped hold the Somalis back from Harar and Diredawa while the Soviets prepared to air- and sea-lift a billion dollars worth of arms and equipment and 18,000 Cubans, who did the brunt of the fighting that pushed the Somalis back across their own borders in early 1978.

These dramatic developments turned the political relationships of the region upside-down. Revolutionary Ethiopia had finally become a Soviet client state. Somalia, which had first come to depend militarily on the USSR in the mid-1960s, and a Soviet ally committed to socialism after Siad Barre came to power in 1969, had no alternative but to seek a close Western relationship and became dependent on conservative, anti-Soviet Arab states for military and economic support. Sudan had traveled the better part of the distance from dependence on Moscow to close association with the United States since the beginning of the 1970s. All this left the Eritrean insurgents in a peculiarly contradictory position.

## Defeat on the Threshold of Victory[27]

Moscow could no longer be a primary source of inspiration and support for any group of Eritrean insurgents, nor could states closely allied with Moscow such as Libya and South Yemen be relied upon. They had, in fact, long since become allies of Mengistu. Other radical Arab states were more equivocal.

On the ground the Eritrean insurgent groups, taken together, controlled at least 90 percent of the province's territory. They had for all practical purposes achieved de facto independence through their own fighting ability. Had they been able to occupy Asmara and Massawa and form a unified government, they might have gained international recognition in 1970. By the end of that year, however, Ethiopian forces had regained control of all but the northern fringe of the province. How did the insurgents turn near-victory into defeat?

At bottom, the problem goes back to the fundamental fragmentation of Eritrea—it is not a nation and Eritreans are not a nationality. The Derg's assault on Eritrea had created a greater sense of cohesion than had ever existed before in the territory, but it was a *negative* sense of being together under attack and against oppression. A *positive* sense of commitment to a constructive purpose never became fully developed. The more active the insurgents became in Eritrea the more acute were the strains between field commanders and exile leaders in both separatist organizations. Crucial developments in 1975 predetermined the failure in 1978.

The ELF-RC had held its second congress in the countryside between Keren and Agordat in May 1975. Previous leaders were voted out as "bourgeois opportunists" and a group of young, mostly Iraqi-trained Muslims took over the leadership. They were supported by a group of largely Christian Tigrean recruits, some of whom had defected from the EPLF. Most of these men were convinced of the desirability of insurgent unity.

Since 1974 Osman Salih Sabbe's links with the EPLF field command had become tenuous. While they became more Marxist, he saw an opportunity, following the Ethiopian Revolution, to base the Eritrean struggle on support from conservative Arab states. Saudi Arabia promised generous assistance, and Egypt and Sudan were favorably inclined. In June 1975 Osman began negotiations with the new leaders of the ELF-RC. They continued in Baghdad and Beirut and culminated in September in Khartoum with the signing of a unity agreement between the entire exile leadership of the EPLF (with Wolde-Ab Wolde-Mariam as head) and the ELF-RC. In subsequent months all EPLF field groups rejected the agreement. They denounced Osman as a traitor and condemned those who had joined in creating "unity" in the Eritrean movement as "feudalist compradors and bureaucratic capitalists."

During the next two years the EPLF became more Marxist and revolutionary and more effective in the field than the ELF-RC. There was still occasional cooperation between fighters of the two groups. Once territory was under their control, EPLF political officers concentrated on organizing it along self-sufficient socialist lines under the slogan "revolution before unity." The Yenan-style austerity combined with a sense of adventure appealed to idealistic young Eritreans and foreign journalists alike.

The EPLF held its first congress in January 1977 and adopted an eleven-point "National Democratic" program establishing guidelines for the future Eritrean state.[28] It was to be a "People's Democracy" governed by a revolutionary socialist regime essentially identical to the one Derg Marxists hoped to set up in Ethiopia.[29] It renamed itself the Eritrean People's Liberation Front and established a classic Marxist command structure with a forty-three-member central committee and thirteen-man politburo. As its insignia it adopted a nine-bullet motif signifying the nine languages of Eritrea. In doing so it rejected the fiction that Eritrea was part of the Arab world. The EPLF retained substantial Muslim membership, but its dynamism derived mainly from young Christians.

Osman Salih Sabbe did not fit smoothly into the ELF-RC and was resented by Christian elements in it. Making good use of the money the Saudis supplied, he laid the basis for a third Eritrean organization and by early 1977 claimed 2,000 guerrillas in northwestern Eritrea sustained by an impressive support structure in the Sudan. In April 1977 near Agordat he assembled the first congress of the Eritrean Liberation Front-Popular Liberation Forces (ELF-PLF) and called for mutual recognition by all three insurgent organizations on the basis of a program that placed unity and consolidation of independence before all other issues. Eritreans were doing so well against Ethiopian forces by this time that they took military success for granted. In June the EPLF and the ELF-RC announced formation of a "National Democratic Front" which also included the TPLF and the Ethiopian People's Revolutionary party (EPRP), a civilian Marxist group which was challenging the Derg. Osman's ELF-PLF was excluded.

Divisiveness among leaders of the three Eritrean separatist organizations encouraged division among the rank and file, and, dizzy with the successes they had achieved against Derg forces, various subfactions of all groups spent more and more of their time vying for position. Subgroups shifted loyalties en masse and fratricidal clashes with heavy casualties became frequent during the fall of 1977. During the period when the Derg's forces were under maximum pressure from Somali invaders in the south and barely able to hold a few remaining strong points in Eritrea, the insurgents concentrated on fighting each other. Asmara lay open to capture by a coordinated joint operation. Rival groups feared each other too much to undertake it. At Massawa EPLF forces drove Ethiopian forces back onto the two outer islands and held all mainland positions, but they were unable to pursue their near-victory to conclusion. At the end of the year Russian air and sea bombardment reduced mainland Massawa to rubble and the insurgents were forced to retreat northward. Ten years later the ruins of mainland Massawa stand as a grim monument to Soviet crassness and insurgent ineptitude as Ethiopian party and government officials try to bring this historic old port back to some semblance of economic health.

## Reassertion of Derg Dominance

With the Somalis defeated by the beginning of March 1978, Mengistu turned his attention to Eritrea and ordered offensives to relieve pressure on Asmara and Massawa.[30] He was too impatient. Nothing was achieved. Before Ethiopian forces could reassert themselves in Eritrea, serious political differences with Ethiopia's major benefactors, the Soviet Union and Cuba, had to be faced and compromises made. The whole political history of 1978 is too complex to recount here,[31] and the disagreements that arose among the Derg, the Soviets, and the Cubans over Eritrea as well as the broader issue of Ethiopia's future political development remain to be elucidated in detail. But as in other aspects of Horn politics in the past, there are reasons to believe that the Soviets were not of one mind on how to proceed.

Factionalized as the Eritrean insurgents were (two new groups broke off from the three existing ones in the summer of 1978) it was evident that the EPLF was the most dynamic. Politically it was a maturing Marxist-Leninist vanguard party with the advantage of battle-hardened civilian leadership. A comparable party remained to be built in Ethiopia. Some Soviet ideologues apparently still doubted the long-term viability of military-based socialism in Ethiopia. They had little sympathy with Mengistu's determination to destroy the EPLF, which held promise of turning Eritrea into a classic people's democracy. The Cubans refused to participate in crushing a Marxist movement which they had helped nurture for more than a decade. Their stance may not have been entirely motivated by considerations of morality; it offered the Soviets the reinsurance of a convenient alternate course.

The Soviets would have preferred to see the Derg negotiate a settlement with the EPLF, but it did not control all of Eritrea. The Derg feared the implications of any negotiations on its precarious position in Tigre and Gondar, where the TPLF and the EDU, respectively, were still far from defeated. During a visit to Moscow in April 1978 Mengistu persuaded the Russians to support an offensive to reassert Ethiopian control over Eritrea. They insisted on important conditions: the Ethiopians would have to rely entirely on their own manpower; they would have to accept Russian direction in preparation and execution of the offensive; they would have to set a timetable for creating a Marxist-Leninist vanguard party in Ethiopia.

When the offensive finally got under way in July, it resembled the great Soviet drives against Hitler's armies in the final stages of the Second World War: slow, systematic build-up with air and artillery bombardments, then masses of troops moving forward on a broad front. All major Eritrean towns except Keren were captured by mid-August. When Keren fell after another long and costly siege at then end of November, 80 to 90 percent of Eritrea was back under Addis Ababa's control. Tens of thousands of refugees had fled over the Sudanese border. The population that remained was dour; some cities, such as Massawa, were almost deserted.

### Deadlock and Stalemate, 1979-1987

For the better part of a decade the Eritrean drama continued in slow motion with little change and a good deal of repetition. The main features of the situation can be briefly summed up:

Addis Ababa has kept large military forces in Eritrea—more than 100,000 men, five to six times the number required in Haile Selassie's time to maintain a higher degree of control over the province. Periodical "final" offensives have invariably failed to overcome the insurgents or prevent them from interdicting major roads throughout the province. The insurgents gained the strength to recapture Barentu and Tessenei in 1985, but were unable to retain them. Militarily the war remained a stalemate with little prospect that either side could win on the battlefield. Large-scale desertions, including officers, show that Ethiopian army morale has generally been lower than that of the insurgents.

On the ground, the EPLF has been dominant. Exile Eritreans continue to be split into many factions and among the rank and file Marxist commitment is not as strong as among the organization's leadership. In the northern portions of Eritrea which the EPLF has been able to hold continually it has built a socialist egalitarian society and administrative structure which has attracted the admiration of journalists, academic enthusiasts, and a number of European leftist politicians.[32] Enthusiasts' judgments to the contrary, "liberated Eritrea" is neither economically self-sufficient nor free of social and political strain.

The EPLF has no resources of its own and few can be generated in territory it controls in Eritrea. Syria and Iraq have continued to support the EPLF. It also benefits from conservative Arab support but resents support which conservative Arabs also continue to give to rival Eritrean groups. Arms flow to the insurgents in Eritrea has gradually declined but the shortfall has been more than made up by weapons and supplies captured from Ethiopian forces.

Cuba has become irrelevant to the Eritrean situation as its forces in Ethiopia have been reduced. The Russians have maintained strong support for the Derg, supplying Ethiopia with almost $3 billion in additional weapons and related military supplies from 1979 through 1985.[33] The Ethiopian military position in Eritrea would be untenable without large-scale Soviet aid. The Soviets have never, however, given up hope for a negotiated solution of the Eritrean problem. They have inspired several mediation initiatives by the East German and Italian Communist parties. These efforts have not only been unsuccessful but have given rise to persistent suspicions among Ethiopian regime officials that Moscow may still be providing support and advice to the EPLF and hopes eventually to bring about some kind of amalgamation of the EPLF and the WPE.

While Addis Ababa was able to maintain a military hold on Eritrea and to exercise administrative control over all main population centers until the spring of 1988, it was unable to impose most of its socialist reforms on the province and made little effort to do so. It has made strenuous efforts to obtain more production from Eritrea's nationalized industries. There is evidence of modest recent increases in Eritrean industrial and agricultural production through early 1988, but the area is chronically susceptible to drought and was severely affected in the 1980s. Given the substantial increase in population that appears to have taken place in Eritrea over the past two decades despite continual insurgency, war, famine, emigration, and flight of refugees the province, which was never self-sufficient, must have a greater net food deficit than ever. Large shipments of Western grain reached Eritrea in 1984–1985, going both to government-held[34] and insurgent areas, and shipments continued to arrive through 1988. Information on the functioning of the Eritrean economy is sparse but a sizable unofficial economy, including exchanges between insurgent- and regime-controlled areas, seems to persist.

Eritrean separatists have made no progress toward gaining international recognition. The Organization of African Unity (OAU) strongly supports Ethiopia's position. The EPLF's strong commitment to Marxism has reduced what slight chances might at various times have existed for gaining unofficial support of major Western governments. The "Second and Unity Congress of the EPLF-ELF (CL)" which was held in EPLF-controlled territory in northern Eritrea 12-19 March 1987 produced a substantial modification of the 1977 National Democratic Program, but the new program still aims at establishing a "People's Democratic State" with a government-directed economy and includes many other Marxist features. On the whole, however, the EPLF's program is now more moderate than that which the WPE is attempting to implement in Ethiopia.

## Does Eritrea Have a Future?

No one can visit Eritrea, as I did in March 1987, and fail to be depressed by the stagnation which more than two decades of insurgency and war have visited upon this geographically dramatic territory. Even though lacking easily exploitable natural wealth, its strategic situation has prompted a succession of ruling powers—Italy, Britain, Ethiopia—to make and maintain investments which give the region a modern infrastructure superior to most of Africa. Many of the prerequisites for self-sustaining economic growth still exist here and more could be created by constructive political, economic, and social policies.

Eritrea has the potential to become an African Switzerland, where geographic contrasts and ethnic and religious differences could contribute to a sense of common purpose: unity in diversity. Though the territory has often been compared negatively to Lebanon (as I have done)[35] such a comparison also has its positive side. Eritrea is similar to Lebanon in its advantageous location on the shore of a sea busy with international trade. The political balance in Lebanon was delicate but remarkably successful until foreign powers and ideological fanatics disrupted it. People who live in areas such as these can learn to live together and accommodate, as Eritreans did at many times in their past, but it is difficult for all groups to resist the lure of gaining special advantage through outside sponsorship. Switzerland has enjoyed centuries of security and prosperity not only because of its peoples' determination to defend their status but also because the country's neighbors have all realized that its neutrality brings each of them too many advantages to risk disrupting it. Eritrea's recent history presents the opposite kind of picture.

In acquiescing in Italian colonial domination of northern Ethiopia, Menelik II secured his empire's northern frontier for half a century while he laid the basis for political consolidation and modernization in the rest of the country. Rejoined to Ethiopia following World War II, Eritrea made a major contribution to the country's development. Tens of thousands of Eritreans found opportunities for work in other parts of the country, and large numbers of them continue to do so. In Eritrea colonialism and the process of extrication from it left a complex legacy. Brilliant leader and statesman that he was on many counts, Haile Selassie was unable to transform the restored Ethiopian relationship with Eritrea into a self-reinforcing partnership.

The mistakes of the imperial regime nevertheless pale in comparison to those of the Marxist military men who have turned Ethiopia into a "People's Republic" that combines features of both Maoism and Stalinism. Recent history has made the problem of Eritrean adjustment to the rest of Ethiopia more difficult but no less necessary.

The events of the past decade have demonstrated that Ethiopia is far from falling apart, though it would be rash to conclude that we have seen the end of the political commotion which the 1974 Revolution unleashed in the country. Five things are nevertheless clear: (1) No government capable of acquiring and maintaining control in Addis Ababa and over a significant portion of Ethiopia will acquiesce in the loss of Eritrea. The kind of concession Menelik II would make in 1896 is impossible a century later. Governments, even juntas who rule people's democracies, must now give greater weight to elite, if not mass, opinion. (2) No major foreign power will support the Eritrean separatists' aspirations. No international organization has the power to do so. In the real world of international politics any foreign government capable of exerting major influence in this part of the world is going to make the same set of calculations the Soviet Union made in 1977, though less crassly perhaps, when confronted with the necessity of choosing. It is going to opt to support Ethiopia over the risky alternative of gaining predominance over a fragment of it. (3) The political and economic case for continued Eritrean association with Ethiopia is and will remain strong. (4) The political and economic case for Ethiopian accommodation to Eritrea's special characteristics and historical circumstances is equally strong. (5) Eritrea cannot be ruled indefinitely by force, nor can its economic potential, which remains very great for Ethiopia, be realized by coercion.

I returned from a visit to Eritrea in March 1987 with two combinations of impressions deeper than all others:

First, the province was very much alive and functioning comparatively better than many parts of Africa in spite of the vicissitudes it has experienced. Physical destruction is minimal in Asmara, greater in Massawa, but less serious than the general stagnation in economic development that has persisted for more than a decade and a half. Nevertheless utilities and services work, schools function, transport operates, and industrial establishments are by no means all idle. Reporters who visit "liberated" Eritrea marvel at the way life is maintained there under adverse circumstances. It is no less remarkable that life continues as well as it does in those areas under Ethiopian government control. The credit belongs less to the Ethiopian military forces than to Ethiopian civil administrators and, above all, to the Eritreans themselves.

And second, Eritrea's greatest asset is its people. Divided as they may be by ethnic affiliation, language and religion, they are naturally gifted and have a talent for working together in adversity. They keep agriculture going.[36] They try to make industries work. If these were still privately operated rather than part of a cumbersome nationalized system, they would be much more productive. Eritreans keep trade, much of which is still private, flowing. Asmara is crowded with young men of military age. They flee from insurgent-held and insurgent-penetrated areas to avoid being drawn into guerrilla service. The adventurousness of the guerrilla struggle which fascinated their fathers and older brothers holds less appeal for them. They flock to Asmara's high schools and its overcrowded university and enroll in courses in engineering, computer science, medicine, and management. If they fail to get into formal classes, they turn to the city's libraries, stocked with books in English from the US and the rest of the English-speaking world. Their priorities are no longer political but economic: they want to acquire the skills to be productive in the modern world.

Seeing these young men filling library reading rooms on weekends symbolized for me both the tragedy and the hope of Eritrea. Given the chance, they could provide the talent and skill for an economic renaissance in Eritrea and all of Ethiopia. If they can find no outlet for their aspirations in their homeland, a large portion of them will sooner or later find their way abroad to join the tens of thousands of Eritreans who are already more or less permanently settled in the Middle East, Europe, and America and who now contribute substantial funds to support insurgency.

Marxism is irrelevant to the problems of these young men and they know it. It is irrelevant to the real problems of Eritrea though the region has been doubly victimized by it. So is the Soviet Union. The Russians have played all sides of the Eritrean game for a quarter of a century, and Eritreans have always been the losers. What do the Soviets want out of Eritrea? Separatists who complain that the Soviets "betrayed" them by shifting support to the Derg in 1977 were self-deluded. The Soviets, the Cubans, Qaddafy, and all the others who originally stoked the insurgency saw it merely as one of several ways of weakening Ethiopia to gain a grip on it. But the grip they have gained is both tenuous and costly. Moscow has put almost $10 billion in arms into Ethiopia during the past decade.[37]

Can Gorbachev, who is trying to revitalize Soviet policies both at home and abroad, afford to continue to invest Soviet resources so unproductively? No wonder he is pressuring Mengistu to compromise in Eritrea, rationalize his economy, and make the Ethiopian Revolution self-supporting. It is a daunting challenge.

The Soviet Union has become a status-quo power in Ethiopia, desperately trying to maintain hegemony over a country Russians have coveted since tsarist times. In this context, the Soviet approach to Eritrea is a damage-limiting operation. Nothing would please Moscow more than to be able to arrange a Marxist marriage between the WPE and the EPLF with the aim of consolidating a Marxist system in a secure, united Ethiopia.[38] The course of events in Eritrea has taken unexpected twists and turns during the past half century, so this one cannot be ruled out. But neither does it seem very probable.

Marxism in Eritrea as well as in Ethiopia rests on brittle and flimsy foundations. EPLF successes against Ethiopian forces in the spring of 1988 were not as much a function of EPLF strength as of Ethiopian military weaknesses and low morale, compounded by Mengistu's brutal treatment of military commanders who failed to deliver victory. Massive mobilization by Addis Ababa, combined with tactical withdrawals from outlying towns, made it possible for Ethiopia to stabilize its hold on the Eritrean highlands by the summer of 1988.[39] Politically, however, the defeats which EPLF forces administered to government forces in March 1988 had the effect of reinforcing separatism, so no progress has been made toward a political settlement. While there is little prospect that Ethiopian forces can reduce Eritrea to submission, there is extremely little likelihood that the guerrillas can take and hold the highlands around Asmara which constitute the political heart, the communications hub, and the major industrial base of the province. When Haile Selassie's armed forces became disgruntled in 1974 at the stalemate in Eritrea, they helped generate the ferment that led to the overthrow of the imperial regime. The rigid security controls which the Soviets have helped Mengistu build to keep dissatisfaction in his armed forces in check have so far operated to prevent this kind of development. But there is no reason to believe that history might not still, in some way, repeat itself.

Without Soviet arms, Mengistu could not maintain his position in Eritrea. Ironically, however, it appears to be primarily these same Soviet arms, captured or appropriated in other ways from the Ethiopian government forces, that now sustain the guerrillas. Were the Soviets to stop supplying arms, both sides would eventually suffer and might be driven toward a negotiated settlement. The Soviet Union thus faces a major policy challenge in Eritrea, and in Ethiopia as a whole. The United States does not.[40] Eritrea dramatizes the dilemma the Soviets face in trying to keep Marxist-Leninist regimes in power in other parts of the Third World as well.

As long as President Mengistu persists in trying to build a Stalinist system in Ethiopia, the United States must bide its time, but it faces no fundamental policy challenge. The US Congress is likely to continue to authorize provision of a major share of the food needed to sustain Ethiopians, including Eritreans, threatened with starvation resulting from conflict and economic mismanagement. The United States and its democratic allies are the only source of development assistance and productive investment that can heal the damage Marxism has inflicted on the Horn of Africa; Soviet models for development and modernization are discredited. The Free World can help Ethiopia, including Eritrea, get free enterprise and a market economy operating again and lay the groundwork for creation of an open, pluralist society—a process well under way when the country fell into the hands of dogmatic military revolutionaries.[41] These men have raised the aspirations of all Ethiopians for a better life but they have delivered stagnation, misery, and disaster. Neither, for all their Marxist rhetoric and demonstrated capacity to maintain themselves under harsh conditions in least productive parts of the province, have the Eritrean guerrillas demonstrated a real capacity to build and operate a dynamic economic system that can guarantee human rights and basic freedoms. What both the Eritrean Marxists and those in Addis Ababa have demonstrated is the poverty and pointlessness of Marxism as a formula for either political reconciliation or social and economic progress.

## Notes

1. The Derg was officially titled the Provisional Military Administrative Committee (PMAC) and the government it established the Provisional Military Government of Ethiopia (PMGE) replacing Haile Selassie's Imperial Ethiopian Government (IEG). Socialist was soon added to the new government's title, resulting in PMGSE, which continued in use until September 1987 when the country was declared the People's Democratic Republic of Ethiopia (PDRE).
2. Haggai Erlich, *The Struggle over Eritrea, 1962-1978* (Stanford, CA: Hoover Institution, 1983), p. 1.
3. Stephen H. Longrigg, *A Short History of Eritrea* (Oxford Clarendon Press, 1945), is still the best brief history available.
4. Assab is now administered separately from the rest of Eritrea. It forms a special administrative region directly under Addis Ababa.
5. From which the present journal of the Eritrean People's Liberation Front (EPLF) takes its name.
6. The PMGSE, to underscore Ethiopia's historical position in Eritrea, celebrat-

ed the 100th anniversary of the Battle of Dogali in January 1987 with a seminar to which prominent historians from several countries (including Israel) were invited. A new monument, capped by a large red star, was dedicated at the site.
7. The first British chief administrator of Eritrea, Stephen Longrigg, concluded his well-researched and thoughtful history cited above with a recommendation for partitioning the territory between Sudan and Ethiopia (pp. 168–175). His final successor, who oversaw the complex process of devolution of British rule and establishment of the federation, produced a masterly record of the entire period of British administration: G. H. K. Trevaskis, *Eritrea, A Colony in Transition, 1941–1952* (London: Oxford University Press, 1960). Both books remain essential reading for those concerned with the Eritrean problem.
8. See Erlich, *Struggle*, pp. 4–10.
9. The Unionist party held 32 of the 68 seats in the Eritrean Assembly elected in 1952 which sat until 1956. Four other parties shared the remaining seats.
10. Haggai Erlich, "The Eritrean Autonomy, 1952–62: Its Failure and Contribution to Further Escalation" in Yoram Dinstein, ed., *Models of Autonomy* (New Brunswick, NJ: Rutgers University Press, 1981).
11. Erlich, *Struggle*, p. 8. Erlich points out that the revised 1955 Ethiopian constitution made no mention of Eritrea or the federation at all.
12. Eritrean insurgents had access to no significant internal monetary or material resources to sustain guerrilla operations. They lacked a capability for seizing arms and supplies from Ethiopian government forces. Without substantial and dependable outside support the Eritrean guerrilla movement never could have expanded beyond the level of conventional banditry.
13. Erlich, *Struggle*, p. 32.
14. Paul B. Henze, "Arming the Horn, 1960–1980" in *Proceedings of the Seventh International Conference of Ethiopian Studies* (Lund, Sweden, 1982), African Studies Center, Michigan State University, East Lansing, MI, 1984, pp. 637–656.
15. By Vice President Spiro Agnew who came to Addis Ababa during the first days of July 1971.
16. They implemented in less than a year and at minimum cost a shift to recognition of Ethiopia's territorial integrity and acknowledgement of both its role and its potential as the major power in its region. The Soviets made the same shift in 1977 but under much more awkward and less auspicious circumstances, at enormous expense, and with much less assurance of ultimate gain.
17. Erlich, *Struggle*, p. 31.
18. Paul B. Henze, "Getting a Grip on the Horn" in Walter Z. Laqueur, ed., *The Pattern of Soviet Conduct in the Third World* (New York: Praeger, 1983).
19. James Firebrace with Stuart Holland, MP, with a Preface by Neil Kinnock, MP, *Never Kneel Down: Drought, Development and Liberation in Eritrea* (Trenton, NJ: Red Sea Press, 1985), p. 30.
20. For background on the concept of the Marxist-Leninist vanguard party, see Korbonski & Fukuyama, eds., *The Soviet Union and the Third World* (Ithaca, NY: Cornell University Press, 1987), p. 30 ff.
21. *The Ethiopian Herald* (Addis Ababa), 28 August and 7 September 1974, as cited in Erlich, *Struggle*, p. 49.

22. For a version of these events by a high-level defector, see Dawit Wolde Giorgis, *Red Tears* (Trenton, New Jersey: Red Sea Press, 1988), pp. 18-20.
23. The Derg claimed 2,321 insurgents killed and 324 wounded in the Asmara operation alone compared with 38 dead and 134 wounded for the Ethiopian army. The EPLF claimed that 2,000 Ethiopian troops had been killed. Claims on both sides were always greatly exaggerated. For comments on the difficulty of determining insurgent strength and casualties on both sides see Erlich, *Struggle*, pp. 72 and 137.
24. This section is based on more comprehensive accounts of this period I have given in *Rebels and Separatists in Ethiopia: Regional Resistance to a Marxist Regime,* RAND/R-3347-USDP, Santa Monica, CA, December 1985 and "Eritrea: The Endless War" in *The Washington Quarterly,* 9/2 (Spring 1986), pp. 23-26.
25. On this and subsequent developments in Eritrea, see the account of Dawit Wolde Giorgis, *Red Tears*, pp. 69-120. Dawit was assigned governor of Eritrea in 1979 and remained until 1983. He had served as a junior army officer in Eritrea during the years 1962-1968.
26. David A. Korn, *Ethiopia, the United States and the Soviet Union* (London: Croom Helm, 1986), pp. 16-18. The Soviets had by this time been dangling the prospect of a military relationship before the Derg for more than a year, but were unsure of the staying power of Derg leaders most favorable to them—Mengistu and his group. There were probably differences among Soviets on strategy in the Horn. Somalia, where they were solidly established, to some looked a better bet than Ethiopia. The EPLF held promise as a Marxist-Leninist Vanguard party. The Derg had been unable to establish a viable party and Mengistu had little enthusiasm for one. It was galling for Mengistu who was committed to a military solution in Eritrea to have to acquiesce in what amounted to an ultimatum from the US Recollection of this sequence of events must account in part for Mengistu's persistent anti-Americanism in subsequent years.
27. A more comprehensive discussion of the developments discussed in this section can be found in Erlich, *Struggle,* pp. 85-96.
28. The text of this program can be found in Basil Davidson, Lionel Cliffe and Bereket Kabte Selassie, eds., *Behind the War in Eritrea* (Nottingham, UK: Spokesman, 1980), pp. 143-150.
29. The Derg had proclaimed a program for "National Democratic Revolution" in April 1976 but its implementation was to be postponed until conditions were more propitious. A separate nine-point program for Eritrea was issued in May. It included "regional autonomy" for all Eritrean nationalities—seven national districts were envisioned. Critics denounced the plan as an effort to eliminate the Eritrean problem by eliminating Eritrea.
30. Meanwhile he had his deputy, Lt. Col. Atnafu Abate, executed in November 1977. The cause seems to have been acute disagreement over the developing Soviet alliance and, perhaps, policy toward Eritrea. See Erlich, *Struggle,* pp. 110-112.
31. There is no single, complete account of this fascinating period on which the revelations of recent high-level defectors are shedding additional light. For key aspects of these developments insofar as they are known, see Erlich, *Struggle,* pp. 110-120; Korn, *Ethiopia*, pp. 97-98; Paul B. Henze, *Russians and the*

*Horn: Opportunism and the Long View* (Marina del Rey, CA: European American Institute for Security Research, 1983), pp. 44–46.
32. See, e.g., Thomas Keneally, "In Eritrea," *New York Times Sunday Magazine,* 27 September 1987. Some of the most comprehensive and balanced eyewitness reporting on the insurgency in Eritrea (as well as on other topics relating to Ethiopia) has appeared in the *Neue Zuercher Zeitung* (Zurich), e.g., "Der Vergessene Krieg in Eritrea," 20 November 1986, and "Andauernder Krieg in Tigre und Eritrea," 24 April 1987.
33. US Arms Control and Disarmament Agency, *World Military Expenditures and Arms Transfers, 1986,* Washington, D.C., 1987.
34. The British Military Administration estimated Eritrea's population at 757,000 in 1943 (Longrigg, *Short History*, p. 173). The Ethiopian government estimated it at 2,131,000 in 1968 (Mesfin Wolde Mariam, *An Atlas of Ethiopia*, Addis Ababa, 1970). The PMGSE census of 1984 concluded that the population stood at 2,614,699. How so specific a count could be made of the population of an area over which Ethiopia was not exercising complete control is not clear. On the other hand, Eritrean separatists claim a far higher population, ranging from "over 3.5 million" upward Bereket Habte Selassie, *Conflict and Intervention in the Horn of Africa* (New York: Monthly Review Press, 1980), p. 38.
35. "Africa's Lebanon," the concluding section (pp. 34–35) of "Eritrea The Endless War" in *The Washington Quarterly,* Spring 1986.
36. See, e.g., Dawit Wolde Giorgis, *Red Tears*, pp. 163.
37. 1984 dollars as calculated by the US Arms Control and Disarmament Agency, *World Military Expenditures and Arms Transfers, 1987,* Washington, D.C., 1988.
38. A curious book filled with anti-Western rhetoric and devoid of criticism of the Soviet Union which nevertheless purports to be pro-Eritrean appears to be, in effect, an exposition of the solution the Soviets would prefer in Eritrea: Tesfatsion Medhanie, *Eritrea, Dynamics of a National Question,* Amsterdam, 1986.
39. Both sides in Eritrea have built redoubts which have proven invulnerable to being overrun by the other. The EPLF has built an elaborate WWI-style trench system in the north which protects the area where it has established its underground command post, hospitals, manufacturing facilities, and support services that regularly impress visiting journalists. This redoubt has been repeatedly attacked by air (probably with Soviet pilots assisting the Ethiopian Air Force) but without serious impact on EPLF ability to maintain operations. On the other hand, Ethiopian government forces have always proven able to maintain control of the central highlands—the area around Asmara— and have never lost the ability to maintain at least daytime use of the highways from Asmara to Massawa and from Asmara south to Tigre. These highways, like the Asmara airport, are subject to harassing attacks by the EPLF from time to time, but without lasting effect. The areas between these two redoubts—about 80% of Eritrea—are contested and subject to varying degrees of interpenetrating control by both sides. Economic life continues in these areas without tight control by either the EPLF or the government.
40. The United States needs to change no policies toward Eritrea nor toward Ethiopia as a whole. The US has always recognized Ethiopia as a significant

power in the region. Its policy toward Eritrea has always favored association with Ethiopia but with recognition of Eritrea's special status.

41. Without fundamental policy changes, Ethiopia is doomed to face new famines and worsening economic crises during the years ahead. It is thus bound to become an increasing source of embarrassment to Moscow. Gorbachev is known to have spoken very harshly to Mengistu during the latter's visit in July 1988. Mengistu was not invited to the 1988 celebrations of the Great October Socialist Revolution. For an exposition of Ethiopia's economic predicament see Paul B. Henze, *Ethiopia's Economic Prospects for the 1990s,* RAND N-2857-USDP, Santa Monica, December 1988.

# 2

# Angola

*Michael Radu*

**The Evolution of the Conflict**

From January to March 1961, a spontaneous, bloody, largely racially motivated rebellion broke out in northern Angola, then a Portuguese colony. It was rapidly crushed by Portuguese air and land attacks, but not before thousands of white civilians and many more thousands of blacks were killed. By 1962, renewed opposition to Portuguese rule had become apparent as the first two major Angolan black organizations, the União das Populaçoes de Angola, later in the year to become the Frente Nacional de Libertacao de Angola (FNLA), and the Movimento Popular de Libertaçao de Angola (MPLA), became active as politico-military organizations. The former was ethnically based among the northern Bakongo people and received its initial support from neighboring Zaire, where many influential Bakongo live; the latter sprang from the Angolan branch of the Stalinist Portuguese Communist party, drew most of its leadership from educated non-whites (those of mixed blood) and acculturated blacks, and received most of its support from the urban population of Luanda's slums and the Mbundus of that city's hinterland. In 1966, dissident elements of the FNLA, led by that organization's "foreign minister," Jonas Malheiro Savimbi, established the União Nacional para ao Independencia Total de Angola (UNITA), which claimed to represent an ideological alternative to both the pro-Soviet MPLA and the allegedly pro-Western FNLA. In addition, UNITA could truly claim to be the only pro-independence organization to include central and southern ethnic groups like the Ovimbundus, Chokwes, and Owambos, as well as the Cabindans from the far north.

In military terms, none of the three rival organizations made any significant headway against the Portuguese; by 1974 they had spent most of their forces against one another. In fact, by the beginning of 1974, the three Angolan insurgency forces had been reduced to little more than isolated, vulnerable, and ineffective roving bands being slowly but surely eliminated by the Portuguese "hearts and minds" campaign and the spectacular economic development of Angola. Writing at the end of 1973, Al Venter, one of the best analysts of guerrilla warfare in Africa, defined the military situation as follows: "There is in fact very little actual fighting in Angola, largely because the guerrillas are divided, not numerous (probably fewer than 10,000 effective combatants), badly equipped and poorly led."[1]

In April 1974, in a reaction against Lisbon's colonial wars in Guinea Bissau, Mozambique, and Angola (in that order), the Portuguese military staged a successful coup. Despite initial confusion, the new military regime was soon brought under the (actual) control of a combination of Communist fellow travelers, starry-eyed Third World proponents, and Socialist and Social-Democratic captains, majors, and lieutenants; each had a different idea about whether Portugal should identify itself with the West, the Third World, or the Soviet bloc. Since, unlike those in Mozambique or Guinea Bissau, the Angolan independence forces were neither united nor effective, their fate was largely determined by the vagaries of Portugal's chaotic ideological, political, and ultimately cultural struggle for identity.

The result was that the outcome of the intra-Angolan rivalries was in part decided by the most consistent, best-financed, and most aggressive of the Portuguese political forces—the Communists and their allies. The new Portuguese regime's high commissioner to Luanda, Admiral Rosa Coutinho, provided the MPLA with the help that made the conquest of Luanda possible and the ensuing civil war unavoidable. During his tenure, Portuguese armories were emptied for the MPLA, and the demoralized Portuguese army units in Angola did nothing to stop that organization from taking over Luanda and openly receiving arms shipments from the Soviet Union, Eastern Europe, and Cuba.[2] Even in 1975, however, as Jonas Savimbi has pointed out, the outcome could have been different: "[Everyone] was so weak that after 6 months it [the war] would have ended.... Our weakness was a guarantee of a general reconciliation. It was the Cubans' entry into the game which altered the entire context."[3] That Savimbi's assessment was correct was amply demonstrated at the time by the truly spectacular impact of exceedingly small groups of professional military men on the outcome of the clashes between the guerrilla groups. A few dozen (at their maximum strength) second- or third-rate mercenaries almost delivered Luanda into the hands of the FNLA;[4] a few inexperienced and poorly armed South African battalions, principally made up of draftees, were surprisingly effective on behalf of UNITA and FNLA; and a few elite units of the Cuban military decided the outcome of the battle for Luanda.

Thus, by the end of the summer of 1975, under the indifferent or impotent eyes of the homesick Portuguese, the MPLA was able to build up its strength upon the perception that its superior (and Soviet-bloc- or Portuguese-provided) weapons would decide the outcome of the struggle for power. The fact that none of the three Angolan groups could seriously or credibly claim any military success was unimportant at that point. Mercenaries and a few South African units fought on the side of FNLA and UNITA respectively,[5] against rapidly increasing numbers of Cuban regulars, who were logistically supported by the Soviet Union, her Warsaw Pact allies, and even a normally neutral country like Yugoslavia. Ever since the late summer of 1975, the continuing Angolan "civil war" has been supported and manipulated by external forces and has involved individuals or units from some twenty countries from four continents.[6] Only wishful thinking, hidden agendas, or abysmal ignorance can explain the view that the Angolan war is an "indigenous" conflict. Whether one likes it or not, since 1976 Angola has been a focus of the Soviet-American, totalitarian-democratic conflict.

What could be described as Angola's second civil war—following the anticolonial and internecine clashes between the three pro-independence groups of the 1962–1974 period—essentially lasted less than one year, from the summer of 1975 to the late spring of 1976. It began with clashes between MPLA and FNLA forces in Luanda and became open warfare after the former's forcible expulsion of both FNLA and UNITA from the capital by July 1975. FNLA retreated into its Bakongo northern redoubts close to the friendly Zaire border; UNITA, the weakest of the three groups, retreated into its central and southeastern strongholds. By November 11, 1975, Independence Day, there were as many as 10,000 Cuban troops in Angola, and FNLA's mercenary-led offensive against the capital was a disaster. The noise of the multiple rocket launchers turned FNLA's ill-trained soldiers into a frightened mob; Holden Roberto's allies, the Zairean "elite" units, performed no better and turned to rape and pillage as they retreated. FNLA was finished as a fighting force, and so, it appeared, was UNITA. Indeed, once the South African Defense Force (SADF) units pulled out by February 1976, Savimbi's men were rapidly routed by the MPLA's Cuban forces. The independent republic proclaimed by the FNLA and UNITA at Huambo on November 11 lasted only as long as it took the Cubans to fill the vacuum left by the departing South Africans and was never recognized by any foreign government.

By the beginning of 1976, it seemed that the Cubans, the Soviets, and their MPLA protégés had won. In fact, however, geography, international politics, and national realities ensured that a new round of civil strife was inevitable.

There was a major difference between UNITA's and FNLA's defeats in the center and northern regions respectively. FNLA's frontal mass attacks on well-protected MPLA-Cuban defenses north and east of Luanda resulted in the physical destruction of Holden Roberto's forces, and his movement never recovered. The magnitude of the defeat, combined with Holden Roberto's long-standing neglect of political mobilization and his absentee leadership, ensured that only a minimal FNLA infrastructure remained in the areas evacuated by the fleeing soldiers and cadres. Thus, while Bakongo resistance to the MPLA regime continued, it never regained its momentum. Writing in 1985, the usually well-informed *Johannesburg Star* described the remnants of the FNLA as follows: "[They] roam the bush dressed in rags. They go into battle armed with only two bullets each and no transport or logistical support."[7] One FNLA element, though, Daniel Chipenda's ex-MPLA, mostly Bakongo force, was cut off by a Cuban-MPLA advance southwards in the first months of 1976 and took refuge in Namibia. There they were soon retrained, re-equipped and, under South African and Portuguese officers, forged into what is now, as the thirty-second Battalion of the SADF, one of the most effective counterinsurgency units in the world.[8]

By contrast, and in another demonstration of Savimbi's military and political acumen and ruthlessness, UNITA did not try to meet the Cuban-MPLA behemoth head-on in its advance southwards in early 1976, and thus avoided the kind of catastrophic casualties suffered by the FNLA. It withdrew from the advancing Communist forces and melted into the bush, saving its cadres and strength, but it also made sure that most known or suspected MPLA cadres or sympathizers in the third of Angola's territory that was UNITA controlled or influenced were annihilated.[9] In the north the MPLA had at least a marginal success in establishing its own administrative and political infrastructure, but in the Huambo area and the southeast it had to start from scratch.[10] Meanwhile, UNITA retained and soon started rebuilding its own political infrastructure in the region. Similar attempts by the MPLA failed, and none was more important for the future of the war than the collapse of the ODP (Organização do Defenção Popular, or People's Defense Organization), with which the militias intended to provide a first line of defense against any possible resurgence of UNITA. In July 1979, ODP units in Bailundo, in the

Huambo province, rebelled, and subsequent clashes with FAPLA (Popular Armed Forces for the Liberation of Angola — MPLA's army) resulted in some one hundred deaths. By the end of that month all civilian governors of the provinces of Moxico, Bié, Huambo, Benguela, Kwanza Sul, Cunene, and Cuando-Cubango were replaced by military commanders.

The almost total collapse of provincial military command structures following the fall of the Nito Alves group in 1977, the change in South Africa's attitudes, and the successful escape of almost all top- and middle-level UNITA commanders after the 1976 debacle largely explain UNITA's sudden and massive resurgence in 1978–1979.

In military terms, South Africa's change of attitude became apparent in October 1977. Until then the SADF considered the MPLA-supported South West Africa People's Organization (SWAPO) little more than a nuisance; as late as 25 October 1977, SADF spokesman Major-General Wally Black described the Namibia conflict as a "corporal's war" of some one hundred engagements per year, all involving small units.[11] Two days later, however, a SWAPO group of at least eighty engaged SADF forces for three days in northern Namibia, with sixty-nine insurgents and six South Africans dying in combat. It was the largest military clash in Namibia since 1915, and it forced Pretoria into a reconsideration of its approach, which resulted in the decision to launch preventive strikes across the northern borders of Namibia, in Angola, and to a lesser extent in Zambia.[12] Operation Reindeer in May 1978 involved a number of ground and airborne attacks deep into Angola, including one airborne raid on Cassinga that netted almost 1,000 SWAPO guerrillas and trainees killed, captured, or wounded.[13] Operations Protea (August 1981) and Askari (1983) were even more massive and resulted in larger SWAPO casualties and, unlike Reindeer, also involved significant FAPLA losses and huge amounts of military hardware and supplies captured.[14]

Reliable data and actual results indicate that neither FAPLA nor SWAPO was in any condition to resist or even inflict significant losses on the South Africans, and the ratio of casualties was always overwhelmingly in SADF's favor, sometimes as high as 50 to 1. SWAPO was clearly unable to put up any significant resistance, while FAPLA's morale collapsed the moment it had to leave heavily defended positions. Such facts simply do not square with the view of those Western academics who consider FAPLA a respectable force.[15] With little experience in significant fighting of any kind and with its history as a minimally effective insurgent force against a weak enemy (Portugal), FAPLA cannot be expected to be effective simultaneously against both a conventional, superiorly trained foe (South Africa) and against a large irregular, experienced enemy (UNITA). Sympathizers who claim anything else are ignoring an obvious reality: in terms of training, morale, organization, technical competence (including the capability to maintain its equipment), and sheer numbers the FAPLA is decidedly vulnerable and probably doomed.

One of the many reasons for this predicament is the MPLA's ideology and thus its arbitrary reading of recent Angolan history. The MPLA believed its own propaganda regarding the "defeat" of the South Africans in 1975–1976 and persuaded other OAU members to accept that fallacious and dangerously unrealistic interpretation. It also retrained its forces based upon the perception that the main threat to the "Angolan revolution" is "racist South Africa," and that UNITA is just a "puppet" of Pretoria. The South African assaults on south-central Angola starting with Reindeer served to reinforce the MPLA's ideological bias in favor of building a strong conventional army. It is worth stressing this point because, as in the case of Mozambique at about the same time, and for similar reasons, the massive retraining and rearming of FAPLA for a conventional warfare against expected South African onslaughts occurred at precisely the same time a massive unconventional challenge was being prepared.

The events following the defeat of 1976 may have seemed to Chinese-trained Savimbi to be a repeat of Mao's famous "Long March" of 1933–1934. The remnants of UNITA's groups fled to Zambia, Namibia, and perhaps Zaire. That country's Mobutu Sese Seko, however, played only a minimal role in helping UNITA recover. In the wake of the two Angolan, East German, and Cuban-sponsored Katangese invasions of his Shaba province in 1977 and 1978, Zaire promised to crack down on anti-MPLA Angolan groups, and did a very thorough job of destroying the FNLA. UNITA, however, was not very much hurt. On the other hand, it is hard to believe that Mobutu's close ties to Morocco, which saved his rule in 1977 in Shaba, had nothing to do with UNITA's ability to obtain King Hassan's help.[16]

The result of Savimbi's political acumen and flexibility was that, between 1976 and 1978, UNITA troops underwent massive retraining in Morocco, China, and Namibia. This was largely subsidized by Saudi Arabia and other Gulf states, Beijing, and Pretoria. Equally important if not more so, was Savimbi's decision to remain inside Angola rather than try to lead his organization from the safety of a foreign capital, as had Agostinho Neto and Holden Roberto. That decision strengthened UNITA morale, solidified Savimbi's control over the movement, and helped convince many rural Africans that he had the "magic" to win against apparently impossible odds.

UNITA actions against the new Cuban-supported regime in Luanda had never ceased completely, but they increased significantly in 1978, when the first Morocco-trained cadres returned. One indication was the number of attacks along the Benguela Railway, which jumped from three a week in 1978 to one a day by the following year,[17] to a few a day by 1987. The persistence of UNITA's underground organization was demonstrated in January 1979, when UNITA commandos blew up 500 meters of track in the Huambo train station.[18] By then, the "Long March" of Savimbi's people was clearly over; South African attacks had created a huge swath of FAPLA-SWAPO-free territory in Cunene and, by eliminating SWAPO's capabilities in Zambia, enabled UNITA to take advantage of the gap created between the FAPLA-Soviet-Cuban positions in Lubango to the northwest, the SADF-controlled Cunene to the south, and the Zambian border. The *terra aõ fim do mundo* (the "land at the end of the world", the Portuguese term for the bush and dry savannahs of southeastern Angola) became a natural UNITA stronghold, Savimbi's Hunan. It was at that time that UNITA began building Jamba out of the sands, to be the "provisional" capital of a new, free Angola. It could afford to do so since by late summer 1978, following the first annual FAPLA-Cuban offensive, Savimbi had proved that he could parade 4,000 sympathizers on the outskirts of Menongue.[19] The Huambo attack demonstrated that the soldiers trained in Morocco were competent, and their performance encouraged South Africa to provide further commando and special-force training. UNITA's successes also convinced the South Africans to support Savimbi despite their doubts and suspicions. By 1979 UNITA was on the offensive, while the MPLA continued to believe its own propaganda and to consider Savimbi's men nothing more than "South African puppets" and "bandits."[20]

### The Nature of the Regime

Although it formally proclaimed itself a Marxist-Leninist "vanguard" party only in 1977, the MPLA has been a Marxist-Leninist organization since its inception. Indeed, some of its founders, including Agostinho Neto, Lucio Lara, Henrique Teles "Iko" Careira, and Carlos Rocha were members of or heavily influenced by the Portuguese Communist party (PCP), historically one of the most dogmatically Stalinist in the world. In fact, the PCP's *de facto* Angolan branch, the Communist party of Angola (PCA) disbanded in 1956, when the MPLA was founded, and some of its cadres went over to the new group.[21]

The leadership of the MPLA has been from the very beginning dominated by minority elements: asimilados, and mestiços. The first were educated blacks who enjoyed full Portuguese citizenship, and made up only a minuscule proportion of the urban population; the latter were in a still more privileged position, compared with the African masses, and often possessed considerable wealth. Among the original leaders of MPLA, Mario and Joaquim Pinto de Andrade and Agostinho Neto were asimilados; Lucio Lara, Careira, and Viriato da Cruz were mestiço. All came from urban backgrounds in a country whose nonwhite population by 1960 was overwhelmingly rural. Where very few blacks spoke Portuguese or had any education, Neto, Mario de Andrade, and Viriato da Cruz were well-educated poets who wrote in Portuguese.

The political leadership of the MPLA was, at least until 1979, highly unrepresentative of the Angolan population, and the make-up of the rank-and-file membership posed problems as well. Until 1977, the MPLA was a Mbundu-based organization. In fact, the only region of Angola where the MPLA managed to maintain a significant guerrilla presence against the Portuguese was in the Dembos Mountains in the Mbundu heartland. On 27 May 1977, however, an attempted coup d'etat against the MPLA leadership was staged by the former leaders of the Dembos guerrillas, all black racialists and all highly popular members of the Mbundus. Led by ex-Politburo member Nito Alves, the coup was crushed by Cuban forces, and its leaders, including Alves, José van Dunem, Jacobo Caetano ("Monstro Imortal"), and Eduardo Evaristo ("Bakaloff") were hunted down and killed.

From the point of view of the MPLA leadership, the putschists were "factionalists" and "ultra-leftist deviationists."[22] MPLA fellow travelers like Basil Davidson[23] and most of the Western media, however, claimed that the plotters were "regionalists," or Mbundu "tribalists."[24] Both were partially correct. Nito Alves was, until his purge in the fall of 1976, the most radical MPLA Politburo member, in control of the Luanda (mostly Mbundu) lumpenproletariat of the musseques (slums), the champion of "people's power" ("poder popular"), a parallel movement seen as threatening by the established MPLA ruling group.[25] In addition, Alves was widely perceived by MPLA rank-and-file supporters as the foremost guerrilla commander. Of the other leaders, José van Dunem was the former chief of staff, and "Bakaloff" the political commissar of the army. All were purged in October 1976, as were far-left Portuguese communists in MPLA ranks, including Cita Vales. Thus, in the period from October 1976–May 1977, the MPLA lost the support of its far leftist elements and the lumpenproletariat of Luanda, that of large sectors of the rural Mbundu followers of Alves and van Dunem, as well as that of significant sectors of the military, with large numbers of political commissars and officers being ruthlessly purged and eliminated after the May 1977 coup attempt.

The 1976–1977 purges were the largest and most extensive in MPLA's history, but far from the only ones. Indeed, as early as 1962–1963 the Viriato da Cruz and Mario de Andrade groups were purged by Agostinho Neto, and in 1973–1974 the guerrilla forces led by Daniel Chipenda joined the FNLA after Chipenda was himself purged. It is important to note that both in the case of Chipenda and that of Nito Alves the losing faction was also the one with a significant military record and following, while the winners were those who had never participated in actual fighting. The pattern of apparatchiks consistently defeating guerrilla leaders in factional struggles was made possible by the organization's continuous reliance upon foreign forces. The Congolese army and the Cuban advisers in Brazzaville during the 1960s allowed Lucio Lara and Neto to kill their opponents once they were caught in the Congo; Cuban troops made the role of Chipenda irrelevant in 1975 by winning the civil war for Agostinho Neto and put down Nito Alves' putsch in 1977.

The MPLA's violent history of factionalism demonstrates a continuous need for foreign support for the organization to survive, as well as a steady weakening of the group's popular base of support. The MPLA itself admits that its membership has declined dramatically over the past decade. In an interview given after the second MPLA Congress in 1985, non-voting Politburo member Antonio Jacinto do Amaral stated that, in 1975, as a "broad front" the group, had 200,000 members; that number shrank to 30,000 by 1977, when it officially became a "vanguard party," and of those some 10,000 were purged before the 1980 Extraordinary Congress. Attempts to increase the number failed until 1984–1985, just before the Second Congress, and by the end of 1986 "the party . . . [had] over 35,000 members, mainly workers."[26] This admission itself reveals the MPLA's lack of significant popular support. According to the World Bank, in 1980 (the latest year for which figures are available), only 10 percent of Angola's labor force was employed in industry, with an additional 17 percent in services.[27] In addition, by do Amaral's own admission, "Some provinces still have no industry at all and, consequently no working class,"[28] but "for some time after independence . . . the peasants . . . remained outside our field of vision. Our internal enemies . . . were quick to take advantage of this omission."[29]

More important in terms of a future "negotiated solution" to the present civil war, MPLA's history of Stalinist-type purges can only be interpreted as a bad omen for its coalition and reconciliation partners. Furthermore, MPLA's record in keeping agreements with other Angolan forces is far from encouraging.

These considerations clearly underscore the ideological, political, ethnic, and social isolation, as well as the diminishing support for the MPLA. Nevertheless, and despite its dependence on foreign troops for its survival, the MPLA has engaged in its own form of "internationalism" since 1977, not only by providing safe haven, training, and weapons to groups trying to overthrow the governments of Zaire, Rhodesia, Namibia, and South Africa, but also by maintaining a 600-strong expeditionary corps of its own in São Tomé e Principe, keeping in power the corrupt, inept, and dictatorial regime of Manuel Pinto da Costa.[30]

*The Anti-UNITA Coalition*

The Angolan regime's precarious survival is ensured by a miscellaneous combination of regular and semi-irregular forces of different national origins, levels of training, motivation, and discipline. FAPLA itself is said to number some 53,000 regulars, including 24,000 conscripts and 50,000 ODP members. In addition, the unarmed spy network of the "Popular Vigilance Brigades" is active in the cities and, to a lesser extent, the rural areas still under government control.[31] With some 540 tanks, mostly Soviet-made T-34s, T54/55s, T-62s and light PT76s, over 400 armored personnel carriers, and 148 combat aircraft,[32] it is, on paper and by African standards, a formidable force.

The Cuban Fifth Army, which until its 1987 sudden reinforcement of 15,000 included between 28,000 and 45,000 combat personnel, trainers, and advisers, is under the independent command of a high-ranking Cuban general and is generally deployed in cities such as Luanda, Huambo, Menongue, Lubango, and Benguela, and at strategic installations such as the Cabinda and Zaire oil fields, the Cambambe dam, and points along the Benguela railway. In addition, the Cubans (and Portuguese mercenaries) often fly "Angolan" aircraft, increasingly so since the 1986 introduction of stingers by UNITA.

There are also 500 to 1,500 East German military personnel, under the command of a general, principally involved in security, intelligence, and communications work, as well as at least 1,000 Soviets, who are concentrated in the main ports of Moçamedes, Namibe, Luanda, and Benguela, and operate Luanda's airfield, fly ASW missions over the South Atlantic, and control the major Lubango air defense installations. In addition, there is a scattering of Warsaw Pact personnel (Romanians, Poles, Czechs, and Hungarians), a significant number of North Koreans (variously estimated at between 1,000 and 4,000), and a few hundred mercenaries, most of them Portuguese leftists still recruited today by Rosa Coutinho.

The Soviet-bloc regulars are supplemented by the forces of three "national liberation movements": the ex-Katangese mercenaries of the FNLC (National Front for the Liberation of the Congo), the ANC ([South]

African National Congress), and SWAPO, numbering approximately 500, 1,000, and 9,000, respectively.[33]

There are a number of essential factors to be considered when examining the anti-UNITA or pro-MPLA military coalition: (1) even based on a conservative estimate, the total of foreign troops in Angola, whether from the Soviet bloc, under its control or dependent upon its support, is at least as large as that of the FAPLA forces; (2) the foreign troops supporting the MPLA are far better equipped, supplied, disciplined, and trained than FAPLA's and are concentrated in the country's vital points, including Luanda and Cabinda. Also, only foreign technicians can keep the Soviet-made equipment operational; and (3) on at least one occasion, the Nito Alves coup of May 1977, foreign troops, specifically the Cubans, decided the outcome of power struggles within the MPLA. There is absolutely no reason to believe that they will not do so again if the interests of Havana or Moscow are threatened. An unjustifiably optimistic approach, like that adopted by the US State Department in general and by former Assistant Secretary of State for African Affairs Chester Crocker in particular, assumes that the present MPLA leadership might make concessions beyond what is acceptable to Havana or Moscow; a realistic analysis, however, has to conclude that the Luanda government is no more a free agent vis-à-vis Cuba or the Soviet Union than the one in São Tomé is vis-à-vis Angola.

The political and diplomatic implications of these hard realities have not received the attention they deserve. For example, one of the "mysteries" that has puzzled observers at least since the 1978 resurgence of UNITA and the beginning of the massive, annual South African forays into Angola has been the consistent and largely successful efforts of Cuban forces and Soviet personnel to avoid head-on clashes with the SADF and direct and massive ground involvement in FAPLA's post-1977 annual drives against UNITA. With the exceptions of the SADF Protea operation, which resulted in the deaths of four Soviet advisers and the capture of another, and the sporadic killing or capture of Cuban airmen shot down by UNITA, very few Soviet-bloc personnel have been casualties of FAPLA's offensive operations.

This reluctance to engage with either UNITA or the SADF speaks volumes about the real aims and intentions of the Soviets and Cubans in Angola. The official Soviet and Cuban explanation for their military presence there has been that it was forced upon them by "imperialist" and particularly "racist South African aggression." The military field record, however, shows that it was precisely during the SADF operations in Angola that the Cubans were most reluctant to fight. The actual pattern of Cuban military deployment in the country's major economic and political centers, which are not threatened by the South Africans, clearly indicates that the real goal is maintaining control over Angola rather than checking any "racist aggression" from the south. In addition, the Cuban, and particularly Soviet reluctance to risk major losses, a certain result of any frontal confrontation with the South Africans or UNITA regulars, is revealing. The only explanation of such behavior, and of the Soviet and Cuban insistence on MPLA's paying its military bills, to the tune of some $7 to $8 million a year, even at the risk of losing territory to UNITA, is that for Havana and Moscow, Angola counts as a strategically important, but not vital outpost.

The Cubans have participated in combat in Angola since the mid-1960s, when small groups infiltrated Cabinda from Congo Brazzaville. Havana's presence suddenly increased after the Portuguese coup, but, with the exception of a few engagements with the SADF by the end of 1975 (which they lost for the most part), the Cubans avoided large-scale combat operations. The pattern of deployment mentioned above also guaranteed that Cuban combat casualties were smaller than they would have been otherwise. In addition, the Cubans occasionally, and increasingly as the war continued, sent some of their least professional or ideologically trusted troops and officers to Angola, including those that are being punished for various offenses. Colonel Pedro Tortolo, for example, the commander of the Cuban forces in Grenada during the 1983 US landing, was demoted and sent to Angola, where he was killed in action (Castro's "Eastern Front"?); Col. Tomas Benitez Martinez, former FAR (Revolutionary Armed Forces—Cuba's military) commander, was demoted in the 1970s for incompetence, but was later sent to Angola as commander of the Cuban forces. While there, he lost many helicopters, one large transport plane, and three MIGs in one day in 1984.[34] Occasionally, however, experienced and competent officers are temporarily posted to Angola, including such well-known names as Harry Villegas (one of the survivors of Che Guevara's Bolivian misadventure), Leopoldo Cintra Frias, and Arnaldo Ochoa Sanchez (a guerrilla in Venezuela during the 1960s); until recently the latter two were both seen as politically reliable and influential, and both were Soviet-trained. As a rule, however, the Cuban officer corps in Angola tends to be less than competent and is closely monitored politically. It includes a disproportionate number of blacks and is tightly controlled from Havana.[35] These factors and apparently decreasing morale explain the unimpressive performance of the Cubans in Angola. Cuban casualties, after a sudden peak of a few hundred killed by the South Africans in 1975–1976, declined steadily until 1978–1979 and have risen drastically every year since. The most recent and best-informed source estimates that 10,000 Cubans have been wounded or killed, are missing, or have died of diseases contracted in Angola.[36]

While it is true that the Soviets and East Germans have a far smaller military presence in Angola than the Cubans, that fact only partially explains the low level of their casualties. There are only a few, mostly unconfirmed reports of East German military personnel dying in Angola; the number of Soviets killed since 1975 seems to have been no larger than a few dozen. The major reason for these figures is that Soviet personnel do not participate in combat, and their protection is the foremost priority whenever they leave their fortified residences. Land convoys always place Soviets in the rear, in BTR-60 armored personnel carriers provided with escape hatches and powerful guns, unlike the "export model" BRDM-2 vehicles available to FAPLA, which lack even escape hatchways.[37] During a failed operation along the Comassa River near Cuito Cuanavale in 1986, wounded and ill Soviet personnel were evacuated in twelve hours; FAPLA wounded were evacuated only after twenty days.[38] Naturally, such episodes and the subordinate role of FAPLA officers to their Soviet and Cuban counterparts, the latter's far better pay and living conditions, and racial animosities account for the numerous documented instances of clashes, including some violent ones, between Angolans and their "internationalist" allies.

## UNITA's Organization

*Logistics*

As is always the case with militarily successful guerrilla organizations, UNITA's major strength lies in its logistical capabilities. Since about 1980 the movement has grown most of its own food in the "liberated areas" of the southeast; it has also been able to buy Zambian produce and grains in the border areas, supplemented by canned goods from various countries, including South Africa, the United States, Brazil, and France. This is ironical indeed at a time when Angola is importing most of its food and facing widespread shortages of staples in government-controlled territory.

The main suppliers of weapons are government forces (through capture), the international black market, South Africa, and the United States, with the latter providing only an insignificant amount in terms of value. Many insurgent groups, from El Salvador to Cambodia and from Peru to the Philippines claim, for propaganda purposes, to rely primarily on captured weapons, but UNITA actually does so. UNITA forces travel along the poor roads of the Angolan southeast in East German IFA and

Soviet GAZ, URAL, and ZIL trucks, are armed with Kalashnikov rifles, and are currently using Soviet-made mobile missile launchers, armored cars, and even tanks. Some were admittedly captured by the SADF and transferred to UNITA, but for the past two or three years, the South Africans have been more interested in selling Soviet weapons to countries like Somalia or Iran for hard currency than giving them to Savimbi's organization. Eye witnesses in Jamba testify that UNITA's impressive repair shops are geared exclusively toward Soviet-bloc vehicles and weapons.

Western weapons are bought or obtained through surreptitious arrangements, often directly from the United States.[39] Nevertheless, and with the major exception of the US-supplied stinger antiaircraft and TOW antitank missiles that have been supplied by the Central Intelligence Agency since the summer of 1986, UNITA has been, at least since 1983, self-sufficient in terms of weaponry. It pays for SADF-captured items of Soviet equipment, largely with revenues from precious wood, diamond, and ivory exports, as well as Middle Eastern funds, and it provides the bulk of its fighters' weapons from the enormous amounts of equipment it captures from FAPLA.[40]

UNITA is subsidized by sympathetic governments, particularly Saudi Arabia, Kuwait, the UAE, and probably Gabon, with funds channeled through Morocco, South Africa, Zaire, and Senegal. Private supporters in Portugal, West Germany, United States, France, and Brazil, among others, also provide aid, and there is semi-official financial aid from the US government. The organization's own "exports" of wood, ivory, and diamonds, as well as excess Soviet weapons also provide income. Finally, UNITA logistics have long depended upon the inability of Zaire and Zambia to control their borders, and South Africa's self-interested permission to use Namibian territory. By 1986 even the officially pro-MPLA People's Republic of Congo implicitly admitted that it could not (or would not) prevent UNITA's penetration of its territory.

*The Economics of War*

Although economic installations under MPLA control are described as legitimate military targets, UNITA refrains from destroying hydroelectric dams, ports, and oil installations, hoping to one day inherit them. Political considerations also play a major role in this decision, particularly in regard to the operations of the American oil companies, even though such companies as Chevron and Texaco make it possible for Luanda to pay for the war. The major exception to this strategy is the Benguela railway, which links the Zambian and Zairean copper belts with the Atlantic; it has been kept largely inoperable since 1975. To some extent the aim was to deny the MPLA revenues; in addition, it put pressure on the opportunistic Zambian president, served as a symbol of UNITA's strength, and served South African interests by maintaining and even increasing the dependence of Zambia and Zaire on South Africa's railway network.

## Leadership and Structure

Most of what is known about the ideology, strategy, and goals of UNITA originates with the statements or writings of Jonas Savimbi, rather than institutional sources, although it is often difficult to distinguish the two. In part this is the result of Savimbi's ability to articulate ideas and concepts better than his colleagues; in part it is the natural result of UNITA's being a highly personalistic organization, with Savimbi as the founding father, the ideologue, strategist, and commander in chief.

Unlike the mujahedeen, contras, and Eritreans/Tigreans, UNITA has a well-established leader of undisputed authority. While the Khmer Rouge has a strong and united collective leadership, with Pol Pot as primus inter pares, UNITA's is more clearly personalistic. Savimbi is the unchallenged leader and exercises strict control over all his forces. Such a style of leadership has important consequences for the nature, effectiveness, and survivability of UNITA. Because Savimbi insists on total strategic control over the military element of the organization, he is physically present whenever a major operation is under way. The presence of a top leader among the fighters is one of the important causes for UNITA's effectiveness and high morale. At the same time, Savimbi's willingness to risk residing in Angola most of the time has also had an important effect on UNITA's and his international credibility, although his persistent efforts to control every aspect of UNITA's diplomacy makes it less effective than it would otherwise be.

Perhaps the most serious potential liability deriving from Savimbi's leadership style is the ever-present danger to his life. Apparently, he was almost killed in 1979 by the Cubans, although the bodyguards that protect him are reputed to be the best in the world. This problem is compounded by the facts that Savimbi has no natural successor and UNITA does not have the institutional mechanisms needed for a painless transition to a post-Savimbi leadership. More importantly, none of his trusted lieutenants possesses his charisma, human relations skills, political genius, or strategic acumen. Nor do they enjoy the kind of deep ethnic loyalty Savimbi does. The UNITA leadership is not only or even primarily differentiated by ethnicity but by functional divisions. The most important of those are between the political and the military leaders, despite Savimbi's consistent and partially successful efforts to combine the two functions at all levels. Even among the political cadres some differences and resentments exist between the internal and external activists. So far Savimbi has succeeded, by force of his personality, political cunning, and appeals to the self-preservation instincts of all concerned to minimize or at least dampen the impact of such cleavages, but it is uncertain whether UNITA could retain its present cohesion without him. This is a fact well understood by MPLA's friends, whether Cubans, Soviets or Western fellow travellers, if not by the MPLA itself, and thus explains the latest public relations campaign accusing Savimbi of physically eliminating such would-be rivals and dissidents as Vakulukuta, Chingungi and others. Such "human rights abuses" are nothing but MPLA propaganda ploys, briefly repeated by the *New York Times* during 1989. Whether some of those allegations of Savimbi's ruthlessness are true (most are not) or not, is besides the point. Indeed, factionalism, often and naturally difficult to distinguish from political or personal corruption, is generally deadly to anticommunist guerrillas. Whether that problem is solved democratically or not is a matter of defining "democracy." In other words, was allowing Mathew Arnold's proclamations a proof of "democracy" or merely suicide for the revolutionary cause?

One should point out, however, that a politico-military organization of UNITA's durability, size, and effectiveness cannot but drastically transform mentalities, expectations, and inter-ethnic relations. An incipient "southern Angolan" nationalism may have developed during the past decade, the result of a violent and protracted war against Luanda. It was encouraged, reinforced, and to a certain extent rooted in the peculiar historic and cultural traditions of the Ovimbundus as well as in the fact that the Portuguese administrative control and cultural impact in the southeast were minimal, at least outside Huambo and the plateaus. The fact that UNITA has largely succeeded in depicting its war as one against alien intruders—the Cubans, the Soviets, and the East Europeans—has provided what would otherwise have been little more than an expression of Ovimbundu/Chokwe provincialism or "tribalism" with overtones of nationalism. This explains the slow but steady advances UNITA propaganda has made, as well as the very presence of a N'Zau Puna in its ranks.

Since Savimbi started his propaganda among the Ovimbundus in the late 1960s and his total war against Luanda twelve years ago, a majority of UNITA's rank-and-file fighters have never been exposed to or influenced by events outside their war-ravaged land. In addition, equally large numbers of fighters, including most local, regional, and even national leaders, grew to adulthood in the middle of the war and learned only the skills of the warrior. Because, unlike the FAPLA draftees, UNITA fighters are all volunteers, such considerations have a decisive impact upon morale. Regardless of the type, intensity, and length of formal military training undertaken in Angola or abroad, a basic difference between FAPLA and UNITA fighters remains: FAPLA soldiers must be taught how to make war; UNITA's soldiers only need to learn how to use the latest weapons in what they have been doing for most of their lives.

*Ethnicity and Popular Support*

Angola experts have consistently maintained that UNITA is a tribal, Ovimbundu-based organization, that the MPLA is Mbundu, and that FNLA is Kikongo; not surprisingly, the repetition of these ideas over more than a decade has almost obscured the far more complicated truth and has failed to take dramatic changes into account. To begin with, Angola's ethnic groups and tribes are not identical, nor are they always hostile to each other. Second, at least two developments during the past twenty-five years raise serious questions as to the continuing relevancy of the traditional, "tribal" approach to ethnic realities in the country.

The first of those developments is the rising importance of ideology, a factor far too often dismissed by Western apologists for both the MPLA and UNITA. In the case of the MPLA, the role of Marxism-Leninism has proved to be more important than simple ethnic or racial politics, although the two factors are to some extent related. Although a relatively small minority (about 20 percent of the total population) the Mbundus have been heavily urbanized, largely due to their proximity to Luanda and the relatively developed Luanda-Malange corridor. Not coincidentally, a disproportionately large proportion of the pre-independence asimilados were Mbundus who studied, plotted with, and befriended the even larger proportion of educated Africans made up of the mestiçoes. The result was that the MPLA, an urban, Luanda-based organization, has had an internationalist outlook and has been led by asimilados as well as mestiçoes since the beginning.

The Bakongo (or Kikongo) of northern Angola, far western Zaire, and western Congo, on the other hand, come as close as any other African ethnic group to fulfilling European definitions of nationhood. The memory of the old Kongo kingdom of the fifteenth and sixteenth centuries instilled a sense of identity and pride that has prevented the FNLA from ever really accepting the other anti-Portuguese organizations as legitimate. Finally, the situation in central and southern Angola has always been unusual, a fact that is essential for an understanding of UNITA's present actions, composition, and aims.

To begin with, the Ovimbundu did not come under Portuguese control or influence until more than three centuries after the first Portuguese settlements were established on the coast. The Ovimbundu were therefore more "African"-oriented than the more Portuguese-influenced Mbundus and Kongos and enjoyed a long-standing dominance over and understanding of their weaker eastern and southern neighbors, the Ganguela, Lunda, and Owambo of today's northern Namibia and western Zambia.

The ethnic geography of Angola today indicates that UNITA cannot be a purely "Ovimbundu" movement and hope to survive in its present "liberated areas." The Ovimbundus are concentrated largely on the high plateaus of Huambo and in parts of Bié—and decidedly not in the *terra aō fim do mundo*, Moxico, or the southeastern reaches of Cuando Cubango, all inhabited by Ganguela, Chokwe (Quioco), and Owambos. The Ovimbundus, of whom Savimbi is one, support UNITA, but the organization has also survived and flourished for years in clearly non-Ovimbundu areas. Finally, none of the ethnic groups mentioned above can properly be described as "tribes." The Owambos are divided into tribes, as are the Chokwes and the Ovimbundus themselves, but the differences among them are more comparable to the differences between North Carolinians and Texans or Provençales and Ile de France inhabitants than they are to those between Frenchmen and Germans. It is only by understanding these facts that one can understand UNITA's leadership and political and military structure. UNITA's second-ranking political leader, its secretary-general and Savimbi's right-hand, for example, is an aristocratic Cabindan, Miguel N'Zau Puna; the party's watchdog, Secretary of the Control Commission Ernesto Mulatto, is a Bembe from the north; the southern front commander, Vakulakuta Kashaka, is a Kwanyama (a tribe of the Owambos, to which SWAPO chieftain Sam Nujoma also belongs), and the northern front leader and secretary for military mobilization is a Mbundu, Colonel Antonio Dembo.

The base of operations on the northern front is in the Dembos Mountains northeast of Luanda, the pre-1974 MPLA's only real guerrilla stronghold. In fact, during the anti-Portuguese war, the Dembos Mountains MPLA guerrillas also produced Nito Alves and Ernesto Gomes da Silva, "Comandante Bakaloff," the most successful MPLA guerrilla leaders. Both were killed by the MPLA following their failed coup of May 1977,[41] but their deaths left a vacuum which is now beginning to be filled by UNITA. Similarly, the incompetence, irrelevance, and personal remoteness of Holden Roberto and other former FNLA leaders left the Kikongo guerrillas of Zaire and Uige leaderless—and thus increasingly prepared to accept UNITA leadership as long as it also provided weapons and a viable strategy, as UNITA has done since 1985.[42]

The new Angolan nationalism also worked in UNITA's favor. It was forged in the central and southern areas of the country in a reaction against the MPLA and Cuban/Soviet/East European intervention. In response, the MPLA, at its congress in Luanda in December 1985, did purge prominent mestiçoes from the party's politburo and central committee, most prominently Lucio Lara and "Iko" Careira; but most Angolans saw the entire exercise in racial rather than ideological terms and did not believe it would change the structure of power in Luanda. The most important Ovimbundu personality to join MPLA's ranks is still Daniel Chipenda, a former soccer star and MPLA commander in the east during the anti-Portuguese war, but he is in Portugal and publicly unhappy with the offers of the Luanda regime.[43]

Unlike the MPLA, UNITA has placed Cabindans, Chokwes, Kongos, and even Mbundus and Kwanyamas into clearly sensitive positions, military as well as political. This is not only an indication of Savimbi's political savvy, but also of his sensitivity to far deeper national realities. He is succeeding as an Angolan nationalist, and UNITA's nationalist aims have taken priority over its former friendships to the extent that the fight against MPLA has been extended to the Kwanyama-dominated SWAPO. The very presence and role of a Kwanyama as a leader in the UNITA army fighting SWAPO indicates that Kashaka is secure in his decision to trust Angolans rather than Ovimbundus alone, a claim that certainly cannot be made on behalf of the MPLA regime.[44]

### The Geography of the War

The UNITA strategy since the organization's post-1977 revival has been one of centripetal advance from the periphery to the centers of the country. Before 1974 the heavy concentration on the provinces of Moxico and Cuando Cubango on the Zambian border was decided by events beyond UNITA's control. Since Zaire was hostile to it and supportive of FNLA, the eastern and northern border provinces of Lunda, Malange, Uige, and Zaire were off-limits to UNITA. Similarly, oil-rich Cabinda was hostile territory, since the neighboring People's Republic of Congo was supporting MPLA, and the local secessionists of the Front for the Liberation of the Cabinda Enclave (FLEC) were no friendlier to UNITA than to its two major rivals. As for the southern provinces of Cuando Cubango, Cunene, and Moçamedes along the Namibian border, they were carefully watched by the South Africans, themselves interested in keeping them clear of guerrillas, whether anti-Portuguese or their own SWAPO foes.

What was left then were Moxico and parts of Cuando Cubango, on Zambia's border. Kenneth Kaunda was never a reliable ally of UNITA (or of anyone else for that matter), and Moxico had been penetrated by MPLA elements. Given these conditions, Savimbi's only alternative was a series of direct thrusts westward, toward the provinces of Bié and Huambo, where the bulk of his organization's ethnic support lies. That meant few, long, and vulnerable supply lines and greater risk of detection by the Portuguese.

The beginning of the second Angolan civil war witnessed dramatic changes in the political and military geography of the border areas. Cowed by the implicit Cuban-MPLA threats and duly impressed by the Communist victory in the first civil war, Kaunda became, formally at least, a supporter of Luanda and an enemy of Savimbi. Furthermore, distracted by his involvement in the Rhodesian civil war, the Zambian president was in no position to also antagonize his western neighbor. Similarly, after seeing his FNLA protégés destroyed in 1975 and his own territory invaded by Angolan-based and Cuban- or East German-trained Katangan rebels in 1977 and 1978, President Mobutu was in no position to support UNITA or allow it access through his territory.

Only in the southeast, in the *terra aō fim do mundo*, were the post-1976 prospects brighter for UNITA. There, in the remote, sandy savannahs of Cuando Cubango, UNITA was soon able to establish a permanent presence and receive direct and indirect protection from the Namibia-based South African forces. By October–November 1977, the southeastern Cuando Cubango was permanently lost to the Luanda government. From that safe base UNITA has slowly but steadily advanced northward along the borders, first in Moxico, then, by 1984 in Lunda, and the following year in Malange, Uige, and Zaire.

At the same time UNITA was establishing itself along the periphery of the country, it was also pushing toward the interior from the east and north, aided by South African pressure on Cunene, in the south. It is very likely that, at any given time during most of the past four years, there have been more SADF/SWATF and SWAPO elements in Cunene than FAPLA personnel. Thus, since 1987, UNITA has had practically free access to all the peripheral areas of Angola, with the exception of the largely uninhabited, waterless southwestern province of Namibe.

The position of FAPLA's defense lines also demonstrates the reality of its having practically lost the border areas: the defense line in the south, centered on the formidable air defenses of Lubango, runs from the ports of Namibe and Lobito along the railroad to Menongue, and it is never closer than 200 kilometers from the Namibian border. To the southeast of Menongue, in February 1988, the government was on the brink of losing control of the provincial capital of Cuando Cubango, Cuito Cuanavale, following a siege by UNITA after the collapse of the 1987 FAPLA offensive. It took massive Cuban reinforcements and, ultimately, the negotiated solution reached in New York at the end of that year to save the city.

Along the eastern borders, government forces remain in the major cities and the provincial capitals of Moxico and Lunda, but have lost most of the hinterland and all control over border crossings. Indeed, with the fall of Cazombo to UNITA at the end of 1983, the entire Zambian border and long stretches along the Zairean border have come under total guerrilla control, as is indicated by the aftermath of the December 1984 UNITA occupation of the diamond mining town of Cafunfo in northwestern Lunda. The foreigners captured there, including sixteen Britons, forty Portuguese, and fifty Filipinos, were taken along on a month-long march to Jamba, 1,100 kilometers away.[45] The fact that such a large group was unmolested by government forces clearly indicated UNITA's control over the entire length of the eastern border areas. In the northern border areas the situation is much the same: the capitals are in government hands, but the heavily forested hinterland and most of the actual border are not, despite Luanda's efforts to strengthen its control by having the Soviets build a major base at Soyo, near the oil fields of the Zaire province.

By the end of 1985, UNITA had access to the entire national territory of Angola, with the exception of the Namibe province.[46] On 19 April 1984 a UNITA sabotage team placed an explosives-laden truck in front of a Huambo hostel used by Cuban and Soviet advisers, killing some 200.[47] In July of that year UNITA attacked installations in Cabinda and blew up two ships in Luanda's harbor; in September 1985 train engines were also sabotaged in Lobito's harbor. Thus, since the end of 1985 the war has been extended to include virtually the entire territory of Angola.

The strategy of Savimbi has also become increasingly clear since the end of the first massive FAPLA offensive in the southeast in the fall of 1985. As previously mentioned, his was a "Maoist" strategy of protracted people's war, working toward the cities from the countryside and aiming at the core regions of the country: the food-producing central plateaus around Huambo, the coffee areas of Malange, Uige and Luanda, the coast, the diamond mines of Lunda, and the oil fields of Zaire and Cabinda. As Savimbi himself describes it, "from the countryside and the villages, we can surround the towns and thus limit the action of the foreign forces of occupation to protecting the towns, leaving in the hands of the national resistance all the countryside, all the villages and all the food."[48] UNITA has been increasingly successful in achieving these aims, although it never completely gave up its attempts to maintain a presence and operational capability in the urban areas. The UNITA presence in Luanda itself was implicitly acknowledged by the government when it executed the "bandits" caught in that city in 1978, and in Huambo, the second largest city, at the same time.[49]

Since then, UNITA has expanded its underground in Luanda and has become increasingly active in Huambo. In April 1984 the most spectacular UNITA urban attack to date took place in Huambo—a Middle East-style car bomb was exploded in front of the main Cuban-Soviet headquarters resulting in many casualties.[50] The next month UNITA claimed another attack on Huambo, targeting government installations and Cuban forces,[51] and in October 1986 its forces attacked the Cabinda Town airport, badly damaging the control tower and its equipment.[52] This attack has been dismissed as another example of a South African commando operation disguised as an UNITA attack, similar to another well-documented one in 1985, which resulted in the capture of a South African officer. By 1986, however, UNITA's commando capabilities were well-established, as was its ability to infiltrate Cabinda, its ties with the remnants of the FLEC, and the ethnic support it had won, symbolized by Miguel N'Zau Puna.

### Cuito Cuanavale and the Changing Nature of the War

On hindsight, it is clear that the 1987–1988 battles for the southeast represented a qualitative, dramatic new step in the evolution of the Angolan war. For the first time FAPLA elite units faced UNITA's regulars on a large scale and, again for the first time, the former were on the defensive. Although FAPLA's performance had been generally poor until then, many observers, including those in the South African military, had given them better grades when on the defensive in well-prepared and fortified positions.[53] The clear implication was that even in the best circumstances FAPLA cannot withstand UNITA frontal onslaughts—an ominous signal for the post-Cuban future of the MPLA.

On the other hand, and in all fairness, UNITA regulars' impressive performance at Cuito Cuanavale was also influenced, and in a major way, by the presence on its side of the best artillery weapons in the world: South Africa's G-5 and Valkiri long-range guns. By contrast, once FAPLA was defeated at Cuito Cuanavale, it took elite Cuban units, dispatched all the way from Havana, to create a diversion to the southwest strong enough to momentarily stop UNITA's siege of Cuito Cuanavale. The lesson of all this is that once the Cubans are out of Angola, as they should be by 1991, according to the 1988 New York agreements, FAPLA and UNITA's forces would repeat Cuito Cuanavale all over the country, with predictable results.

In November 1987 an estimated 18,000 elite FAPLA troops reached the most advanced point in the attack on Mavinga: the southern bank of the Lomba River. The importance of the attack was clear to both sides: the fall of Mavinga to government forces would deny UNITA the use of its airstrip and enable FAPLA's aircraft to attack Jamba at will; the failure of the attack would mean that the rains would force a rapid and long withdrawal from the exposed region of the Lomba, perhaps as far as Cuito Cuanavale, which might lead to the loss of that town. Given the stakes, it is not surprising that both sides invested all their resources in the battle. UNITA's force was estimated at some 8,000 heavily armed regulars, in conventional formations, supported by a small South African artillery unit and, in all likelihood, elements of the SADF's Thirty-second Battalion. FAPLA received more direct support than usual from the Cuban expeditionary corps, and the offensive was under the overall command of a Soviet general. It was the largest conventional battle in sub-Saharan history since the Anglo-Boer War, and the government lost it badly. In addition to its immediate military and strategic importance, including the subsequent siege of Cuito Cuanavale by UNITA, the Lomba victory marked an important advance for Savimbi. He not only fielded 8,000 regulars along the Lomba River, but also intensified medium-scale attacks throughout the eastern half of Angola and smaller-scale attacks in the northern regions. What was once a regionally based guerrilla organization has proved itself as the army of the counterstate established by Savimbi. It has an effective national strategy and presence and has proved that the best FAPLA units cannot withstand its regulars. That has been abundantly demonstrated by the outcome of the 1987–1988 conventional battles in the southeastern regions, the most important being those at the Lomba River and Cuito Cuanavale.

The UNITA siege of Cuito Cuanavale, which started in January 1988, was the logical result of its previously mentioned victory along the Lomba River. Cuito Cuanavale's airstrip and installations were the most advanced outposts available to FAPLA and the Cuban expeditionary corps for tactical air support in any future operation against UNITA's strongholds in the *terra aõ fim do mundo*, including Jamba and Mavinga. With Cuito Cuanavale lost, the closest such outpost would have become Menongue, some 300 kilometers from Mavinga, almost 500 kilometers from Jamba, and well north of the 15th parallel. Even by jet fighter that distance would have drastically limited the range and effectiveness of air attacks against UNITA positions and made attacking aircraft more vulnerable to South African air force counter-attacks from the bases at

Rundu and Grootfontein in Namibia. Furthermore, the loss of Cuito Cuanavale, combined with UNITA pressures on Cangombe, northeast of Menongue and along the Benguela Railway, would have threatened Menongue itself, and with it FAPLA's already shaky claim to the entire southeastern third of Angola.

Even though FAPLA retained Cuito Cuanavale, following the arrival of massive Cuban reinforcements and the negotiations leading to the New York agreements, any major FAPLA offensive in the southeast during 1988 became unrealistic. Thus, while the New York agreements saved Cuito Cuanavale for the Luanda regime, with no 1988 offensive to defend against, UNITA was also able to expand its operations in the rest of the country. By the end of the rains in 1989, any FAPLA offensive may well have to be directed toward easing the looming siege of Huambo rather than checking UNITA's expansion from its southeastern strongholds. Such considerations have previously affected FAPLA's morale, as was indicated by their use of chemical weapons against UNITA forces at Lucusse and Cassamba late in 1987, despite the obvious risk of detection by the well-equipped SADF advisers posted with UNITA's forces. That was also the best-documented, but least-publicized instance of the use of Soviet-made chemical agents against anticommunist insurgents to date.[54]

The strategic importance of Cuito Cuanavale to both sides explains the ferocity of the fighting around the town. Of the three major elements on the Luanda side, the MPLA, Cuba, and the Soviet Union, the first two seemed clearly convinced that the battle of Cuito Cuanavale was decisive. The Soviets, on the other hand, have taken a decidedly more sanguine attitude and have been the first to evacuate their personnel from the area, apparently followed by the Cubans. On the opposite side, while all indications are that Savimbi is well aware of Cuito Cuanavale's importance, he also wants to minimize his casualties and therefore to avoid a frontal attack on the demoralized FAPLA defenders. South Africa seems interested in helping UNITA occupy the town, although the specific aspects of that commitment are still unclear. South Africa may contribute highly sophisticated and effective artillery, particularly her G-5 howitzers, the best in the world with an effective range up to 39 kilometers.[55] As for the United States, the weakest link in the anti-Luanda coalition, it appears that the Mavinga-Lomba River victory has convinced the State Department that a "negotiated solution" should be easier than ever to achieve. Under-Secretary of State for African Affairs Chester Crocker's trip to Luanda in January 1988 seemed centered on working toward a withdrawal of Cuban forces and a "national reconciliation" between the MPLA and UNITA, as if the failed government offensives of 1985-1987 had never occurred. Worse still from the point of view of US diplomacy, Savimbi is not naive, and he is under strong pressure from the rank and file, as well as from his colleagues in the UNITA leadership, to treat Lomba River and Cuito Cuanavale as steps toward victory rather than bargaining chips. Pretoria is eager to demonstrate that it has no debts to pay to the Reagan administration, which in its view took too meekly submissive an approach to the emotional campaign for sanctions. Despite their peaceful rhetoric, then, both UNITA and South Africa are fully aware of the fact that they are military winners: the former at Lomba, the latter in its war against SWAPO.

On the other hand, however, Fidel Castro's 1988 offensive in the southwest and the bombing of Ruacana, during which South Africa suffered a modest number of white casualties, allowed Havana also to claim military victory. South Africa and Cuba were able thus to save face and protect their respective ideological flanks at home. But they were also reluctant to engage in a decisive confrontation among themselves, and so the road to negotiations was open. Nevertheless, in light of his previous triumphalistic threats to stay in Angola until the death of apartheid, it was Castro who made the most painful decision and had the hardest time justifying the compromises he accepted in New York on 22 December 1988.

A double military stalemate thus followed the siege of Cuito Cuanavale and the Cuban attacks in the south on the one hand and between UNITA and the MPLA coalition in most of the country on the other. This was paralleled by a steady shift in the diplomatic balance of forces between UNITA and the Luanda regime, a shift that had a major impact on MPLA's reluctant acceptance of the New York compromises.[56]

## The Politics of the Insurgency

When Jonas Savimbi started his second war against the MPLA and its Cuban expeditionary force supporters, he and Holden Roberto's FNLA had the support of almost half of the OAU member states. Since neither controlled Luanda, however, they lost the political battle in the OAU for recognition. In February 1976, by a thin margin won by the likes of Idi Amin of Uganda and the insistent lobbying of pro-Soviet regimes, the OAU recognized the MPLA as the legitimate government in Luanda.

It was a clear and apparently decisive victory for the MPLA and Havana; but the fickleness of African political elites and governments and their respect for power soon altered perceptions of civil war in Angola. While all OAU member states recognized the MPLA (Senegal, the last holdout, did so in 1980), a solid minority continued to maintain informal ties with UNITA, some even providing discreet financial and logistical support.[57] Zaire and Zambia, although they seem friendly to Luanda and its foreign protectors, have made a virtue of their own weakness and allowed UNITA to operate along and inside their borders.

FAPLA's failed annual offensives of 1984-1987, the US Congress's success in forcing the Reagan administration's hand by repealing the Clark Amendment and then providing aid to UNITA in 1985, and the persistent and intelligent diplomatic efforts of UNITA itself produced a significant shift in African attitudes toward the Angolan conflict by 1987. In that year, UNITA missions visited Congo, Cameroon, Gabon, Chad, Niger, and Benin and were received by foreign ministers or even heads of state; Egypt, Zaire, Ivory Coast, Senegal, and Cameroon continue to provide discreet help; and Kenya, Mali, the Central African Republic, Chad, and Niger moved decisively toward a "neutral" attitude.[58] By far the most shattering blow to Luanda's consistent attempts to isolate UNITA in Africa, however, came from Nigeria, which had been one of the MPLA's strongest supporters. At the end of 1987 Lagos publicly announced that it considered the conflict in Angola to be a civil war and offered to "mediate" between Luanda and Jamba.[59] The list of African countries now explicitly recognizing UNITA as a legitimate contender in a civil war includes almost one-third of the OAU membership (and more if states naturally wary of communism like Malawi, Botswana, Lesotho, Comoros, Swaziland, Liberia, and Guinea are included). Among those countries, Luanda is losing its diplomatic battle to isolate UNITA, to label it as a South African puppet, and to describe the war as one between black Africa and "racist" South Africa. Indeed, Egypt, the Ivory Coast, and Nigeria are states of major importance within the OAU, and their attitudes are bound to influence wavering and small states so far rhetorically committed to Luanda's position. Equally important, if not more so, is the position of countries like Congo and Benin, both self-proclaimed Marxist-Leninist regimes, both linked to the MPLA by treaties of friendship and cooperation, and both closely aligned with Soviet positions in international affairs. If the views of Luanda, Abidjan, Rabat, and Cairo can be dismissed as pro-Western (although not very credibly or realistically), and perhaps even as "neo-colonial," that is clearly impossible in the case of the revolutionary regimes in Porto Novo and Brazzaville. After losing the racial argument (Luanda vs. Pretoria) and the nationalist one (Angola vs. foreign-supported "gangs"), the MPLA is now losing the ideological one ("socialism" vs. reactionary, tribalist forces). Congo's attitude is the most significant, since that country served as a staging point for Cuban forces involved in Angola since the mid-1960s, has had a treaty of friendship and cooperation with Moscow since 1980, and is one of Angola's neighbors. The fact that Benin, Congo, and even largely pro-Soviet Mali now keep their distance from the MPLA indicates that the deterioration of Luanda's diplomatic and political posture can no longer be sustained by the views of individual leaders, traditional ideological attitudes, or the reflexive African hostility toward South Africa. Savimbi has clearly overcome the MPLA propaganda describing UNITA as a South African puppet. He insists that UNITA's dependence on Pretoria is the result of African indifference and opportunism and that once his options are wider he will be able to act as the Angolan nationalist he has always been.

Black African states and the OAU, important as they might be in other ways, are of secondary importance insofar as a solution to the Angolan civil war is concerned, in that their attitudes reflect, rather than influence developments on the battlegrounds of Angola. The real actors controlling military developments are, with the exceptions of FAPLA and UNITA, outside the scope and direct influence of "African opinion": South Africa, the Soviet Union, Cuba, and the United States.

For the Soviets, Angola was once a self-sufficient, self-financed asset in a strategic area of Africa. Oil revenues from US companies paid for Soviet weapons and for the cost of Cuban troops. Prior to the sharp decline in oil prices in 1982–1983, Luanda paid for most of its Soviet-imported weapons in cash; its payments for the Cuban troops today remain by far Havana's largest source of hard currency, between $500 and $800 million. The post-1984 annual offensives, however, cost the Soviets some $3 billion in military equipment shipped to Angola at the very time Luanda's ability to pay, whether in cash or in kind, declined drastically. Indeed, oil revenues dropped dramatically, despite increased production. The export of other commodities, including diamonds, sugar, iron, and coffee, also declined as a result of guerrilla activity. By 1984 MPLA was in debt to Moscow, and the debt increased exponentially as Soviet military hardware arrived and was largely lost, captured, or proved ineffective during the annual offensives against the UNITA "bandits."[60]

An assessment of these financial considerations and Moscow's unwillingness to risk a direct confrontation with the South Africans has led the Soviets to proclaim their support for a "negotiated solution" in Angola.[61] There were clear indications that the Soviet command in Luanda in 1987 did not see the possible fall of Cuito Cuanavale as the disaster Havana and Luanda did, and there are signs of a Soviet attempt to disengage from Angola along the lines defined by Gorbachev regarding Afghanistan. Edvard Shevarnadze and Africa expert Anatoly Adamishin, as well as Gorbachev, have made statements to the effect that a "negotiated solution" in Angola is desirable.[62] Soviet representatives have met with

UNITA's in Western Europe, and Soviet diplomats have met with Savimbi's Paris representative, Armindo Lucas "Gato."[63] As in Afghanistan and Cambodia, the Soviets under Gorbachev seem to be prepared to negotiate with their opponents, or their satellites' opponents, as long as those opponents are militarily strong, present a long-term, self-sustaining opposition, and enjoy consistent diplomatic support among Western and Third World governments. Looking reasonable in such circumstances is a low- or no-cost option that also allows foreign observers to blame the anti-Soviet forces and their supporters for the continuation of bloodshed.

From Havana's point of view, however, the Angolan war will help to determine the importance of Fidel Castro's role in contemporary history. That the MPLA is Cuba's main source of foreign currency and a convenient dumping ground for Castro's unemployed are also important factors, but they are secondary to Fidel Castro's personal ambitions, despite the unpopularity of the Angolan expedition among Cuba's party apparatus and ordinary citizens. More importantly still, both Fidel and Raul Castro see a possible defeat in Angola as a decisive setback in their perceived zero-sum game against the United States, and thus as a threat to their own rule in Cuba. Moscow, despite its different and more sanguine assessment of the situation in Angola, has little leverage over Fidel Castro's egomaniac Angolan policy, and is not prepared to replace the huge MPLA subsidies to Cuba with its own. Hence, neither Moscow nor Luanda can actually "deliver" Castro in any negotiations over a "political solution" to the Angolan war.

Similarly, Washington's (or at least the State Department's) hopes for a "political" and "negotiated" solution to the civil war are dependent upon the cooperation of Savimbi and Pretoria, both of whom have their own objectives in Angola and neither of whom is decisively dependent upon the United States for pursuing them.

### UNITA's Future and Peace in Southwestern Africa

UNITA was not a part, was not mentioned, and apparently was only superficially consulted by the United States during the process leading to the New York agreements between South Africa, Cuba, and the MPLA regime. Those agreements involved a total and rapid South African disengagement from Namibia, thus denying UNITA access to air and heavy artillery support and allowing for the possibility that its deadly enemy, SWAPO, would take power in Windhoek.[64]

Some of the other negative results of the New York agreements, as far as UNITA was concerned, were the provisions banning any South African military support for Savimbi and the very fact that he was not directly involved in the negotiations. Thus South Africa renounced any aid to Savimbi, and MPLA did the same regarding the ANC; the difference is that once Pretoria left Namibia it would have no physical means to aid UNITA, while MPLA could always return to its long standing support for the ANC, including hosting that organization's concentration camps on Angolan soil.

Worse still, strategically, logistically, and politically, UNITA will, at best, be dependent upon Washington and Zaire as its lifelines: those are perhaps the worst possible allies, in terms of long-run reliability. Indeed, the State Department has for years regarded support for UNITA as a mistake imposed upon them by a misguided Congress. Supply lines from the United States, through Ascension Island and the upgraded Kamina air base in Zaire's Shaba Province are long, often unreliable, and always costly, not to mention the additional problem of transferring supplies from Kamina to UNITA's core areas. Not surprisingly, soon after it became clear that South Africa would soon be out of the picture as a supplier of Savimbi as a result of the New York agreements, there were rumors that UNITA would shift its headquarters from Jamba to the far northwest, closer to Zaire but far from its zones of maximum strength.

Finally, even on the best of circumstances, that is supposing Congress succeeds in consistently forcing the State Department into support for UNITA, US military supplies, unreliable, logistically unwieldy, and limited as they are, are basically defensive in nature. They include stingers and TOWs, both defensive weapons more likely to prolong rather than end the civil war in Angola. A number of observers have even gone so far as to conclude that the New York agreements signal the coming to an end of the Savimbi saga. Indeed, as one noted, the agreements allowed the consolidation of the MPLA regime, particularly in light of the probable SWAPO electoral victory in Namibia, and the "neutralization" of Savimbi.[65] That is a clearly alarmistic view, although partly true. In fact, the tripartite MPLA-Cuban-South African agreements also provided some opportunities to UNITA, despite their being largely damaging to it.

Indeed, on the positive side, the New York and related agreements, those between Havana and the MPLA in particular, provide for the actual withdrawal of Cuban troops from combat on behalf of FAPLA.[66] Thus, by 1 August 1989, Cuban troops are to be redeployed north of the 15th parallel, and by October 31 the same year they are to be stationed north of the 13th parallel.[67] Furthermore, as SWAPO discovered to its chagrin after its April 1989 attempt to invade Namibia, open disregard of those agreements is likely to bring disapproval even from old friends.

As far as the MPLA is concerned, the issue of UNITA remains one of dealing with "bandits" and "foreign puppets": in other words, MPLA wants law and order, and as such will treat UNITA like ordinary criminals. At best, individual UNITA members are to be granted amnesty, as provided by the Luanda law that began to apply on February 1989. In no circumstances is UNITA to be treated as a legitimate political contender and negotiating partner, and Savimbi in particular is never to be accepted as a political figure deserving to be treated seriously. In fact Luanda and its allies abroad, including ultra-liberal US congressional figures, have engaged in an intensive campaign to discredit both Savimbi and UNITA.[68] Furthermore, discreet but promptly leaked attempts to remove Savimbi by having him leave for a "golden exile" in Morocco or the Ivory Coast indicate Luanda's desperate attempts to deprive UNITA of its main asset at almost any cost.

As for UNITA in general, and Savimbi in particular, they try to make the best of the bad deal represented by the New York agreements. While categorically rejecting Luanda's offers of amnesty, Jamba consistently reiterates its willingness to negotiate with the regime. Some arrangements with the Cubans, including the release of Cuban prisoners and a de facto cease fire between UNITA and Havana's forces were announced by Savimbi at the same time as the intensification of military operations along the Angola-Namibia border.[69]

It remains to be seen whether UNITA will once again adapt to the changing military and political circumstances that have resulted from the New York agreements. Its history suggests that it will succeed in doing so and that it will continue to fight. If the Cuban troops do indeed leave Angola by 1991, the chances are that fighting between UNITA and the regime will escalate and generalize, with the former in a good position to reach yet another stalemate, more favorable than the situation prior to the major battles of 1987. What does not seem likely to happen soon is a truly negotiated end to the civil war.

## Notes

1. Al J. Venter, *The Zambesi Salient. Conflict in Southern Africa* (Old Greenwich, Ct.: Devin-Adair, 1974), p. 155. Venter's book, together with *Angola*, by Douglas Wheeler and René Pelissier (London: Pall Mall, 1971), are the only ones in the abundant pre-1975 literature on Angola to escape the dominant bias in favor of the guerrillas, particularly the MPLA.
2. Rosa Coutinho's ties with the MPLA continue to this day. His contributions to the survival of the Luanda regime were for many years demonstrated by his recruiting of Portuguese mercenaries to fight against UNITA or to protect vital installations in Luanda and Lunda province.
3. Interview in *Le Figaro*, 17 February 1984, p. 2.

4. Anthony Mockler, *The New Mercenaries* (London: Sidgwick & Jackson, 1985), pp. 149–234, provides an accurate, objective, and professional analysis of the role of European mercenaries in Angola and is one of the very few such analyses available.
5. A good first-hand description of the misgivings the South Africans and their soon-to-be-elite Thirty-second Battalion of ex-Chipenda, MPLA Angolans had regarding UNITA is provided by that unit's first commander, Jan Breytenbach, in *Forged in Battle* (Capetown: Saayman & Weber, 1986), pp. 10–34. Breytenbach was also the commanding officer of the Cassinga operation of 1978.
6. Since 1975 the following countries have been mentioned as sending troops, advisers, or weapons to various Angolan fighting groups: On the MPLA side: the Soviet Union, Cuba, Ethiopia, Congo, Mozambique, Zambia, Nigeria, Guinea, Vietnam, North Korea, East Germany, Hungary, Tanzania, Brazil, and France. On the FNLA, and particularly the UNITA side: Morocco, Senegal, Gabon, Zaire, South Africa, China, and United States. In addition, FAPLA is supported in the field by SWAPO, the ANC, ex-Katangans, and Portuguese mercenaries; UNITA has consistently used small numbers of West European mercenaries, mostly Portuguese, as pilots.
7. *Johannesburg Star*, 6 January 1985. The author of the report, David Mills, also expressed his surprise at the determination and high morale of the ragtag Bakongo fighters under the leadership of a white Angolan, Alberto Villela. When UNITA started penetrating the north in 1986–1987, it attracted these committed, ragtag groups. They provide it with local intelligence, acceptance, and knowledge of the terrain—all invaluable contributions.
8. For some interesting (but South African government-approved) insights into the formation of that unit, see Breytenbach, *Forged in Battle*.
9. Even sympathetic observers like Fred Bridgland mention massacres of MPLA cadres in Huambo and Bié. See Fred Bridgland, *Jonas Savimbi. A Key to Africa* (New York: Paragon House, 1987), pp. 190–191.
10. It is interesting to note that the most important former MPLA opponents and dissidents who defected or betrayed their political past and their supporters were former FNLA cadres, including such former top FNLA leaders as Johnny Eduardo Pinock, Eduardo Val Neto, and Daniel Chipenda. In contrast, disaffected UNITA cadres, few as they were, choose the West rather than Luanda for their exile.
11. Willem Steenkamp, *Borderstrike* (Alberton: Galago Publishers, 1983), p. 6.
12. Ibid., p. 3.
13. Ibid., p. 103.
14. Protea alone resulted in some $250 million worth of Soviet equipment, most of it still in crates, being captured by the South Africans. Most of it was transferred to UNITA.
15. See, for instance, Christopher Coker, *South Africa's Security Dilemmas* (New York: Praeger, 1987), pp. 30–32. Despite its flaws, Coker's assessment is more balanced than that of most US academic Africanists.
16. Senegal, UNITA's long-standing and most consistent supporter in black Africa, is also close to Rabat, politically and ideologically, and South Africa has always had good, albeit discreet ties to Morocco.
17. *Africa Confidential*, 14 February 1979, p. 1.
18. Ibid.

19. Ibid.
20. It does seem, however, that Cuban, if not MPLA perceptions of UNITA are changing; the most recent Cuban Communist party messages to MPLA describe UNITA as a "counterrevolutionary movement," quite a spectacular upgrading of the groups's importance. *InformAfrica*, January 1988, p. 5.
21. John Marcum, *The Angolan Revolution*, vol. 2 of *Exile Politics and Guerrilla Warfare* (1962–1976) (Cambridge, Mass. and London: M.I.T. Press, 1978), p. 15; Keith Sommerville, *Angola. Politics, Economics, and Society* (London and Boulder, Colo.: Frances Pinter, 1986), p. 24.
22. See Claude Gabriel, *Angola: le tournant africain?* (Paris: La Brche, 1978), pp. 325–329.
23. West Africa, 18 July 1977.
24. *Le Monde*, 29 May 1977; *Jeune Afrique*, 10 June 1977; and *Afrique-Asie*, 25 July 1977.
25. Gabriel, *Angola*, pp. 320–324.
26. Antonio Jacinto do Amaral, "Recruiting the Finest People," *World Marxist Review*, November 1986, p. 11.
27. World Bank, *World Development Report 1986*, (Washington, D.C.), 1986, p. 239.
28. Ibid.
29. Ibid.
30. *The Military Balance 1987–1988* (London: IISS, 1987) estimates the FAPLA strength on the islands at 500; the better-informed *InformAfrica* (December 1987, p. 12) estimates it at 600. In either case, the number is enormous for a country with a 1985 population of less than 90,000.
31. *The Military Balance*, pp. 119–120.
32. Ibid., p. 120.
33. The figures for the ANC are from *The Military Balance*, p. 120; those for SWAPO are from SADF sources consulted by the author.
34. *General del Pino Speaks*, (Washington, D.C.: Cuban-American Foundation 1987), p. 13.
35. This is in part a public relations decision, but blacks have often volunteered for service in Angola to advance their otherwise slow and uncertain careers in the white-dominated FAR.
36. Michael Radu and Arthur J. Klinghoffer, *Southern Discomfort. Soviet military activities in Sub-Saharan Africa* (New York: Holmes and Meier, 1989); *General del Pino Speaks*.
37. *InformAfrica*, September 1987, p. 16.
38. Ibid.
39. In March 1987 the Cape Verde government banned Saint Lucia Airways from landing at the Sal Airport because it had been transporting arms to UNITA illegally.
40. For example, during the failed 1987 FAPLA offensive against Mavinga, 217 vehicles and 26 armored cars were captured, destroyed, or put out out of action by UNITA (*Janes' Defence Weekly*, 24 October 1987, p. 950), most of which now serve as spare parts for UNITA armorers and mechanics. Knowledgeable estimates put the total value of FAPLA equipment losses after the battles for Mavinga at $300 million. (*InformAfrica*, December 1987, p. 16.)
41. See the consistently pro-MPLA description of these events in Sommerville, *Angola*, pp. 163–164. The similarly biased Wolfers and Bergerol do however

provide a quantitative assessment of the impact of the Alves coup on the MPLA: "The Central Committee was now reduced by around one-third of its pre-coup membership: three members have been murdered by the factionalists, five have been named in the conspiracy, and two suspended." Michael Wolfers and Jane Bergerol, *Angola in the Front Line* (London: Zed Press, 1983), p. 98.
42. Bridgland, *Jonas Savimbi*, pp. 470–471.
43. *InformAfrica*, 31 October 1987, p. 6.
44. Even Sommerville, indiscriminately sympathetic to MPLA as he is, admits that the Ovimbundu have been underrepresented in the MPLA leadership, with Transportation Minister Faustinho Muteka the only "prominent" Ovimbundu in the cabinet. Sommerville, *Angola*, p. 102.
45. See Bridgland, *Jonas Savimbi*, p. 428. For a dramatic, first-hand description of the events as seen by an unwilling participant, see Glen Dixon, *Hostage*, (Alberton, South Africa: Galago Publishers, 1986).
46. It should be pointed out that the harbor of Namibe was attacked in 1986 by South African Navy units and special forces, although UNITA was not involved.
47. Bridgland, *Jonas Savimbi*, p. 433.
48. Foreign Broadcast Information Service (FBIS), *Africa*, 30 August 1983, p. U1.
49. Sixteen "bandits" and South African "puppets" were publicly shot in Huambo in December 1978. *Africa Contemporary Record*, 1977–1978 (London, 1978), p. B487.
50. The casualty figures vary, depending on the source. According to Luanda and Havana, twenty-four civilians were killed, including fourteen Angolans. According to UNITA, no civilian casualties occurred, and the victims included three Soviet lieutenant-colonels, thirty-seven Cuban officers, and many FAPLA officers. *Le Point*, 30 April 1984, p. 26.
51. FBIS, *Africa*, 8 June 1984, p. U1.
52. *InformAfrica*, 28 February 1987, p. 3.
53. Briefing of the author by SADF officers in northern Namibia, September 1986.
54. *International Defense Review*, January 1988, p. 11.
55. *The Washington Times*, 16 June 1987; *International Defense Review*, May 1987.
56. The text of the relevant documents leading to and including the New York agreements of December 1988 can be found in *Strategic Review for Southern Africa*, vol. XI, no. 1, 1989, Pretoria, pp. 81–94.
57. Most of these states are Francophone, a fact that seems to imply that France, which retains significant influence over its former colonies, never acted seriously upon its alleged hostility to UNITA and friendship for the MPLA. Senegal (particularly under Leopold Sedar Senghor), Gabon, Cameroon, Ivory Coast, Togo, and Niger are among the discreet friends of Savimbi; Morocco is far less discreet. Among English-speaking states, Kenya, Liberia, and Malawi also belong to the first category.
58. *InformAfrica*, June 1987, p. 8.
59. Ibid., January 1988, p. 6.
60. Ibid.
61. Ibid.

62. Ibid.
63. Ibid.
64. Text in *Strategic Review for Southern Africa*, vol. XI, no. 1, 1989, pp. 88–90.
65. Jaime Suchlicki, in *The Cuban Revolution at 30*, The Cuban American National Foundation, Washington, D.C., 1989, p. 77.
66. See the Appendix to the New York agreements, signed between Angola and Cuba, in Ibid., 93–94.
67. Ibid.
68. The spearheads of the anti-Savimbi campaign in Washington are prominent Democratic congressmen Howard Wolpe, Stephen Solarz, and William Gray. *Washington Post*, 25 April 1989. In the US Senate, on the other hand, pro-Savimbi feelings are very strong, with two Democratic members, Denis DeConcini and Robert Graham among UNITA's best friends.
69. *FBIS*, 15 February 1989, p. 8. Savimbi also admitted that, just prior to December 22, South Africa has provided his organization with one year supplies of gasoline and two years supplies of weapons and ammunition.

# 3

# Mozambique

*Jack Wheeler*

### FRELIMO'S Background and Nature

When the famous Portuguese explorer Vasco da Gama sailed around the Cape of Good Hope and into the Indian Ocean, he made a landfall in March 1498. He and his crew were so well treated by the local Arab ruler, Sultan Musa-bin-Iqi (Moses, son of the weaver), that Portuguese who began settling along the coast in the sixteenth century referred to the entire territory by the Sultan's name, transliterated as Moçambique (or Mozambique by the British and French). A Y-shaped country of more than 300,000 square miles (about twice the size of California)[1] with a present-day population of some 14 million, Portuguese East Africa received independence from Portugal in 1975, with governmental power turned over to the FRELIMO Marxist guerrilla movement (unelected to this day) led by Samora Machel, who declared the country's name as The People's Republic of Mozambique and placed a depiction of a Soviet AK-47 Kalashnikov on the national flag.

FRELIMO, *Frente de Libertacao de Moçambique*, Mozambique Liberation Front, was formed in June 1962 in Dar Es Salaam, Tanzania, by a uniting of three Mozambican nationalist movements: UDENAMO, *União Democratica Nacional de Moçambique*, led by Adelino Gwambe and Fanuel Mahluza, of Mozambicans working in Southern Rhodesia[2] and Nyasaland;[3] MANU, Mozambique African Nationalist Union, led by Matthew Mmole, made up of expatriates in Tanganyika;[4] and UNAMI, *Uniao Africana de Mocambique Independente*, led by Urias Simango, headquartered in Blantyre, Nyasaland.

Dr. Eduardo Chivambo Mondlane was elected president of FRELIMO.

Born in Gaza province in 1920, Mondlane attended Northwestern University in Illinois, earning his B.A. in 1953 and his Ph.D. in 1960 in sociology. As the first black Mozambican to achieve a doctorate, Mondlane enjoyed considerable prestige among his countrymen. He had married a white American, Janet Johnson, joined the faculty of Syracuse University as an instructor of sociology, and worked as a research officer at the United Nations Department of Trusteeship at the time he assumed the FRELIMO leadership.[5]

Mondlane was a political moderate whose writings were center-left and free of Marxist cant.[6] While many in FRELIMO held similar views, the movement also contained strident Marxists, such as the virulently pro-Soviet Marcelino dos Santos, and a young Maoist, Samora Moises Machel.

Machel, whose father Moises Malangatane Machel was known to be "loyal to Portuguese rule,"[7] and reputed to work for PIDE, the Portuguese colonial secret police,[8] had worked in the Rand gold mines in South Africa, where he was allegedly known by his fellow Mozambican mineworkers as a *tsotsi*, a pickpocket or petty thief.[9] After joining FRELIMO in 1964 (Machel was not among FRELIMO's founders) he was sent to Algeria for guerrilla training where he became acquainted and enamored with the "little red book" of Mao Tse-Tung.

As a protégé of Marcelino dos Santos, Machel developed bitter ideological quarrels with FRELIMO members opposed to Marxism, including FRELIMO's military commander, Filipe Magaia. On 10 October 1966, Magaia was assassinated by a member of Machel's sympathizers, Lourenco Matola,[10] whereupon Machel was elevated to Magaia's position. Over the next two years, other non-Marxist leaders of FRELIMO, such as Paulo Kankhombe and Jaime Siguake, were liquidated, evidently at the direction of Machel and dos Santos.[11] By the time of FRELIMO's second congress in July 1968, the movement had swung sharply left, hailed the aid it received from Cuba and other "socialist" countries, and had joined the World Peace Council and a number of other communist front organizations.[12]

The last remaining obstacle to a full Marxist takeover was Mondlane himself. On 3 February 1969, a bomb exploded at the FRELIMO headquarters in Dar Es Salaam, killing Mondlane. An investigation reported that Mondlane received a package postmarked from Moscow with a book, in Russian (Cyrillic) script and printed in the Soviet Union, containing a bomb. When Mondlane opened it, the bomb detonated.[13]

An eyewitness has recently, however, contradicted this version. Agostinho Murrial, one of FRELIMO's original members, and at the headquarters at the time of the assassination, testifies that:

On the day in question, Dr. Mondlane went to the post office and brought back the mail himself. There were several parcels, and he placed it all on his desk. He then walked around his desk and sat in his chair. Almost immediately upon sitting down, there was an explosion which blew off the lower half of Dr. Mondlane's body; from above the desk level—the chest, hands, face—the body was intact. Dr. Mondlane was killed, not by a parcel bomb, but by an explosive planted in his chair when he went to the post office. It was obviously done by somebody in FRELIMO. My conviction is that it was done by "The Algerian Gang," the Marxists in FRELIMO, such as Marcelino dos Santos, Samora Machel, and Joaquim Chissano, who, of course, ended up taking over the movement after Mondlane's death and drove the remaining moderates out. I must also voice my strong suspicion that Dr. Mondlane's wife, Janet, played a direct role in the assassination. She had become a member of dos Santos' clique (which we called "the Algerians") and quite committed to Marxism. She showed no sorrow or grief whatever at Dr. Mondlane's funeral, which I attended, and remains to this day a high official of the FRELIMO government, residing in Maputo."[14]

Marcelino dos Santos, the Soviets' primary agent in FRELIMO, could not become heir to Mondlane, as he was *mestizo* with *café au lait* skin. Samora Machel, whom Portuguese intelligence described as "uneducated and barely literate"[15] became—contrary to FRELIMO's own statutes requiring election by a party congress—president of FRELIMO.

FRELIMO had begun guerrilla activities in the Cabo Delgado province from camps across the Rovuma River, which forms the border between Tanzania and Mozambique, in September of 1964. By the early 1970s, the guerrillas had penetrated past the Zambezi, from Tete province and down into Sofala near Beira, but never beyond.[16]

In April 1974 a radical left-wing group of Portuguese officers called the Armed Forces Movement (FAM) overthrew the government of Marcelo Caetano (successor to Antonio Salazar who had ruled from 1932 until two years before his death in 1970) in Lisbon, quickly announcing it intended to hand governmental power in Mozambique to FRELIMO. On 25 June 1975, independence was formally granted to Mozambique by Portugal. Without an election or referendum of any kind, Samora Machel was installed as the president of The People's Republic of Mozambique.

Machel's first state visit outside of Africa, in May 1976, was to the Soviet Union. In Moscow, he stated his intention was to transform Mozambique into "the first fully Marxist state in Africa." A military agreement was signed between the two countries.[17] At FRELIMO's third party congress in February 1977, Machel declared FRELIMO to be a "revolutionary vanguard" party of orthodox Marxism-Leninism: "There can be no 'African socialism' nor 'Mozambican socialism'; there can be no socialism other than scientific socialism." Machel concluded by announcing that: "Our struggle is to destroy all vestiges of feudalism and colonialism, but fundamentally to crush capitalism, which is the most advanced form of exploitation of man by man."[18] The following month, Nikolai Podgorny, president of the Soviet Presidium, arrived in Maputo[19] to commemorate the signing of a twenty-year Treaty of Friendship and Cooperation between Mozambique and the USSR.[20]

Machel's ideology was put into practice with a vengeance. FRELIMO was declared to be the sole legal party, with the politburo of the party administering the state and government apparatus.[21] Thirty days after independence, 25 July 1975, Machel proclaimed at a rally the immediate nationalization, with no compensation whatsoever, of all private educational institutions, hospitals, clinics, funeral parlors, and legal practices, ordering armed soldiers to proceed at once to these establishments to bar the (now previous) owners from entering and removing anything.[22] All private medical practice was declared illegal and doctors were forbidden to make house calls. Of the 336 registered physicians in Mozambique at independence, 20 remained in the country a year later.[23] February 1976 saw the formal nationalization of all privately owned buildings and property, all rental income from which would henceforth go to the government.[24]

By 1976, 90 percent or well over 200,000 of Portuguese Mozambicans, many of whose families had lived in Mozambique for generations and even centuries, had fled the country.[25] The family of Lucinda Pires, from Tete province, is perhaps typical. In an interview with the author, she related,

> We were hopeful for the future of an independent Mozambique. But our illusions were shattered during the months of transition government prior to independence, when FRELIMO got its first taste of government power.
>
> Machel's first project was the systematic elimination of the black and white middle class of Mozambique. So many knocks on the door late at night came at the residences of businessmen or property owners, with the man being told he was an enemy of the people, shot dead on the spot, and his family told his (and their) property now belonged to the government, that it is no mystery why we all left. Every country that has experienced a communist takeover has had a mass exodus, and Mozambique was no exception.
>
> Today, Mozambique is listed as one of the world's poorest nations, a plight which the FRELIMO regime continues to blame on the Portuguese exodus. This excuse reminds me of the apocryphal child who murders his parents, then demands leniency from the court on the grounds that he is an orphan.[26]

But at least the Portuguese settlers could leave. For the black Mozambicans who had to remain behind, their fate was bleak. Shortly after independence, at the end of October 1975, Machel instituted a "campaign against prostitution and banditry." The first wave of arrests netted 5,000 people.[27] One of those arrested was young Antonio Isaac of Maputo.

"In November, 1975, he has testified," on coming out of the cinema, I found FRELIMO trucks outside. Near the lorry, soldiers of the people's militia could be seen arresting almost everyone coming out of the cinema. People without any documents were arrested for vagrancy and those with their identification papers were accused of being 'reactionaries.' I did not have papers with me, so I was taken in as a vagrant."[28]

The Mozambican people were told by Machel that he had uncovered countless "enemies of the people" in their midst, entire classes of them in fact: the *internal bourgeois*, the *reactionary*, the *imperialist*, and the *colonial agent*. In order to correctly "mobilize and organize the masses," Machel told them, these enemies must be ruthlessly rooted out. It was your "revolutionary duty" to inform the government as to who they were, even if they were members of your own family. Thousands were denounced by their neighbors and relatives as former agents of PIDE, the Portuguese colonial secret service.[29]

When the jails quickly overflowed, Machel set up a number of "re-education centers" (seven were in Niassa province alone) — concentration camps that Machel called "Centers for Mental Decolonization: laboratories for the transformation of man." The camps were run by SNASP (the Popular National Security Service), trained and organized by East Germans, and which also operated the "People's Revolutionary Military Tribunals," responsible for filling up the laboratories with "infiltrados" (fifth-columnists) and "counterrevolutionary parasites."[30]

Antonio Isaac was sent to the Mitelela camp near Lichinga in Niassa province, where he, as all other prisoners, did forced manual labor (such as cutting down trees) from 4:00 a.m. to 5:00 p.m. every day, with one single meal per day at 2:00 p.m. consisting of filthy corn porridge and rotten beans (his description is eerily similar to the Khmer Rouge camps). Anyone attempting to escape, seen as lazy or insubordinate, or incurring the displeasure of the camp commanders for any reason was summarily shot.

The most infamous of all the concentration camps set up by Machel were the extermination centers of Chaiamite and Ruarua in the Cabo Delgado province. Reverend Daniel Sithole, deacon of the São Leonardo Catholic parish at Mussorize, Manica province, was sentenced to Ruarua for protesting the arrest of his parishioners. His portrait of conditions at Ruarua, or "Mozambique D" is chilling:

Every morning, instead of breakfast, prisoners get six strokes of the cane each. At noon they get twelve and before retiring to cells at night they get 20 strokes of the cane. This was done every day. . . . When the security men come to inspect the underground cells, they usually point the muzzles of their guns to the cells and just open fire against anybody they choose to kill. Fellow prisoners are not supposed to remove the body without the order to do so. The body remains in the cell for two to three days before the order comes from the command post to remove the dead body. The body is not buried. It is taken and thrown away near the camp. The decomposing flesh is eaten by hyenas and other wild animals at night.[31]

As the Reverend Sithole reports, the skulls and bones of thousands of Machel's victims are today strewn over the plain at Ruarua, bleaching in the African sun. Intelligence estimates state that between 200,000 to 300,000 Mozambicans have been imprisoned in Machel's Gulag, in which well over 75,000 have died.

### The Origins and Evolution of Renamo

The son of Chief Manguande of the Changane-Ndau tribe, Afonso Maccacho Marcetta Dhlakama, was born on New Year's Day in 1953 at the town of Chiba Bava in Sofala province. At the age of 19, young Afonso was recruited by his uncle Samuel to join FRELIMO (Samuel Dhlakama is presently with the ministry of health in Maputo). It was March of 1972, and Afonso had just deserted from the Portuguese colonial army. He had been conscripted the year before, after finishing school at the Zobue Catholic Mission Seminary in Tete province.

The young Afonso was militarily trained at Nachigwa in southern Tanzania and sent to FRELIMO's Marrupa Central Base in Niassa province in July 1973. From there he was promoted to company commander at Cuengwere Base, in Niassa. After independence from Portugal, Dhlakama was appointed head of logistics for the FRELIMO army in Sofala province, and from his vantage point in Beira for the ensuing two years, he saw that his country had not gained independence at all, but that it had merely switched, as had Angola, from being a colony of Portugal to being a colony of the Soviet Union.

This was not the society Dhlakama fought to achieve. As he looked around at the horror of Machel's social engineering with the camps; the wholesale attempt to destroy the tribal way of life by forcing villagers into communal farms (similar to Julius Nyerere's *Ujamaa* in Tanzania); the Khmer Rouge policy of forcing thousands of "unemployed parasites" and "marginals" in the cities into completely undeveloped remote countryside, dumping them into an area of straight bush to build a village and farm land from scratch; the East German-organized spy and informer network disenabling anyone from trusting a fellow citizen, even a brother or a son; the endless and ubiquitous forcefeeding of childish Marxist propaganda; and Russians running everything, ordering Mozambicans around as chattel, far worse than the Portuguese—Dhlakama decided he had to fight again.[32]

But how and with whom? It was then he decided to find Orlando Christina. A white Portuguese whose father had settled in Niassa province, Christina became fascinated with the peoples of northern Mozambique, learning Ajaua (or Yao) fluently and marrying an Ajaua woman under traditional rites, by whom he had a son. After a stint in the colonial army, he became a big game hunter and guide in Niassa.[33]

Over the years, Christina also became an outspoken advocate of Mozambican nationalism. When pressured, along with other big game hunters, to join army intelligence at Nampula, he fled to Tanzania in 1963 to join FRELIMO, as did other white Mozambicans who sympathized with the democratic ideals of Dr. Mondlane. Becoming disillusioned by the Marxism and anti-white feelings of the "Algerians" at FRELIMO headquarters in Dar Es Salaam, he returned to Mozambique in 1964, only to be arrested as a subversive by the Portuguese colonial police.

Christina appealed to a man whom he had guided on big games hunts to get him out of jail, a Beira businessman named Jorge Jardim who personally knew Antonio Salazar.[34] After his release in 1965, Christina became Jardim's personal assistant. With the Marxist takeover of FRELIMO complete following Mondlane's assassination in 1969, and Salazar's death in 1970, they became convinced that Mozambique would someday be independent, and that if FRELIMO took over it would be a totalitarian disaster. A Portuguese civilian settler effort was made to create an indigenous black Mozambican army, which ended in fiasco for Christina, as the colonial army resisted every attempt to make it autonomous. A Col. Costa Campos formed a special forces unit called *Grupos Especiais* (GEs), and as the unit's "political advisor," Christina proceeded to tell the recruits they were fighting for an independent Mozambique, free from control of both Portugal and FRELIMO.

Marques' revealing observation is that Christina had evidently began to see himself as a Lawrence of Arabia figure, possessed with the romantic idea of guiding Mozambicans—especially the tribes of the north, such as the Yao, Nyanja, and Macua, of whom he was so fond—to the future.

Quickly falling out with Campos,[35] Christina went to Malawi in 1972, where Jardim arranged with his friend President Kamuzu Banda for him to train Banda's militia, the Malawi Young Pioneers. Moving to Rhodesia after FRELIMO gained power, he was unable to convince the Rhodesians that a Soviet Mozambique was a threat until Machel closed the border in March 1976. With that, permission was quickly forthcoming to let Jardim finance Christina in setting up a radio station called *Voz da Africa Livre*, Voice of Free Africa, which started broadcasting from Gwelo, Rhodesia in June 1976. As FRELIMO began giving open sanctuary and support to Robert Mugabe's and Joshua Nkomo's ZANLA and ZIPRA guerrillas attacking Ian Smith's regime in Rhodesia,[36] Smith was happy to allow radio broadcasting in Portuguese denouncing the "Communist tyranny" now in Mozambique.

Smith was soon conducting a border war with FRELIMO. Elite units of the Rhodesian Army conducted extensive across-border antiterrorist raids, while an Angolan-born Colonel Oscar Cardoso led a group of black Mozambican colonial troops called the *Flechas* (Arrows), who were responsible for a number of atrocities upon Mozambican villagers near the Rhodesian border.[37] Cardoso attempted to recruit Christina, who subsequently disagreed with his methods and disassociated himself from Cordoso.

After listening to the clandestine broadcasts of the Voice of Free Africa, Dhlakama made his decision. Gaining a safe-conduct pass to Machiponda on the border with the pretense of inspecting how to stop FRELIMO deserters escaping out of the country (a document signed and stamped by FRELIMO party headquarters was necessary for anyone traveling anywhere in Mozambique), he left Beira in June of 1977, slipping into Rhodesia to find Christina. (FRELIMO was to later claim Dhlakama was caught embezzling army funds and cashiered—totally fabricated charges in keeping with its policy of calling any opponent a thief, robber, counterrevolutionary, colonial fascist, imperialist agent, and CIA spy.)

He was also looking for a man he had once met in Beira, through whom he had heard about Christina's radio talk. Christina brought Dhlakama to a remarkable young man, Andre Matadi Matsangaisse, from Chirawa in Manica province, and revered today as Commander Andre, the founder of RENAMO. Having fought extensively with FRELIMO as a platoon commander, upon independence Matsangaisse was assigned to the Engineering Corps in Beira. Shortly thereafter, however, Matsangaisse, a charismatic and fiery orator, began vocally denouncing the new regime for bringing dictatorship instead of democracy to his country. When he tried to organize a protest movement among his fellow soldiers, he was arrested and sent to the Sacuza concentration camp in Sofala province.

Escaping from Sacuza in October 1976, Matsangaisse went to find the people behind the Voice of Free Africa and ask them for help. "You are doing much talking," he told Christina when he met him, "and what your radio says is true. But I am willing not just to talk but to fight, to take up arms against FRELIMO. Will you help me?"

Christina took Matsangaisse to meet Peter Burt of the Rhodesian Central Intelligence Organization (CIO). Burt recognized a solution in Matsangaisse to an increasing problem created by Christina's radio. In addition to thousands of Mozambican refugees who had fled the totalitarianism of the Machel government, hundreds of disaffected FRELIMO soldiers had entered Rhodesia attracted by Christina's radio as moths to a flame. But the Rhodesians did not know what to do with them, particularly as no born leader had emerged — until Matsangaisse.

Rhodesia's situation with Mozambique had become serious. By closing the border (thus all trade and traffic through the Beira corridor, Rhodesia's vital lifeline to the Indian Ocean), and helping the ZANLA and ZIPRA guerrillas to the utmost, Machel had virtually declared war on Rhodesia.[38] Giving support and sanctuary to an anti-Marxist, anti-FRELIMO guerrilla movement seemed a fair quid pro quo. Burt asked Matsangaisse what was the first thing he would like to do. "Give me some men, and I will free all those imprisoned in the camp I escaped from," Andre replied. "Most of them will join me."

With Burt's approval, Christina took Andre to refugee camps near Umtali. From there, Andre recruited a small band of former FRELIMO soldiers who felt as he did. Armed only with machetes and pangas, and a few light arms provided by the CIO, Andre proceeded to lead them on a daring raid attacking the Sacuza camp in April of 1977 to free his fellow prisoners. The raid was successful and the camp overrun, whereupon he asked the liberated inmates to join him in a Second Struggle for National Liberation: "FRELIMO has sold out the revolution to the Soviet colonialists. Machel's dictatorship is worse than the Portuguese. Now we must fight for democracy and the independence of Mozambique all over again. Are you with me?" When they shouted yes, the Mozambique National Resistance — *Resistencia Naçional Moçambicana*, RENAMO — was born.

Of the 500 prisoners released at Sacuza, 300 followed Matsangaisse back to Rhodesia. The success of the Sacuza raid prompted Jack Berry (who had succeeded Burt as head of the CIO Mozambique Desk) to assign one of his deputies, Rick May, as project officer for assisting the new guerrilla movement. May, in turn, asked the Rhodesian Army for help. Capt. Bob MacKenzie and his C Squadron of the Rhodesian SAS (Special Air Service) were assigned to provide training on an ad hoc basis for Andre's men. An American from San Diego, California, Mackenzie had been involved in counterinsurgency operations ("coin-ops") for the

SAS since 1970, and before that he had participated in numerous special operations against the Viet Cong while in the 101st Airborne in Viet Nam. A training facility was set up at Odzi, near the Mozambican border.

But neither the CIO nor the SAS had any money in their budgets for the fledgling RENAMO. Christina got Jardim and other wealthy *retornados* (Portuguese Mozambicans who had fled to Portugal) to finance the purchase of arms, supplies, and the costs of running the Odzi sanctuary training camp. It was as this was getting under way that Dhlakama arrived in June 1977. A strong bond quickly developed between Dhlakama and Matsangaisse, and soon Dhlahama became the latter's second in command.

There are conflicting reports regarding the extent to which the newborn resistance was assisted and trained by the Rhodesians. In an error-riddled paper on "The MNR" prepared for the Center for Strategic and International Studies at Georgetown University, Africa scholar Colin Legum claims that the role is extensive; the argument is often made, in fact, that the MNR or RENAMO was created and totally controlled by the Rhodesian military. Yet in a book cited by Legum as a primary source, *Top Secret War* by Col. Ron Reid-Daly, commander of the Rhodesian Army's elite counterinsurgency Selous Scouts, there is no mention of the MNR in the entire text.[39] The Selous Scouts' purpose was to track down ZANLA and ZIPRA guerrillas *within* Rhodesia, and had, in fact, almost nothing to do with RENAMO, which was assisted instead by the Rhodesian SAS, a small, entirely separate unit for conducting operations against ZANLA and ZIPRA sanctuaries in Zambia and Mozambique.[40]

An accepted necessary condition of successful guerrilla war is a sanctuary in a neighboring country. The Afghan Mujahedin use Pakistan. The Eritreans use Sudan. The Nicaraguan contras use Honduras. But the Pakistanis did not "create" the Mujahedin, and neither did the Rhodesians create RENAMO. Internal oppression and political tyranny with the grossest violation of human rights, supported by an imperialist foreign power, created an indigenous resistance—whether in Afghanistan, Eritrea, Nicaragua, Angola, or in Mozambique.[41]

The Rhodesian government had every reason to provide a sanctuary for RENAMO, as the Mozambican government was providing a sanctuary for Marxist guerrillas trying to overthrow it. But the fact remains that the Mozambique National Resistance was created, and its activities were conducted, by Mozambicans.

For a little more than the first two years of its existence, RENAMO operated out of camps at Odzi. The SAS would take RENAMO guerrilla teams to the border in trucks, drop them off, and pick them back up again when their mission was completed. The teams would normally operate inside Mozambique on their own, unaccompanied by any SAS personnel, from two days to six weeks. Their primary objective was to develop a network of local support among the villagers of Manica province. Militarily, their targets were FRELIMO military and government facilities; ambushing military convoys and capturing weapons; and attacking the "re-education centers" to free the prisoners (many of whom, particularly ex-FRELIMO guerrillas, joined the resistance). During this time, the exploits of Andre, involving considerable personal bravery, became widely known not only in Manica, but throughout Mozambique due to Christina's radio.

There was an occasional joint SAS-RENAMO operation, such as the spectacular destruction of much of the Munhava oil storage depot at Beira, on 23 March 1979, commanded by SAS Capt. Bob MacKenzie.[42] But for the most part, joint SAS-RENAMO activities inside Mozambique were limited to RENAMO providing guides every so often for SAS attacks on ZANLA sanctuary camps.[43] Most of RENAMO's weapons were captured, but the CIO was able to supply some light arms with Jardim's money.

What the Rhodesians really supplied was training at Odzi. It was nothing elaborate, and actually quite informal. Captain MacKenzie had been trained in Vietnam to teach guerrilla warfare techniques to indigenous peasants (such as the Montagnard hill tribes). He devoted whatever time he could spare to teaching his methods to Andre and his men, giving Andre his collection of US special forces pamphlets and field manuals, augmented with British Army instruction booklets.

By September of 1979, Andre's force had grown to 600 men. Their successes against the FRELIMO army and their popularity among the rural villagers throughout Manica and extending into Sofala had given Andre the confidence that RENAMO could establish a permanent headquarters deep inside Mozambique. He selected a place with which he was familiar as a FRELIMO guerrilla, a 6,000-foot-high plateau in the Serra da Gorongosa mountains of Sofala.

Rick May authorized a small SAS contingent of a dozen men, led by Lt. Charlie Buchan, to accompany Matsangaisse, Dhlakama, and 200 RENAMO guerrillas on the three-week-long trek to Gorongosa. During the same month, September 1979, Andre sent another third of his force, 200 strong, commanded by Lucas ("Luke") Mushlangu and with no SAS accompaniment, to establish a permanent base at Gogoi in the Sitatonga mountains of southern Manica, from which to expand RENAMO operations into Gaza. The remaining third of 200 fighters stayed at Odzi.

"We knew that RENAMO was doing quite well militarily, because we were intercepting FRELIMO army transmissions," MacKenzie reports. "And we knew, from our own men on the ground, how popular RENAMO was becoming with local villagers, who were quite terrified of FRELIMO and were happy to have somebody trying to get rid of them."

Things seemed to be going very well for the resistance movement. Optimism and morale were high as they settled into their Gorongosa camp. But on October 17, Andre decided to attack the FRELIMO garrison of a Gorongosa Town, at the base of the mountains. Personally leading a charge upon a fortified position which included a Soviet tank, he was killed.[44]

Dhlakama, as Matsangaisse's deputy, assumed command of the guerrillas, who were stunned at the loss of their leader. But Dhlakama was able to rally his men, launching a series of successful operations against FRELIMO soldiers in Sofala. MacKenzie was authorized to send a new SAS team to Gorongosa for intensified training; led by Lt. Rich Stannard, they arrived in December 1979.

SAS support for RENAMO was now codenamed Operation Bumper, and under Stannard's tutelage, the proficiency of RENAMO activities improved considerably, resulting in the capture of substantial amounts of FRELIMO army weapons, ammunition, and materiel. Operation Bumper was short-lived, however, lasting less than three months, for Rhodesia was rapidly becoming Zimbabwe. Britain reasserted colonial control over the country in December, and new elections (invalidating those that elected Bishop Abel Muzarewa the previous April) were held in February 1980, with Robert Mugabe the declared winner. Christina's Voice of Free Africa was taken off the air, and the SAS was soon to be dissolved.

To be caught in a vise between Machel and Mugabe with no sanctuary whatever was untenable for RENAMO. Dhlakama sent a message to Christina: would Rick May ask his counterpart in South Africa Military Intelligence to provide a sanctuary for RENAMO? May's request received a positive answer. In March of 1980, Dhlakama left Gorongosa for the Sitatonga base at Gogoi. The last operation of the SAS, under the direction of Captain MacKenzie, was to secretly (i.e., without the knowledge of Mugabe or the British) take three truckloads of equipment and the remaining RENAMO men at Odzi (the rest had gone by foot) to the border to be picked up by SADF (South African Defense Force) Puma helicopters and ferried the thirty-five kilometers to Sitatonga. Christina and his staff took an Air Rhodesia flight from Salisbury (not yet renamed Air Zimbabwe and Harare, respectively) to Johannesburg.[45] By May, the Voice of Free Africa was broadcasting again from Phalaborwa in the northern Transvaal, adjacent to Kruger National Park.[46]

A short time after Dhlakama arrived at Sitatonga, "Luke" Mushlangu challenged Dhlakama's leadership of RENAMO. But contrary to some reports, there was no "gun battle" between the two.[47] The issue was put to a vote among the more than 600 guerrillas in the camp,[48] and Dhlakama was the overwhelming choice.[49] In a ceremony at Sitatonga, Afonso Dhlakama was formally installed as president and supreme military commander of RENAMO in June 1980.

The following month, in July, FRELIMO forces attacked and overran the Sitatonga base at Gogoi. Hundreds of RENAMO guerrillas were either killed, captured, or deserted. Dhlakama fled 150 kilometers south to a small base called Garagua on the Save River, which forms the border between Manica and Gaza provinces. Down to a few hundred followers, the outlook for the liberation movement was bleak.

But Capt. Bob MacKenzie and 80 percent of his men in the SAS (127 men) had requested transfer to the SADF (South African Defense Forces), proposing they form a second reconnaissance commando unit under SAMI ("Sammy," South African Military Intelligence) to, among other tasks, assist RENAMO. Gen. Pieter van der Westhuizen, director of SAMI, approved the proposal, appointing SADF Col. Charles van Niekerk as liaison officer between the training unit and RENAMO. By October 1980, a small training team of SADF commandos had parachuted into Garagua, and regular air drops of weapons and materiel were being made by SADF C-130s. The training teams were on a six-week rotation and numbered from eight to ten men.[50]

Political and economic conditions in Mozambique had by now so worsened that Dhlakama discovered he had as many recruits as he had weapons. Using the network of local support he and Andre had created among rural villagers, he quickly established a string of bases throughout Manica, western Sofala, southern Tete, and northern Gaza provinces. With the Voice of Free Africa broadcasting instructions on how to join RENAMO, the liberation movement was soon inundated with thousands of volunteers, many of them defectors from the FRELIMO army. By the end of 1980, RENAMO had close to 10,000 men under arms; Orlando Christina had been appointed secretary-general, and a third-generation Mozambican of Goan ancestry who had worked for Jorge Jardim, Evo Fernandes, had opened up RENAMO's first European mission near Lisbon.[51]

Dhlakama spent much of 1981 strengthening and expanding RENAMO's relations and support network with local villagers. A large portion of support came from the *regulos*, traditional rural village chiefs upon whom Machel was waging war in his effort to create "a new socialist man" in Mozambique. Dhlakama found most everyone in the rural countryside agreeing with him when he and his men told them: "FRELIMO is worse than the Portuguese ever were. The colonials exploited us, but at least the Portuguese did not try and destroy our traditions and our traditional way of life because they are so-called reactionary."

The RENAMO message was one of Mozambican nationalism vs. Soviet colonialism; of defense and respect for the traditions and beliefs of the various Mozambican cultural and religious communities vs. a violent contempt for them;[52] of democracy vs. Marxist dictatorship; and of the right of every Mozambican to earn his living as he sees fit vs. forced communal slavery.

The message also came out of the barrel of a gun, pointed at the economy and FRELIMO's capacity to govern. The key targets became the railway lines from Maputo and Beira to Zimbabwe, attacked for the first time in October 1981; the oil pipeline from Beira to Mutare (ex Umtali) in Zimbabwe, also in October; the main paved roads, especially along the coast; and the power lines from the Cabora Bassa dam on the Zambezi which supplies South Africa with seven percent of its electricity. The power lines were first cut in November 1980[53] and twice in 1981.

Machel's response to Dhlakama's offer to negotiate a democratization of Mozambique was to daily denounce the insurgents as "armed bandits" and "creatures of racist South Africa," and to increase the controls and East German surveillance over the people.

The major setback for RENAMO came in 1981 at the end of the year, when FRELIMO forces overran the Garagua base on December 7.[54] Having had advance warning of the attack, via a burgeoning number of informers within FRELIMO ranks, Dhlakama had already abandoned the base, moving RENAMO headquarters back to Gorongosa. On December 17 RENAMO forces captured a British scientist, John Burlison, in the Gorongosa Game Park. Held captive for 158 days, he was released inside Zimbabwe on 5 May 1982, after walking some 800 kilometers through the Mozambique bush. He personally encountered over 1,000 armed RENAMO guerrillas, all of whose officers acknowledged Dhlakama as their leader, were "anti-communist," and wanted to replace the FRELIMO regime with a government "more sympathetic to private enterprise." He reported that was "well-treated," that the guerrillas "seemed to be popular" among local villagers, that he "never encountered" FRELIMO forces and never saw "any white people at all with the guerrillas."[55]

From the entrenched Gorongosa headquarters, Dhlakama rapidly expanded RENAMO's area of operations, capitalizing on the widespread disillusionment with FRELIMO. By the end of 1982, RENAMO had a local village support base and over fifty guerrilla camps launching attacks on FRELIMO targets throughout all of Manica and southern Tete, almost all of Sofala, Gaza, and Inhambane to within fifty kilometers of the

Limpopo River. On 15 August 1982 RENAMO officials crossed the Zambezi River, and in a formal ceremony signed an agreement with Jimo Phiri, leader of a group of anti-FRELIMO guerrillas in Zambezia province, *Africa Livre* (Free Africa), merging it into RENAMO. By year's end, RENAMO's operational zone extended to the southern third of Zambezia.

Of the more than 1,500 military actions recorded by RENAMO in 1982, the most spectacular was the blowing up of thirty-four oil storage tanks in Beira harbor on December 9, causing damage estimated at $20 million and a severe fuel crisis in Zimbabwe.[56] Although a virtual repetition of the famous attack on the Munhava Depot in 1979, this operation was evidently conducted solely by RENAMO personnel, however extensively prepared and trained for it by a SADF team in Gorongosa.

Nineteen eighty-three saw a series of successful FRELIMO offensives against RENAMO in the south, particularly in Maputo and Gaza provinces, coupled with rallies that paraded captured RENAMO guerrillas for humiliation and public execution. At one such rally at Chibuto, Machel exclaimed, "Those who supply information to the bandits [RENAMO] must die with the bandits. Those who feed the bandits must die with the bandits. Those who deal with the bandits must die with the bandits. Our mission is not to wound, but to kill!"[57]

Against these losses, RENAMO continued activity in Gaza. One such action was an attack on the Mangoro barracks on March 30, killing three Cuban military advisors and twenty-seven FRELIMO soldiers.[58] RENAMO conducted a number of offensives itself, such as "Red August" and "Black September" (the former culminating in the capture of twenty-four Soviet technicians in Morrua in Zambezia); expanded throughout all of Zambezia and Nampula, and all of eastern Tete to the Malawi border; and increased attacks in Sofala and Manica, focusing on FRELIMO convoys and trains. By the end of 1983, RENAMO's "zone of active operations" reached throughout the entire country save for the two northernmost provinces, Niassa and Cabo Delgado, western Tete, and southern Maputo. The FRELIMO army commander for Inhambane province admitted that at least 3,500 guerrillas were operating in Inhambane alone.[59]

RENAMO's major loss of 1983 was the assassination of Orlando Christina by an unknown gunman on April 16 on a farm near Pretoria. Evo Fernandes was appointed secretary-general of the movement that December.

Another political setback was a major disinformation campaign orchestrated by the Soviets, featuring a diplomatic offensive by FRELIMO, launched with a tour in October 1983 by Samora Machel to six countries in Western Europe. During the tour, the Soviets circulated a rumor that

Mozambique would "loosen" its ties with Moscow and become "genuinely non-aligned" if it received enough economic and military aid from the West.[60] This strategy, devised to persuade the West to pay for keeping Machel and FRELIMO in power, was well received, especially so by Chester Crocker, U.S. Department of State assistant secretary for African affairs under Ronald Reagan.

After a number of consultations with South African Foreign Minister Roelof "Pik" Botha, the most important being in February 1984 in Pretoria, Crocker convinced South Africa to sign a nonaggression pact with Mozambique on 16 March 1984. Known as the Nkomati Accords, its purpose was to stop South Africa's support of RENAMO, in exchange for Mozambique's stopping its support of the Africa National Congress or ANC, headquartered at the time in Maputo.

Until Nkomati, SADF assistance to RENAMO had been considerable, including special-operations training for a limited number of RENAMO personnel at the Reconnaissance Regiment barracks at Phalaborwa. In anticipation of the assistance cutoff, and in defiance of Foreign Minister Botha and Chester Crocker's express wishes, SAMI Director General Westhuizen ordered a massive resupply of military materiel, mostly taken from stocks of Soviet weapons captured in SADF raids on SWAPO camps in Angola, air dropped to Gorongosa and other RENAMO bases in the weeks prior to March 16.

After Nkomati, however, virtually all material assistance to RENAMO from South Africa ceased, although Colonel Niekerk did continue for a time as liaison. The Voice of Free Africa closed down. As a Marxist, Machel was convinced that without the "external conditions" of South African support, RENAMO, as nothing more than an "extension of South African armed forces,"[61] would evaporate into the bush. "We have turned off the tap," observed Machel of his reason for signing Nkomati. "All that is left is the water which is already in the pipe."[62]

It came as a rude surprise to Machel and all adherents to the "South Africa-backed bandits" theory that the opposite occurred as RENAMO increased its activities more than ever. Instead of a perceiving Nkomati as a setback, Dhlakama chose to see it as an opportunity to prove to the world that RENAMO was a genuine indigenous liberation movement, and was neither a creation nor a puppet of South Africa.[63]

Before a month had passed after Nkomati, the American Embassy in Maputo was warning its personnel that the Maputo-South Africa main highway was not safe from RENAMO attacks, while RENAMO blew up Maputo's power station so that the capital was without electricity for a week.[64] By July, RENAMO had extended its activities throughout western Tete, and halfway up Niassa and Cabo Delgado provinces, establishing a substantial degree of cooperation with the Maconde tribe of Cabo Delgado. Predominantly Moslem, the Macondes formed the bulk of FRELIMO's fighters prior to independence, but were now quite alienated from the regime.[65]

Rather than withering away, RENAMO emerged stronger than ever at the end of 1984. Its zone of active operations had spread across the entire country, encompassing all ten provinces. The movement claimed "consolidated control" over the entire rural area of seven provinces: Nampula, Niassa, Zambezi, Tete, Manica, Sofala, and Inhambane, and had an estimated force in excess of 15,000 armed guerrillas in addition to a support network of at least 10,000 sympathizers.

Obviously, the $450 million in economic and military aid the Soviet Union had given FRELIMO from 1978 to 1982 had been insufficient.[66] Since late 1982, some 700 Zimbabwean soldiers had been guarding the Beira pipeline,[67] but they had not been able to stop the attacks. As a result, Machel intensified his effort to convince the West he could be "weaned away" from the Soviets if only his regime was provided with enough money and assistance to defeat RENAMO.

The most enthusiastic response from Machel's entreaties came from Chester Crocker, and from Margaret Thatcher, whom Machel had met on his October 1983 trip. On 16 January 1985, the State Department announced it would seek funding for a "limited military assistance relationship" between the U.S. and Mozambique.[68] On 5 July 1985, the British ambassador to Mozambique, Eric Vines, announced the granting of $650,000 in military aid to FRELIMO, with British military instructors to train and equip FRELIMO army officers in a Zimbabwe training camp.[69]

President Ronald Reagan welcomed Samora Machel into the White House on 19 September 1985. As a prelude to the meeting, a helicopter-borne assault of 12,000 troops from the Zimbabwe National Army and 8,000 FRELIMO Army soldiers was launched at the end of August, overrunning RENAMO's Gorongosa headquarters. Dhlakama and his men retreated with small losses, killing two of the Soviet officers who led the attack.[70]

But the invasion force bogged down in the October rains. RENAMO was soon conducting serious attacks throughout the entire country, and by January 1986 there were newspaper stories such as "Mozambique Rebels Return to Offensive."[71] On February 14, the Gorongosa headquarters was recaptured, with the BBC reporting, "the Mozambique FRELIMO government forces have been suffering serious setbacks in its war against RENAMO."[72]

By the middle of 1986, it had become clear that the FRELIMO government and military was incapable of defending itself and required substantial numbers of foreign troops and military advisors to be kept in power and not be overthrown by RENAMO.[73]

Subsequent efforts by Joaquim Chissano, taking over the FRELIMO leadership after the death of Samora Machel in a plane crash on 19 October 1986 (both the aircraft and its pilot were Soviet), have failed to alter this predicament.[74]

### Renamo Today

*Leadership and Command Structure*

The leadership of RENAMO remains centered upon Afonso Dhlakama, as both president and supreme military commander of the liberation movement. He looks younger than he is (he was thirty-six in 1989), so that journalists who have interviewed him invariably comment upon his intelligence and professorial demeanor. Married in 1980, he lives at the Gorongosa headquarters with his wife, Dona Rosario, and his two daughters, Belhina and Albertina (born in 1982 and 1985). As both a devout Catholic and son of a tribal chieftain, he possesses a deep reverence for Christian justice and values as well as for traditional African society and customs.[75]

The National Council provides RENAMO's political leadership. Chaired by Dhlakama, it has ten departments, the secretaries of which were (in 1988) the following: Vincente Ululu (administration), Albino Faise (education), Francisco Mota Moises (information), Felipe Soares (health and welfare), Agosto Chaviro (agriculture), Mario Luis Gonzaga (youth affairs), Artur da Fonseca (foreign affairs); Dhlakama himself is both secretary of defense and ideology. The post of secretary-general was abolished July 1986.[76] All members of the National Council reside at Gorongosa, with the exceptions of Fonseca, who lives in West Germany, and Moises, who lives in Canada.

Foreign representation is limited to representatives in Washington, Professor Luis Serapiao; Bonn, Horacio Leven; and Lisbon, Manuel Frank.

The Military Council of RENAMO is also chaired by Dhlakama as commander-in-chief. Under him are three chiefs-of-staff for the north, central, and south military regions: General Dick (for Niassa, Cabo Delgado, Nampula, Zambezia, and Tete; or from the Rovuma to the Zambezi rivers); General Ismail (for Sofala and Manica; or from the Zambezi to the Save rivers); and General Domingos (for Gaza, Inhambane, and Maputo; or from the Save to the Swaziland/South African border).

Under the chiefs-of-staff, who reside at Gorongosa, are ten provincial leaders with the rank of general-commander, who are responsible for all operations within each province. Nearly every province has a large central base coordinating insurgent activities, training recruits, and providing administrative facilities for medical, health, education, agricultural, and other programs. Most general-commanders reside full-time at their respective central bases, but some reside, at least part-time, at Gorongosa.

Each province is divided into regions, with a regional base and commander; within each region are a number of smaller bases and garrisons, occupied by anywhere from a dozen to several hundred men. Interaction between the guerrillas and the local population mostly takes place on the garrison level. Garrisons provide police support for the local tribal authorities, working within the traditional system of governance through local *regulos* or tribal chiefs. RENAMO health and education cadres also work out of the garrisons setting up small clinics and schools for the local villagers.

The smallest unit of RENAMO is the section (what we would call a squad), of 8 to 12 men, led by a section leader (equivalent to a sergeant). Three sections, comprising about 30 men, form an operational group or platoon, led by a platoon commander (equivalent to a corporal). Three operational groups form a zonal group or company, led by a company commander (equivalent to a lieutenant), containing about 100 men, including a nurse, radio operator, and artillerymen with mortars and heavier weapons.

Three zonal groups make up a battalion of 300–400 men led by a sector commander (equivalent to a captain), while three battalions comprise a brigade led by a regional commander (equivalent to a major). In addition to this structure, there are at Gorongosa four elite "strike battalions" of around 500 men each, which conduct specific missions assigned to them by headquarters, and assist provincial forces in major operations. Gorongosa also commands a "special forces" unit of some 200 men, which conducts assassination, sabotage, and reconnaissance missions with 3-man teams spread throughout the country.

Current estimated strengths of RENAMO forces is around 25,000 men under arms, with several thousand more "irregulars" who are incorporated into the fighting as the need arises and as the weapons become available. The FRELIMO army has an estimated strength of some 30,000.

*Communications, Logistics, and Transport*

The small bases and garrisons communicate between each other and to the regional bases via courier either on foot, bicycle, or motorcycle. The motorcycle courier system is reportedly well-developed, particularly between the regional bases and each province's central base. A radio network exists between many regional bases and their central base, and between all provincial central bases and Gorongosa, using old South African and Rhodesian radios supplied years ago, such as Syncal-30 radios and Mortley-Sprague hand-cranked generators, or British radio equipment captured from Zimbabwean forces.

Tactical communications equipment, such as walkie-talkies, is quite rare and limited to occasionally captured devices. The lack of such equipment, according to an observer for *Janes' Defence Weekly*, causes "coordination during operations (to be) often non-existent."[77]

The logistical system is based almost wholly upon self-reliance on the garrison, and often the regional level. There is neither a central logistical base for materiel at Gorongosa, nor at most provincial central bases, only personnel recording where materiel was captured and where it is stored. Apparently, RENAMO relies almost totally on what it is able to capture in attacks on FRELIMO targets.[78]

RENAMO has mined and dug up most roads, preferring its own network of trails and paths or those trod by local villagers. Not possessing fuel supplies, such as South Africa provides for UNITA in Angola, the vehicles, trucks, tanks, etc., it has captured are rarely used. Supplies, captured weapons and materiel, are transported by teams of porters on foot. Guerrilla fighters, moving from one sector to another, also travel by foot.

*Combat Tactics, Morale, Weaponry, and Materiel*

In general, there are two basic models of guerrilla warfare strategy. One is the Russian model, advocating attacks on urban targets, particularly the capital city, going directly for the power centers. Quite often, this strategy entails purposeful urban terrorism, terrorism being consciously perpetrated violence upon known noncombatants as a means of demoralizing (i.e., terrorizing) the citizenry at large, in order to weaken their resistance and confidence in their government's ability to protect them. The PLO (Palestine Liberation Organization) and the ANC (African National Congress), both Soviet-backed, would be examples of this strategy.

The other model is the Chinese, as developed by Mao Zedong. This is a rural strategy, which entails gaining control of the countryside, finally to such an extent that all sources of supply to the cities are cut off, causing their collapse and ultimately that of the capital itself.

The first necessary condition for the successful implementation of this strategy is the cooperation and support of the rural population. The guerrillas must be able to, in Mao's famous dictum, "swim like fish in the sea" of local villagers. Without this support, the guerrilla movement must fail, as did Che Guevara in Bolivia, who thought the rural peasantry would spontaneously rally to him, and so began fighting without first soliciting local support; the Viet Cong also failed with, extensive terror tactics against peasants and hill tribes (remember that it was an invasion of the North Vietnamese Army which conquered South Vietnam).

RENAMO uses the Chinese model, as does every other anti-Soviet insurgency now in operation.[79] The reasons are twofold: it was the model used by FRELIMO against the Portuguese in northern Mozambique due to Samora Machel's Maoist persuasion,[80] and it was the model used in training by the Rhodesian SAS. Thus a great deal of stress is put by Dhlakama on RENAMO forces working with and gaining the support and cooperation of local villagers. Virtually every independent observer who has actually travelled through RENAMO-held territory comments favorably on the guerrillas' relations with the civilian peasantry.[81]

Combat tactics are commonly not much more than a simple headlong assault on a selected FRELIMO position, more often that not routing the opposition. Morale among RENAMO combatants is universally reported to be exceedingly high. "Their confidence is unshakable," reports *Jane's* while "FRELIMO troops [are] demoralized, unskilled, and unable to stop the rise of the resistance."[82]

A key element in the Chinese strategy is ambushing and closing down roads and goods distribution systems; another is attacking the infrastructure upon which the urban centers depend, such as factories, electric power stations, and government agricultural centers. All of these are key RENAMO objectives throughout the country. A primary target is the road, rail, and oil pipeline of the Beira Corridor, which must be protected by several thousand Zimbabwean and other foreign soldiers.[83]

The overall strategy is, according to Dhlakama, "maintain[ing] pressure all over the country, launching a lot of small-scale attacks to force the enemy to the country, launching a lot of small-scale attacks to force the enemy to disperse his forces."[84] Towns are frequently captured, but always abandoned whenever a major government effort is launched for the town's retrieval.

One flaw in the Chinese strategy is that it was developed by Mao in the 1930s when air power and transport were insignificant as compared to today. FRELIMO has come to rely almost entirely on air power and transport to attack RENAMO positions and to resupply both its personnel in the field and inland urban centers. Thus a sufficient number of (and proficient training in) effective antiaircraft weapons has perhaps become a necessary requirement for modern implementation of the Chinese strategy. RENAMO has captured a small number of 12.7-mm.

"Dashaka" and 14.5 "ZPU" Soviet heavy machine guns, and a handful of Soviet SAM-7 "Strela" portable missiles. This is woefully inadequate to cope with FRELIMO's air power, resulting in the government's only military advantage over the insurgents.

The other basic problem RENAMO faces is severe equipment shortages of virtually everything. *Jane's* has called RENAMO "probably the most 'ragtag' army in the world."[85] Supplies of weapons, ammunition, motorcycles, and all materiel are captured, and everything is used until it disintegrates. Thus, almost all weapons are Soviet-bloc: E.g., AK-47s, RPD machine guns, RPG-7s, 82-mm. mortars, 122-mm. B-11 rockets, and all in short supply, with precious little ammunition and cleaning oil a rarity. There are intelligence reports, however, that claim RENAMO is currently capturing substantially more weapons from FRELIMO forces than in the past.[86]

Allowing peasants to grow crops and raise animals freely in RENAMO areas of control, however, has resulted in food being in relative abundance: there have been no reports of starvation or famine by observers in RENAMO territory. FRELIMO, on the other hand, received $75 million in famine relief from the United States in 1987, none of it to go to RENAMO-controlled areas, and $185 million in economic and emergency-relief aid in 1988.[87]

*External Support*

Like epic poets whose descriptions are often repetitive formulas (such as Homer's "Hector of the flashing helmet" and "Achilles of the loud warcry"), journalists and scholars can sometimes unthinkingly repeat a facile formula and become unable to provide a description of an individual or organization apart from that formula. Thus it has become commonplace for much of the media to automatically repeat the formula "South Africa-backed" with any mention of RENAMO.

Yet no observer who has travelled with RENAMO forces in Mozambique has reported evidence of such backing.[88] Evidently SADF and SAMI officers' feelings towards the Foreign Ministry are bitter about this. "If it were up to us," confides a top officer in SAMI, "we would back RENAMO to the hilt. But we cannot, not since the Nkomati Accord." Evidently, much of SADF and SAMI have the same regard for the South African Foreign Ministry and its minister, Roelof "Pik" Botha, as many American conservatives have for the US State Department and Chester Crocker. "Pik Botha," asserts the same SAMI officer, "has convinced Pretoria to sacrifice RENAMO to save the sacred cow of Nkomati."[89]

With the lack of evidence of South African support, there has been intense speculation on where external aid to RENAMO may be originating. Much of it has centered on the Comoro Islands. Certain intelligence sources are convinced that Saudi Arabia is providing assistance, and perhaps other moderate Islamic states such as the UAE, Oman, and other members of the so-called Safari Club originally put together by King Hassan of Morocco to help Savimbi in Angola after the Cuban-led Shaba Offensive in 1978.

According to this scenario, the Saudis, the Omanis, and others were so incensed over Machel's mistreatment of Moslems in Mozambique that they have authorized C-130 supply flights to the Comoros, where the weapons and materiel is offloaded onto Britain-Norman Islanders and flown to RENAMO strips in Cabo Delgado.[90] The problem with this speculation is the lack of any evidence for it on the ground in RENAMO-held Mozambique.

A more plausible scenario is that RENAMO does not receive substantial external support from any source. The FRELIMO army has in certain ways ceased to be an army at all, with many of its units turning into bandit gangs, starving in garrisons cut off by RENAMO, clad in tattered uniforms or begging for food from villagers (e.g., along the border with Malawi).[91] The massacre in Homoine on 18 July 1987 is an example: FRELIMO soldiers garrisoned there had not received any food deliveries for six weeks and went on a rampage, killing many civilians.[92] Thus the rate at which RENAMO captures FRELIMO weapons and supplies, as I mentioned above, is now high and likely to go higher.

*Political Program and Ideology*

The other formula automatically repeated by much of the media and certain scholars when they mention RENAMO is that the movement "has no political program," that its goals and purposes are "vague," "murky," and "obscure." The persistence of this formula is puzzling in the face of a clearly stated "Manifest and Program" adopted by RENAMO in 1981, which has been published in an English edition and publicly distributed.

RENAMO does not possess an all-encompassing ideology detailed in a blueprint for control of an entire society as typified by Marxism-Leninism. But its political program and objectives are not rendered murky, obscure, or nonexistent because it advocates democracy instead of Marxism or free enterprise instead of socialism.

The immediate demands of the liberation movement are two in number and quite clear: The withdrawal of all foreign military and advisory personnel from Mozambique, specifically all Zimbabwean and Tanzanian soldiers, and all Soviet, Cuban, and other Soviet-bloc advisors; and the relinquishment of a forcibly-held monopoly of governmental power by FRELIMO, and a new government freely chosen from competing political parties through internationally supervised elections.

It is worth noting that Dhlakama has acknowledged that the second demand implies that should the FRELIMO party freely and honestly win such an election, RENAMO would fully abide by it. "If (Joaquim Chissano) wants to be leader of Mozambique, he must be elected," Dhlakama avows. "If the people of Mozambique choose him above other candidates in a free election, so be it."[93]

RENAMO is evidently fighting not to impose a specific ideology upon Mozambique society, but rather to let the Mozambican people choose the type of social and economic system they want under a democratic framework — a choice they have never been given in their history.

The major failure of RENAMO in the political realm is its lack of a public relations campaign articulating its motives and purposes to the media and foreign diplomats. Interviews of Dhlakama report he has little comprehension of the importance of public relations, of developing a competent political organization and representative network in foreign capitals.[94]

This problem has been endemic from the inception of RENAMO. According to João Marques, the Rhodesian CIO intentionally "created a division between the military (RENAMO) and the politicians (the Voice of Free Africa), with the two having no direct contact between them, and in fact were prevented from doing so by the CIO . . . [thus] up to 1980, the two factions grew separately, with the military (RENAMO) becoming increasingly independent."

An additional source of the problem is the lack of a sanctuary, and thus ready access to the outside world. Every neighboring country to Mozambique is either militantly hostile to RENAMO (Zimbabwe, Tanzania, Zambia) or refuses to allow RENAMO to set up a political office which can serve as a communication channel for messages and press releases, and a conduit for inserting journalists and observers into RENAMO territory (Malawi, Swaziland, South Africa).

No other major anti-Soviet insurgency in the world has this problem, that is, the lack of a sanctuary. Virtually all journalists and observers entering RENAMO territory have done so by sneaking in through Malawi, whose attitude towards RENAMO varies from looking-the-other-way ambivalence to hostility (in fact, when I attempted to enter Mozambique from Malawi in 1986, I was arrested and prevented from doing so by the Malawi secret police). It is thus more difficult to enter and gain an on-the-ground knowledge of RENAMO territory than it is any other major anti-insurgency (in Afghanistan, Nicaragua, Angola, Ethiopia, and Cambodia).

## Summation and Assessment

Within the phenomenon of armed resistance to Soviet colonialism—the world of anti-Soviet, anti-Marxist, pro-West, pro-capitalist democratic liberation movements—RENAMO presents an extraordinary paradox. It is perhaps the archetypal example of the phenomenon, possessing to a greater degree than the others all of the qualities just enumerated. Certainly it is the most explicit advocate of free enterprise, claiming to see a necessary connection between political freedom and economic freedom—and not just for the society at large but also for the individual citizen. It is capable of outright military victory. Yet it is the pariah of anti-Soviet liberation movements, condemned and maligned almost universally by the media, receiving the least external support, and the most wholly self-contained, possessing no sanctuary.

In 1988, media and State Department condemnation reached virtually hysterical levels, accusing RENAMO guerrillas of massacring pregnant women, such as at Homoine, or of eating children. To squelch emerging support for RENAMO in Congress, the State Department issued the "Gersony Report," a transparently biased and politically motivated document accusing RENAMO of massive human rights violations.

Written by State Department consultant Robert Gersony, it alleged, based on interviews with Mozambican refugees, that RENAMO was conducting a war of mass terror and brutality against the people of Mozambique, and that its guerrillas had murdered over 100,000 Mozambicans. This report was uncritically accepted as gospel by the major media. Yet its scholarship was sophomorically sloppy. The figure of 100,000, now quoted as established fact in most every story about RENAMO, was a pure extrapolation based on a handful of accounts of refugees who were not sure at all who attacked them. Many of Gersony's interviews were conducted in FRELIMO camps; all of his interviews were done through SNASP (FRELIMO secret police) interpreters. Gersony made no attempt to visit areas of Mozambique under RENAMO control; no interviews were done with refugees in RENAMO areas who had fled FRELIMO tyranny.

The report's almost total bias against RENAMO and for FRELIMO invalidates its objectivity. The nationwide atrocities committed by FRELIMO, with the "reeducation" camps, the "people's tribunals," the public floggings, the forced collectivization and "Operation Production" causing the death by starvation of tens of thousands, the murder and torture by SNAPS of countless Mozambicans accused of lacking sufficient revolutionary zeal, and on and on year after year, is blithely ignored. According to the Institute for Human Rights in Frankfurt, FRELIMO currently has imprisoned over 10,000 political prisoners and has "slaughtered an unknown number of Christians in Tete and Zambezia provinces."[98]

There is no mention by Gersony of the numerous credible reports that a renegade Rhodesian Army officer named Lionel Dyke has been leading a collection of "pseudo-gangs" composed of soldiers of the Zimbabwean Army Sixth Brigade. At the direction of Zimbabwe CIO (Central Intelligence) Director-General Emmerson Munangawa in liaison with SNASP secret police, Dyke's units commit atrocities on civilians with the express purpose of blaming them on RENAMO, a technique used by FRELIMO when they fought the Portuguese.[99] Malawi intelligence has confirmed to the author (June, 1988) that the practice of FRELIMO soldiers disguising themselves as RENAMO guerrillas and committing atrocities upon civilian villagers is systematic and widespread.

Gersony's account is wholly at odds with almost all observers who have actually visited RENAMO territory, which Gersony was forbidden to do by the State Department. French journalist Eric Gérard, for example, after an extensive sojourn with RENAMO in early 1988, reported that RENAMO was "highly disciplined and drew on considerable local support." Gerard "rejected reports of rebel massacres against the population . . . if these charges were true the rebels would have lost all popular support and there would not be refugees flooding into their areas."[100]

The timing and context of the public release of the Gersony Report is disturbing. In early March of 1988, Afonso Dhlakama instructed Evo Fernandes to make the arrangements for him to visit West Germany, France, England, and the US. Evo traveled to South Africa where South African Military Intelligence (SAMI) gave him the money needed for Dhlakama's trip. SAMI did this on its own, as the South African Foreign Ministry was under enormous pressure by Crocker not to cooperate with or assist RENAMO in any way. By the first week of April, the schedule was set: Dhlakama was to arrive in Washington on April 22 for a series of press conferences, media (especially television) interviews, and meetings with various senators and congressmen. He would continue on to West Germany on April 26 to meet with Franz Josef Strauss and other West German officials, then continue on to Paris and London. For the American and European publics, it would be their first opportunity to see Dhlakama, to hear his and RENAMO's side of the story, to judge for themselves the goals and policies of the Mozambique resistance.

Dhlakama's precise schedule remained a closely guarded secret, for if

SNASP discovered it, they would, it was feared, make every effort to assassinate him. A week before Dhlakama's arrival in the United States, the head of the Mozambique Information Office in Washington, Tom Schaaf, who was coordinating the schedule, began to worry about the possibility of the State Department using some pretext to order Dhlakama's arrest and deportation to the Mozambican capital Maputo, a death sentence for Dhlakama. Schaaf persuaded Robert MacKenzie, executive director of Freedom Inc., an organization promoting democracy in the Third World, who had access to Crocker to test Crocker out. MacKenzie saw Crocker on Friday, April 15 and asked him how opposed would he be to a visit by the RENAMO leader to Washington. Startled, Crocker wouldn't answer. He was now alerted.

The next day, Saturday, April 16, Crocker asked to see South African Ambassador to the United States, Peter Koornhof. Crocker was, in Koornhof's words, "fuming, threatening, and very excited." Crocker said he knew Dhlakama was being helped by South Africa in coming to Washington, called this a "hostile act," and demanded to know Dhlakama's exact schedule. All this was news to Koornhof, who truthfully denied all knowledge.

On the evening of Sunday, April 17, the following day, Fernandes had a dinner meeting in Cascais, a Lisbon suburb, with two Mozambicans carrying credentials from FRELIMO leader Joaquim Chissano authorizing them to initiate negotiations with RENAMO. They were Alexandra Xavier Chagas and Macias Natividade, and in reality they were working for the Director of the D-13 (External Affairs) branch of SNASP, Joao Carlos Esteira. At 11:00 p.m., Fernandes left the restaurant with them and was never seen alive again. Apparently abducted to extract Dhlakama's schedule from him so a hit upon Dhlakama could be made, Evo's body was found four days later. There were five bullet holes in him, but an autopsy revealed he had been savagely beaten and tortured before he died. Almost every bone in his body had been fractured, while he was still alive. Dhlakama, hearing of Evo's disappearance, canceled his trip. The day after Fernandes' abduction, April 18, the State Department released the Gersony Report.

And even though the State Department will hold formal meetings with Oliver Tambo of the Soviet-supported African National Congress, and recognize as the legitimate government of Cambodia a coalition that includes the Khmer Rouge, it continues to refuse to have any contact with RENAMO whatsoever. Any questions former President Reagan raised as to why the United States is supporting a Soviet-Marxist regime against an anti-Soviet democratic insurgency were met with reassurances that the CIA has agents within the FRELIMO government with certain knowledge that the regime is just about to abandon Moscow and turn to the West at the first opportunity.

Nonetheless, the most pessimistic of independent observers view the current situation as a stalemate, with the Zimbabweans preventing a RENAMO victory as the Cubans prevent a UNITA victory in Angola; but the FRELIMO regime is far too weak to overcome the guerrillas (as is the MPLA in Angola). It has become clear on all accounts that victory for FRELIMO over Dhlakama's forces is totally unrealistic.

A principal obstacle to a RENAMO victory may be the belief on Dhlakama's part that a coup is imminent within the FRELIMO military that will overthrow Chissano and negotiate to form a transition government with RENAMO. This belief may be causing Dhlakama to hesitate to pursue an all-out military victory. One objection he gives, however, to an investment of Maputo is that without sufficient artillery and antiaircraft weapons, the masses of troops required for such an attack on the capital would be subject to devastating air and armor attacks.

It is my opinion that after a thorough analysis of the historical and current situation in Mozambique, one must conclude that the achievement of peace in Mozambique can only be done through a negotiated settlement between FRELIMO and RENAMO, with FRELIMO acceding to RENAMO's two principal demands, that a transition government be formed, and that internationally supervised elections be held and be freely contested by competing political parties. Surely if democracy should be attained by all South Africans it should also be obtained for Mozambicans.

It is often objected that RENAMO, if it came to power, has no capability or the trained personnel to govern the country, that the country would quickly fall into chaos and anarchy.[101] To this it must be riposted that the goal of RENAMO is not to govern the country but to establish, by armed force if necessary, a democratic framework through which the Mozambican people can choose their government. Further, much of the country has already fallen into anarchy. FRELIMO has already shown a murderous incompetence for governing far beyond anything RENAMO could achieve.

And lastly, it must be taken into account that while FRELIMO never established itself south of the Zambezi, RENAMO's accomplishment of coordinating and conducting an insurgency throughout a country twice the size of California, involving complex logistics and C3 (command, control, and communications) without a sanctuary, with little or no external support, without motorized transport, and under the most primitive conditions, is an organizational achievement that is a tribute to RENAMO's leadership and Afonso Dhlakama's capacity to lead and govern.

It must be recognized by RENAMO's opponents and critics, particularly those in the State Department, that RENAMO is a genuinely indigenous revolt not led by sophisticated politicians but mostly by rural people who simply want, and are willing to fight for, an end to Marxist tyranny, people who are not anybody's puppets—certainly not the "Boers," as they call the South Africans—but who are inspired by the values and ideals of the West, of democratic pluralism and individual rights. Surely, Western leaders and diplomats should cease treating them as pariahs and give them a sympathetic hearing.

At the time of this writing (November 1988), it is not known what the policy of the incoming Bush Administration will be towards Mozambique. There are preliminary indications, however, that it will be more balanced and neutral. Should Secretary of State Baker and his new assistant secretary for African affairs advocate an end to the war through sincere negotiation and democratization, rather than the war's continuation and a FRELIMO military victory as do their predecessors, peace may come at last to Mozambique.

## Notes

1. Due to the distortion of the Mercator projection, the type of world map with which most are familiar, the enormous size of Africa is ill-appreciated. You can fit the entire Soviet Union (8.6 million sq. mi.) and the entire continental United States (that is, without Alaska, 3.0 million sq. mi.) both into the 11.7 million sq. mi. of Africa. The coastline of Mozambique is 1,700 miles, as long as from Portland, Maine, to Miami, Florida.
2. The British internally self-governing colony of Southern Rhodesia (named after Cecil Rhodes in 1895) was part of a Federation with the British Protectorates of Northern Rhodesia and Nyasaland from 1953 until 1963, when Northern Rhodesia gained independence as Zambia and Nyasaland as Malawi. Dropping the "Southern," Rhodesia declared itself unilaterally independent in 1965. A black-majority government, led by Robert Mugabe, was elected in 1980, whereupon the country's name was changed to Zimbabwe, named after the ruins of a civilization that flourished in the area 1,000 years ago.
3. The British Protectorate of Nyasaland ('Nyasa' is a Chichewa word for 'lake'; part of the Great Rift Valley, Lake Nyasa, now called Lake Malawi, is the third largest lake in Africa) gained independence as the Republic of Malawi in 1963. Malawi derives its name from the Maravi, a Bantu people who came from the Congo some 600 years ago. It has been governed since independence by Dr. Hastings Kamuzu Banda, who received his medical degree in the United States in 1937.
4. German East Africa, or Tanganyika, was mandated to Britain after World War I, and received independence in 1961. In 1964, it formed a political union with Zanzibar, and was renamed as the United Republic of Tanzania. Led by Julius Nyerere until 1985, the country's president is Ali Hassan Mwinyi.

5. Biographical note, Eduardo Mondlane, *The Struggle for Mozambique* (London: Penguin, 1969).
6. Ibid.
7. F. X. Maier, *Revolution and Terrorism in Mozambique* (New York: American African Affairs Association, 1974), p. 12.
8. Author interview with ex-member of FRELIMO, Swaziland, Sept. 1983.
9. Ibid.
10. Ibid.
11. Ibid. As African scholar Thomas Henriksen puts it, these killings "arose from a jostling of power [due to] the progressive radicalization of FRELIMO." *Revolution and Counter-Revolution in Mozambique* (Westport, CT: Greenwood Press, 1983) p. 135.
12. Mondlane, pp. 196, 212.
13. Maier, *Revolution and Terrorism*, p. 11; Henriksen, *Revolution and Counter-Revolution*, p. 135. An investigation of the Tanzanian police claimed the bomb was assembled in Lourenco Marques by Portuguese intelligence (PIDE), but a thorough search of PIDE files for evidence of "crime of fascist oppression and colonialism" by the communist government of Portugal after the 1974 *coup d'etat* found no evidence for the assassination of Mondlane by PIDE. (Andre Thomashausen, "The National Resistance of Mozambique," *African Insight*, February, 1983, p. 125).
14. Testimony taken in Nairobi, Kenya, August, 1987; on file at the Freedom Research Foundation, La Jolla, California. Other FRELIMO members present corroborate Murrial, and believe the bomb was brought into Mondlane's office by Veronica Nammiva with the help of Chissano, head of security at the time. They also note that Janet Mondlane was crazed with jealousy over her husband's passionate affair with an American woman living in Tanzania named Betty King.
15. Maier, *Revolution and Terrorism*, p. 12.
16. I.e., FRELIMO never, throughout its insurgency, established a presence in the entire southern half of Mozambique.
17. David Rees, *Soviet Strategic Penetration of Africa* (London: Institute for the Sutdy of Conflict, 1976), p. 12.
18. David & Marina Ottaway, *Afrocommunism*, 2nd Ed. (New York: Holmes & Meir, 1986), pp. 75–76.
19. The capital of Mozambique, renamed from Lourenco Marques after independence. It is worth noting that the names of the major boulevards and plazas in the capital were renamed after Communist heroes: Karl Marx, V. I. Lenin, Ho Chi Mihn, Fidel Castro, and others.
20. Delegations and congratulatory messages were exchanged between Moscow and Maputo on the 10th anniversary of the Treaty of Friendship and Cooperation, which "enshrines our relations and strengthens in all fields (our) fraternal cooperation." (From the message sent by the FRELIMO Party Central Committee to the CPSU Central Committee, *Maputo Domestic Service*, 31 March 1987; translated in *FBIS*, Southern Africa, 1 April 1987, p. U6.
21. Background Notes: Mozambique (Washington, D.C.: United States Department of State, May 1985), p.4.
22. *Boletim da Republica*, Maputo, 29 July 1975.
23. J. Hanlon, *Mozambique: The Revolution Under Fire* (London, Zed Books, 1984), p. 56.
24. Ibid.

25. Background Notes: Mozambique, *US Department of State*, p. 5.
26. Author interview, Pretoria, South Africa, September, 1984.
27. See *Noticias de Lourenco Marques*, official communique of the Mozambique Ministry of Interior, 1 November 1975.
28. Testimony on file at the Freedom Research Foundation, La Jolla, California.
29. Act No. 7/74 issued by FRELIMO on 7 October 1974, specified that any public servant accused of "collaboration" could be summarily dismissed. See also, Hanlon, *Revolution Under Fire*, p. 58ff; and D. Joseph, "Zur Rechtsentwicklung in der Volksrepublik Mocambique," Staat und Recht (East Berlin), May, 1981, p. 443.
30. Interview of Jorge da Costa, National Director of Security (head of SNASP) for the FRELIMO government, who defected in 1982. *Scope* (Johannesburg), 11 February 1983, p. 32ff.
31. Testimony on file at the Freedom Research Foundation, La Jolla, California.
32. The following account of the origins of RENAMO is taken principally from the author's interviews of two sources, who are neither in touch with each other, nor are they aware the author knew the other, yet whose accounts tally to a remarkably detailed degree. One is Joao Marques, a white (Portuguese) Mozambican who was Orlando Christina's personal assistant from the inception of the Voice of Free Africa to Christina's death in 1983. He has been quite generous with translated sections of his manuscript, to be a book on RENAMO. The other is Robert MacKenzie, formerly a captain in the Rhodesian Special Air Service and major in the Second Reconnaissance Commando of the South African Defense Forces.
33. Christina was born 13 October 1928, in Lagos, Algarve, Portugal. As a law student in Lisbon, his political activities with the left-wing Democratic Unity Movement (MUD) put him under threat of arrest by PIDE, whereupon his mother sent him to join his father in Vila Cabral (now Lichinga), Niassa, in 1947. He was drafted into the Portuguese colonial army in 1950.
34. Often reputed to be extremely wealthy, Jardim was neither a millionaire nor owned significant property while he lived in Mozambique from 1953 to 1974. He was, rather, the managing director of an asbestos company in Beira. He did possess a family relationship with Salazar, whom he called his "godfather."
35. Christina was not, as sometimes claimed, the leader to GEs, nor of the GEPs, the special paratroop forces, formed after Christina broke with Campos. Another common accusation, originated by Samora Machel, was that Christina was a PIDE agent. Marques (see above, note 32), who is quite forthcoming about Christina's faults and was the closest person to him for several years, strongly denies this. In addition, a search of PIDE's files after 1974 provided no evidence of any connection.
36. The Zimbabwe African People's Union (ZAPU) was formed in 1961 by Joshua Nkomo, Ndabaningi Sithole, and Herbert Chitepo. ZAPU guerrillas, armed and trained with Soviet support, were called ZIPRA, the Zimbabwe People's Revolutionary Army. The Zimbabwe African National union (ZANU) was formed in 1963 by Sithole and Robert Mugabe in a break with Nkomo. ZANU guerrillas, armed and trained with Chinese support, were called ZANLA, Zimbabwe African National Liberation Army. Mugabe became undisputed leader of ZANU/ZANLA in 1975 and formed an alliance with Samora Machel. In March of 1976, Machel closed Mozambique's border to Rhodesia, particularly to all rail/road traffic and the oil pipeline from Beira, and ZANLA guerrillas began offensives in Rhodesia from sanctuary camps in

Tete, Manica, and Gaza provinces in Mozambique. ZIPRA guerrillas operated from Zambia and were allowed to infiltrate via Tete, but without much success, as they were Matabele, who are in southern Zimbabwe, while Mugabe and his men are Shona, of the tribe who inhabit the border with Tete.
37. See below, note 43.
38. In a September 1985 speech to followers in Chimoio, Machel claimed that FRELIMO had at one time "5,000 men fighting alongside ZANU [ZANLA] in Zimbabwe." FBIS-MEA, 10 September 1985, p. U1.
39. Colin Legum, "The MNR,"*CSIS Africa Notes*, no. 16, 15 July 1983. The article contains a very large number of errors and is seriously misinformed in numerous instances. Legum confuses Matsangaisse with Dhlakama as a quartermaster in the FRELIMO army after independence (p. 2); and vice versa in thinking both were born in Manica (Dhlakama is from Sofala) (p. 3); wrongly asserts Dhlakama was an officer in the Portuguese army (p. 2); and unquestioningly repeats FRELIMO's false charges against Dhlakama that he was "cashiered" for theft, when Dhlakama still possesses his safe-conduct pass issued in June 1977 for Machipanda (p. 2). The errors are too many to enumerate here, but for other examples, see below: notes 43-47, 49.
40. Interview with Robert MacKenzie, San Diego, September 1987. See also Barbara Cole, *The Elite: The Story of the Rhodesian Special Air Service* (Transkei, South Africa: Three Knights Publishing, 1984), p. 92. In the Cole book, MacKenzie is referred to as "McKenna."
41. It might be noted that FRELIMO existed and came to power because it was given sanctuary by Tanzania, and Mugabe's guerrillas survived and came to power because FRELIMO, which was also Tanzanian-backed, offered them safe havens, military support and even fighters to their cause. On the other hand, Mugabe's credentials as a Marxist-Leninist, for better or for worse, have nothing to do with his pre-1979 debt to FRELIMO, with his present role as the dominant warlord of the Beira Corridor or the controlling pro-government force in Mozambique played by the Zimbabwean military today.
42. For a vivid and detailed account, see Cole, *Special Air Service*, pp. 260-270.
43. Colin Legum mistakenly asserts RENAMO acted as guides for the Selous Scouts, who only operated inside Rhodesia. He also accuses RENAMO of confining their initial activities to terrorizing civilians, and "did not seek to engage the Mozambican army." ("The MNR," p. 2.) According to Captain MacKenzie, this is the opposite of the truth. Legum had evidently confused RENAMO with the *Flechas* of Oscar Cardoso (see p. 12). It is the *Flechas of Top Secret War*, not the "MNR" or RENAMO. Reid-Daly recounts that after independence from Portugal, Cardoso (incorrectly spelled by Daly as "Cardosa") and the remainder of his *Flechas* (most had been shot or imprisoned by FRELIMO), some 40-odd men, escaped into Rhodesia. An attempt was made to incorporate them into the Selous Scouts, but after a few months, due to a lack of numbers—there were less than three dozen men—and lack of morale, the unit was disbanded. (Lt. Col. Ron Reid-Daly, *Top Secret War,* Alberton, South Africa: Galago Publishing, 1982, pp. 160-165). CIO chief Ken Flower, in a self-serving book, implies a connection between the *Flechas and* RENAMO, but in no other way substantiates it; not one name of any RENAMO member or leader is ever mentioned. (K. Flower, *Serving Secretly* [Alberton, South Africa: Galago Publishing, 1987] pp. 300-302.)

44. One of MacKenzie's men was an eyewitness to Matsangaisse's death. Again, Legum's account has it backwards: he asserts Matsangaisse was killed in a FRELIMO attack on the RENAMO base in Gorongosa ("The MNR," p. 2). There was no such attack.
45. Legum asserts that "two South African Dakotas flew the MNR headquarters staff from their camp at Bindura, while . . . the staff of the MNR's Voice of Free Africa were picked up by a South African C-130 at Mutare," and that "both of these operations were witnessed by the British military team." ("The MNR," p. 2). Dhlakama and his staff were in Mozambique this entire time, while Christina, his staff, and remaining MNR personnel were at Odzi, not Bindura. Joao Marques, Christina's personal assistant, suspects that what the British team saw was the evacuation of the Selous Scouts from Murare and Muzorewa's Auxiliaries from Bindura.
46. Legum is incorrect in asserting that the "MNR headquarters" was established at Phalaborwa ("The MNR," p. 2). While Christina set up the radio there, Dhlakama and his staff remained inside Mozambique. Dhlakama, in fact, has remained inside Mozambique, except for a small number of brief and very occasional trips to Europe or South Africa continuously since September 1979.
47. Legum, "The MNR," p. 2. Both MacKenzie and Marques independently verify there was no such event.
48. Total RENAMO strength had grown to more than 900 men (A. E. Thomashausen, "Mozambique: 10 Years' Independence," lecture, South African Institute of International Relations, Johannesburg, 8 February 1986; text on file at the Freedom Research Foundation in La Jolla); the remainder were in camps in Manica and Sofala.
49. Legum's claim that Mushlangu (spelled "M'lhanga" by Legum) was backed by the Rhodesians is vehemently denied by MacKenzie, who reports that Mushlangu was strongly disliked by the SAS men, whereas they were quite supportive of "Alphonse," as they called Dhlakama. Marques reports that Legum's assertion that after the nonexistent "gun-battle," Mushlangu was "missing and presumed dead" is also false. Marques personally saw Mushlangu in Manica with RENAMO forces in 1982.
50. Most of the Rhodesian SAS men were soon to become dissatisfied with serving in the SADF. Within a year, only seven of the original 127 remained in the SADF "recce" commando. Although promoted from captain, Major MacKenzie left the SADF in July 1981 to serve in Transkei for three years with Ron Reid-Daly, former leader of the Selous Scouts.
51. After Jardim passed away in 1979, it is thought that Fernandes then secured financial backing for RENAMO from millionaire industrialist Manuel Bulhosa, one of the wealthiest men in Portugal whose oil refinery in Maputo and other investments had been nationalized by FRELIMO. Both Fernandes and Jorge Correira, the RENAMO press spokesman in Lisbon, worked for Bulhosa's publishing house, Bertrand. See *Africa Confidential* (London), 28 November 1984.
52. Of a population of over thirteen millions, about 12–15% are Christian, 25–30% Sunni Moslem, and the remainder native animists.
53. A "graduation exercise," said Major MacKenzie of his team's demolition course.

54. Sapa-Reuter, 8 January 1982.
55. *The Rand Daily Mail* (Johannesburg), 29 May 1982; *The Johannesburg Star*, 4 June 1982.
56. *The Financial Times* (Johannesburg), 1 July 1983.
57. *The Johannesburg Star*, 1 March 1983.
58. *Agence France Presse*, 4 April 1983.
59. *The Johannesburg Star*, 13 January 1984.
60. Pentagon intelligence source.
61. *The Johannesburg Star*, 21 January 1984.
62. *The Johannesburg Star*, 20 March 1984.
63. Author interview with Afonso Dhlakama, September 1984.
64. *The Johannesburg Star*, April 11 and April 12, 1984.
65. E.g., while upwards of 30% of Mozambique's population is Moslem, only one Moslem, Abdel Magid Osman, sits on FRELIMO's ruling Politburo as finance minister. The leader of the Moslem community in Portugal, Vali Mamede, had reportedly assisted in a reputed "secret airlift" of arms and supplies from Oman and Saudi Arabia via the Comoro Islands to RENAMO forces in Nampula and Cabo Delgado (*London Observer*, 2 December 1984).
66. *Time*, 30 January 1984.
67. *Agence France Presse*, 24 August 1984.
68. *New York Times*, 16 January 1985.
69. *Mozambique News Agency* (AIM), 5 July 1985.
70. Lt. Nikolai Vasovshokov and Sgt. Gregor Guessev. *Washington Times,* 12 September 1985.
71. *The Washington Times*, 24 January 1986.
72. *BBC World Service*, "Focus on Africa," 25 February 1986. See also, *The Washington Post*, "Capture of Camp Strengthens Insurgents in Mozambique," 2 March 1986.
73. See *Washington Times*, "Private Armies Protect Projects in Mozambique," 22 October 1986. Current Malawi intelligence estimates as of November 1988, are 5,000–8,000 Tanzanians and 12,000–15,000 Zimbabweans (the numbers fluctuate according to offensives), 3,000 Zambians, 1,000 Malawians, 1,500 Cubans, and 2,000 Soviets and East Germans. The FRELIMO army numbers around 30,000.
74. See *The Washington Times*, "Anti-Communist Guerrillas Gain Ground in Mozambique," 20 August 1987.
75. See the lengthy interview of Dhlakama in *Pretoria News*, 5 May 1986.
76. Evo Fernandes continued to be one of RENAMO'S principal representatives in Europe.
77. *Janes' Defence Weekly*, 12 July 1986, p. 20.
78. Ibid.
79. UNITA in Angola, the Mujahideen in Afghanistan, the contras in Nicaragua, the EPLF and TPLF in Ethiopia, the KPNLF and ANS in Cambodia, and the ELOL in Laos.
80. It should be noted that this strategy was not particularly successful because of FRELIMO's penchant for terrorist tactics among recalcitrant villagers and staging atrocities to be blamed upon the Portuguese. FRELIMO only marginally operated south of the Zambezi, and by early 1974 had been pushed out of Tete almost up to the northern Zambia border by the Rhodesian SAS.

81. Kindra Bryan, "My Three Month Trek Out of Africa," *Washington Post*, 23 August 1987. Ms. Bryan, a missionary, was captured by RENAMO forces on 13 May 1987, and walked through several hundred miles of RENAMO territory. She reported that "the soldiers seemed disciplined and well organized and seemed to have a good relationship with the villagers, who, in turn, seemed to recognize them as the government." Sharon Behn, "Behind Rebel Lines in Mozambique," *The Los Angeles Times*, 20 March 1987. Paul Moorcraft, "The Savage, Silent Civil War," *Army*, April 1987. Peter Godwin, "RENAMO's Hard Men Rule Over the Bush," *The London Sunday Times*, 5 April 1987. Godwin quotes a Zimbabwe Army sergeant in Zambezia province: "These RENAMO are good. They control the countryside. The local people support them." The author's own observations inside Mozambique in June of 1985 coincide with these reports.
82. *Janes' Defence Weekly,* 12 July 1986, p. 21.
83. See note 72.
84. *Janes' Defence Weekly,* 12 July 1986, p. 21.
85. Ibid.
86. Personal source in the intelligence community.
87. *Los Angeles Times*, 16 August 1987; US State Department figures.
88. See sources in note 81.
89. Personal communication.
90. See note 65.
91. Author interviews of Malawi villagers and Mozambican refugees on Malawi-Mozambique border in 1984, 1985, and 1986.
92. Personal source in Pentagon intelligence. Headline stories around the world repeated uncritically Maputo's accusation that RENAMO perpetrated the massacre, when eyewitnesses reported that the attackers were "wearing uniforms." If it is anything RENAMO guerrillas do not have it is uniforms.
93. Author interview with Afonso Dhlakama, September 1984.
94. Also consider the comment of an interviewer of Dhlakama for the BBC: Dhlakama "doesn't have [much of an] idea about PR work and projecting the image of his organization, which is probably why it has such a poor world image. Everybody has only heard about [RENAMO] from FRELIMO . . . [so] they come over as a disparate group of bandits. They [RENAMO] are in fact not like this at all." See *BBC World Service*, "Focus on Africa," November 1986. Dhlakama has taken an initial step to correct this problem by authorizing a Mozambique Information Office and a US representative, Dr. Luis Serapiao (professor of African Studies at Howard university), in Washington (address: P.O. Box 1995, Washington, D.C. 20013; phone 202/546-0023).
95. See note 90.
96. *Newsweek,* 24 August 1986, p. 29. Atrocities have been committed by both FRELIMO and RENAMO troops, as in most guerrilla wars. Mutilation of local FRELIMO officials has occurred. All RENAMO commanders are, however, under Dhlakama's strict orders not to mistreat local villagers.
97. R. Gersony, *Summary of Mozambican Refugee Accounts of Principally Conflict-Related Experiences in Mozambique* (Washington, D.C.: Dept. of State, April 1988).
98. *The Wall Street Journal,* 12 August 1987.
99. Author interview of ex-FRELIMO member Jose Francisco, December 1987.

100. *Africa Confidential* (Lisbon), April 1988, p. 3. See also note 81.
101. While this is a serious objection that must be dealt with, the objection that RENAMO should not be supported because if it won, FRELIMO would take to the bush and start the whole cycle of guerrilla warfare anew is not; one can only characterize it as frivolous. Such an attempt by a defeated and demoralized FRELIMO, with less morale than it possesses now, with no sanctuary (a shutdown of the Beira Corridor would quickly disabuse Mugabe, should he still retain power, of providing one), and a probable avalanche of popular hostility towards it (especially in rural areas) would be preposterous.

# 4

# Cambodia

*Justus van der Kroef*

### Background

Of all the anticommunist resistance movements described in this book, the one active in Cambodia today probably is the least effective. In terms of its composition, organizational structure and leadership, its tactics and long-term strategic objectives, the resistance and guerrilla movement directed against the present Hanoi-installed, Communist government of Cambodia (the People's Republic of Kampuchea — PRK) is beset by debilitating anomalies and mutually conflicting objectives. The involvement in various degrees, moreover, of the superpowers and of Cambodia's noncommunist regional neighbors in seeking a solution to the Cambodian problem has had the effect of further deepening the policy paradoxes and internal conflicts within the anti-government resistance movement. This, in turn, has benefitted the PRK regime, and particularly its Vietnamese ally and de facto suzerain, for whom the prolonged stalemate on the Cambodian question has consolidated their power.

Indeed, among the active, broadly publicized, anticommunist insurgent organizations in the world at present, the one in Cambodia offers the anomaly that its largest component faction, popularly known as the Khmer Rouge (Red Khmer or "Red Cambodians"), that is "Democratic Kampuchea" and its 40,000-man "National Army," is Communist as well, though it currently proclaims Marxism-Leninism to be inapplicable to its policies. The DK also is de-emphasizing the role of its onetime premier Pol Pot, as well as his direct involvement in the conduct of its "National Army's" current military operations. However other, non- or anticommunist factions in the Cambodian resistance, mindful that the DK's principal diplomatic supporter and armorer is People's China, not only remain skeptical of the DK's ideological basis and policy direction, but also have repeatedly complained in recent years that the DK's forces have been attacking their noncommunist resistance allies. On 7 May 1987, Prince Norodom Sihanouk, Cambodia's longtime (1941-1970) ruler, after denouncing from Pyongyang (one of his frequent residences) the attacks on his own forces by what he termed the "SS Khmer Rouge," declared in protest that he was stepping down for one year as the head of the "Coalition Government of Democratic Kampuchea" (CGDK), the organizational matrix of the present Cambodian resistance.[1]

The prince's action not only underscored the polarization existing between the component factions of the Cambodian resistance, but also left the movement without a transcendent head and a broadly recognized symbol of the Cambodian resistance in the eyes of the international community, raising more questions about the resistance's viability.

The anomalies of the Cambodian resistance have been accentuated also by a seeming unwillingness on the part of the superpowers and Cambodia's regional neighbors in Asia to break the diplomatic deadlock by undertaking new meaningful initiatives and, above all, as in the case of the USSR and People's China, by exerting leverage on their respective clients, the Socialist Republic of Vietnam (SRV) and its PRK dependent, and the DK faction of the CGDK respectively. In other words, as I will further argue, both super- and regional powers in Asia find the Cambodian conflict *at its present level of violence* quite advantageous to their own policy interests in the region. These powers, therefore, are little inclined to seek either a compromise leading to peace (even if a formula could be found in the near term) or mount a decisive military breakthrough. But, heavily dependent as the CGDK is on disparate foreign supporters, both Communist and noncommunist, this in turn tends to shackle the Cambodian resistance still more to its present state of division and disrepair.

## The Origins and Evolution of the Insurgencies

Decades before the establishment of the CGDK in 1982, Cambodia already had known armed anticommunist groups. Some of these groups, such as those in the fifties and sixties, were in a state of confrontation with both Communist guerrilla forces, like the Khmer Rouge, and the then prevailing "neutralist" Sihanouk government in Phnom Penh.

These groups emerged against a background of complex historical factors. Cambodian nationalism and resistance to French colonial rule, later spurred on by Japan's march through much of Asia during the Second World War, already had given impetus in 1940 to the formation of various "Independent Cambodia" (Khmer Issarak) committees. In these fledgling nationalist organizations, Marxists and anticommunists at first had found it possible to bury their ideological and long-term policy differences for the sake of the larger cause of Cambodian independence. But in the turbulent aftermath of the war, as French colonial power gradually declined, the Issarak movement under Vietnamese Communist influence veered ever more sharply to the Left, eventually providing much of the rank and file of the Communist "Khmer People's Revolutionary Party" (KPRP) founded in 1951. At the same time, separate Communist parties also emerged in Laos and Vietnam.[2]

Reaction to these developments was not late in coming. In 1956, Song Ngoc Thanh, a senior Cambodian nationalist, twice prime minister but political foe of Sihanouk (whose policies Song deemed vacillating and too subservient to Vietnam's Communist pressures) formed the first so-called *Khmer Serei* (Free Khmer) organization.[3] It was designed in the first instance to be a political fulcrum for Cambodia's middle class and other more conservative Cambodian elite elements. As Hanoi's ambitions in the later fifties to use Cambodian territory in its conquest of South Vietnam quickly led to ever further Vietnamese encroachments on Cambodian territory, giving new impetus as well to Cambodia's own Hanoi-trained Marxist revolutionaries, an embattled Sihanouk, with rapidly diminishing success, tried to preserve his country's independence. His evident attempts to curry favor with the Left, including a ministerial appointment for Khieu Samphan,[4] one of Pol Pot's collaborators, earned the prince the ever more solid opposition from conservative military, business, and landed elites. And far from stabilizing his country, Sihanouk's periodic accommodation of the Left only succeeded in further aggressively polarizing political currents.

The Khmer Serei, now often dubbed by Sihanouk the *Khmer Bleu* (Blue Khmer), supplied by the Thai military and the US Central Intelligence Agency, evolved into a full-blown, anticommunist guerrilla movement which at its peak in 1968 numbered some 8,000. Operating from base camps in South Vietnam and in Cambodia itself, and attacking the Hanoi-allied Cambodian Communist guerrillas first named Khmer Rouges by Sihanouk, the Khmer Serei units under US Special Forces' direction, recruited their followers from dissidents within Sihanouk's own 35,000-man, largely ineffectual army (Force Armée Royale Khmer), as well as from ethnic Cambodians living in Thailand and South Vietnam. Khmer Serei units were central to the coup by Lon Nol which in March 1970 overthrew the regime of Sihanouk. The anticommunist coup came after it had become apparent that the prince was having no success in persuading either Moscow or Beijing to mitigate Hanoi's steady encroachments on Cambodian territory, provoking much-debated US intervention, as it strove to conquer South Vietnam and contain the Khmer Rouges (more properly at this time, the guerrilla forces of the Kampuchean Communist party, or the "Revolutionary Army of Kampuchea").[5]

Whatever one's judgment of the historic role of the Khmer Serei, and of Lon Nol's avowedly anticommunist "Khmer Republic" and the circumstances of its collapse in 1975, there is little doubt that both reflected a significant, indigenous, anticommunist orientation in Cambodian politics and culture. The well-known, because much-publicized, horrors of the subsequent *Democratic Kampuchea* (DK) regime that took over from Lon Nol in 1975, and of the policies of onctime DK premier Pol Pot, therefore did not spawn anticommunist opinion or movements in Cambodia, but merely added another bloody dimension to an already existing Cambodian ideological power struggle. From the very beginning Hanoi played a dominant role in that struggle, shaping the whole Indochinese, including Cambodian and Laotian, Communist movement. As early as October 1959, Son Ngoc Thanh, in his Manifesto of the Khmer Serei Movement, had charged Sihanouk with allowing the "Communization" of Cambodia, calling specific attention to those from various social strata in Cambodia, from "high school and normal school students" to "porters and dockers," who "have gone over to North Vietnam in order to join the Khmer Communist Army" being trained there.[6] The time was to come when Sihanouk himself, despite his efforts at collaborating with leading Cambodian Communists, both before and after the fall of the Lon Nol regime, found himself under arrest within weeks after the 5 January 1976 proclamation of Pol Pot's new "Democratic Kampuchea."

During the DK's brief three-year existence, both a polarization within the Left and a realignment of the struggle between Left and Right was to take place, both of which shaped the Cambodian resistance today. There were boundary disputes and ever-sharper armed clashes between Communist Cambodian and Vietnamese units and mutual charges of border violations: on 7 January 1978 the DK radio in Phnom Penh claimed that more than 29,000 Vietnamese troops had been killed in battle with the DK's National Army since September 1977, but that Hanoi still was unlawfully encroaching upon some 400 square miles of DK national territory. As the horrifying brutalities of Pol Pot's social and economic reform policies became known abroad, the evidently explicit rejection by Pol Pot and by other central leaders of the Kampuchean Communist party of Hanoi's historic guidance in Indochinese communism and of Hanoi's self-assumed role as the leader of the three Indochinese states provided the impetus for Vietnam's invasion in force of Cambodia. It also led to the overthrow of the DK regime during the closing weeks of December 1978 and the first week of 1979.[7]

Meanwhile, tens of thousands of Cambodian refugees, among them diehard loyalists of Lon Nol's Khmer Republic, as well as followers of Sihanouk, began swarming to safety near or across the Thai-Cambodian border in the wake of the DK victory. They set the stage for the emergence of anticommunist resistance organizations. Thai military commanders at the border, reportedly joined by elements of the US Central Intelligence Agency, began rebuilding a new Khmer Serei movement among the human flotsam of the refugee border camps. Development of such a new Khmer Serei was given an additional boost by some army circles in Bangkok and by US technical military personnel in Thailand, who perceived the border-based Khmer Serei as offering the possibility of developing a *human wall* of anticommunist Cambodians, drawn from the steadily growing refugee camp population. It was believed that neither the DK, nor later its successor regime, the Hanoi-installed government of the "Kampuchean United Front for National Salvation" (KNUFNS), would feel free to attack such a human wall with any ease, particularly as the refugees were an object of growing international humanitarian concern amidst the general outcry over the horrors of the Pol Pot era. Thus it came to be believed in some Bangkok army circles that there also would be an implicit strengthening of the national security interests of Thailand — Southeast Asia's new "frontline state" — in what was now generally designated "the Third Indochina War."

Shortly the battle lines of Cambodia's present civil war came to be drawn. As some 180,000 Vietnamese troops, additional hundreds of Vietnamese party cadres, and eventually thousands of Vietnamese farmers ensconced themselves in the new "People's Republic of Kampuchea" (PRK), remnants of the DK's "National Army," supplied by People's China with the connivance of Thai military and business circles, and initially still led by Pol Pot as military commander, almost at once began launching a new "people's war." Vietnamese military encampments in Cambodia and supply lines of the nascent "Khmer People's Republic Armed Forces" (KPRAF), the PRK's fighting arm, quickly became targets of DK guerrilla attacks.[8]

The prospect apparent in the first half of 1979 that the indigenous Cambodian resistance to Vietnamese expansion threatened to become primarily a struggle between "Left and Left" (i.e. between the Beijing-supplied DK remnant and the Hanoi- and Moscow-backed PRK) spurred non- and anticommunist Cambodian political leaders into exile, and their representatives and followers into the refugee camps. It also spurred alarmed members of ASEAN (Association of Southeast Asian Nations) to formulate plans for a *third alternative* political strategy in Cambodia. This strategy came to mean first of all the creation of a firm, new, organizational matrix for avowedly non- or anticommunist Cambodian resistance fighters, a matrix far more disciplined and structured than the floating bands of Khmer Serei in the chaotic border refugee nation. Second, it meant persistent mobilization of international support, e.g. in the United Nations, for such a Cambodian resistance, and formal recognition of it as a countergovernment by sympathetic and concerned countries. Implicit in such a third alternative strategy would be winning world support for a new political arrangement in Cambodia, acceptable first of all to the Cambodian people themselves and secondly to Cambodia's neighbors, Communist and noncommunist. In short, a third alternative resistance organization, if militarily and politically viable, would, it was believed, be able to exert sufficient leverage on all sides in the dispute to move toward compromise.

Those Cambodians and others seeking realization of some or all of these objectives were to travel a rocky road, however. For one thing, the jealousies and divisions among the major non- or anticommunist Cambodian political leaders in exile (a condition that unhappily in short order also manifested itself among the refugee groups in the Thai-Cambodian border camps) initially seemed to doom the third alternative approach from the start. For the "new Khmer Serei" there remained the hard reality that as of 1979, the largest (about 40,000), reasonably well-organized and best-equipped force fighting the Vietnamese occupier and its PRK client regime in Phom Penh was the DK and its odious leader Pol Pot, well placed in mountain range strongholds in southwestern Cambodia and in more shifting guerrilla camps along the Thai-Cambodian border. To veteran anticommunist Cambodian political figures, and to foes of Sihanouk's many attempts to find an accommodation with the Khmer Rouge and the KCP during the sixties, any alliance now, either with the DK or with Sihanouk, seemed out of the question.

On 9 October 1979 Son Sann, standing among his followers in a refugee camp just inside Cambodia, announced the formation of the first third alternative organization, the "Khmer People's National Liberation Front" (KPNLF). The KPNLF was designed to be both a political and military organization. But for some time its military capacity hardly need have concerned the Vietnamese. Numbering at its foundation perhaps no more than 2,000 or so (usually persons of some education with little or no military experience who had held minor bureaucratic or professional positions in the Cambodia of Sihanouk in the sixties, or later, in Lon Nol's "Khmer Republic," as well as a sprinkling of former Lon Nol military) the KPNLF quickly gained enduring logistical support from senior

Thai military commanders and Western intelligence agencies. But efforts to bring the crusty, old (then seventy-one), Son Sann into an alliance with Sihanouk at first proved as unavailing as overtures by Pol Pot's DK colleague, Khieu Samphan, to forge links with the prince.

Both the US and People's China, from the beginning, were directly involved in creating such a closer alliance between the principal Cambodian opposition figures. Beijing, for example, where Sihanouk periodically has found a residence and considerable personal and family assistance over the years, persuaded him to hold a futile meeting with Samphan in Pyongyang in early February 1981 to explore an alliance. Less than a year before, in early March 1980, the US already had sought to promote the cause of Son Sann, inviting him to Washington for extended but equally inconclusive unity discussions with the prince.

For both China and the US there were growing new strategic concerns over the Cambodian issue. As with the passing months the whole concept of a viable Cambodian resistance movement seemed to be fading because of the disunity among principal Cambodian factional leaders, both the SRV and PRK became emboldened to denounce ever more vociferously the threat posed by large numbers of hostile refugees—indeed an emerging refugee nation of more than a quarter million people—along the Thai border. Charges that the refugee camps, including those inside Thai territory, had become recruiting and operational staging grounds for the anti-Vietnamese Cambodian resistance, and that Bangkok was aiding resistance leaders, henceforth were to be Hanoi's diplomatic stock-in-trade.[9] This, coupled to gradually increased armed border clashes between Thai and Vietnamese military as a result of disputes over the exact location of the frontier between the two countries, had the result that the idea of the possible advantages of a protective human wall of border camps rapidly lost support in Bangkok strategic circles and among Bangkok's allies in the US as well.

The danger that the Third Indochina War might spill over into Thailand, setting the stage for renewed Chinese intervention, and also drawing the US into another Southeast Asian land war, all gave new impetus to the proposition that the Cambodian conflict, and the organization of a strong Cambodian resistance, should be a matter of primary concern for the Cambodians themselves.

Yet it was external pressure that ultimately provided the breakthrough in the unification of Cambodian resistance factions. That pressure came particularly from the ASEAN countries, where there was a mounting concern over Beijing's ability, shown at recent international meetings on the Cambodian question, to protect the interest of its DK client—indeed to the point of seemingly getting the DK accepted as the only legitimate alternative to the Hanoi-backed PRK.[10] After the above-noted failure of the Sihanouk-Samphan meeting in Pyongyang in February 1981, ASEAN members with the strong, quiet backing of the US redoubled their efforts to bring the DK, Son Sann's KPNLF, and Prince Norodom Sihanouk and his various organizations into a formal alliance. Between an ASEAN-arranged conference held in Singapore in early September 1981, among the three persistently contentious Cambodian leaders, and the latter's ultimate acceptance of a "coalition government" at yet another conference in Kuala Lumpur on 22 June 1982, there were threats by several ASEAN countries that they would withdraw their support for the DK at the United Nations.[11]

The UN was critical of the hopes of the Cambodian resistance, thanks to annual, ASEAN-sponsored and promoted resolutions in the UN General Assembly that continued to legitimize the DK as the lawful occupant of Cambodia's seat. Through this acceptance — despite the odious memory of the Pol Pot regime — major powers, including the US, felt justified in maintaining diplomatic recognition and, in some cases, in providing humanitarian or other assistance to the DK regime as well. Beijing, too on occasion had exerted its influence on Sihanouk and his followers (similarly the recipients of considerable Chinese largesse over the years) in order to ease their objections to joining Samphan and the DK. However, the tugging and pulling among the three factions in the Cambodian resistance coalition left their regional supporters under no illusion. The Third Alternative was not turning into a "Third Force," as Malaysia's Foreign Minister Ghazali Shafie already had put it in December 1981, but into a "Third Farce."[12]

The 22 June 1982 Kuala Lumpur declaration created a "Coalition Government of Democratic Kampuchea" (CGDK), an entity subsequently recognized with overwhelming majorities among the members of the UN General Assembly in annual Assembly seating votes as the legitimate successor to the DK in that international body and its ancillary organizations. Sihanouk became president of the CGDK, and Son Sann premier. The DK's president and premier (after Pol Pot's 1979 resignation), Khieu Samphan, became CGDK vice president "in charge of Foreign Affairs," a potentially pivotal position which Samphan thus far has chosen to fulfill with quiet, almost reclusive discretion. Each of the three CGDK leaders retains full authority over his respective organizations, which, over time, have continued to be fully autonomous.

In the absence of common CGDK policy setting or deliberative bodies, or any attempt on the part of the three main CGDK leaders over the years to refine a common program, the whole Cambodian resistance movement has suffered. It is perhaps best to characterize the CGDK as a loose federation, presumably united by the common policy objective of (1) getting the Vietnamese out of Cambodia, in the first instance by means of a commonly accepted political settlement, rather than through primary reliance on the use of force, although "people's war" as a tactic to achieve a Vietnamese withdrawal has been viewed generally as permissible, and (2) establishment of a new Cambodian government acceptable to the community of nations. The text of the Kuala Lumpur agreement forming the CGDK is woefully short on the specifics of policy implementation. It speaks vaguely about an "eventual modification" of the CGDK structure, presumably through democratic means. But the agreement particularly and repeatedly stresses the autonomy and "freedom of action" of the coalition partners and even notes that in the event of an "impasse" among the parties, "Democratic Kampuchea" will have the right "to resume its activities as the sole legal and legitimate state of Kampuchea" and as a member of the UN.[13]

Clearly, each of the three wary coalition partners came to the CGDK with its own political-ideological antecedents. These, for the sake of reaching the above-cited policy objectives, often have been muffled or even declared officially suspended. Thus, the KCP, once it came to power in 1975, displayed through the institutions and policies of the DK in the Pol Pot era (1976–79) a distinctive ideological character, made up of a Robespierrist or radical Rousseauism in its social and reform policies and a terror-filled Stalinist application of Leninist concepts of state and governance.[14] This ideological mélange, which led to vast suffering and death through forced labor, malnutrition, neglect, and mass executions, was never wholly accepted by all KCP cadres in the DK. With the Vietnamese invasion in force in December 1978, and the advent of the PRK, it increasingly came to be de-emphasized if not repudiated de facto by the new leaders of the DK, including Khieu Samphan, presently heading the DK guerrilla countergovernment movement in Cambodia. In addition, in recent years, the DK has sought periodically to refurbish its image and to make itself appear more ideologically malleable and acceptable to potential noncommunist allies. As early as November 1980, for example, the DK's own foreign minister, Ieng Sary, during a Jakarta interview, even asserted that "we are prepared to hand over power to anyone capable of driving the Vietnamese out of Kampuchea," and he indicated that Sihanouk or even Son Sann would be an acceptable leader.[15]

The time was soon to come when the DK's president (presidium chairman) Khieu Samphan would announce a much harder line, according to which, in effect, any potential ally would be required to submerge its interests in those of the DK.[16] In fact, even the preservation of the name "Democratic Kampuchea" in the new, post-Kuala Lumpur coalition government has been seen by some observers as one of those symbols so critically important to the DK as it agreed ultimately to join a common Cambodian resistance front.

But the actual importance of such symbols to the DK may well be doubted. In strict Leninist fashion it is and has been the preservation and operational independence of the DK's organizational weapon—its party cadre power base and its National Army—that have been far more important to Pol Pot and his colleagues. Indeed, in order to maintain that power base, not least through continued (if grumbling) acceptance of it as an organization and as a needed element in the Cambodian resistance among coalition partners and foreign supporters in ASEAN and the West, Pol Pot's colleagues even have been prepared to repudiate their formal Communist affiliation and demote Pol Pot himself. Thus, on 1 December 1981, the DK's China based-radio transmitter, "The Voice of Democratic Kampuchea," (VODK) announced that the KCP had dissolved itself "permanently."[17] Subsequent VODK broadcasts declared that the Communist ideology was not pertinent to Cambodia's current liberation struggle against the Vietnamese occupation forces. However, these same broadcasts always were quick to note that the DK *government* and National Army would continue to carry out their "historic mission" to drive out the Vietnamese enemy.[18]

As for Pol Pot, though he had relinquished the DK premiership to Samphan on 17 December 1979, at a special KCP congress, he remained at first commander-in-chief of the DK's 40,000-man National Army. His continued prominence drew fire from both anticommunist supporters of the Cambodian resistance coalition, including the US, and from Vietnam and its PRK client. The latter two not only found it easy to dismiss the whole Cambodian resistance as consisting of mere "Pol Potists" who had long since been rejected by the Cambodian people, but also to devalue the cascade of political compromise formulas put forth by ASEAN and other powers designed to end the conflict. To meet this criticism and also to identify a scapegoat for the severe DK military losses in Vietnamese dry season military offensives in 1984–1985, the DK's radio announced that on 24 August 1985 Pol Pot had stepped down as the Khmer Rouges's commander, and that presently he only would hold the post of "Director of the Higher Institute of National Defense."[19]

It seems as doubtful that Pol Pot's real power in DK affairs has been clipped significantly by his formal departure as DK military commander as that his various, much publicized, but somehow undefined illnesses are slowing him down. It is true, however, that in the past three years a serious factional split has been developing among second-echelon DK leaders over the question of submerging the DK (for the time being!) in a better organized, more closely coordinated, general Cambodian resistance movement, presumably headed by Sihanouk or by Sihanouk's son, Prince Norodom Rannaridh, which could win greater international respect. Ta Mok, staff chief of the National Army, has supported Pol Pot in a hardline, uncompromising stance. Longtime KCP Politburo member Son Sen, who in 1985 succeeded Pol Pot as the National Army's Commander, and onetime DK Foreign Minister Ieng Sary, repeatedly have favored a more flexible, accommodationist approach.[20]

DK President Khieu Samphan sides now with one, then with the other faction. Samphan, like the DK's main supporter (and to its critics the real master of the DK, namely People's China), has made numerous gestures of closer cooperation with the rest of the Cambodian resistance—by supplying them weapons, agreeing to broadbased political discussions among the PRK and all CGDK factions on an equal footing, even declaring a readiness to accept a "liberal capitalist economy and parliamentary political system" in a new, post-settlement Cambodia.[21] But the DK's (and People's China's) real, unrelenting commitment is to the preservation of an independent, armed, DK political organization, capable of shaping whatever settlement process ultimately is accepted among Cambodians. It is Ta Mok who, according to Sihanouk, has been the principal obstacle to better relations between the National Army and the prince's own followers. Indeed, according to Sihanouk, "Ta Mok can't bear to see Sihanouk's face" even on the badges worn by the prince's own guerrilla fighters.[22]

Division and personality clashes also have sapped the strength of the KPNLF. I might emphasize first that in its way, the KPNLF is ideologically as doctrinaire as the DK's hardliners. Son Sann's followers are avowed anticommunists who reject not only the Communist antecedents of the DK, but also whatever quondam Communist tenets to which the DK still may and (considering the importance of its Chinese ally to the DK's survival) in fact still must be subscribing. But equally odious to the crusty septuagenarian Sann is Sihanouk and his, for want of a better term, political pragmatism. That pragmatism, it will be recalled, even allowed for having Khieu Samphan and other Communists from time to time in the prince's cabinet. To Sann, Sihanouk's open collaboration with the KCP in the early seventies, and, subsequently, the prince's international campaign in November 1975 to win support for the DK forever disqualify him as participant, let alone leader of an anticommunist crusade. Just as the question of collaborating more closely with the prince divides Khmer Rouge leaders, so it led toward the close in 1985 and all through 1986 of seriously debilitating confrontations between younger KPNLF "pragmatists," among them KPNLF Commander in Chief Sak

Suthsakan and Staff Chief Dien Del, on the one hand, and Son Sann and his principal supporter, senior guerrilla commander Chea Chhut, on the other.[23]

Sann's unwillingness to accord greater prominence to a distinctive, nonmilitary, political arm within the KPNLF, which would be able to compete with the political cadre structures of the other Cambodian coalition partners on the post-settlement Cambodian scene earned him, additionally, the opposition of Hing Kunthon and Abdul Gaffaer Peang. The latter, as leaders of the KPNLF's "civilian affairs" section, had been attempting to develop just such a political arm for the KPNLF. And, as in the case of Pol Pot's resignation as DK "National Army" commander, so too the rift in the KPNLF involved as well dissatisfaction within the military rank and file over Son Sann's tactics, and particularly over the losses which the KPNLF, like the Khmer Rouges, sustained during the Vietnam dry season offensives in 1984–1985.

The dispute within the KPNLF led to the virtual suspension of its already limited military operations. The "Joint Military Command" between the KPNLF and the Sihanoukist units, which had coordinated some small-scale guerrilla probes between these two noncommunist coalition partners collapsed. Increasing concern over the KPNLF's future, accompanied by quiet fence-mending efforts, was voiced in US congressional and administration circles, as well as among the Thai military command. Meanwhile, Sam kept expelling his KPNLF opponents, but in January 1986 he himself was barred by his rivals from entering KPNLF camps at the Thai-Cambodian border.[24] KPNLF supporters residing in France — among the group's wealthiest contributors — also exerted pressure on Sann, accusing him of having become increasingly autocratic and having surrounded himself with "fawning aides."[25]

Though Sihanouk affirmed that Son Sann would remain as CGDK premier, and the DK's radio in mid-February 1986 appeared to back Son Sann's side in the dispute, the KPNLF rift dismayed the coalition.[26] Already at the close of January 1986, a KPNLF spokesman bravely declared that the rift within the organization was being healed, that Son Sann would stay on as KPNLF president, and that there would also be significant changes among KPNLF military commanders. Whatever the compromise that was being effected, in March 1987 Son Sann loyalists in the KPNLF issued another communique saying that the split had been ended after Son Sann reportedly had a cordial meeting with Sak Sutsakhan at the so-called Site-2 Cambodian refugee camp near the Thai-Cambodian border.[27] There have been no similar pronouncements by various other KPNLF factional leaders, however, some of whom, like Abdul Gaffaer Peang, remain expelled from the organization. It is apparent that the rift within the KPNLF continues to affect the organization's viability, also among its guerrilla fighters rank and file. In the first half of 1987, a large number of KPNLF soldiers reportedly abandoned the organization and joined Sihanouk's growing *Armeé Nationale Sihanoukiste* (ANS) instead, though small KPNLF patrols and guerrilla units have continued their periodic forays inside Cambodia. By May 1987, KPNLF field headquarters, in a communique received in Bangkok, declared that its armed combat force was down to only 8,000, from a high of over 20,000 soldiers only a few months earlier.[28]

The Cambodian resistance's third and smallest coalition partner, the forces of Prince Sihanouk, appeared in mid-1987 to be rising in popularity and strength, for reasons I will note. As was his wont in the past, Sihanouk today presides over an array of small heterogeneous support groups, including the 5,000-man ANS, of which his son Rannaridh now is the operational commander. Before the 22 June 1982 Kuala Lumpur conference and the birth of the CGDK, the prince's major support groups had been the so-called Moulinaka (an acronym for *Mouvement de Liberation Nationale du Kampuchea*) founded in 1979 and the FUNCINPEC (an acronym from the French name for "National Union Front for an Independent, Neutral, Peaceful and Cooperative Cambodia").

The latter group first emerged in 1977 in Paris and Beijing, after Sihanouk's falling out with the DK leaders whom he previously had supported. Initially, and until pro-Sihanouk refugees in Thailand and at the Cambodian border began to provide it with some organizational substance, FUNCINPEC seemed to consist more of the aspirations of Sihanouk's immediate circle, including his expatriate Cambodian following, to revive the Khmer United National Front (FUNK). The latter had been the main Sihanoukist organization after the prince's 1970 deposition by Lon Nol. And although FUNK also had its own independent fighting arm, the military side at the time had been left primarily to the Khmer Rouges. Sihanouk seemed to see his anti-Lon Nol resistance role at the time more as that of a political unifier in a common struggle.

Initially, after the Vietnamese capture of Phnom Penh in January 1979, Sihanouk conceived of his new resistance task in similar terms — a tactic which early on had led to criticism by hardline anticommunists like Son Sann and to the formation of the KPNLF. In response, Sihanouk, by 1981, had begun to develop his ANS force. But even today, at a strength of about 5,000, it is the smallest of the three fighting arms in the CGDK, despite a recent influx of disgruntled KPNLF followers. As late as September 1985, just before the division within the KPNLF leadership broke fully into the open, Sihanouk was still quoted as saying that he would like to merge his own movement with the KPNLF, and that the latter's commanders would be given the top posts in the fused organization.²⁹ Sihanouk added, however, that he recognized that there were still obstacles to such a merger. And, as has been noted, within the KPNLF itself there are those who regard close collaboration with the prince as anathema.

Sihanouk's evident reluctance over the years to develop a large, strong, armed resistance group of his own (though he has the funds and popularity to do so) probably has stemmed from a belief that the DK would never cease to put primary logistical emphasis on building and maintaining the strength of its own organizational weapon, the National Army, and (its now covert) party cadre structure, and neither would the DK's main armorer, People's China. Therefore, in Sihanouk's calculation despite periodic Khmer Rouge gestures of rapprochement toward her other coalition partners, the DK, with or without Pol Pot, means to be in a commanding condition to shape any future Cambodian settlement. From the prince's perspective one either can contest the DK, as the KPNLF under Son Sann essentially had been doing, despite the CGDK alliance, or one can, in the manner of the prince's own long political career, be pragmatic and attempt to find agreement with various changing facades and formulas of compromise, such as the CGDK itself, all directed toward one goal and the prince's own unswerving objective: the survival of Cambodia, its people and culture, and with as much peace and independence as circumstances will allow.

Though younger Cambodians who have lived through the Pol Pot and the current PRK era reportedly have become more skeptical toward him, Sihanouk, by all accounts today, remains the most popular and the most broadly acceptable alternative political figure (or figurehead) in the country. The DK and Beijing know this as do the Vietnamese and their PRK ally. Hence these Sihanoukist tactics, resting as they do primarily on adroit political footwork and on the aura of a historic and symbolic prestige require that the prince and his following first of all constitute no military or organizational threat to any other Cambodian resistance partner, and also that he and his organization, despite avowals of closer cooperation, know how and when to keep their distance and maintain their own organizational independence.

All this to be sure has meant the pragmatic gyrations which, for one, Son Sann and his KPNLF supporters find unacceptable. The point should be made, however that Sihanouk, as in the past, appears to be under little or no illusion about his Communist allies, and that he has attempted to use them as much as they have sought to use him. The most recent course of Sihanouk's relations with the DK exemplifies this. Having been appointed by his father to the position of commander-in-chief of the ANS in early February 1986, Prince Norodom Rannaridh already felt confident to declare in late September of that year, in a press interview, that though there had been clashes between the Khmer Rouges and Sihanoukist forces in the recent past, and that on the battlefield "cooperation has often been lacking," matters had now changed for the better. Since the beginning of 1986, in fact, according to Rannaridh, there had been "genuine" collaboration "in all fields." Indeed, the DK's National Army and Sihanouk's ANS on 28 March 1986 even "jointly conducted a major operation" against Battambang city, deep inside Cambodia. ANS relations with the Khmer Rouge had changed, Rannaridh said, because "they have realized they need us."[30]

The trouble with this sort of talk is that Sihanouk and the ANS appear to find it useful to accentuate or deflate their difficulties with the DK, depending on their political objectives, and sometimes they meet each other coming and going on the same subject of DK cooperation within a matter of days. Were Rannaridh's reassuring words in September 1986 spoken while he was mindful of the possibility of a new, forthcoming, Vietnamese dry-season military offensive against the refugee border camps and resistance strongholds, necessitating the latter's more coordinated defense? Perhaps, but his words still rang a little strangely. Only four weeks before Rannaridh had referred to the emergence since the beginning of 1986 of "genuine" ANS-Khmer Rouge collaboration, his father, in another press interview on the Thai border, had sharply accused the Khmer Rouges once again of attacking and killing their resistance allies in Cambodia. Sihanouk added on this occasion that, despite his own recent statements that the three Cambodian resistance factions were unified and cooperating, nevertheless there was "bloodshed" between the Khmer Rouge and its two noncommunist coalition partners.[31] These recent attacks, Sihanouk said, with characteristic use of the graphic phrase, showed that the Khmer Rouges are still "monsters."

Meanwhile other resistance leaders, commenting also on the continuing rifts within the CGDK, focussed on what was seen as the principal stumbling block in any future negotiations among the parties designed to reach a comprehensive Cambodian settlement, and that is the DK leadership's unwillingness to give up or even scale down their organizational weapon, particularly their National Army. Amidst the constant search during 1986–1987 among ASEAN, Hanoi and its allies, and European and Asian powers for new compromise formulas to settle the Cambodian problem,[32] the question of how to neutralize the DK's military power in a new post-settlement Cambodia emerged as the key issue, not only for the two noncommunist factions of the resistance but obviously for the Vietnamese occupiers of Cambodia and their PRK client government as well, according to these CGDK resistance sources.[33]

Even as his ANS commander and son Rannaridh all during 1987 was going ahead to forge new cooperative military ventures with the Khmer Rouges and the KPNLF, Sihanouk found it useful to belabor the alleged perfidy of his DK ally. This culminated in his 7 May 1987 announcement from Pyongyang that he was leaving the CGDK presidency for one year. In a telegram to his ASEAN supporters the prince declared that the Khmer Rouges not only had failed to keep their promise not to attack the ANS but also, as he said he had recently learned "with sorrow," there had been grave violations of human rights by the Khmer Rouges in the border refugee camps under their control.[34]

It is difficult to credit this explanation as the real reason for his temporary withdrawal as CGDK leader. Earlier Rannaridh had informed his father that Khmer Rouge forces, as so often in the past, had attacked the ANS again. But this information appears to have been part of a routine series of ANS operational reports, and it cannot now be determined if the attack had been a recent isolated incident; certainly Rannaridh himself did not take the occasion then to criticize the Khmer Rouges. Moreover, a Sihanoukist spokesman in Bangkok, at the time of the prince's withdrawal announcement, declared that although the Khmer Rouge had repeatedly attacked ANS units in previous months, on 22 April 1987, both forces jointly had attacked a Vietnamese military installation inside Cambodia, killing thirty-eight Vietnamese soldiers. Sihanouk, however, soon expatiated on the reasons for his resignation. He charged that some "sponsors" of the CGDK were deliberating aiding the DK at the expense of his own movement. It was not clear what countries or parties he meant by the term sponsors (informed analyses included People's China, the US and ASEAN). But, Sihanouk charged, their "secret services" were attempting to denigrate his credibility. He added that "secret" diplomatic maneuvres, which also involved the USSR, were being undertaken by these foreign powers with the connivance of the PRK and its Hanoi backers. Their aim was to establish a new regime in Phnom Penh, a modified Khmer Rouge version presumably acceptable to the Vietnamese. Such a regime could bring the Cambodian conflict to an end. The new regime already was being dubbed the *Khmer Rose* (Pink Khmer) in some quarters. Sihanouk's own part in any such future compromise regime "would be honorary at best." Some other observers appeared to support Sihanouk in these contentions also.[35]

Whether or not such a hidden Khmer Rose initiative was being undertaken then or later, and whether it was more likely to be successful than its many predecessors, is perhaps of much less significance than that Prince Sihanouk had come to feel, once again, the need for new diplomatic action of his own. Such action, as before, required that he put distance between himself and his DK ally. In this the ASEAN foreign ministers also obliged the prince: at their Singapore meeting the ministers decided to send a letter to DK leader Khieu Samphan rebuking the Khmer Rouges for their attacks on Sihanouk forces. Already in February 1987 emissaries of UN Secretary General Javier Pérez de Cuellar, possibly with the quiet backing of the US and People's China, had begun to develop a new "four-point proposal," calling for the partial withdrawal of Vietnamese forces, the formation of a new national coalition regime under Sihanouk, followed by a full withdrawal of Vietnamese forces, and, finally, the holding of general and free elections in Cambodia.[36] Even before the proposal was formally discussed during the late June 1987 ASEAN Foreign Ministers meeting in Kuala Lumpur, and in other Asian capitals, Sihanouk already had indicated his support for it. From Sihanouk's perspective his own campaign to distance himself from the present Khmer Rouge became imperative in order to prevent a kind of compromise Khmer Rose regime emerging in Phnom Penh, in which his own future role would be minimal at best. Given his previous experience of cooperation with the DK (during 1975-1977), he had little reason to think he and his followers would thrive in a new Khmer Rose arrangement. After all, the DK's basic organizational weapon was intact. And much of Pol Pot's old DK organizational structure would be retained, including some of the old KCP comrades-in-arms, such as present PRK President Heng Samrin, who later had broken with the DK.

For Sihanouk, a much newer image needed to be projected by any compromise settlement in Cambodia—one where his own position and that of his FUNCINPEK loyalists would be secure. As Sihanouk wrote to then Indonesian Foreign Minister Mokhtar Kusumaatmadja—ASEAN's official dialogue partner with Hanoi on the ASEAN issue—in early June 1987, "The struggle of the coalition government will be difficult to achieve if the Cambodian people no longer like their (i.e. Khmer Rouges) actions and if people do not see any difference between the coalition government and the Phnom Penh government."[37] As Sihanouk, then, perceived it, a modified Khmer Rouge regime in Phnom Penh, whatever its name, would be a recipe for disorder even if it could be achieved. Though Pol Pot and some of his close associates were gone, both the old DK power structure and Heng Samrin and his Vietnam-backed party would still be in place. In any case, such an arrangement would leave little room for leadership by Sihanouk himself.

By his 7 May 1986 temporary resignation as CGDK head and simultaneous renewed sharp criticism of the Khmer Rouge, Sihanouk meant to position himself independently of unwanted consequences of the Khmer Rose idea and the United Nations' "four-point proposal." But the net effect of the prince's actions was, once again, to make the CGDK hostage to the endless diplomatic maneuvering and factional jockeying for power before and after an anticipated Cambodian settlement, rather than turn it into an effective armed resistance movement. Developing such an effective resistance, despite the CGDK's internal problems, seemed to be more the policy approach of Prince Norodom Rannaridh.

For the CGDK as currently constituted, and for the elements in the Cambodian Resistance movement generally, power evidently does not flow from the barrels of guns so much as from the stratagems at the diplomatic conference table. In short, the primary purpose of the Cambodian Resistance movement thus far—certainly in terms of its superpower and regional backers—is not to defeat the Vietnamese, even through a protracted "bleed them white" style of people's war and even if that were possible. Rather, it is to be a political presence and a reference point in regional and other international diplomatic maneuverings and negotiations on the Cambodian issue.

### The Military Performance

The wonder is that given this constricting framework, and the quarrels and conflicting aims between and within the leadership personnel of the principal Cambodian resistance factions, the CGDK has been able to survive militarily at all. However, not only did it survive, but it still constitutes a tactical strike force which, though it is nowhere near to being able to inflict serious harm to the Vietnamese and their Cambodian allies in the "Khmer People's Revolutionary Forces" of the Heng Samrin regime, still is strong enough so that it must continually be reckoned with. The reason lies in a strategy beloved of Mao Zedong, Ho Chi Minh, and other Communist guerrilla leaders, namely to secure for the guerrilla strike force a relatively secure, protected rear base or border zone that the enemy finds either logistically difficult or politically unwise to enter and clear out.

That protected rear base for the CGDK, from the beginning, has been the Thai border. Vietnamese reluctance to engage in a hot pursuit of the resistance forces across that border for a sustained anti-CGDK military operation stems in part from their unwillingness to aggravate an already tense Thai-Vietnamese military confrontation. The Vietnamese are particularly unwilling to risk Beijing inflicting a "second punitive lesson" (as the Chinese call it) on Hanoi. Recall that the Chinese invaded Vietnam in force in mid-February 1979, occupying SRV territory until mid-March when they withdrew. In recent years visits by Chinese military leaders to Bangkok have brought the Thais the possibility of a repeat performance if the Vietnamese were to be so unwise as to attack Thailand or threaten the Khmer Rouge camps.[38]

As a result, even before the 1979 Vietnamese occupation of Phnom Penh, the Thai-Cambodian border had seen the gradual emergence of a floating, camp-housed "nation" of more than a quarter million people, straddling the frontier and maintained with the aid of international relief organizations. In this no-man's-land atmosphere, however, the line between refugees and anti-Vietnamese Cambodian rebels became increasingly more difficult to draw. Within constantly shifting camps and bases, a "third alternative" found its uncertain rank and file. The three principal CGDK resistance groups not only did their recruiting here, but developed their regular military command intelligence and training system, supervised from Bangkok, Pyongyang, Beijing, Paris, or other world capitals by the small, frequently permanent expatriate Cambodian military, business, or diplomatic elites that lead the factions of the CGDK and their respective fellow travelers.[39] The more blatant overt resistance movement encampments always have been described by Thai military as being located just within the Cambodian border and, therefore, technically not Thailand's responsibility. But ethnic Chinese and other Thai citizens or residents; conniving Thai and Vietnamese military on opposite sides of the border; Cambodian entrepreneurs, some in the camps and others in Cambodia itself, engaging in a lucrative overland and coastal-waters smuggling trade between Thailand and consumer-goods-starved Cambodia; Chinese arms suppliers operating with tacit Thai approval—all these have contributed to the emergence of a flourishing, border-zone black market in whose continuance many have a stake.

Meanwhile, refugees from Cambodia, Laos, and Vietnam, fearful of the journey by sea as "boat people," continue to trickle daily into the border zone, or seek political asylum in Thailand or, if fortunate, eventually in third countries. Since 1975, some 550,000 refugees have sought safe haven in Thailand and in Bangkok, as in other world capitals compassion fatigue makes more long-term entrances increasingly unlikely.[40] The result: more human flotsam at the teeming border—the base of the CGDK. Each Vietnamese dry-season military campaign, aimed at clearing up the border zone of potentially new encampments and combat staging grounds of the Cambodian Resistance movement, produces a new influx of refugees into Thai border areas. After the danger lapses, the recent refugees are shifted again by the Thai authorities at or back across the border—but not before some have been drawn into the rebel-refugee "nation."

I need not emphasize that amidst such poorly supervised refugee movements the opportunities for profitable enterprise, particularly through affiliation or contacts with a resistance group, are many. In such Thai border towns as Klong Yang in Trat province, Cambodian traders regularly make contact with their Thai suppliers and overland or by longboat off the waters of Trat, Thai consumer goods enter Cambodia.[41] Supplying the Cambodian resistance camps straddling the border north of Klong Yang occurs in much the same way. Other Thai border towns or sites, with Thai military approval, manage to fulfill similar functions for adjacent rebel-refugee camps. The camps also afford enterprising Cambodian refugee merchants something of a protective site to do business. A number of local Cambodian resistance commanders in the camps take their cut from these transactions.

The political differences and leadership infighting at the apex of the CGDK all have led to more desertions from the Cambodian resistance forces, particularly since 1987. Sometimes, as I discussed earlier, there are desertions from one to another CGDK armed group (e.g. from the KPNLF to the ANS), and sometimes too, according to regular announcements by the PRK government, numbers of "deceived" former residents of the border camps decided to "return" to the government fold. Perhaps even more serious to the cause of the resistance, however, and indicative again of the CGDK's problem of morale and discipline, especially as it affects the long-term inhabitants of the "border nation," is the emergence of criminality among ex- or deserted Cambodian resistance fighters at the border. The following press report in mid-1987 is suggestive:[42]

> Another danger for visitors and local people (at the border—VDK) is the growing number of Kampuchean guerrillas who have taken to banditry in border areas. Eighteen bandits, most of them former guerrillas of the anticommunist Khmer People's National Liberation Front have been killed by Thai soldiers. Four Thai civilians and one soldier have lost their lives in attacks on vehicles on border roads.
>
> There are also numerous cases of rape, kidnapping, and robbery, some of the attacks being on Westerners working for aid agencies. The Thais have now established a new force comprising police, army, village volunteers and civil officials, to counter these attacks and some border roads are now closed at night.

The relative fluidity of the resistance camp sites, due to their exposure to enemy attack, the changing tides of refugee influx, the limited cadre structure (at least until 1982) of the resistance movement, the time needed to develop a regular logistical support supply system with the aid of initially reluctant Thai military, and the continuous intra- and inter-leadership clashes—all these impeded the growth and efficiency of the resistance fighting units. By 1982, however, a number of relatively stable, "regimental" or "battalion" headquarters of different CGDK factions had emerged, usually not far from the major Thai border town of Aruanyaprathet. Satellite command posts operate in alternate locations further north of Aruanyaprathet all along the "elbow" region near and at the Thai-Laotian border. Left to themselves, some of these resistance headquarters sites, at the end of 1982, had acquired a seemingly permanent appearance, with fenced off barracks, considerable communications equipment, small hospitals, schools, shrines, and so on.

Thus Nong Chan camp at the time had become perhaps the major operational headquarters of the KPNLF, housing the Force's then 3rd, 7th, and 9th battalions, as well as a Special Forces unit. Nong Chan at this point had nearly half, and the largest single concentration of KPNLF forces. The residents apparently had come to believe that although they were technically inside Cambodian territory, whence periodically they launched small forays and patrols further inland, they need not be concerned that so much of their admittedly limited strength was so heavily concentrated in one area. Some thirty miles away from Nong Chan lay Phnom Chat camp which housed the DK National Army's 5th regiment, and a principal Khmer Rouge border command center as well. The bulk of the DK's forces, then as now however, remain scattered throughout or near the Cardomom Mountain range, south of Battambang, with relatively easy access to the Gulf of Thailand and maritime supply lines. Khmer Rouge "battalion" strength units also were reported at the time at the satellite camps of Chamkar Kor and Prey Moin, just across from the Thai village of Kok Tahan. Finally, O Smach, colloquially known as "Sihanoukville," a camp about eighty miles just inside Cambodia located north of Aruanyaprathet, began serving as the headquarters and principal training ground for the ANS. In late 1982 it was perhaps the least developed of the resistance movement's staging areas, and it appeared at first that the prince, despite the recently formed CGDK, still had serious reservations about maintaining much of a military force of his own at all.

Sihanouk's reluctance may have been prescient. All these campsites were overrun by the Vietnamese in the first of their major dry season military offensives against the Cambodian resistance during the early months of 1983.[43] On January 31 an assault by some 4,000 light-artillery and tank-supported Vietnamese troops left much of the KPNLF's Nong Chan camp devastated. This was followed by similar attacks on the Khmer Rouges' Phnom Chat site on March 31 and on O Smach on April 4. Thousands of Cambodians, from these and adjacent camps, fled to (mostly temporary) refuge in Thailand.

Yet, from a tactical military point of view, the Vietnamese assault, accompanied subsequently by ever more intensified Vietnamese efforts to seal off as much of the border as possible, Maginot line style, through mine fields and heavy patrolling, proved to be as much of a failure for Hanoi as it was for the Cambodian resistance. The 1983 offensive should have persuaded CGDK leaders of not relying so heavily on stationary border camps for command, intelligence, and recruitment functions of their forces. But within months, presumably in the expectation that the Vietnamese would not be back, a new string of resistance-controlled border camps and operational staging grounds had sprung up. As for the Vietnamese army and its KPRAF ally, all that had been accomplished by the 1983 dry season campaign was a brief respite from guerrilla attacks. Destroying or bottling up the Vietnamese's CGDK enemy would have meant achieving effective control of the highly porous Thai-Cambodian border and/or obtaining through military or political means an end to the Cambodian resistance's de facto "protected rear base," that is, Thailand. As we have seen, too many people — on the Thai, Vietnamese, or Cambodian side — were beginning to have a stake in the "border nation," with its profitable no-man's-land trade ventures. As for an all-out containment of the rebels, neither Hanoi nor Phnom Penh, as I wrote earlier, has been willing to risk a wider war with Thailand and its accompanying threat of renewed Chinese intervention. Closer Thai-Chinese military cooperation in supplying and training the CGDK resistance in the period since 1984, as well as other signals of warming Thai-Chinese military relations — such as Beijing's agreement in March 1987 to sell Chinese T-69 tanks to the Bangkok government at "friendship prices" — all make a Vietnamese military removal of the Cambodian resistance threat less and less likely.[44]

In short order, therefore, there was a repeat of the old CGDK tactical pattern. Despite their continuous inter-leadership squabbles and the failure of one international diplomatic ploy after another to solve the Cambodian problem, the three CGDK quickly began reconstructing their headquarters on the border. New major KPNLF camps and First and Second Battalion head-quarters emerged at Nong Chan, Rithisen, and Ampil camps, all located a few miles within Cambodian territory, and all just across, again, from Aruanyaprathet. Further south, Phum They village and the adjacent Phnom Malay base area rapidly became the Khmer Rouges's major border headquarters outside the Cardomom range. The National Army's reconstituted 5th and 9th regiments were located at Phnom Malay, Northeast of Ampil, at the Tatum site just within Cambodian territory, the ANS (now growing quickly since Sihanouk's son Rannaridh assumed operational command) shortly became the Sihanoukists' new field headquarters. In retrospect one may wonder at the seeming indifference or even insouciance of CGDK factional forces about the possible consequences of yet another, even more severe Vietnamese dry season attack in the future. But given their continued logistical dependence on the refugee nation and on the border environment for their survival, it is not readily apparent what tactical alternatives the Cambodian resistance had.

Between 23 November 1984, when the Vietnamese attacked the KPNLF's Nong Chan camp, and 11 March 1985, when they overran the ANS's Tatum camp, another Vietnamese offensive once again decimated most of the major border encampments of the resistance. Once again thousands were pushed across the frontier into temporary havens inside Thailand. At the same time there came in the next two years a steady intensification of Vietnamese skirmishes with the Thai forces over control of strategic border zones, such as the Chong Bok pass, believed by the Thais to be inside Thai territory but claimed by the Vietnamese.[45] There was as well a further Vietnamese-PRK consolidation process of control at the frontier, in part through the construction of new access roads, command posts, and improved communications systems. Hanoi unmistakably was signalling to Bangkok, the Cambodian resistance, and their Chinese backers that it would no longer permit any repetition of a "protected rear base" strategy without exacting a heavy price. Continuing to lay hundreds of mines along the nearly 460 miles of Thai-Cambodian border, and moving in force across from Thailand's southern coastal province of Trat, whence many access passages into Cambodian territory begin, Hanoi accelerated its interdiction strategy, striking with heavy firepower (supplied by Soviet-made helicopter gunships) against the CGDK.

The sustained 1985 Vietnamese "mop up" and interdiction policy produced a crisis within the Cambodian resistance, aggravating a deepening leadership struggle within the KPNLF, and eventually a significant change in guerrilla tactics, particularly within the Khmer Rouge.[46] Though the latter's Phnom Malay bases complex had been badly damaged by the Vietnamese in an assault that had begun on 23 November 1984, within a few weeks the DK's National Army seemed to have recovered significantly, drawing on its reserves in its own protected rear-base area in the Cardomom mountains. Switching to long-range patrol tactics, based on Vietnamese and current Philippine counterinsurgency experience, the Khmer Rouge units, well supplied by its Chinese allies, now increasingly began distancing themselves from the border. They moved about the interior of Cambodia in smaller units, equipped with increased firepower, including light mortars and improved rockets. The units made sure they never stayed in any place long enough to become targets of a concentrated attack. Maintaining as much self-sufficiency as possible, the Khmer Rouge also sought to develop "people's friendship" (i.e. supplies and political support) with the local rural population. That effort proved less successful, however, as the odious reputation of the Khmer Rouge regime had not been forgotten.

Despite flare-ups of ANS-Khmer Rouge fighting in 1986–1987 several joint patrols took place, some as far as Phnom Penh, and all in the context of the new mobile approach of the resistance. The Sihanoukist presence with the DK guerrillas on occasion also helped to soften popular anti-Khmer Rouge sentiment. Operating independently, meanwhile, some ANS and KPNLF units began adopting similar mobile tactics, striking around the town of Battambang and the Tonle Sap lake marshlands. By early 1987, CGDK mobility seemed to have brought the Cambodian resistance movement to a new stage. Both a growing ANS, and the Khmer Rouge appeared to be vying with each other in extending the range of "deep penetration" operations. Meanwhile, refugee-rebel border camps and villages, in many cases, by late 1986 had become primarily rest and recreation areas. CGDK units, according to their own reports, now were harassing Vietnamese troops in their provincial garrisons with quick, hit-and-run attacks, blowing up a landing strip here or ambushing a convoy there.

But how significant actually were these military resistance actions? Something of the scope of resistance operations may be gleaned from "battlefield communiques" regularly issued by the Khmer Rouges's clandestine transmitter. Even from this admittedly biased (and almost impossible to verify) source, and bearing in mind as well that the DK's National Army still is overwhelmingly the Cambodian resistance movement's principal armed component, one does not get the impression of major military strikes that are likely to alter the balance of power inside Cambodia any time soon. At the close of April 1987, for example, DK forces claimed to have "completely liberated" four Vietnamese military-held posts in the Kompong Thom area, including a Vietnamese "company" position, a "battalion" position, a "township which was assaulted" and a "district seat" of local government plus "six villages"—at a total cost of only ten Vietnamese dead and fifteen wounded. There also had been a destruction of "seventeen weapons," among them AK rifles as well as "six barracks."[48] How long the areas remained "liberated" has not been disclosed. And, given the nature of the CGDK's quick strike-and-withdrawal tactics, it seems unlikely to have been very long.

Then, at the end of June 1987, the DK claim was that a Vietnamese train had been destroyed along the Phnom Penh-Battambang railway, and somewhat earlier there was a DK transmitter summary that in fourteen "battlefield" areas, from Komg Som to the "northeast," more than 1,300

Vietnamese soldiers had been killed or wounded over an unspecified period of time, but presumably since the beginning of the year.[49] Nothing of a similar scope has been reported from the ANS, whose current long-range patrols are much more episodic and on a smaller scale. As for the KPNLF, it was reported in the Thai press in mid-July 1987 that there were flurries of attempts being made to revitalize its armed operations, described as still largely "paralyzed" because of the organization's prolonged leadership crisis.[50] KPNLF Commander-in-Chief Sak Sutsakhan reportedly was seen as "indecisive" by his subordinates.

Particularly in 1986–1987 there were indications that fresh weapons, including antiaircraft artillery and antitank rockets and launchers were being supplied to all factions of the resistance under the terms of earlier agreements with Beijing.[51] There has been heavy reliance traditionally on Chinese-made small arms and mortars. But the resistance remains confined to a relatively low level of easily transportable firepower, suited to highly mobile guerrilla-style operations, not to sustained, fixed-position artillery duels or even to combat by armoured units. Tactical innovations have been confined to such matters as increased use of demolition teams, or improved systems of on-the-ground combat communications, making possible more easily simultaneous attack from different directions on limited size targets. Whether, together with the relentless diplomatic pressure in various international forums and the relative economic isolation forced on Vietnam and the PRK regime, such a style of "slowly-bleed-the-enemy-white" warfare is likely to be effective remains very much to be seen.

### The International Politics of the Conflict

In the view of some authoritative observers, to be sure, the attacks by the CGDK, particularly the periodic "battalion size" Khmer Rouge operations in the Thai-Cambodian border provinces, throughout Battambang, and as far east as Kompong Speu, definitely are curbing Cambodia's recovery. Indeed, the CGDK's strikes are said to be slowing economic growth significantly and the country seems to be "exhausted" and "teetering between rebirth and decay" as one writer has put it.[52] Severe inflation, periodic shortages of food and of basic consumer goods except on the flourishing black market, power failures, stagnation of much of the industrial sector due not least to the isolation of the country from major foreign sources of development capital, overbureaucratization—all these are aggravated by the dislocating effects of the CGDK insurgency.

And yet nothing suggests that Cambodia's PRK regime is any nearer collapse now because of the seemingly endless struggle within and over

Cambodia than is the PRK's own mentor, Vietnam. Rather, authoritative on-the-scene reports suggest that in this, Indochina's third protracted war, Hanoi remains convinced that it will emerge victorious, and that neither the "bleed-white" strategy of China, nor the strategy of economic and diplomatic-moral isolation pursued by the United States, will work. As the editor of the Vietnam Communist party's newspaper *Nhan Dan* remarked in a press interview in late June 1987: "Vietnam might be the world's poorest country, but its morale will never collapse," and he added that the "Vietnamese are very patient people. We will do what we have to do and no one can dictate."[53]

Neither the changes and reforms in the Vietnamese party leadership and economic policies announced in Hanoi in mid-1987, nor the much anticipated meeting of the new Vietnam party secretary general Nguyen Van Linh with Soviet Secretary Mihail Gorbachev in Moscow in early June 1987 have done anything to indicate that (1) despite their past complaints about Hanoi's use of Russian aid the Soviets now are ready to exert pressure on Hanoi to change course by curtailing their nearly $3 billion annual aid to Vietnam, or (2) that Moscow herself is committed to pursue a fundamentally different course in the Cambodian conflict. To be sure, Gorbachev in his meeting with Linh stressed the desirability of "all national patriotic forces" in Cambodia to contribute to a solution to the conflict. Who might be among these "patriotic forces" the Soviets carefully have not specified. But Hanoi, meanwhile persists in showing no desire to meet with Sihanouk to bring about a broad-based conference of all Cambodian factions; insists, furthermore, that there can never be any discussion with what it calls the "genocidal Pol Pot clique" (i.e., the Khmer Rouge faction); and has made it clear that it expects no real change in her relationship with the United States until after the Reagan administration departs the White House.[54]

Evidently the Vietnamese and their PRK allies in Phnom Penh prefer the present stalemate, however that may retard and debilitate Cambodia's — and Vietnam's — economic development, rather than seriously contemplate modifying their present control structure over Cambodia. Unless the existing level of violence inside Cambodia were to escalate significantly and the Cambodian resistance — organizationally and strategically — were to become a much more formidable threat, it is unlikely that the present grin-and-bear-it determination in Hanoi and Phnom Penh will change. Meanwhile, as Thai military sources have emphasized, Soviet military assistance — exemplified by the steady chain of Soviet vessels that offload their cargoes of tanks, armoured personnel carriers, petroleum, and other war-related materials at the Cambodian port of

Kompong Som—remains a major factor in keeping the Vietnamese army going in its Cambodian occupation.⁵⁵

Nor is there any indication that, despite Hanoi's assertions to the contrary, the Vietnamese occupation will soon end. In mid-July 1987 in a press interview Vietnam party secretary general stressed once again that "It is certain that Vietnamese troops will withdraw completely from Cambodia by 1990."⁵⁶ The 1990 date not only is well beyond US policy changes anticipated by Hanoi following the 1988 presidential elections, but, also Hanoi's previous announcements of troop withdrawal from Cambodia generally have been found to be nothing but a public-relations smokescreen. An analysis in May 1987, for example, by Bangkok's Chulalongkorn University's Asian Studies Institute, and based on interviews with defecting Vietnamese soldiers, shows persuasively that new Vietnamese military regularly are sent into Cambodia to replace troops that leave the country.⁵⁷ A full and genuine Vietnamese military withdrawal from Cambodia remains, however, a major Chinese *sine qua non* for an acceptable settlement of the Cambodian conflict. In mid-1987, Beijing's leading daily, in a comment on Vietnamese policy, reiterated that if "the new Vietnamese leadership" really wished to "extricate itself" from its present difficulties, then stopping "the war of aggression against Cambodia," as well as a commitment to "withdraw its troops" would be the only way.⁵⁸ Until then, presumably, and, indeed, until whatever ultimate Cambodian settlement suits Beijing is achieved, it is evident that the Chinese intend to maintain their particular arm of the present Cambodian resistance, the Khmer Rouge. China's leader Deng Hsiao-ping intimated as much when he declared that China "unconditionally supports Democratic Kampuchea's struggle for independence until it has won final victory."⁵⁹ Deng used the old name of Cambodia's post-1975 regime—"Democratic Kampuchea"—not its present name accepted in the United Nations and denoting the alliance of the Cambodian resistance, "Coalition Government of Democratic Kampuchea."

Was this merely an inadvertent slip? Perhaps. But the present, relatively low level of combat engaged in by the Cambodian resistance, whatever faction is involved, suggests that the stalemated condition of the Cambodian conflict generally, to which such low-intensity protracted warfare tactics contribute, has its own rationale. It underscores that the real purpose of the CGDK's armed forces today is not a steadily building crescendo of military success and liberation over the Vietnamese occupation force and its PRK ally. Rather the CGDK's purpose is (1) to maintain various Cambodian factional organizational interests whose main point of agreement is their opposition to the Vietnamese PRK regime in Phnom

Penh, and (2) to permit these interests to jockey for power in any political settlement of the Cambodian conflict and especially in its immediate post-settlement politics.

In this process, I will note in conclusion, the superpowers' policy perceptions are likely to be decisive, whatever the Cambodian resistance itself may desire. An example is to be found in the position of the United States toward the Cambodian conflict. In July 1981 at the United Nations Conference on Kampuchea, and again in May 1987 at the Tokyo Conference on Peace, Security and Economic Cooperation in Asia, US State Department spokespersons emphasized that creating a "neutral" regime in Cambodia was the desired objective, along, however, with the rights of Cambodians to determine their own political destiny through "free elections."[60] The contradiction in this US position seemed to keep on escaping the Reagan administration. For what if, for example, the Cambodian people, given the free opportunity to do so, should choose a government that is not "neutral," but one that, given their experience with various Communist regimes in recent years, in fact leans toward the West? Or even is avowedly anticommunist, as most of its neighboring Southeast Asian governments are?

It would appear, then, that if the fractured Cambodian resistance wishes to move toward genuine liberation and self-determination, its ultimate enemy may turn out to be a *realpolitik* compromise consensus ("coalition government"; "neutralism," "Finlandization"?) among the resistance movement's own respective superpower patrons. Illustrative again was the movement toward an interim, new quadripartite coalition regime in Cambodia, evident throughout 1988. The United Nations General Assembly on 3 November 1988 adopted a resolution (122 in favor, 19 against, with 13 abstentions) once again calling for Vietnam's withdrawal from Cambodia and urging a reconciliation of all political factions under Sihanouk's leadership. Significantly, the resolution also demanded that Cambodia not return to the "universally condemned policies and practices of a recent past" — a direct allusion to the Pol Pot era. Though China voted in favor of the resolution, its spokesmen during that year indicated that Beijing expected the Khmer Rouge to play its rightful role in any future coalition regime in Cambodia. During the UN General Assembly debates, for example, China's foreign minister, Qian Qichen, declared that "we stand for a quadripartite coalition in Kampuchea. We are against the exclusion of any of the four factions from it or the exercise of power by any one faction alone."[61] Earlier, in mid-August 1988, General Secretary Zhao Ziyang of the Chinese Communist party already had declared that the Khmer Rouge should not be allowed to resume power "exclusively."[62] It might be noted also that during the discussions surrounding the drafting of the 3 November 1988 UN General Assembly resolution, Beijing first strenuously had objected to any condemnation of the Khmer Rouge in the resolution's wording, ultimately settling for the nonspecific wording cited above. China, as US and ASEAN diplomatic sources periodically during 1988 reported, was ready to accept the exile of Pol Pot, and some of his close associates like former DK Foreign Minister Ieng Sary and senior combat commanders Son Sen and Ta Mok (both of whom retain senior posts in the present Khmer Rouge power structure). But it also has continued to make it plain that it will go on supplying the Khmer Rouge with weapons so long as the last Vietnamese has not left Cambodia.[63]

Clearly, China means to keep its hand in Cambodian affairs — whether there is a settlement or not. And the Khmer Rouge themselves, meanwhile, are pushing their own guerilla encampments deeper into Cambodian territory, empressing refugees from the Thai border camps into their service, catching weapons, and showing every indication that they are prepared to seize power as soon as the opportunity presents itself in the aftermath of the Vietnamese withdrawal.[64] Whether as a result of this known Khmer Rouge political-military infiltration, Hanoi will keep its often stated promise to pull back by 1990 all of its remaining forces — still estimated to number about 100,000 by the end of 1988 — likely will become more uncertain during 1989. Already by mid-1988 it was becoming apparent that Khmer Rouge guerrillas were scaling down their armed forays and attacks on Vietnamese and KPRAF troops, concentrating instead on infiltrating villages with their agents.[65] Securing a widening range of districts — especially in Battambang, Preah Vihear, and Siem Reap provinces in the northwest of Cambodia, and sending "show the flag" patrols out as far as Kah Kong province in the south, and Mundulkiri in the east — had become an ever-more preferred Khmer Rouge tactic by the close of 1988. Indeed, so potentially threatening had the Khmer Rouge military incursions and logistical "battle girding" inside Cambodia become that the Sihanoukist ANS and the still badly divided KPNLF, the two resistance partners of the Khmer Rouge against the Vietnamese and its Heng Samrin-led PRK regime, were said to be receiving PRK help in facilitating the crossing of the mine-strewn Thai-Cambodian border by the Sihanoukist and KPNLF forces in order to deploy their units as a counterweight to the Khmer Rouge.[66] With Hanoi's military departure by 1990, if it comes, there may well erupt what probably would be called the "Fourth Indo-China War," a conflict to which Beijing hardly would be indifferent, even if Pol Pot and his close associates were not directly involved. According to Western diplomatic and military attachés at the end of October 1988, the Khmer Rouge have stockpiled arms and supplies "enough for 2-year use."[67]

And what of Moscow's position, and particularly that of its client Vietnam, and, in turn the latter's client, the PRK? "Reconciliation" meetings of the CGDK's on-again-off-again leader, Prince Norodom Sihanouk, and the PRK's premier Kun Sen were held at the prince's suggestion at Fère-en-Tardenois, near Paris on 2 December 1987, and again at Saint Germain-en-Laye, on 20–21 January 1988. Moscow pressured Hun Sen to attend. But these meetings were noteworthy primarily for articulating the PRK's concern for a Khmer Rouge ("Pol Potist") return to power after a Vietnamese military withdrawal, and for the squabbling over just how a new "coalition" government in Cambodia could be formed if at all after the departure of Hanoi's troops.[68] Like the previous discussions, held between Hun Sen and Sihanouk at Fère-en-Tardenois, on 8–9 November 1988 (this time with the suspicious KPNLF leader Son Sann also in attendance) little was accomplished beyond the agreement of the parties on the need for some kind of international supervision of any future elections. It was also agreed that the superpowers and concerned nations in the region should hold an international conference to guarantee Cambodia's future sovereignty and "nonalignment" status. Hun Sen stressed through all his discussions with his CGDK opponents that "all Cambodian parties," except for the "ringleaders of the genocidal Pol Pot regime" would be allowed in the "national reconciliation" process. But the Khmer Rouge would have to lay down their arms, and in the meantime "the political and military status quo in Cambodia," i.e., the PRK regime's authority, would be "maintained."[69] All during 1988 the PRK and its Indochinese allies had been sounding the same theme. At a Phnom Penh conference of the Foreign Ministers of Vietnam, Laos and the PRK in mid-July 1988, for example, emphasis again had been placed on the PRK's effective control of Cambodia today, and on the allegedly "firm and complete confidence" of Cambodians in their present "authentic new regime."[70] At the end of June 1988, as talk in ASEAN circles about a new "reconciliation" government for Cambodia had been intensifying, PRK President Heng Samrin already had declared that he did not intend to accept the "dismantling" of the PRK.[71]

All this could only be viewed as a blow to the tireless efforts of the ASEAN countries, and particularly the group's official "interlocutor" (dialogue partner) with Hanoi, Indonesia, to bring the warring Cambodian factions along with Vietnam to face-to-face discussions and compromise. On 25 July 1988, at the West Java hilltown of Bogor, and in the Indonesian capital itself, the three CGDK factions, Vietnam, and ASEAN representatives argued, proposed, and counterproposed solutions to the Cambodian problem. After three days of deliberations, no common communique was agreed to, and this much-touted "Jakarta

Informal Meeting" (JIM) could do no more than accept a formula for future meetings by establishing a joint *working group*. On 17 October 1988 such a working group did in fact meet again in Jakarta. But the CGDK's strongest faction, the Khmer Rouge, sent no representative, probably in protest to the condemnation of the Pol Pot regime voiced during the original JIM. The Khmer Rouge by now seemed more intent than ever to dig itself in for a new post-Vietnam occupation struggle, rather than put confidence in diplomatic discussions. Even at the previously cited 8–9 November 1988 Fère-en-Tardenois conference the Khmer Rouge refused to send its principal leader, Khieu Sampan; one of the DK's lower ranking diplomats, Ok Sakun, made a token gesture of an *acte de presence*, but did not participate with Sihanouk, Hun Sen and Sann in the discussions. This November 1988 meeting proved fruitless anyway, the participants mainly agreeing to setting up yet another working committee meeting. They also hoped to convene an "international conference" on Cambodia at some unspecified date. After the 8–9 November 1988 meeting the PRK's Hun Sen blamed China for a continuing stalemate in the Cambodian problem, declaring that Chinese pressure was preventing Sihanouk from signing any agreement "because Beijing does not want to drop the Khmer Rouge under any circumstances."[72]

The Cambodian deadlock increasingly was having a divisive effect on ASEAN also. Thailand, looking to Beijing for protection as Thai troops almost weekly skirmish with Vietnamese forces along the Thai-Cambodian border, appears much less compromise-driven than Indonesia, which long has viewed Hanoi as a potential future ally against a modernized and possibly aggressive China. Meanwhile, a steady thaw in Sino-Soviet relations, and even a round of discussions between the USSR and China in Beijing in early September 1988 on the problem of how to resolve the Cambodian issue, thus far have produced no new breakthroughs. In alarm over the continuing stalemate, ASEAN representatives scheduled a meeting in December 1988 to see "what can be done" in the words of Malaysian Foreign Ministry secretary general Yusuf Mitan.[73]

And amidst all this fruitless tugging and hauling, the US State Department, at the close of September 1988, announced that the Reagan administration, now in its fading hours, suddenly had decided to triple its aid to Sihanouk's ANS and Son Sann's KPNLF presumably in an effort to "curb" the influence and expanding power base of the Khmer Rouge.[74] Planned was an increase in assistance from $3.5 million in 1988 to perhaps as much as $15 million for the coming fiscal year. Apart from the almost ludicrous tardiness of this gesture — not to mention its likely futility, given the divisions between and within the two noncommunist Cambodian resistance groups — there swiftly followed another embarrassment. To expressions of official outrage in Bangkok, there came disclosures that the Thai military and their business associates had stolen perhaps as much as $3.5 million from the millions of dollars in nonlethal aid that the United States reportedly has been providing the Sihanoukist and KPNLF elements of the CGDK over the last five years; indeed, the US aid level already had risen to about $12 million a year in 1985 and had leaped by 50 percent annually since then.[75] The affair strained US-Thai relations and further raised the question whether or not there are too many interests, ranging from the superpower's own long-term strategic concerns to Cambodian factional elites and their respective local and regional political and military supporters, that have a stake in keeping the Cambodian problem going on and on. But in Cambodia itself and among the thousands of refugee camp dwellers strung along the Thai border the prospects of either victory or a workable compromise seem as far away as they were a decade ago.

## Notes

1. Agence France Press despatch, Beijing, 15 May 1987 (Foreign Broadcast Information Service reports, hereafter *FBIS,* 19 May 1987, p. H2).
2. David P. Chandler, *A History of Cambodia* (Boulder, Colo.: Westview Press, 1983), pp. 176-183.
3. Ben Kiernan and Chantou Boua, *Peasants and Politics in Kampuchea 1942-1981* (London: Zed Press, 1982), p. 201. On Son Ngoc Thanh see, e.g., Michael Vickery, *Cambodia 1975-1982* (Boston: South End Press, 1984), pp. 254-255.
4. Michael Vickery, *Kampuchea. Politics, Economics and Society* (London: Frances Pinter Publishers, 1986), p. 16.
5. Craig Etcheson, *The Rise and Demise of Democratic Kampuchea* (Boulder, Colo.: Westview Press, 1984), pp. 86-89.
6. From "Manifeste du Mouvement Khmer Serei," in *Documents et écrits se rapportant au Khmer Serei*, mss., Olin Library, Cornell University, Ithaca, N.Y.; also cited in Ben Kiernan, *How Pol Pot Came to Power* (London: Verso Publishers, 1985), p. 186.
7. Nayan Chanda, *Brother Enemy: The War After the War* (New York: Harcourt Brace Janovich, 1986); and Elizabeth Becker, *When the War Was Over: The Voices of Cambodia's Revolution and its People* (New York: Simon and Schuster, 1986).
8. Justus M. van der Kroef, "Cambodia: From 'Democratic Kampuchea' to 'People's Republic,'" *Asian Survey*, August 1979 (vol. 19, no. 8), pp. 731-750.
9. See, e.g., Radio Hanoi, 9 April 1983 (*FBIS*, 11 April 1983, p. K1), and *Quan Doi Nhan Dan* (Hanoi), 9 November 1986 (*FBIS*, 12 November 1986, p. K3).
10. I have discussed this ASEAN concern in my "Kampuchea: The Diplomatic Labyrinth," *Asian Survey*, October 1982 (vol. 22, no. 10), pp. 1009-1033.
11. Radio Kuala Lumpur, 2 February 1982, and Agence France Presse despatch, Jakarta, 20 February 1982 (both in *FBIS*, February 3 and March 1, 1982, pp. K3 and I2 respectively).

12. OANA/Bernama despatch, Kuala Lumpur, 15 December 1981 (*FBIS*, December 18, 1981, p. 02).
13. Text of CGDK agreement in Agence France Presse despatch, Bangkok, June 1987 (*FBIS*, 21 June 1987).
14. Justus M. van der Kroef, "Political Ideology in Democratic Kampuchea," *Orbis*, Winter 1979 (vol. 22, no. 4), pp. 1007–1030.
15. *Le Monde* (Paris), 26 November 1986 (*FBIS*, 6 December 1980).
16. See, e.g., the DK policy statement broadcast over "The Voice of Democratic Kampuchea," 13 October 1981 (*FBIS*, 16 October 1981).
17. Radio Beijing, 7 December 1981 (*FBIS*, 7 December 1981).
18. E.g., Ibid.
19. "Voice of the National Army of Democratic Kampuchea" (clandestine), 1 September 1985 (*FBIS*, 3 September 1985).
20. For different versions of this DK factional split see, e.g., "Checkmate in Kampuchea," *Asia Pacific Context* (Melbourne, Australia), May 1986 (vol. 2, no. 1), pp. 13–14; Jacques Bekaert in *Bangkok Post*, 21 November 1986 (*FBIS*, 26 November 1986), and Barbara Crosette in the *New York Times*, 7 December 1986.
21. *Asiaweek* (Hongkong), 26 July 1985, p. 7.
22. Nayan Chanda, "Cambodia in 1986: Beginning to Tire," *Asian Survey*, January 1987 (vol. 27, no. 1), p. 117.
23. *Far Eastern Economic Review*, 24 October 1985, p. 44.
24. *Bangkok Post*, 4 January 1986, and Agence France Presse despatch, Hongkong, 3 January 1986 (both in *FBIS*, 6 January 1986).
25. *The Straits Times* (Singapore), 2 January 1986.
26. Ibid., 15 February 1986, and Agence France Presse despatch, Beijing 11 January 1986 (*FBIS*, 13 January 1986).
27. Agence France Presse despatch, Bangkok, 27 March 1987 (*FBIS*, 27 March 1987), and The *Straits Times*, 1 February 1986.
28. *Asiaweek*, 5 July 1987, p. 37.
29. Agence France Presse despatch, 30 August 1985 (*FBIS*, 3 September 1985).
30. In a press interview with *Avanti!* (Rome), 28–29 September 1986 (*FBIS*, 7 October 1986).
31. Agence France Presse despatch from Bang Saen, Thailand, 28 August 1986 (*FBIS*, August 1986).
32. See, e.g., by Justus M. van der Kroef: "'Proximity Cocktails' and 'Provisional Salvation': Cambodia's Tortuous Course," *Issues and Studies*, April 1986 (vol. 22, no. 4), pp. 120–139; and "Crafting a Cambodian Compromise: 'Eight Points, Three Points, Two Points, No Point,'" *Asian Thought and Society. An International Review*, July-November 1986 (vol. 11, no. 32–33), pp. 231–244.
33. Agence France Presse despatch by Michael Adler from Bangkok, 31 May 1986 (*FBIS*, 4 June 1986).
34. The *Nation* (Bangkok), 13 May 1987.
35. Agence France Presse despatch, by Jacques Tondre, Bangkok, 19 May 1987 (*FBIS*, 20 May 1987).
36. The *Bangkok Post*, 26 June 1987, and the *Nation* (Bangkok), 28 June 1987.
37. The *Philippine Star* (Manila), 24 June 1987 (italics supplied).
38. See, e.g., the warning on 30 January 1985 of People's China's Foreign Minister Wu Hsueh-ch'ien in Hsinhua despatch, Hong Kong, 30 January 1985 (*FBIS*, 31 January 1985).

39. I have described some of the details of this process and system in my "Refugees and Rebels: Dimensions of the Thai-Kampuchean Border Conflict," *Asian Affairs. An American Review*, Spring 1983, pp. 19-36. Data in this and the following paragraphs are based on close personal observation of Cambodian refugee and rebel camp conditions during my annual journeys to the border areas since 1982.
40. *Indochina Chronology* (Institute of East Asian Studies, University of California, Berkeley), January-March 1985, p. 12. See also Rob Burrows, "Thailand-Vietnamese Refugees, Past and Present," *Refugees* (United Nations High Commission on Refugees, Geneva), July 1985, p. 16.
41. *Nation* (Bangkok) 23 June 1987, p. 5.
42. The *Australian* (Sydney), 2 July 1987, report from Nam Yuen, Thailand. See also The *Nation* (Bangkok), 6 and 9 June 1987 (*FBIS,* 10 June 1987).
43. Justus M. van der Kroef, "Kampuchea—Protracted Conflict, Suspended Compromise," *Asian Survey,* March 1984 (vol. 24, no. 3), pp. 314-334.
44. The *New York Times,* 26 July 1987, p. 7.
45. See, e.g., *Bangkok Post,* 25 June 1987.
46. This discussion draws heavily on information supplied the author by Thai military and ANS and KPNLF resistance leaders during interviews in Bangkok and Arvanyaprathet in early June 1986. See also *Asiaweek,* 14 June 1985, p. 31.
47. See e.g., the report in *Economist* (London), 24 May 1986, p. 44; and *Asiaweek,* 13 July 1986, p. 28, and 5 July 1987, p. 37.
48. Voice of the National Army of Democratic Kampuchea (Clandestine), 21 April 1987 (*FBIS,* 23 April 1987).
49. Voice of the National Army of Democratic Kampuchea, 5 June 1987 (*FBIS,* 15 June 1987).
50. *Nation* (Bangkok), 19 July 1987 (*FBIS,* 21 July 1987).
51. Information supplied the author by Thai military circles in Bangkok, July 1987.
52. Murray Hiebert, "Cambodia: Guerrilla Attacks Curb Development," *Indochina Issues* (Washington, D.C.), September 1986, pp. 1-6.
53. Reuter's despatch by Joseph de Rienzo, Hanoi, in *Nation* (Bangkok), 27 June 1987.
54. *Far Eastern Economic Review,* 11 June 1987, p. 24; and 23 July 1987, p. 26.
55. *Straits Times,* 22 May 1987.
56. *FBIS,* 13 July 1987.
57. *Straits Times,* 14 May 1987.
58. Renmin Ribao (Beijing), 8 July 1987 (*FBIS,* 10 July 1987).
59. *Beijing Review,* 23 December 1985, pp. 7-8.
60. "US Interests in Asia," *Current Policy* (US Department of State, Bureau of Public Affairs, Washington, D.C.), no. 295, July 1981, pp. 1-4; and "East Asia and the Pacific: An Era of Opportunity," *Current Policy,* no. 971, May 1987, p. 2.
61. Xinhua despatch, United Nations, New York, 28 September 1988 (*FBIS,* 29 September 1988).
62. *Straits Times,* 18 August 1988.
63. *New York Times,* 14 November 1988.
64. Ibid., April 1, October 23, and November 13 and 20, 1988; Agence France Presse despatch by Jacques Tondre, Hong Kong, 14 March 1988 (*FBIS,* 15 March 1988); *Far Eastern Economic Review,* 22 September 1988, p. 23.

65. Clayton Jones from Phnom Penh, *Christian Science Monitor,* 15 June 1988.
66. *Asiaweek,* 11 November 1988, p. 31.
67. *FBIS,* 1 November 1988.
68. For an analysis of the Hun Sen-Sihanouk and follow-up ASEAN meetings discussed in this paragraph, see Justus M. van der Kroef, *Cambodia: Diplomatic Stalemate and Initiative* (forthcoming).
69. Radio Hanoi, 8 November 1988 (*FBIS,* 9 November 1988).
70. Radio Phnom Penh, 13 July 1988 (*FBIS,* 14 November 1988).
71. *Straits Times,* 29 June 1988.
72. *Le Figaro* (Paris), 9 November 1988 (*FBIS,* November 14, 1988).
73. Xinhua despatch, Beijing, 12 November 1988 (*FBIS,* 16 November 1988).
74. *New York Times,* 29 September 1988.
75. Ibid., 1 November 1988; *The Washington Post,* 30 October 1988; *The Far Eastern Economic Review,* 27 October 1988, p. 17; *Naeo Na* (Bangkok), 2 November 1988 (*FBIS,* 2 November 1988).

# 5

# Afghanistan

*Anthony Arnold*

*An uncommonly cruel war, causing terrible human suffering, has been waged for more than seven years in Afghanistan. The Soviet army should be withdrawn without delay so that the Afghan people can settle their domestic problems for themselves.*

— Andrey Sakharov, May 1987.

## Introduction

Of the countries considered in this book, Afghanistan stood out in 1988 for three reasons: First, the anticommunist struggle there was perceived both domestically and internationally as a "just" war, the defense of an indigenous people against the expansionist designs of an aggressive neighbor. Only in Cambodia was there a similar unequivocal case of military invasion and occupation by a neighboring power. To the outside world, this factor bestowed an automatic legitimacy on the Afghan and Cambodian resistances that other anticommunist movements, which were often seen as "civil" wars, had to struggle continuously to achieve and sustain. The outrage Afghans felt at having been invaded by an alien power was an important psychological factor in maintaining their fighting spirit.

Second, the Afghan resistance was also solidly rooted in an ideology— Islam. Whereas other anticommunist movements relied on a variety of appeals, including nationalism, human rights, and even (in the case of the Cambodian Khmer Rouge) a Maoist form of Marxism-Leninism, the Afghans' main sustaining motivation was their religious faith. Many believers attributed their difficulties to a form of divine retribution, a punishment for having permitted insufficiently devout governments to develop during the precommunist era. The religious common denominator is the single most important unifying influence among the otherwise contentious Afghan resistance factions.

Finally, it was only in Afghanistan that the USSR itself was massively engaged with its own combat units against the resistance. Elsewhere it maintained advisers, but it relied on either indigenous or other surrogate forces for combat.

Of these three factors, only the first was novel for the Afghans. True, they had been fighting powerful foreign invaders in *jihads* (holy wars) for centuries, but they had fought alone, without international support or even international awareness. The anticommunist resistance was thus merely the continuation of a long tradition, but one that was little-known in the outside world.

In Afghanistan, the essential problem of politics—indeed of any collective human effort—was always unity. The mountainous terrain hinders communication and encourages local self-sufficiency. Throughout most of the country, the population survives on an agricultural subsistence economy. The basic social building blocks thus tend to be small communities or groups, usually the village and the family, cemented by an overall social code and close personal loyalties. To the extent that there are larger groupings—linguistic, ethnic, social, or religious—their internal cohesions tend to be much weaker, especially in the absence of personal connections.[1]

These larger divisions do exist, however, and they complicate the problem of unity even further. Afghanistan had two main languages, Pashtu and Persian (Dari), several minor languages, and innumerable dialects. Ethnically, the country is home to Pashtuns (40 percent), Tajiks (30 percent), Hazaras (10 percent), Uzbeks (10 percent), and numerous smaller minorities, including Turkmen, Kirghiz, Kazakhs, Arabs, and others.[2] Except, however, for Hazaras and a few tiny minorities, each of these ethnic groups had its population center in a neighboring state; compared to Afghanistan, there are more Pashtuns in Pakistan, more Baluch in Pakistan and Iran, and more Tajiks, Uzbeks, Turkmen, Kirghiz, and Kazakhs in Soviet Central Asia.

In terms of religion, the country is more than 99 percent Islamic, but it is divided into about 80 percent Sunni and 20 percent Shia. Socially, there is a three-way split between urban dwellers, sedentary farmers, and nomads, with long-standing mutual suspicion on all sides. There is a deep cleft in the villages between the government representative and local citizens, a difference that for decades found expression in distinct ways of speaking, dressing, and even walking.[3]

Finally, there is the venerable tradition of feuding, which finds expression not only on an inter-tribal but an intra-tribal or even intra-family basis.

Despite these splits—and contrary to popular belief—Afghans were not forever at each other's throats. Even the traditional feuds tend to be low-key affairs, broken by frequent periods of peace and even cooperation. The leaders (*khans*) are the same local figures who are in charge when there is no fighting, and they have little or no influence outside their immediate communities.[4]

Within the framework of a jihad, however, a new set of rules and leaders came into play. A jihad was a general, not a local phenomenon, and it involved setting aside (at least temporarily) tribal and local animosities. The leaders were charismatic figures who arose from outside the tightly knit local hierarchies—they were never khans—and were thus able to take charge without suspicion of wanting merely to promote the ambitions of individual communities. Uniting many mutually antagonistic groups was, however, no short or easy task. The local khans, of course, were rarely inclined to aid the outside leader, who was perceived as a threat to their own power.

### Origins of the Anti-Soviet Resistance

In the 1950s, the USSR began trying to win Afghanistan with a program of economic aid and military assistance. There followed a matching political effort, exemplified by the emergence of a pro-Soviet People's Democratic party of Afghanistan (PDPA) in the 1960s.[5] The appearance of the PDPA, founded on 1 January 1965, alarmed the religious community, which began to organize its own forces.

Following adoption of a constitution in 1964, four loci of political power became distinguishable within the narrow band of politically aware Afghans.

1. *Royal Family.* The royal family, hereditary rulers for centuries, continued to hold power, even after the monarchy was overthrown in 1973. (President Daoud, who deposed the king, was the monarch's first cousin and brother-in-law.)
2. *Politicians.* Various foreign ideologies, ranging from pro-Maoist through social democratic to ultra-nationalistic, found expression in proto-parties. The PDPA was part of this group. Their common failing was the inability to reconcile the state they hoped to build with the values of the society in which they hoped to build it.
3. *Traditionalists.* The traditional religious community was made up of

mullahs and Islamic intellectuals who believed that their contribution should be what it had always been: the formation and interpretation of law, which the state should be obliged to carry out.
4. *Islamists.* Finally there were the Islamists, also religious in orientation but immediately concerned with practical matters of politics and economics, as well as judicial matters. Unlike the others, they were seeking some completely new approach that would combine the traditional values of their country with political power.[6]

All of these trends suffered from the pandemic Afghan political disease of factionalism. The Traditionalists, largely Pashtuns, were prisoners of tribal loyalties and animosities. The Islamists split into radical and moderate wings. Even the royal family had its internal divisions. Perhaps the most noticeable split, however, came in the ranks of the PDPA, where two factions each laid claim to the party's name while excommunicating the other. They were commonly known by the names of their respective organs, *Parcham* (Banner) and *Khalq* (Masses). In 1973, Parcham made common cause with a disaffected member of the royal family, Mohammed Daoud, and together they overthrew the monarchy, declaring a republic in its stead.

Daoud immediately began to persecute both Traditionalists and Islamists, as well as those politicians who favored less radical approaches than the PDPA's. An uprising in 1975 by the more radical Islamists gave him an excuse to imprison and execute most leaders of all three groups (including innocent moderates) who still remained in the country, a reprisal that all but wiped out a generation of potential leaders. They would be sorely missed in the resistance movement that began to coalesce against the communists three years later.

Daoud's Parchami supporters and would-be manipulators might have been forgiven for smugness as they witnessed this purge, but their own turn was coming. Having rid himself of potential opponents on the right, Daoud took on the left. Parchamis found themselves moved from post to post in Kabul, suddenly dispatched overseas as ambassadors, or simply fired for alleged (and probably real) malfeasance. Their replacements tended to be from the estranged branch of the royal family, with whom Daoud was clearly making amends.

These developments could not have pleased Moscow, which had probably counted on seeing the PDPA seize power on Daoud's demise. Still less popular in the Kremlin were the changes in Daoud's international posture. He patched up his relations with Pakistan, solicited aid from Iran and Saudi Arabia, cut back the number of Soviet advisers in Afghanistan, and made arrangements to shift the training of his military officers from the USSR to India and Egypt.

Daoud had not fulfilled Soviet expectations, and they undertook to get rid of him. The first step was to reunite the feuding Parcham and Khalq PDPA factions, an effort that succeeded in July 1977 after at least one failure. Not ten months later, in late April 1978, a coup dignified as the "Great Saur Revolution" won out over Daoud loyalists by a close and bloody margin, sending the president and many members of his family to their graves. Afghanistan slipped over into the Soviet camp.[7]

This fact was not immediately recognized by most Afghans, who treated the change as just one more example of *padshahgardi*—the "king game," as sudden leadership shifts had long been called. Such changes had never had much effect on the citizens' daily existence, and there was no apparent reason to believe that the latest violent example would be any different from those that had occurred before.

Most politically alert Afghans and knowledgeable foreigners, however, immediately understood that the coup was indeed intended to be a revolution. Nur Mohammed Taraki, the new leader, was well known as the Marxist-Leninist chief of the Khalqi wing of PDPA, whereas his second-in-command, Babrak Karmal, was the Parchami chief. In order of influence, all of the important cabinet posts were divided evenly between Parcham and Khalq representatives.

Those Islamists still at large inside the country immediately went into exile or hiding, as did most Traditionalists and non-communist politicians. Most who fled abroad settled in Pakistan, a few went to Iran, and a handful (largely politicians and members of the royal family) emigrated out of the region. The new Afghan authorities rounded up most of those who failed to act swiftly, and many were summarily executed. Between April 1978 and December 1979, when the Soviets invaded, some 50,000 to 100,000 persons simply disappeared in Afghan prisons.[8]

Only a few months after Saur, even the most politically unaware Afghans began to understand that this was no simple padshahgardi but an attempt to change the very fabric of their society. The government not only announced its program of reform (an accepted ritual for any new regime) but instantly began trying to implement it without regard for regional custom or local political autonomy. The reforms (such as land redistribution, women's rights, and annulment of farmers' debts) were progressive in appearance, but they upset deeply ingrained economic and cultural patterns, cherished as much by those the reforms were supposed to benefit as those they were intended to penalize.[9]

Even before the more radical reforms were promulgated, the first stirrings and rumblings of armed resistance were being felt. In a remote and mountainous part of Kunar Province, a government military post was overrun in July 1978, and by October all of eastern Nuristan had fallen to a loose alliance of tribal forces. In the words of one insurgent, it was their intent "to drive this Russian crumb-licker [Taraki] from our Islamic soil." By December parts of the Hazarajat in central Afghanistan had purged themselves of all government representatives and established a de facto independence that was still extant in 1987. In March 1979, local insurgents took over Herat, Afghanistan's third largest city, massacring Soviet advisers and their families as well as PDPA officials. In April, the northern province of Uruzgan erupted, and from then until the Soviet invasion in December, uprising followed uprising in one province after another, across the whole country.[10]

As time went on, some of this ferment was abetted by members of one or another of the pre-Saur, noncommunist trends that were regrouping and concentrating in Peshawar, Pakistan. At the outset, however, the exiles were generally in even worse disarray than was their wont. Daoud's rapprochement with Pakistan and Saudi Arabia in the two years before his overthrow had cut a good deal of support from the older Islamist exiles, who in 1976–1977 had already been weakened by their split into moderate and radical wings. The more recent emigres, though already starting to organize in their own groups, had to devote considerable energy just to survive. Well into 1980, "their influence hardly radiated beyond the refugee camps in Pakistan or in a few of the border provinces of Afghanistan."[11]

Thus, most of the initial anticommunist activity inside Afghanistan was merely a spontaneous, uncoordinated, grassroots reaction against unpopular reforms brought to the villages by arrogant intellectuals from Kabul. In general, those entrusted with the task were students who had lost whatever connections they had once had with village life, and who accepted the dictates of Marxist ideology with blind faith.

Many of them promptly paid for such ignorance with their lives. The government's literacy campaign, for example, used Soviet texts that outraged the deeply held religious beliefs of the rural population. In May 1978, less than a month after Saur, the first assassinations of teachers sent to preach the new gospel were reported.

Other DRA emissaries had the task of humiliating, dispossessing, and in some cases executing rich landowners. Usually, however, the local people who were supposed to benefit from the punishment of their "oppressors" related far more sympathetically to the victim of official wrath — who was often a member of the community and personally related to many of its citizens — than to the reformer.[12]

Subsequent Soviet propaganda has justified the USSR's 1979 invasion on the grounds that the United States, using exile groups in Pakistan, had launched an "undeclared war" against the fledgling DRA. Aside from unsubstantiated reports of the US furnishing a few medical supplies and some simple communications equipment, there is no evidence to support such allegations. It was the DRA's own misguided policies that led to the people's rejection of the new government.

Moreover, resistance field commanders from the outset exercised great independence. Although almost all of them were under the nominal supervision of one or another exile group in Pakistan and Iran, the nature of the war and the poor transborder communications meant that they operated on their own. They were dependent on the exiles to champion their cause and to act as a conduit for externally supplied weapons, but they were leaders in their own right and carried far more weight among their compatriots remaining in Afghanistan than did their exile "supervisors."

**The Exile Opposition in 1987**

When the 1978 "Saur revolution" occurred, the split among Islamist exiles in Pakistan between the radical *Hezb-e-Islami* (Islamic Party—IP), and the more moderate *Jamiat-Islami Afghanistan* (Islamic Society—IS) had already occurred. The names were significant. Although both were Islamist, the Leninist-style, cadre IP "party," justifying its right to absolute authority over all Afghans in the name of ultimate Islamic purity, placed politics above religion; its sole aim was to seize and monopolize power at whatever cost. The IS "society," on the other hand, called for a fight against the common enemy by a broad coalition of Muslims based on their faith and with emphasis on submerging any differences between them.

Immediately after the April 1978 coup, there was a proliferation of other emigré organizations in Peshawar, out of which a number of coalitions were formed and dissolved. The IS, for example, tried to make common cause with some eight small Traditionalist groups by forming a National Rescue Front in June 1978, but it only lasted six weeks before disbanding with mutual recriminations.

By the end of the first year, the IS and IP groups were rivaled by a third major organization, the Traditionalist *Mahaz-e-Melli Islami* (National Islamic Front—NIF), a royalist group with good connections in Pashtun frontier areas facing Pakistan. Both Traditionalists and Islamists then were confronted by new rivals. In 1978, the Jabha-e-Melli Neiat (National Liberation Front—NLF) and *Harakat-e-Enqilab-e-Islami* (Islamic Revolutionary Movement—IRM) entered the Traditionalist lists, and in

1979, a break-away branch of the IP formed a third Islamist group, the *Hezb-e-Islami/Khales* (Islamic Party/Khales—IP/K). Finally, in 1980 yet another Islamist group, the *Itihad-e Islami Barave Azadi Afghanistan* (Islamic Union for the Liberation of Afghanistan—IULA) came into being.[13]

In May 1985, these seven Sunni groups, all headquartered in Peshawar, Pakistan, banded together in a loose association called *Itihad-e Islami Mujahideen Afghanistan* (Islamic Unity of Afghanistan Mujahideen—IUAM). Unlike previous umbrella organizations, two of them bearing the same name, this one was still functioning after three years' precarious existence. The Afghan Shias, although supposedly allied in a "joint headquarters" in Tehran in 1983, had nothing like the IUAM until 18 June 1987, when a "seven-party Islamic Afghan coalition" was reportedly formed there.[14]

The political orientation of the various Sunni groups is exemplified by their leaders, who I will introduce in order of their position on the political spectrum:[15]

- Sayed Ahmad Gailani, who headed the Traditionalist/royalist NIF, inherited his father's spiritual rank of *pir* (old one) and leadership of a Sufi Brotherhood, the Quadiriyya. He married into a branch of the Afghan royal family in 1952, and subsequently became the Peugeot automobile dealer in Kabul. He thus combined royal connections, links with the commercial world and with modern Western capitalism, and the claim to a venerable Islamic heritage. He established an inside track in the resistance by organizing one of the first new groups after the April 1978 coup to help support the internal resistance. Nevertheless, inasmuch as the old regime was considered by most Islamists to have been corrupted by secular rot, Gailani's NIF cornered only a small but loyal following among Pashtuns traditionally associated with the royal family.
- Also related to the royal family but opposed to its secularism and to Western-style economics was Sibqatullah Mojadeddi, who inherited the leadership mantle of the *Naqshbandi* Sufi brotherhood. Mojadeddi's NIF had relatively wide exposure in Western media because of the connections he developed during long years in European exile, a result of his oppositional activities. Mojadeddi was somewhat slower in getting started and only came into his own after the Soviet invasion.
- Mohammed Nabi Mohammedi, whose IRM was Islamist when it was founded in 1979, evolved into a Traditionalist, hoping to attract as many supporters as possible to his group by avoiding ideological demands on them. Unlike the other two Traditionalist parties, his was not purely Pashtun but included Tajiks and Uzbeks as well. Mohammedi succeeded in attracting a mass following in part because he did not

demand absolute ideological or political conformity, but the IRM's detractors claimed that such fuzziness left it open to penetration by *WAD*, the DRA's Ministry of State Security. One of the largest groups in 1980, the IRM later lost considerable ground as certain field commanders shifted their allegiance to the moderate Islamists.
- Sayed Burhanuddin Rabbani's IS, probably the most powerful of the exile groups since the early 1980s, slowly increased its strength through 1988. Rabbani himself, who was born in 1940 in Badakhshan Province, concentrated on Islamic studies in Turkey and Egypt before returning to help found the Afghan Islamist movement in 1958. He was the most moderate of the Islamist leaders, having shown a willingness to compromise with rival groups on both his ideological flanks. His group's major weakness was the fact that it is mostly Tajik and Uzbek, whereas Afghan leaders traditionally have come from Pashtun stock. In the mid-1980s, Rabbani began to build some political support in key Pashtun areas, but his major strength remained in the Tajik/Uzbek minority areas.
- Close to Rabbani in general outlook — and cooperative with him — was the IP/K's Yunes Khales, who broke with the IP in 1979 over the IP's unwillingness to commit its forces to battle. Born in 1919 in Nangarhar Province, Khales was a respected leader among Pashtuns, and his following in this field helped to offset Rabbani's weakness among this ethnic group.
- Abdi-Rab Rasoul Sayaf (IULA) was born in Paghman, near Kabul, in about 1940. In 1972, he was deputy to Rabbani (then the "Amir," leader, of the Islamist movement), but Sayaf's ideological outlook — at least after 1980 — was much closer to Hekmatyar's radicalism, being almost as anti-West as anti-Soviet. In 1975 he was imprisoned in Daoud's roundup of Islamists, and he was only released in early 1980, after the Soviet invasion. He immediately fled to Pakistan, where he at first associated with Hekmatyar but later started his own party, the IULA. The IULA tapped into a rich Saudi-supplied source of weapons, with which Sayaf was said to have bought support among some opportunistic elements in the field.[16] By late 1988, Sayaf's party had dwindled markedly, however.
- The most radical and controversial of the resistance leaders, Gulbuddin Hekmatyar, is a Pashtun born in 1946 in the northern province of Baghlan. His preoccupation with politics prevented him from completing his studies in engineering at Kabul University in the late 1960s. In 1972, accused of having murdered a fellow student, he fled to Pakistan. After Saur, Hekmatyar, who had started with a clear advantage in terms of organization, membership, and local support from the Pakistanis, soon lost popularity due to his attempts to concentrate all power in his own hands and his tendency to hoard his own combat resources when others were committing theirs. Only after the Soviet invasion did he

enter the fray in earnest, and it was some years before reports of his units' fighting other resistance bands instead of the common enemy began to subside. The IP was reputed to be the most tightly disciplined of the exile groups. Although a Sunni, Hekmatyar was at first outspokenly in favor of Iran and its version of an Islamic revolution, and he expressed as much revulsion for "Western imperialism" as for the USSR. He was unabashedly authoritarian and antidemocratic. ("Democracy and Islam do not go together.")[17]

Although the rivalry among the various exile leaders was persistent, it began to heal as the war progressed. Moreover, the gradual increase in the strength of Rabbani's moderate Islamists was an encouraging sign of Afghan grass roots political maturity. In its own way, the fragmentation of the resistance—whatever its costs in efficiency—provided a sort of democratic platform from which field commanders and their followers could choose their allegiances, based on a combination of pragmatic and ideological considerations. Support gravitated neither to the old royalists nor to the extreme radical wing of the Islamists but to the moderates.

Less was known about the Shia exile community, because it was based in Iran, beyond the reach of Western observers. Only Mohammed Asif Mohseni's *Harakat-e-Islami* (Islamic Movement—IM), with headquarters in Qom, was relatively well known, and that is probably thanks mainly to his group's collaboration in the field with Rabbani's IS. Of the others, *Al Nasr* (Victory) and *Shura-e-Enqilab-Ettefaq-e-Islami* (Revolutionary Council of Islamic Unity—RCIU) were both founded inside Afghanistan before the Iranian Revolution, and they had no known external leadership. *Al Nasr* was initially supported by the Iranians, but this aid eventually was shifted to two other groups that were more firmly under Tehran's control: *Pasdaran Jihad Islami* (Islamic Jihad Army—IJA), which was the creature of the Iranian army; and the ultra-radical *Hizbullah* ("God's Party"), which placed itself directly under the Ayatullah Khomeini and maintained an external office in Mashad. *Hizbullah* was directed by a thirty-man council and a five-man "central council" and proclaimed as its goal a "worldwide Islamic Revolution."[18]

### The Mujahideen in the Field

In 1987, the *mujahideen* ("warriors of the Holy War") or *jihad* fell into various categories. Most belonged to bands that owed allegiance to one of the exile groups described above. There was a basic split between the Shias and the Sunnis, with the former concentrated in the central highlands (Hazarajat), and the latter dispersed throughout all the borderlands. Among the Sunnis, Rabbani's IS dominated in most of the northern provinces and spread southward on both east and west flanks. In so doing it established authority over almost all of the Afghan Tajiks and Uzbeks, who were much more amenable to endorsing one organization than were their Pashtun compatriots, who were divided along narrow tribal lines. The southern and eastern provinces, which encompass the Pashtun tribal areas, thus show a patchwork pattern of loyalties.

Although most mujahideen were motivated by patriotism, Islam, and outrage at the alien occupation, a few — particularly among the independents and those nominally allied with Sayaf's IULA — were exploiting the situation for the brigandage that war conditions allowed.[19]

The first fighting, in 1978, was strictly local, as one or another policy of the new regime outraged a community to the point of taking up arms against central authority. The advantage of a locally based resistance lay in the total support that the community would give it, but disadvantages were the responsibility the mujahideen felt for their dependents (who were vulnerable to reprisals) and the lack of incentive to cooperate with other groups. Even after many local resistance groups had established links with the exiles, this factor — especially in the Pashtun areas — tended to dampen enthusiasm on the local level for the jihad.[20]

After the Soviets entered the conflict directly, the massive retaliation against civilians in areas offering resistance increased markedly and led to the evacuation of entire communities as refugees to Pakistan or Iran. On the one hand this partially broke down the civilian infrastructure on which the mujahideen depended, but on the other it gave the fighting men freer rein. With their women, children, and old ones being cared for as refugees abroad, the families of the fighters in the field were no longer hostage to the enemy or a bond holding the fighting men to one locale.

Unlike most other groups, Hekmatyar's IP combat units from the outset rarely stemmed from the areas where they did their fighting. His roving bands did not have to worry about retribution against their families, but neither did they enjoy the wholehearted support of civilians in their areas of operation. Often as unfamiliar with the terrain as the government troops sent to root them out, the IP bands needed such support for both attack and defense.

From these conflicting advantages and disadvantages evolved compromise organizational solutions, best exemplified and known in areas under the control of Ahmad Shah Massoud, one of Rabbani's (and the whole war's) most outstanding field commanders. Many of Massoud's practices were adopted by other successful commanders, such as IP/Kh's Abdul Haq in Kabul Province.

Massoud divided his forces into full-time and part-time troops, the latter on the pattern of the Minutemen of the American Revolutionary War. When not fighting, the Afghan Minutemen were farming or otherwise supporting the resistance. By contrast, the fulltime mujahideen were professional fighting men. Some were organized into *motariks,* fast-moving mobile units that could strike at targets and fade away before retaliatory strikes could be organized.

Massoud's military organization depended on levies of local manpower, which in turn implied a measure of civil rule. By 1984 he had established a civilian infrastructure in his home territory of the Panjshir Valley that included such departments as a court system, tax collection, support for war victims, schools, mosques, a hospital, and a military training academy.[21]

In 1987 it was impossible to set an accurate figure on the total number of mujahideen in the field. Press accounts and exile claims ranged from 90,000 (with only 20,000 active at any one time) up to 500,000. A German estimate at the end of 1984 placed the number of full-time mujahideen at 90,000 to 120,000, with an additional 100,000 to 150,000 part-time guerrillas. In 1987 an American journalist reported from Washington that there were 120,000 mujahideen, whereas a week later the *London Times* gave a figure of 200,000.[22]

Total casualties were equally hard to determine. A German group, Verein fuer afghanische Fluechtlingshilfe (Association for Afghan Refugee Assistance) estimated in 1986 that about one million civilians and 80,000 mujahideen had been killed. In addition, some 45,000 other Afghans were missing and presumed dead, and a further 100,000 had been executed by the DRA. Some 65,000 were thought to be imprisoned. A United Nations report in late 1986 said that 10,000 to 12,000 civilians had died in the first nine months of 1986, compared with 37,000 in all of 1985.[23]

Estimates of casualties on the other side were equally uncertain, though occasionally given with great precision. For example, the resistance press agency claimed in 1987 that 8,321 Soviet and DRA troops were killed in 1986, of whom 3,040 were identified as Soviet soldiers, 1,602 DRA, and the rest undetermined. In 1985 the deaths had totaled 7,920, of whom 1,162 were Soviets, 1,536 were DRA, and the rest undetermined. Defections from the DRA went up from 1,000 in 1985 to 3,541 in 1986. In the first four months of 1987, there were another 2,132 reported defections.[24]

Although none of these figures could be accepted unreservedly, they fell within proper ranges of probability, especially given the more intense fighting of 1986 and 1987. Until 1988, Moscow published no statistics on Soviet losses, and when precise figures of 13,310 killed, 35, 478 wounded, and 311 missing were released in May 1988, they were suspect both within and outside the USSR. For example, as early as July 1986, the *Guardian's* Moscow correspondent advised that "informed Soviet sources" considered the official US State Department estimate of 10,000 dead and 20,000 wounded to be "much too low."[25] Later, Soviet sources were to admit that some 30,000–35,000 Soviet soldiers had perished from disease alone during the war. In any case, the exact death figure was less important than Soviet popular perceptions, which also saw the figures as much higher.[26]

## Goals, Assets, and Strategies

For the resistance, the goals of the struggle were clear and uncomplicated: removal of the Soviet troops, destruction of the puppet DRA regime, and establishment of a new, independent Afghanistan. Although there had been — and doubtless would again be — sharp disagreement among the exiles as to the form of the future government, by 1987 there seemed to be tacit agreement to shelve such arguments until the Soviets had been expelled. Resistance cooperation in the field was improving, with different groups sharing supplies.[27]

By contrast, the Soviet goals, although basically unchanged since 1980, were mutually contradictory and seemed to have become less sharply defined. In 1980, the Soviets were intent on annihilating the resistance, establishing a genuinely popular regime that was firmly cemented in the Soviet camp, and then, perhaps within a year, removing most of the occupation forces used for these purposes. After nearly eight years' effort, they had succeeded in neither of the first two endeavors, but were faced with growing pressures to undertake the third anyway. In 1987 their declared goals — less ambitious but no more realistic — were to abandon gradually their own involvement in the war, having established some kind of friendly Afghan government that could handle its own security. Like the American effort in 1968 to "Vietnamize" the conflict in southeast Asia, however, the attempt to "Afghanize" Moscow's war seemed fated for failure.

The assets that each side could bring to bear to achieve its aims seemed hopelessly unequal in 1980, an apparent imbalance that had been only partly rectified after nearly eight years of war. At the outset, the Afghans had no cohesive resistance organization, no effective propaganda mechanism, no organized security service (and little experience in intelligence operations), no cohesive military organization, and no modern experience in fighting a guerrilla war or resisting foreign invasion. The Afghan "nation" was a weak concept to most of its citizens, for whom loyalties rarely extended beyond the village boundaries. There was, however, the underlying bedrock of Islam and the natural pride and self-assurance of a people who had not been overrun successfully for centuries. There was their natural affinity for weapons and fighting. And there were their familiar mountains, whose fastnesses could help defeat even modern military technology.

The Soviets, for their part, had a massive, modern, fully equipped military machine that within living memory had invaded and destroyed indigenous oppositions in Hungary and Czechoslovakia. Via the world's largest intelligence and propaganda apparatus, as well as by global Communist party connections and Communist front activities, they had achieved a high level of sophistication in deception, subversion, and influence operations.[28] Nevertheless, Marxism-Leninism, though aggressive and crusading in its writs, was not the heart and soul of the individual Soviet soldier in Afghanistan. Though some doubtless believed they were fulfilling their "holy [proletarian internationalist] duty," most probably had little motivation beyond surviving until the end of their tours. Moreover, the very massiveness of the Soviet apparat led to a "cookbook" approach to operations that discouraged initiative by subordinate units faced with swiftly changing conditions.

In line with the simplicity of their goals and assets, the Afghans' strategies were also few and clear: maintain the total dedication of fighting men and civilians to the jihad until victory; sustain Afghan values in the exile groups abroad; achieve unity—or at least cooperation—among the various resistance factions; build international support for the resistance; frustrate the Soviet effort to depopulate the countryside by encouraging people to stay on the land; keep the combat initiative; spread the conflict to the cities; raise the level of fighting so as to increase Soviet casualties (at whatever cost to the mujahideen); and, ultimately, grind down the enemy's willingness to prosecute the war by raising its costs to unacceptable levels.[29]

Strategies attempted by the Soviets were more detailed, but as of 1987 few had succeeded:

- *Military.* Hold key cities and communications lines while conducting periodic ground attacks and continual air strikes against resistance-controlled areas and strong points; isolate and surround resistance forces, cutting them off from their bases in Pakistan and destroying them piecemeal in battle; deter foreign support by air and artillery strikes against border villages in Iran and Pakistan; utterly wipe out Afghan villages in areas where the resistance was active; destroy the resistance's local agricultural support base by razing irrigation works, orchards, housing; displace the rural population in strategic areas, driving it into foreign exile, into the cities, or into other parts of the coun-

try; terrorize any who remained in order to discourage support to the resistance.
- *Political.* Slowly spread government control through the countryside; enhance the DRA's reputation domestically and internationally; "broaden the base" of government by admitting token noncommunists to positions of ostensible (but not real) power;[30] aggressively recruit new members into the PDPA and the National Front (NF—formerly the National Fatherland Front); establish traditional Soviet means of persuasion and coercion, such as front groups, collective farms, secret police; exploit tribal hostilities and buy off tribes, especially those lying across resistance supply lines.
- *Ideological.* Divorce the DRA from "socialism," and project the image of Afghanistan as an independent Islamic republic in the "national democratic stage of development."
- *Economic.* By aid and trade, bind Afghanistan irrevocably to the Soviet bloc.[31]
- *Sociological.* "Sovietize" the Afghan people via broad programs of education, including the dispatch to the USSR of 7- to 9-year-olds for ten years of boarding school.[32]
- *Psychological.* Terrorize and discourage opponents, both civilian and military; convince the outside world of the inevitability of a Soviet victory; stifle all objective reporting about the war; assassinate leading resistance field commanders; dispatch agents among the exiles to fan existing disputes and foment new ones; project the impression of a divided, corrupt, ineffective resistance working in a hopeless cause against an infinitely patient, confident, omniscient, and omnipotent Soviet adversary; show the DRA as the only legitimate and organized force in the country; give the DRA and USSR a "peace-loving" image by: (1) undertaking a false withdrawal of Soviet troops in October 1986; (2) conducting forceful propaganda for a coalition government of "national reconciliation" (including some exile leaders and even the king); and (3) instituting a unilateral DRA cease-fire in January 1987. (Note: All of the above were belied by a much more intense level of combat through the summer of 1987).[33]

## Tactics, Weapons, and Outside Support

Both sides in the war modified their tactics in response to the weapons and equipment available to them and to their adversaries. At first, the mujahideen were almost solely dependent on arms that deserting DRA soldiers brought with them, or those captured in combat. Although there were some heavy weapons among these, the mujahideen had no way of maintaining them, and they had to be stripped of whatever might be useful to a foot soldier before being abandoned or cached. The basic weapon in the first year was the British .303 single-shot rifle, a World War

I issue. Later, the Soviet AK-47 Kalashnikov assault rifle came more and more into use.

For at least the first year, outside support consisted only of a modest supply of small arms, donated by the United States and Saudi Arabia. As time went on, the level of support from both donors increased, and Egypt, which earlier had been given Soviet turn key arms factories, provided stores of Soviet weapons. Despite international outrage over the invasion, some influential voices in Washington were warning that supplying weapons would be the "way least likely to drive the Soviets out of Afghanistan." American aid only began to reach significant levels in 1984.[34]

At first the mujahideen suffered from overconfidence, believing that they could storm and hold fixed objectives. Assaults on strongly defended Soviet positions resulted in heavy resistance losses, and attempts to seize control of Kandahar and Herat, the second and third largest towns in the country, resulted in unacceptably severe civilian casualties and property destruction.[35]

The initial Soviet tactics were at least as awkward. Cumbersome armored sweeps, known in advance to the resistance from informants in the DRA forces, permitted the mujahideen to fade away into the mountains well ahead of the advancing troops. After some time, the Soviets would find it necessary to abandon the ground they had seized, if only to launch other attacks elsewhere. Although they tried to minimize their own casualties, they were not always successful; the guerrillas would harrass retreating columns with sniper fire and ambushes.

As a result of successful resistance attacks on isolated outposts, the Soviets by 1982 had begun pulling in their troops to safe enclaves. They abandoned the Hazarajat completely, leaving those central provinces largely self-governing. For their part, the mujahideen began concentrating on more vulnerable targets such as convoys. The Soviets responded by clearing all cover, including human habitation, from the edges of main roads, to which the resistance replied by night attacks. Both sides used mines to increasing advantage. During 1983, the Soviets began using the SU-25 ground-attack aircraft to supplement their Mi-24 helicopter gunships.

In 1984, thanks to a belated rise in US support, the resistance began to get better weapons. RPG 7 antitank rockets, mortars, and .50-calibre machine guns improved their capabilities, but they still had no effective counter to the gunship, the most devastating weapon in the Soviet counterinsurgency arsenal. The mujahideen were reduced to conducting nighttime hit-and-run operations, or attacking when bad weather grounded the helicopters.

There was growing criticism of the US effort, both for the poor quality of arms provided and for the failure to insure that they reached resistance hands. Allegedly, detonators and other vital parts had been removed from munitions, and there were many duds (up to 55 percent of all mortar rounds, according to one source). The early SA-7s were unreliable and left a white smoke trail that led directly back to the launcher. Later versions, modified by a US contractor, apparently performed better, but they never were a battlefield success. Stocks of ammunition for heavy machine guns were inadequate. Once the arms passed to the Pakistani Interservice Intelligence Directorate for distribution to the mujahideen, they passed out of US control; some 15 to 70 percent of them then disappeared.[36]

In 1984, the Soviets were improving their tactics and raising both the number and quality of their ground forces. Anti-personnel mines were sown by air across supply routes. The Soviet force level increased from 105,000 to 115,000 during the year, and the first *spetsnaz* (special purpose) troops were deployed. For the first time, the Soviets themselves began operating at night and laying ambushes for the mujahideen. The subsequent introduction of night-vision weapons and silencers gave the Soviets a decided advantage that the resistance's familiarity with the terrain could only partly overcome. During the 1984 Panjsher offensive, paratroopers and light tanks were airlifted to the mountain heights in an attempt to cut off the enemy's retreat. Soviet TU-16 long-range aircraft carpet-bombed the valley from bases in Central Asia. Casualties increased on both sides, but there was no change in the overall stalemate.

At the beginning of 1985, the first hard evidence that the mujahideen were at last getting worthwhile surface-to-air missiles began to appear. Decoy flares dropped by Soviet aircraft operating out of Kabul airport were setting occasional fires in the West German and American Embassy compounds.[37] Moreover, rocket attacks on Kabul during the last week of 1984 may have forced the postponement of the triumphal 20th anniversary celebration of the PDPA's founding from January 1 to January 10. By mid-1985, supplies of Chinese-made 107-mm rockets were coming through, and the resistance could launch an all-night attack on Kabul airport with them.[38]

The Soviets, however, were honing their own tactics and continuing to experiment with equipment. By the end of 1985, some 25 percent of all Soviet spetsnaz troops were reportedly posted to Afghanistan, and the capability for launching large assaults on the resistance rose from three simultaneous offensives to five. Victories against resistance besiegers of Khost and Barikot were accompanied by renewed efforts to cut supply lines to Pakistan. Security belts were being constructed around major cities to prevent mujahideen infiltration.[39]

Through 1986 and into 1987, the level of combat rose steadily. In April 1986, a combined Soviet/DRA assault on a resistance stronghold at Zhawar succeeded in routing the defenders, with heavy casualties on both sides. Part of the reason for the success of the operation was the failure of US stinger missiles, brought into action for the first time, to survive the temperature extremes of the battlefield. Nevertheless, the "defeat" of the mujahideen was more apparent than real: they decimated the best (perhaps only) effective DRA combat units, caused heavy casualties to the Soviets, and within two weeks had reoccupied the fortress after the victors withdrew.[40]

In September, following improvements in the stingers, the long-heralded delivery of effective antiaircraft weapons at last gave the resistance an equalizer against the gunships and ground attack aircraft. Not only stingers and the British blowpipe missiles, but Swiss oerlikon 20-mm cannons were starting to flow. As a result, Soviet losses during the last three months of 1986 and on through mid-1987 were running at more than one aircraft per day. Astonishingly, the Soviets did not devise any effective counter to the new weapons except to raise the operational ceiling of some aircraft to 10,000 feet above ground level and to lower that of others to about five meters.[41]

The sudden change in the balance of forces in the air war forced the Soviets to change their ground tactics. The absence of air cover caused them to forego the now-vulnerable armored personnel carriers and revert to traditional infantry tactics. Artillery proved to be a poor and inaccurate substitute for aircraft, and the mujahideen could mass their forces for attack or defense. This had the unexpected side effect of spurring more field cooperation among the resistance groups, which undertook hand-to-hand battles with the enemy. In separate battles near Kandahar and in Paktia Province, badly outnumbered resistance forces fought Soviet and DRA forces to a standstill in July 1987.[42]

## End Note — November 1988

In the year that has passed since the above analysis was written, there have been radical changes in the Afghan situation. What follows is a replacement for a final section that was originally entitled "1987 Appraisal of Resistance Viability." That section reached the conclusion that time was probably on the resistance's side, a position that as late as the end of 1987 was still considered rashly optimistic by many analysts. A year later, it has emerged as an obviously much too cautious assessment.

Although the momentum for a Soviet withdrawal was underestimated, the reasons for it remain valid and are worth repeating for their possible bearing on other situations elsewhere in the world.

The first point was that Afghanistan was only one of a large number of serious problems facing the USSR, whereas the Soviet occupation was virtually the sole national problem facing Afghans. The corollary was that the average mujahed knew exactly what he was fighting for, whereas the average Soviet and DRA soldier had no corresponding dedication.

Second, it was noted that Gorbachev was counting on mobilizing the Soviet people behind his new policies, infusing them with discipline, enthusiasm, and the spirit of *glasnost* (openness). But the war was unquestionably unpopular, and glasnost itself had given rise to more and more grumbling about it, undercutting what little discipline and enthusiasm remained in Soviet society.[43]

Third, Gorbachev no longer had in hand some traditionally Russian assets used by the tsars and commissars of yesteryear in their conquests of Central Asia and the Caucasus: a stolidly docile (if unenthusiastic) population, unlimited time, and infinite patience. For the first time in recent history, the Kremlin was confronted with a foe that had more patience and dedication to victory that it did.

Fourth, there were continuing indications that the CPSU and Soviet state were keeping a careful distance from their Afghan cousins, who were accorded only observer status in Comecon, were not members of the Warsaw Pact, and (after brief recognition as socialists in 1978-1979) were quietly but firmly relegated to the category of "nations in the national democratic phase of development."

Finally, there was the external dimension, the support and encouragement accorded the mujahideen by outside powers such as the United States, Pakistan, China, and Iran.

All of these factors must have played a role in the Soviet decision to pull its troops out of Afghanistan unconditionally, a decision declared by Gorbachev in February 1988 and at this writing still under way.[44] What surprised even the most enthusiastic backers of the *mujahideen,* however, was the stiffness and completeness of the apparent Soviet capitulation.

Soviet investments and commitments in Afghanistan had begun with the economic aid and trade programs of the 1950s, moved on to a political level in the mid-60s (founding of the PDPA), had taken on an ideological coloration in 1978 with the PDPA coup, and finally reached their climax in the military invasion and occupation of December 1979.[45] Now the film was being run in reverse and at high speed. The military retreat meant that neither the already weakened ideological commitment nor the political commitment could be sustained. In late 1988, only the economic connection, the essential foundation for any future politico-ideological expansion into Afghanistan, remained a clear-cut Soviet objective.

Gorbachev has said that the decision to get out of Afghanistan was reached at a secret Politburo meeting in April 1985, two months after he assumed the title of general secretary of CSPU.[46] As far as it goes, this statement is probably accurate; what Gorbachev did not say, however, was that he had given his military a free hand to try to achieve victory over the resistance within a fixed time frame (one or two years), after which, win or lose, the troops would be brought home. This interpretation is sustained by the fact that Soviet offensives against both mujahideen and Afghan civilian targets peaked in 1985, causing the highest single-year casualties of the war, and continued at a furious rate in 1986.[47] It is probable that only the introduction of stinger antiaircraft missiles into the military equation prevented casualties among the Afghans from indiscriminate air attacks from mounting even higher in 1986 than 1985.

In addition to direct military pressure on the Afghans, the Soviets undertook other measures to shore up the Afghan regime and minimize their losses as the deadline for withdrawal approached: they tried to popularize the PDPA and give the appearance of internal political flexibility (while at the same time keeping real political control in PDPA hands); they replaced Babrak Karmal with the former chief of the secret police, Najibullah; they increased pressure on Pakistan via transborder air and artillery strikes and by agent-planted bombs in Pakistani cities; there was a stepped-up campaign to buy off and arm tribes along the main mujahideen infiltration routes in order to interdict resistance supply and troop movements; Soviet troops began distributing consumer goods in Afghan villages; efforts were made to dissuade the United States from supplying stingers and the British from supplying blowpipe surface-to-air missiles to the resistance.

None of the measures was effective. Most Afghans continued to despise the PDPA, which they rightly considered a Quisling government; if anything the replacement of Babrak by the detested former chief of the secret police Najibullah only increased their contempt. The Pakistanis remained calm and dedicated to continuing their support for the resistance. The tribes in the border areas gladly accepted bribes, occasionally fulfilled their side of the bargain, but eventually and invariably turned the guns they had received on the donors. The consumer goods distribution program led to a surge in black marketing and corruption without increasing Soviet popularity. And the flow of hand-held antiaircraft missiles continued unabated.

These failures, all predictable, could have led Gorbachev to postpone his departure deadline. The immense political costs, internal as well as external, to the Kremlin in conceding defeat to the mujahideen were commonly believed to be unacceptable to any Soviet leader. By the end of 1987, few expected Gorbachev to increase the stakes by committing the extra 350,000 troops needed to establish minimal control over the country—but even fewer thought he would accept the price of defeat. Most believed he would continue the attempt to grind down the resistance by a long, slow war of attrition.

The fact that the withdrawal has proceeded (so far) according to schedules is probably the most clear-cut, if still only indirect, evidence of the seriousness of the USSR's internal problems.

## Lessons Learned and a Look to the Future

The credit for getting the Soviet armies out of Afghanistan must be shared by the many players already mentioned, among them Pakistan for its resolute support of the mujahideen, the United States for its belated commitment to a resistance victory, and Mikhail Gorbachev for his realism in accepting the inevitable. But I believe that these participants have done no more than influence the timing of the withdrawal. The Afghans were prepared to go on fighting for generations, if need be, to secure their independence, and in the end they would have been successful, even as they were in ultimately breaking free of the Greek, Mongol, Timurid, Moghul, and British empires. Without that fighting spirit, the other inputs would have meant nothing; with it, the others were welcome auxiliaries but little more.

The foregoing judgment, shared by most Afghans, can and will be discounted by many as Afghanophile posturing, but it has an importance that transcends any arguments over its objectivity. It is vital that the other contributors to the approaching finale of the First Russo-Afghan War understand that the Afghans do not feel beholden to anyone but themselves for their victory.

The Pakistanis must understand that their generous support of the Afghans during these troubled times will not translate into an automatic Afghan acceptance of the long-disputed Durand Line as the border between the two nations.

The United States must understand that its furnishing of sophisticated weapons, while most welcome, will not translate into automatic support of American policies in the post-Soviet period.

The Soviet Union must understand that not only is Afghanistan not worth the price of conquest, but that the Kremlin will have to deal with Afghan leaders in the post-occupation era as equals. This will not come easily to Politburo members.

Besides the principal players, others will also draw lessons. For minority nationalists inside the USSR, especially those in Central Asia, there is new hope for the future. The impact of the Afghan victory may be slow in coming, but it is hard to imagine that there will not ultimately be a serious political fallout from the Soviet retreat.

Conversely, other Marxist-Leninist regimes in the "national democratic stage of development"—as well as aspiring revolutionaries in lands still under noncommunist rule—must feel despair that they can no longer count on all-out Soviet protection. (It is intriguing that South Yemen, a nation even more primitive than Afghanistan, is solemnly considered to have passed this stage and now to be pursuing "scientific socialism." The fact that vital Soviet strategic military bases are located in South Yemen may have something to do with the surprisingly advanced stage of development that the Kremlin accords it, which implies a continued Soviet willingness to defend the country against all external and internal enemies.)

Whether Afghanistan becomes a model for other anti-Soviet national liberation movements depends in part on the regime that eventually replaces Najibullah's. The Soviet hope for a coalition government in which the PDPA plays a dominant or even an incidental role is a vain one, but the shape of the future regime remains unclear.

The old way of ruling amounted to almost complete independence at the village level, with greybeard elders in command. The war chased many of these local leaders into exile, and a whole new generation of young mujahideen field commanders began to administer in their place. With the end of the war in sight, many of the greybeards are now returning, and they have an incentive to cooperate with the regime (especially now that it has offered to share power with them) in getting rid of their local rivals. In many cases, these conflicts will be settled violently and personally, with the villagers themselves making the final judgment.

One resistance commander who has dealt successfully with this kind of jealousy is Ahmad Shah Massoud, who has managed to retain overall control of his region while allowing the most respected former elders to return and resume governing their villages. There are a few other regional commanders with equal vision, and shape of a future Afghanistan may be emerging from their experiments. Superficially, their administrations resemble the old, precommunist system of local rule under a distant central government.

But Massoud and the other regional commanders are much closer to the village level than Kabul's bureaucrats have ever been, and they can be expected to make a much greater impact on all Afghan citizens in their areas. The greybeards will no longer rule with quite such a free hand.

On the other hand, Massoud and the other main commanders will have more independence from Kabul's rule than the provincial governors who have traditionally been the intermediate level of command between the central government and the districts. For one thing, many of them already govern more than one province and thus have bigger constituencies than any governor has had. For another, they have been administering their areas for some time and are not about to relinquish political control to those who have been sitting out the war in Peshawar as exiles, no matter what their former rank.

Pessimists expect an outbreak of internecine warfare when the Soviets depart, optimists a fair degree of collaboration among neighboring regional commanders. The most probable immediate result will be a mixture of the two, with anarchy and bloodshed in areas where no administration has been set up and reasonable calm elsewhere. Ultimately, it can be hoped that a cantonal government patterned on the Swiss model will develop, with the central government responsible for such overall concerns as foreign affairs, international trade, banking, and national defense, but with regional governments in almost complete control of their territories. The old system of independent village rule is probably a fading phenomenon, one of the war's many casualties.

The probable instability that will follow the final Soviet withdrawal will be an enticement for outsiders of all kinds to offer their own suggestions for settling the Afghans' problems. If there is one cardinal lesson that the war has taught the world, however, it is that Afghans are averse to outside interference in their affairs. No matter how painful the process, it must be the Afghans—and only the Afghans—who determine the shape and direction of their future government.

## Notes

1. For a fascinating description of the Afghan community (*qawm*) and other elements of Afghan society, see Oliver Roy, *Islam and Resistance in Afghanistan* (Cambridge, England: Cambridge University Press, 1986), chapters 1 and 2.
2. See Bernard Dupaigne, "Les Peuples," in *Afghanistan: La Colonisation impossible* (Paris: Les Editions du Cerf, 1984), pp. 27-55. No reliable census has ever been taken in Afghanistan. The Pashtuns, once thought to number over 50 percent of a population numbering perhaps 17 million, are now believed by most Western scholars to be only a plurality inside the country.
3. See Roy, *Islam and Resistance,* pp. 10-11. The government man customarily lived in a house set apart from the rest of the village, and there was usually one village elder delegated to communicate with him. His relationship with the other villagers was one of "profound and mutual contempt."

4. Ibid., p. 59.
5. Anthony Arnold, *Afghanistan: The Soviet Invasion in Perspective* (Stanford: Hoover Institution Press, 1985).
6. Roy, *Islam and Resistance,* Chapters 4-8, provides the best elaboration of these short descriptions.
7. There is still dispute in scholarly circles about the Soviet role, if any, in the 1978 coup, but the circumstantial evidence supporting that interpretation is convincing, and it is backed by Babrak Karmal's blunt statement in 1981 to an Indian journalist who was also an old friend: "Russia wanted that there should be revolution here." (Anthony Arnold, *Afghanistan's Two-Party Communism: Parcham and Khalq* [Stanford: Hoover Institution Press, 1983], p. 59, quoting *New Delhi,* no. 24 [April 27-May 10, 1981]: 10.)
8. A small but important percentage of these consisted of Parchamis, for as soon as the coup was accomplished, Parcham and Khalq again were at each other's throats, and this time the Khalqis won decisively. Later, however, the surviving Parchami leaders, who had been exiled as DRA diplomats, returned on the coattails of the invading Soviet forces in early 1980 to establish their own hegemony over party and state.
9. For a closer look at what these reforms were supposed to correct — and how they missed their mark — see Nazif Shahrani and Robert L. Canfield, eds., *Revolutions and Rebellions in Afghanistan: Anthropological Perspectives* (Berkeley: University of California Press, 1984), pp. 10-25 and 291-340. For an excellent description of how Communist officials antagonized the rural population, see Nasir Shansab, *Soviet Expansion in the Third World: Afghanistan, a Case Study* (Silver Spring, MD: Bartleby Press, 1986): pp. 54-59.
10. Roy, *Islam and Resistance,* pp. 99-191; Shahrani, *Revolution and Rebellions,* pp. 77-93.
11. J. Bruce Amstutz, *Afghanistan: The First Five Years of Soviet Occupation* (Washington: National Defense University Press, 1986), p. 89; Roy, *Islam,* p. 78.
12. Shansab, *Soviet Expansion,* pp. 49-50, 58-62. The attrition among progovernment intellectuals was probably higher than is commonly realized. Whereas most of the PDPA consisted of teachers and other intellectuals in 1978, by 1982 they constituted only 5 percent of a party conference of middle and higher leaders that gathered in Kabul. See Arnold, *Afghanistan's Two-Party Communism,* p. 125.
13. Amstutz, *Soviet Occupation,* pp. 92-93, 100, 400-406; Roy, *Islam and Resistance,* p. 120.
14. Amstutz, *Soviet Occupation,* p. 109; British Broadcasting Corporation Summary of World Broadcasts, 25 July 1987, p. FE/8629/i. In addition, minor Sunni — and probably Shia — groups and factions proliferated both inside Afghanistan and in exile. None was known to play a significant role in 1987, however.
15. Information about these individuals is summarized from Roy, *Islam and Resistance,* pp. 127-138 and Amstutz, *Soviet Occupation,* pp. 397-406.
16. Roy accuses Sayaf of furnishing arms to groups more interested in brigandage than the jihad (Roy, *Islam and Resistance,* pp. 135-136). According to an unsubstantiated report, Sayaf had only 2 percent of the fighting *mujahideen* but — thanks to Saudi patronage — received 20 percent of the weapons (Manchester Herald [CT], 11 May 1987, cited in *Afghanistan Forum* 15 no. 4:6.)

17. Amstutz, *Soviet Occupation,* p. 400. In 1987 Hekmatyar criticized Iran for separating the religious and secular establishments, declaring that he would combine both under his own leadership in a post-Soviet Afghanistan.
18. "Forgotten Refugees: Afghans in Iran," *The Middle East,* August 1986, reprinted in *Afghanistan Forum* 14 no. 6: 23-24.
19. Roy, *Islam and Resistance,* pp. 135-136. Like Hekmatyar, however, Sayaf has enthusiastic supporters as well as suspicious detractors. According to the *Pakistani Times* of 2 June 1987 (*Afghanistan Forum* 15 no. 4, July 1987: 8), he personally led *mujahideen* forces into battle with the Soviets in the Jaji region of Paktia Province, and the Soviets tried to capture him with an airborne commando unit.
20. Edward Girardet, *Afghanistan: The Soviet War* (New York: St. Martin's Press, 1985), pp. 69-70.
21. *Christian Science Monitor,* 2 October 1984, p. 1.
22. *Frankfurter Allgemeine Zeitung,* 24 December 1984, p. 8; *South China Morning Post,* 5 January 1985; *Afghanistan Forum* vol. 13, no. 2, March 1985, p. 16); *New York Times,* 18 February 1987, p. A10; *London Times Spectrum,* 25 February 1987, p. 10. Hekmatyar and Mojadeddi have each claimed to control up to 150,000, and Gailani 200,000 (*San Francisco Chronicle,* 18 March 1987, p. E1), but these clearly are exaggerations.
23. *Afhanistan Forum* 14, no. 5 (September 1986): 14; and 15, no. 1 (January 1987): 5. The German estimate may be high.
24. Ibid., 15, no. 2 (March 1987): 11; and no. 4 (July 1987): 5.
25. *Financial Times,* 26 May 1988, p. 3; *The Guardian,* 12 July 1986, p. 1.
26. *San Francisco Chronicle,* 24 October 1988, p. A13. "A Soviet Soldier Opts Out in Afghanistan," Radio Liberty Research Bulletin RL-121/84, 19 March 1984. In late 1981, students in a Soviet non-commissioned officers' school calculated that there had already been some 20,000-25,000 killed in action (Possev 39, no. 6 (June 1983): 15).
27. United Press International, 6 July 1987.
28. A first priority task after the invasion was to rename, reorganize, and retrain the secret police (State Information Service—Khad), which became reputedly the most efficient DRA bureaucracy and was subsequently made into a ministry (Wad).
29. *London Times,* 19 December 1986, p. 5.
30. This policy was in force in 1980, fell out of favor in 1981, and then was revived in 1985. In 1987, it was broadened to include the program of "national reconciliation."
31. Between 1979 and 1986, trade with the USSR tripled. In 1986 an agreement was signed that would raise Moscow's share from 70 to 80 percent of all foreign aid to the DRA. See US Department of State, Bureau of Public Affairs, *Afghanistan: Seven Years of Occupation,* Special Report no. 155, December 1986, p. 15.
32. *Kabul New Times,* November 18, 19, and 20, 1984.
33. United Press International, 14 July 1987; TASS, 14 June 1987; *Manchester Guardian Weekly,* 21 June 1987, p. 13. Soviet peace feelers all included a non-negotiable proviso that whatever post-Soviet government emerged would have to be "friendly" to the USSR. The resistance flatly and unanimously rejected any such provision. Though the Communist "peace" overtures may have been pure deception, intended only to make their side appear reasonable, they

seemed to reflect a steadily eroding DRA position and thus served to bolster resistance resolve during the first half of 1987.
34. *Christian Science Monitor,* 28 May 1980, p. 6; Carl Bernstein, "Arms for Afghanistan," *The New Republic,* 18 July 1981, pp. 8–10. The best compendium of information and references on the arms supply program is Amstutz, *Soviet Occupation,* pp. 199-222.
35. Shansab, *Soviet Expansion,* p. 84.
36. *Wall Street Journal,* 9 April 1984, p. 34; *New York Times,* 24 May 1983, p. 10; *San Francisco Chronicle,* 13 July 1987, p. 13; Amstutz, *Soviet Occupation,* p. 213. According to one resistance spokesman, Pakistani policy was to release sophisticated weapons to the Afghans only when Soviet forces neared the Pakistani border, but not to issue them when the Afghans wanted to go on the offensive elsewhere (*London Times,* 22 July 1987, p. 7). If this ever was Pakistani policy, the fierce inland battles that were raging in the summer of 1987 would seem to indicate that it has been abandoned.
37. *Sueddeutsche Zeitung,* 14 February 1985, p. 1.
38. *New York Times,* 31 July 1985, p. 3.
39. *London Times,* 17 April 1985, p. 8; Shansab, *Soviet Expansion,* p. 103; *Financial Times,* 6 September 1985, p. 3. The spetsnaz figure may be high; crack Soviet paratrooper units of the regular army are sometimes confused with these irregulars who are trained to operate in disguise behind the lines.
40. *Manchester Guardian Weekly,* 3 August 1986, p. 16; *Christian Science Monitor,* 17 June 1986, p. 3.
41. *New York Times,* 17 December 1986, p. 6, and July 7, 1987, p. 6.
42. *New York Times,* 7 July 1987, p. 6.
43. The unpopularity of the war has now been verified from within the USSR. According to a Soviet official, some 75 percent of all letters received by *Izvestiya* from Soviet citizens in 1987 were about the Afghan war, most of them opposing it. (*Financial Times,* 14 May 1988, p. 3).
44. *New York Times,* 9 February 1988, p. 1.
45. Arnold, *Afghanistan,* chapters 4–10.
46. *Washington Post,* 17 April 1988, p. A30.
47. Ibid.; *Wall Street Journal,* 24 August 1988, p. 15.

# 6

# Nicaragua

*Michael Radu*

Of all contemporary anticommunist insurgencies, none has been misunderstood by both its supporters and detractors as the one in Nicaragua. Even more significant is the almost total dependence of the Nicaraguan insurgents upon political, material, and particularly psychological support from the United States, a fact which has provided much ammunition for their detractors. That fact may indeed be the strongest argument in support of the theory that there is a reverse relationship between an anticommunist insurgency's degree of dependence upon a single foreign benefactor, particularly if it is the United States, and its effectiveness and chances of ultimate victory.

From the very beginning, Nicaragua's insurgent forces have admitted their dependence upon US financial support. Paradoxically, as they have grown more effective and numerous the insurgents have used their successes to justify demands for more aid from Washington, thus making themselves even more dependent upon the vagaries of US politics.

### The Origins of the Insurgency[1]

The Nicaraguan anticommunist insurgency was not sparked by the victory of the Sandinista National Liberation Front (Frente Sandinista de Liberación Nacional, FSLN) on 19 July 1979, but by the FSLN's performance in power. The collapse, by the end of 1980, of the political alliance that made that victory possible and the increasingly orthodox Marxist-Leninist policies of the Sandinistas ever since first created the impetus for the resistance and later drew new recruits. Thus, in very short time the insurgency grew far beyond the original nucleus of armed opposition formed from the remnants of the Somoza National Guard (*Guardia Na-*

*cional*). It quickly reached all levels of the Nicaraguan society and, in many rural areas at least, it resulted in the formation of a parallel civil society inexorably opposed to and alienated from the Managua regime.

Like so many societies, whether Western or Third World, post-1979 Nicaragua had its share of frustrated, revengeful, and violent elements, mostly exiles, prepared to engage in violence against the system. Nevertheless, without the widely unpopular and anti-national policies of the Sandinistas those groups would easily have been contained and reduced to ineffective terrorism and propaganda abroad, rather than evolving into a genuine national movement.

The original nucleus of armed resistance against the Sandinistas was centered, not surprisingly, around the guardsmen who escaped death or capture by the victorious Sandinista forces in July 1979. They were professional, proud, and motivated soldiers and NCOs, most of peasant origin from the northern departments, with a sprinkling of senior officers among them.[2] Most of them refused to accept the notion that they had been fairly defeated in the field, and believed that the Sandinista victory had largely been orchestrated from outside Nicaragua—in Washington first of all, but also in Havana, Moscow, Caracas, and San José. Moreover, most of the leaders of the surviving Guardia recognized that they had been badly used by the Somozas and their cronies in the top officer ranks, including most prominently Anastasio Somoza Portocarrero, "El Chiguin," the former dictator's corrupt and incompetent son. Not surprisingly, then, the new leaders of the Guardia remnants were neither the Somozas nor the former top brass but rather those who excelled in the field: mostly NCOs and middle-level officers who had come up through the ranks by fighting FSLN terrorist bands.[3]

Thus, by July 1979, officers like Major Pablo Emilio Salazar ("Comandante Bravo"), the paradoxical hero of defeat, were the undisputed leaders of the growing National Guard exiles in Honduras, Guatemala, El Salvador, and Miami, excluding the politicians and family members of the Somoza regime. Salazar saved the best units of the National Guard fighting in the south by leading their successful escape by sea to El Salvador. In the process, he proved that even the FSLN's allegedly best commander, Edén Pastora Gómez, was no match for a professional force, even when numerically inferior, running out of ammunition, and logistically isolated. The battle for Rivas in the last months of the first Nicaraguan Civil War (1977–1979) and the stalemate Salazar forced upon Pastora, then the darling of Western admirers of the FSLN, also significantly weakened Pastora's claims to a post-Somoza leadership position in the eyes of his more ideologically committed comrades, who were taking

Managua when he was stuck south of Rivas. This, on hindsight, ended Edén Pastora's ambitions as a would-be caudillo; ever since, despite some illusions on the part of the United States and particularly the CIA, Pastora has remained a pathetically ineffective, noisy, and suspiciously destructive (for the resistance) opponent of the Sandinistas.

When Managua fell, Pablo Emilio Salazar embarked with the bulk of his troops on barges, under the noses of the revolutionaries, and led them to El Salvador, and from there to Guatemala, Honduras, and the United States. Some 3,500 of the best guardsmen fled with him, and perhaps as many as 1,500 escaped overland, under the spontaneous leadership of their corporals and sergeants. Almost all the Guardia's senior officers, led by Somoza and his son, had already fled before the end came.

The rump elements of the Nicaraguan military survived through the competence of isolated officers like Salazar and, more often, through the unheralded courage of its NCOs. Some of these NCOs later became committed and courageous counterrevolutionaries as well as ruffians, like Sergeant Pedro Pablo Ortiz Centeno, "Commander Suicida,"[4] once discipline had temporarily collapsed with the absence of officers. That collapse was hurried by the Sandinistas' successful kidnapping, torture, and murder of Pablo Emilio Salazar in Tegucigalpa in 1985.[5] The murder denied the ex-guardsmen their most competent and charismatic leader—and inspired an intense hatred and distrust for the Sandinistas that continues to this day.

Pablo Emilio Salazar's message was taken up by Enrique Bermúdez,[6] and by the end of 1981, a "September 15 Legion," named after Nicaragua's National Independence Day, was formed in Honduras, with a membership of NCOs and former rank-and-file guardsmen. It was led by a few officers and NCOs, all disgusted with the Somozas and full of desire for revenge against the new regime in Managua. It is important to note that nationalism more than simple anticommunism was the dominant idea of the early insurgency: what might be called the "proto-contras" were not "Somocistas" in any meaningful sense of the term. On the contrary, they were as contemptuous of the Somozas as they were filled with hatred for the FSLN.

The Sandinista-ordered murder of Anastasio Somoza Debayle in Asunción, Paraguay, carried out by fugitive remnants of Argentina's Ejercito Revolucionario del Pueblo (People's Revolutionary Army—ERP), was not lamented by the would-be insurgents. Not only was contempt for the dead dictator rampant among the surviving guardsmen, but Somoza Debayle's murder removed whatever bond of loyalty professional soldiers may have felt toward his defeated regime. In addition, the Asunción assassination reminded them of the long arm of the FSLN and of the impotence and incompetence of Somoza's heir, "El Chigüin."[7]

Although it is understandable that some Americans believed that the early *contras* were in fact "Somocistas" in disguise, such claims cannot be credited about the second, and by now the largest contingent of the resistance's military commanders: those who came from the ranks of the Sandinistas themselves. The best-known of these (from 1981 to 1986) was Edén Pastora Gómez ("Comandante Zero"). Lionized by the Western media, the politically, ideologically, and emotionally unstable Pastora played a decidedly destructive role in the history of the Nicaraguan resistance.

### The Nature and Performance of the Regime

Perhaps the best explanation of the Sandinista regime is provided by its leadership's background and ideological evolution. Socially, the core cadres of the FSLN are from middle- and upper-class backgrounds, many are university dropouts, and almost none have had any employment experience. A few examples are significant in this respect. Of the three FSLN founders, Carlos Fonseca Amador was the illegitimate son of Somoza's administrator of rural properties, and Silvio Mayorga and Tomás Borge Martínez were student leaders at the National Autonomous University of Nicaragua (UNAN) in the 1950s, when literacy was under 50 percent and university degrees or even enrollment were status symbols.[8] One of the nine members of the National Directorate, Luis Carrión Cruz, is a graduate of the exclusive Phillips Exeter Academy in New Hampshire. Virtually none of the prominent FSLN cadres come from poor families, and a large number of the most important present and past leaders are from such prestigious and wealthy bourgeois families as Cuadra, Lacayo, Coronel, Chamorro, Cardenal, Gabuardi—what Lenin would have defined as "traitors to their class"—or from established *nouveau riche* Somozista families (such as Castillo and D'Escoto).[9] Their ideology is "the ideology of a group of young people, mostly middle- or upper-class in origin (or at least upwardly mobile due to their education), and . . . never a lower-class phenomenon."[10] While a superficial analysis may suggest that the insurgents' political leadership comes from similar social backgrounds and has its own share of Chamorros, Coronels, and Rappacciolis, the nature of the membership on the two sides in the Nicaraguan civil war and the make-up of the military cadres of the resistance clearly demonstrate the sharp differences between them.

Many of the leaders of the FSLN, including Fonseca, Borge, Mayorga, Oscar Turcios, and Daniel and Humberto Ortega, were initially members of the Nicaraguan Communist party (Partido Socialista Nicaragunse, or PSN) or of its youth branch, the JPN (Juventud Patriotica Nicaraguënse).[11] Some, primarily Carlos Fonseca, had a definite Stalinist ideological bent. Indeed, he glorified the Soviet system in 1957 in his *A Nicaraguan in Moscow* even as Khrushchev was trying to reform it. They broke with the PSN because of their positions to its left, because of their pro-Cuban allegiances, or because the PSN did not engage in the level and type of violence they advocated. Considering the well-known facts about the origins and evolution of the FSLN, it is a tribute to the Sandinistas' ability to impress liberals in the West that the ideological nature of the organization is still debated in Western capitals today.

Because the FSLN, as a Marxist-Leninist "vanguard" party, is an elitist organization, the background of its leaders is far more important than that of the political leaders of insurgent organizations. Thus, according to National Directorate member and hard-line ideologue Bayardo Arce Castaño, a decision was made after the revolution that the FSLN would not "open up the membership to all those people who regarded themselves as Sandinistas," but instead would "adhere to the concept of a party of cadres."[12] Among those cadres, the domination of the National Directorate is total: it appoints leaders of front or "mass" organizations as well as lower-level party cadres, and has "not made much progress in forms of party democracy."[13] There are no plans for a congress in the foreseeable future.

The FSLN membership ranks have evolved as a result of a National Directorate decision made after the July 1979 political takeover. At that time it was discovered that there were less than 150 cadres with more than five years of membership; fewer than 500 had joined before 1977; and only some 1,400 fulfilled the final criterion for membership, having joined the FSLN by the time of the fall 1978 urban insurrections.[14] Most of these had no political experience, and this made it difficult to fill the top positions in the country, including forty ministries, eighteen "mass and social organizations," seventy "strategic enterprises," nine politico-administrative regions, and sixty-one National Assembly positions. The result of the decision to retain the elite nature of the party while expanding its control over national life was based on the notion that "a good collaborator is better than a poor militant."[15]

The structure of the Nicaraguan political system today is defined by its three-tiered division. At the bottom is the level made up of the Conservative, Social Christian, and Social Democratic parties, among others, the Council of Private Enterprise (COSEP), and the center-left union federation CUS. None of the groups involved in the umbrella organization known as the Coordinadora Democratica participated in the parliamentary and legislative elections of 1984, and thus they do not enjoy even the minimal privileges of the legal, parliamentary opposition. The second tier of the political system includes the Independent Liberals, but also a number of Conservative party factions (other than the Cordova Rivas faction, which is simply a Trojan horse within the opposition, controlled or at least manipulated by the FSLN), the Popular Social Christian party (PPSC) and the PC de N. On a number of occasions this opposition group has publicly protested FSLN policies. In July 1987, PLI and PPSC deputies walked out of the National Assembly to protest the arrest of fifteen PLI members.[16] The PC de N, an orthodox Marxist-Leninist party, is consistent enough in attacking the FSLN "distortions" of Marxism-Leninism to join the democratic legal opposition parties, although, naturally enough, it is a determined enemy of the armed resistance. The other far left parties, the PSN, the "Maoist" Marxist-Leninist party of Nicaragua (PMLN), and the Partido Revolucionario de Trabajadores (PRT) and its close ally, the Central American Unification party (Partido de Unificación Centro Americana, or PUCA), are tolerated as long as their irresponsible and irrelevant rhetoric serves to support FSLN claims to be a "centrist" party attacked from both left and right—a tactic highly successful with some American liberals and most West European democratic left parties, especially the Scandinavian ones.

By allowing the far left to compete in the 1984 elections, and by allocating each of the leftist parties the same 2 percent of the vote, the FSLN managed to pose as the party of the "responsible" left; by allowing the "right," including Cordova Rivas' fellow travellers, some 25 percent of the vote, the Sandinistas managed to repeat the history of Eastern Europe in the late 1940s without anyone noticing it—the "people" preferred the "revolutionary" party, although some (carefully controlled) still choose the "bourgeois" parties.

Perhaps the single most important cause of the swelling of the insurgent ranks during the past five years has been the FSLN's effect on the Nicaraguan economy and the spectacular gap between the standard of living of the FSLN *nomenklatura* and the population as a whole. The process of formation of a Sandinista *nomenklatura* progressed rapidly during 1987, and the economic crisis has made the disparities between standards of living increasingly glaring. Top FSLN and EPS officials have exclusive access to special stores providing staples and luxury goods (Soviet cars for instance) at heavily subsidized prices. They also have the right to exchange cordobas for dollars at the official rate,[17] which was C 70 per dollar in January 1987, compared to that of C 3,000 per dollar on the black market.[18] The most prominent cases of personal enrichment, according to high-level defector Roger Miranda Bengoechea, Humberto

Ortega's close associate, are the Ortega brothers themselves, with their Swiss bank account of over $1 million.[19]

By September 1987, the black market exchange rate had reached 13,000 per dollar.[20] On 14 February 1988 a new economic plan was put into effect, including drastic price increases—gasoline went up 1,000 percent for instance—and a new currency was introduced, worth 1,000 old cordobas.[21] Nevertheless, six new devaluations of the cordoba followed during the year, including five by July, each ranging between 50 and 25 percent.[22] The new cordoba, originally set at a 10/1 exchange rate vis-à-vis the US dollar reached 180/1 by July and 320/1 by August.[23]

According to the independent, but sympathetic to FSLN economist Francisco Mayorga of Managua's Central American Institute of Business Administration, in December 1988 the national inflation rate reached 27,000 percent, an almost incomprehensible level "unprecedented in economic history."[24]

The economic situation remains the most dangerous problem facing the FSLN, and it is becoming more critical every month. The inflation rate in 1987 was over 1,000 percent; food was rationed and often impossible to find. The monthly ration of rice, a staple of the Nicaraguan diet, was two pounds at C 40 per pound, but was seldom available; on the thriving black market, however, where it was available, it cost C 800.[25] The cordoba, kept at a stable and plausible 10/1 exchange rate to the dollar until 1978, was virtually worthless; a C 1,000 note, which was worth $100 in prerevolutionary times, was worth 3 cents, and it cost 2.7 cents to print. The new cordoba, a de facto devaluation of the currency by 1,000 percent, was even less acceptable to most Nicaraguans than such barter items as US cigarettes. The GNP is at early 1950s levels, and the monthly income of the average citizen was between one-fifth and one-tenth of what it was in 1980. The public transportation system had collapsed for lack of fuel, vehicles, and parts; traditional Nicaraguan products, such as coffee, sugar, meat, and cotton were impossible to find on the official markets. The government, while blaming the United States for the economic crisis, made no allowances for the needs of the population. Speaking in February, Daniel Ortega defined the "general guidelines" of the regime's economic policies: "First, top priority will continue to guarantee the military defense of the revolution. . . . Second, the goal is to concentrate [on] export goods that will generate foreign exchange, . . . goods that prop up or support the country's military defense, . . . basic goods for the population."[26] With such a point of view, it is no surprise that the government decided to label private-market operations, mostly conducted by peasant women, "speculation" and to crack down on them. As the pro-government *El Nuevo Diário* claimed,

"Profiteering is not a spontaneous upshot of production problems" although it became one with basic supplies absent and declining standards of living. More and more workers were forced to take a second job; the result was that in fifty-nine enterprises in the first half of 1986, absenteeism amounted to 403, 715 man days, according to the government.[27] Nevertheless, "profiteers," or *bisneros*, were still defined as people with "thick skin . . . [and] crooked, corrupt conscience."[29] Despite the regime's attempts to blame the economic collapse on alleged "US aggression," even the Soviet newspaper *Izvestia* claimed that difficulties "are being intensified by parasitism, speculation and swindling."[29] Even some of the many Cuban- or Soviet-bloc-trained experts have had a hard time finding jobs in Nicaragua.[30]

The combination of repression, economic collapse, foreign interference and omnipresence in Nicaragua, and the persistent Sandinista attacks against the Catholic Church and its extremely popular leader, Cardinal Obando y Bravo, all contributed to the rapid growth of the armed opposition's ranks and have defined its nature.

## The Counterinsurgency Coalition

The Nicaraguan conflict has never really been just a civil war, since both sides have relied heavily on external assistance with weapons, expertise, funds, and logistical support. The major difference is one of magnitude and the involvement of foreign personnel. It is significant, for instance, that US financial support for the resistance from 1982 until March 1988 amounted to $189 million;[31] by contrast, and according to the Czechoslovak ambassador to Nicaragua, the economic aid provided by the Soviet bloc in 1987 alone amounted to $425 million.[32] That amount was comparatively small if seen in light of the $2–3 billion aid provided by the Soviet bloc, radical Third World regimes like Libya, Iran, and Algeria, or "progressive" Western governments like the Scandinavian ones. In fact, US aid to the insurgents is not much more than the amount of aid (approximately $125 million) Washington gave to the Sandinistas between 1979 and 1981.

The EPS is by far the largest military establishment in Central America's history, including some 77,000 active personnel in the army, 50,000 militia, 1,000 navy, and 3,400 air force personnel, as well as 2,000 Interior Ministry troops (Tropas Pablo Ubeda).[33] This truly impressive establishment has a dual mission: conventional deterrence, directed at Nicaragua's weaker neighbors and to some extent at the United States, and counterinsurgency. The former mission is manifest in the militarization of the society, including the introduction of the draft in 1982 and the acquisition of some 175 tanks (150 Soviet-made T-54/55s and 25 PT-76s) and 200 APCs,[34] all of marginal usefulness in counterinsurgency. Counterinsurgency operations are overwhelmingly conducted by the eighteen specialized battalions (Batallones de Lucha Irregular, BLIs), one airborne Battalion, the 7,000 border-guard troops (Tropas Guardafronteras, or TGF), and the Pablo Ubeda units of the Interior Ministry. Static positions are protected by the militias, which have also borne the brunt of casualties in the war. The air force is heavily dependent on helicopters — one squadron has four MI-2s, twenty-four MI-8-17s, and twelve MI-24/25s, as well as transport and small plans.[35] Persistent EPS attempts to acquire MIG jet fighters, including training pilots in Bulgaria, have so far been rejected by the Soviet Union as overly provocative, useless for counterinsurgency purposes, and possibly risking a US military reaction.

The number of foreign military personnel in Nicaragua is still a matter of debate; for instance, most US sources claim that there are some 3,000 Cuban military personnel in the country, while a well-informed Cuban defector mentioned only 300.[37] Such disputes, however, are misleading, since in a guerrilla warfare the professional, armed personnel play a limited (albeit essential) role; those involved in intelligence, civic, political, and indoctrination (or "education") activities make almost as much of a contribution as helicopter pilots or BLI fighters. In this respect, the thousands upon thousands of *internacionalistas* now present in Nicaragua are as vital to the Sandinista war effort as are Soviet-bloc military personnel and may do more damage to the insurgents' cause than many a Hind attack helicopter. Such organizations as the US Witnesses for Peace, Hands off the Americas, the Canadian Farmers for Peace, and the Pledge of Resistance are vital weapons, at least in public relations terms. The same is true of those clergymen who take advantage of their clerical garb to provide propaganda, indoctrination, and moral support for the government side in the civil war, whether they are Nicaraguans or, as is more often the case, foreigners.

More or at least equally important in their impact are the often more discreet and certainly more influential *internacionalistas* who have been allowed or indeed encouraged to infiltrate FSLN decision-making bodies or who play a direct military role in the conflict. The list of the former should certainly include Victor Tirado Lopez, a veteran Mexican Communist, now one of the nine members of the National Directorate, and of the original faction of the dominant Ortega brothers as well. The list should also include "Renán Montero Corrales" (Andrés Barahona Lopez), a Cuban-born professional revolutionary, now a Nicaraguan citizen, lieutenant colonel in the Interior Ministry and chief of the fifth Directorate, in charge of foreign intelligence and operations, including support for Latin American revolutionary groups.[38] Cuban, Bulgarian, East German, and Soviet experts advise the FSLN on intelligence and interrogation techniques.[39] Professional terrorists of Argentina (the Montoneros and the ERP), Chile (Movimiento de la Izquierda Revolucionaria, or MIR, and Frente Patriotico Manuel Rodriguez, or FPMR, the terrorist branch of the pro-Soviet Communist party), and Uruguay (Tupamaros) advise on interrogation (torture) and kidnapping techniques, as do Spanish Basques of the ETA and Italians of the Red Brigades, while the Colombian M-19 and FARC seem to have set up channels of communication between Managua and the Colombian cocaine underground through Cuba to the United States—a promising source of funds. Costa Rican Communists are known to have been killed in combat by the insurgents within Nicaragua, and the Hondurans of the Cinchoneros, Lorenzo Zelaya, PRTCH, and Morazanista Marxist-Leninist insurgents, as well as the Salvadoran guerrillas of the various FMLN groups, are not only headquartered in Nicaragua but obtained their first combat experience fighting the contras in northern Nicaragua.[40]

The FSLN side of the war is thus a complex mixture of the Western New Left in its public relations, Latin American terrorist and guerrilla experiences at intelligence and terrorist levels, Soviet-bloc counterinsurgency experience in military terms, and Soviet-bloc conventional arming and general training. The war is an international one involving more foreign ideas, funds, personnel, and practice than any other war against an anticommunist insurgency.

## The Nature of the Insurgency

The Nicaraguan insurgency can be defined as a spontaneous uprising hijacked by US interests beginning in 1982 that has remained, and fatally so, dependent upon the United States ever since. All available data indicate that the overwhelming majority of the combatants are young—most of them far too young to have been involved in the pre-1979 civil war. They are principally poorly educated peasants from the northern, eastern, and central areas of Nicaragua. They are devout Catholics, including significant numbers of women, and they tend to operate in their own home areas. Another important element is the presence of ethnic and racial minorities—Indians and Creoles.[41] Most of the fighters, with the exception of the Indians, joined the insurgent forces after 1982. The standard Sandinista propaganda line describing the contras as "Somocista bandits" has been thoroughly discredited, both within Nicaragua and among knowledgeable people elsewhere;[42] its only consistent supporters remain pro-FSLN fellow travelers and supporters in the West. In fact, simple arithmetic should suffice to discredit such allegations; Managua itself claims to have killed, wounded, or captured almost 6,000 contras in 1987 alone, and a similar number in 1986.[43] These numbers represent more than the strength of the National Guard by the fall of 1978 (some 7,000); in fact, official Sandinista figures claim that some 20,000 contras have been killed since the war began in 1981. One has to assume that many guardsmen suffered the same fate prior to June 1979. Finally, Managua has admitted to having jailed between 2,500 and 3,500 ex-guardsmen[44] (a figure rejected as far too low by neutral observers)[45] since 1979. Adding up these figures results in the paradoxical situation in which at least twice as many "Somocista guardsmen" have been killed or captured since 1979 than there were at the height of the Guardia's strength: some 14,000 by the spring of 1979, a majority of them young, poorly trained, recent recruits who had never engaged in any serious fighting.

The fall-back position for Managua and its Western spokesmen and supporters is that while the contra fighters may not be ex-guardsmen, their leaders and commanders certainly are. This is yet another untenable proposition, contradicted by all known facts. At the political level, none of the National Resistance Directorate members until 1988 were active Somoza supporters, and the overwhelming majority were active political foes of the Somozas. The latter included such figures as Aldolfo Calero, Alfredo César, Alfonso Robelo, and Arturo Cruz, Azucena Ferrey, and Pedro Joaquín Chamorro Barrios. As for the Indian and Creole resistance leadership, not even Managua has claimed that any of its members were pro-Somoza in the past. In fact, as previously mentioned, National Resistance leaders have tended to come from the same elite backgrounds as have many of the Sandinista cadres, and to have opposed the "upstart" Somoza clique for many of the same reasons, albeit with different aims in mind.

The major insurgent force, formerly known as the Nicaraguan Democratic Front (Frente Democratico Nicaraguënse, or FDN), is now the Army of the Nicaraguan Resistance (Ejercito de la Resistencia Nicaraguënse, or ERN). The supreme military commander is ex-Guardia colonel Enrique Bermúdez Varela, who, as military attaché to Washington between 1975 and the end of the old regime, played no role in the first Nicaraguan civil war. In fact, in July 1979 Bermúdez was seriously considered, *by the Sandinistas*, for the position of defense minister.

Of the field commanders, at the height of the insurgency in November 1987, half had had no previous military experience of any kind, one-third were ex-Sandinista fighters or EPS (Ejercito Popular Sandinista, the

FSLN army) defectors, and the rest, or some 17 percent, were ex-guardsmen, a majority of whom had been Guardia NCOs.[46] The obvious conclusion is that after starting as an outburst of revenge on the part of remnants of the National Guard in 1981, the Nicaraguan resistance became a largely peasant army by the next year. It is now a totally peasant force. Most of its military leaders are of the same background as the troops, although the political "leadership" is not.

It was primarily its dependence on the United States's political, military, and tactical support that kept the Nicaraguan insurgency from being as effective, successful, and massive as it could have been. For the Reagan administration to obtain even unreliable, vacillating, and limited congressional support for aid to the insurgents, it had to provide the guerrillas with a facade acceptable to congressional political, "moral," and cultural notions. The result has been that the insurgents' leadership has long remained top heavy with personalities lacking a significant following in Nicaragua and socially and educationally removed from the insurgent forces, sympathizers, and military leaders.

It is highly significant that the Pacific coast cities, where one would expect the exiled "leaders" of the RN to have their following, are the most difficult for the resistance to operate in. The support for the guerrillas in those areas, while not insignificant, is quiet rather than active, and anti-Sandinista sentiments are channeled through the Church and the legal opposition parties rather than through the armed resistance. The gap between most of the political cadres and the fighters is made wider still by the fact that many of the former held high positions under the Sandinistas in the first years after the revolution and some even after the resistance started. Finally, the political ideas and attitudes of many although by no means all the politicians who have joined the resistance are to the left of those of the conservative peasantry making up the rank and file; whether Social Christians, Social Democrats, or confused leftists like Edén Pastora Gomez, many of the political cadres have only the most tenuous understanding of the mentality, beliefs, and aims of those they are to guide. Most of those politicians, however, and once again Edén Pastora is a prominent example, have had such an exaggerated opinion of their own importance that they have been prepared to do political damage to the insurgent cause rather than cease or suspend their personal squabbles. Even some of the most courageous and devoted politicians opposed to the FSLN, like Fernando "El Negro" Chamorro Rappaccioli, gave up the fight for illusory political aims;[47] others left after doing considerable political harm to the anti-Sandinista opposition (Pastora, Cruz, Pedro Joaquín Chamorro); and a handful, including Edgar Chamorro Coronel, actually became supporters of Sandinista propaganda.[48]

Most importantly perhaps was the fact that, with the exception of Adolfo Calero and Aristides Sanchez, none of the politicians involved in the highest ranks of the insurgent leadership felt comfortable with, understood, or even believed strongly in armed struggle. In fact, most of them left the movement because they could not control its military arm. Arturo Cruz for instance, despite his decency and popularity in Washington, was always hopelessly politically naive, a fact that explains why he, of all top political leaders of the insurgency, was the last to break with the FSLN. Nevertheless, he was also the most outspoken in demanding control over the military units in the field, and left when he failed to gain it.

None of these characteristics of the political leadership of the insurgents increased their popularity or credibility with the fighters, but they often provided unnecessary ammunition for the pro-FSLN activists in the United States, or for those opposed to the Reagan administration's Central American policies for partisan or other reasons. Regardless of Reagan administration claims echoed by pro-insurgent congressional and media spokesmen, the tenuous connection between the fighters and the "political leadership," made up principally of ex-politicians with Washington connections was, until their 1988 break, provided by the Calero-Bermúdez team. If there has been any political leader of the insurgency with any credibility among the actual fighters, the Indians aside, it has been Adolfo Calero, the least popular of the RN leaders in Washington's political and media circles. The different political outlooks of the top "political leaders" of the insurgency—ranging from Socialist admirers of Augusto César Sandino and Ernesto "Che" Guevara, such as Edén Pastora, to Social Democrats, to Conservatives like Calero—and the personalistic, fragmented nature of Nicaraguan politics has made a consensus difficult. The result has been that, at least until 1987, the insurgents' political platform stressed rather vague promises of democracy, pluralism, and free enterprise. As Carlos Icaza, a former judge briefly in charge of the resistance's "human rights" affairs, who has described himself as a "true Sandinista,"[49] admitted, "We have people with different political attitudes in the leadership and at the executive level, and to establish one political line would be to lose that variety."[50] That may look like true democracy, but in the context of armed struggle against a determined, skilled Marxist-Leninist foe it sounds more like an irrelevant cacophony, confusing the fighters and the potential allies within the internal opposition, as well as deterring potential support from foreign governments.

Reliance on congressional funding has meant that the insurgents have had to tailor their tactical aims toward political short-term goals directed at congressional perceptions and voting schedules rather than toward a long-term strategy of steady pressure and weakening of the enemy's capacity and will to fight.

Among the highly unusual results of the Nicaraguan insurgency's following American ideas and war-fighting practices, and as a natural result of its addiction to US congressional or administration support, was the existence of the "human rights" office of the RN, an example of how to commit military suicide in the name of a noble political cause. Indeed, the definition of "human rights" as it was imposed by Washington included obligations that few governments in the Third World, even if willing, could possibly fulfill. Among those were formal trials for Sandinista spies and infiltrators, an absolute prohibition against military operations that might in any way endanger civilians, centralized control over field commanders at all times, amounting to permission for "human rights" commissars to second-guess the commanders, and a large bureaucracy dedicated to filing compliance reports for the US Congress. All that was imposed as a precondition for military support when the resistance, naturally enough, had no courts, prisons, defense lawyers, or the means to obtain them.

Another major distorting factor that explains the apparent failure of the Nicaraguan insurgency was the deeply rooted and media-fueled basic American misunderstanding of the nature of guerrilla warfare. Thus, two of the most often heard "arguments" for the claim that supporting the insurgents was a waste of taxpayers' money were that the RN never controlled a town, city, or village, and that the insurgents were guilty of atrocities against civilians.

In fact, guerrilla control over cities is always a characteristic of the last stage of an insurgency, when it has ceased to be an irregular force and has become a competing conventional army, defeating the government in set conventional battles. The very critics using this argument against the RN were also those who were opposed to providing it with the massive aid needed to reach that stage. In fact, in tactical terms, for the guerrillas to occupy a city or town when they have no defense against air or armored attacks would be tantamount to suicide, since it provides a well-defined, static and unprotected target for government attacks. The same critics who dismissed the insurgents' effectiveness were also the same who denied them access to effective and sufficient antiaircraft weapons, such as stinger missiles.

As for the alleged "atrocities" of the Nicaraguan insurgents, they were related to the above mentioned "human rights" standards on one hand and, more importantly, were part and parcel of the massive, persistent, and highly effective Sandinista psychological and political warfare and propaganda targeted at the US Congress, public, and media. Most of such claims were clearly proved to be Managua's inventions propagated by its apologists in the United States;[51] a few were found to be real, and disciplinary measures were taken by the resistance, including the trial and execution of "Suicida," one of the most effective commanders; other such claims were simply the result of tactical circumstances. As a matter of common sense, it is hard to define terms like "atrocities" and "civilian" in any guerrilla warfare context. Executions of informers and infiltrators are a necessary and inevitable reality, and guerrillas seldom, if ever, have the luxury of staging protracted trials and following the niceties of American (peacetime) law. The "civilians" who were supposedly victimized may have been non-uniformed, although in many cases they were armed, political cadres of the regime or foreign fellow travelers like Benjamin Linder, people whose contribution to the government side was often more important than those of EPS soldiers. Finally, the question should have been raised, but seldom was, as to why the resistance managed to replenish and expand its ranks and enjoy massive popular support in many areas if indeed it engaged in a terror campaign against would-be recruits, suppliers, informers, and couriers.

## Insurgency Organization and Structure

The Nicaraguan resistance's order of battle and command structure have changed continuously since 1981, a direct result of numerical growth, the influx of new leaders, and the vagaries of American demands and support. It is thus difficult to define the resistance's structure in general terms, at both political and military levels, but the year 1987 is perhaps the best period to choose in order to understand its organizational trends before the present state of suspended animation. Indeed, the political capabilities of the major armed opposition organization, the Nicaraguan Resistance, changed quite dramatically during 1987, the year of maximum military effectiveness and US financial support.

In May after a bad start at the beginning of the year, when Arturo Cruz resigned in March, a massive restructuring of the organization took place. The United Nicaraguan Opposition (UNO) was replaced by the Nicaraguan Resistance (RN), which consolidated into a single organization practically all non-Indian external opposition groups, armed and unarmed. A congress held in Miami in the first half of May elected a fifty-four-member assembly, which in turn elected eleven members of the new directorate. Some of the top eleven were old leaders of the FDN, like Adolfo Calero, Enrique Bermúdez, and Aristides Sànchez; others were politicians like Alfonso Robelo and Alfredo César or representatives of parties in exile, like Azucena Ferrey of the Social Christian party.[52]

As of the end of 1987 the ERN (Ejercito de la Resistencia Nicaraguense) was organized along geographical and functional lines, much as a conventional army. The main divisions were the northern and southern fronts, with the Atlantic front, mostly made up of Indian resistance groups, only nominally included in the overall military and political structure. The Strategic Command, the overall strategic and general staff leadership, was made up of a seven-man group: Bermúdez, general commander; Diogenes Hernandez Membreno ("Fernando"), personnel chief; Rodolfo Ernesto Ampie Quiroz ("Invisible"), intelligence chief; Victor Sanchez Herdocia ("Licenciado"), operations assistant; Carlos José Guillén Salinas ("Gustavo"), the logistical chief (psychological operations chief) José Francisco Hernandez Altamirano ("Camilo"); and (communications chief), Sebastian Flores Gutierrez ("Florito"); of those, three (Bermúdez, Ampie, and Flores) are ex-guardia professionals, and the others are military amateurs.[53] Following the 1988 internal conflicts among the top military commanders, four of them left the organization, including one of the most competent ones, Encarnacion Baldivia Chavarria ("Tigrillo"). Manuel Adan Rugama Acevedo ("Aureliano") briefly became second in command and was in charge of daily operations in the Honduran camps, until his assassination in Tegucigalpa at the beginning of 1989.[54]

Field operations are coordinated at the level of regional commands, numbering twenty for the northern and ten for the southern fronts, and the four zonal commands of Yatama on the Atlantic front. The regional commands are divided into task forces (*Fuerzas de tarea*), of which in 1987 there were sixty-three in the north and ten in the south.[55] Independent special-support and service units, including air transport, artillery, counterintelligence, military police, medical corps, and naval operations complete the insurgent infrastructure. As a rule, special units and services tend to have a larger proportion of ex-guardsmen among their leaders than the field units, and ex-EPS cadres predominate among the southern front commanders.

The task forces, which started as battalion-size units in 1982 and tended to decrease in strength as they grew in numbers, are the main tactical operational units, largely responsible for their own recruiting, tactical intelligence, and in-field logistics. Usually they retained a minimal underground presence in their specific areas during the periods of withdrawal to Honduras for retraining and resupplying. In a majority of cases (universally in the case of task forces) commanding and executive officers are natives of their operational areas.

Logistics and finances are concentrated in the hands of the strategic command, as is strategic intelligence when US intelligence agencies provide satellite and aerial information. Logistics and finances are among the success stories of the Nicaraguan insurgency, but that very success is also another demonstration of the distorting impact direct US involvement can have on an irregular force. By the end of 1984 a senior insurgent leader boasted that his forces had brought 630,000 pounds of war materiel into Nicaragua in less than ten months, a remarkable feat for any irregular force.[56] The following years, and particularly by the fall of 1987, that amount probably doubled.

The problem, however, is that most of the weapons, ammunition, uniforms, and medicines arrive by air. Air drops are clearly the most efficient way of supplying the insurgents, and supply flights had risen dramatically by 1987. They are also expensive and thus vulnerable to the vagaries of US support, particularly since most of the pilots are US citizens (many of them Cuban-Americans with Bay-of-Pigs experience and memories). Such a direct American role tends to harden congressional opposition to aid to the insurgents, since it involves the risk of American deaths or captures, as indeed has happened. Furthermore, there are also political and diplomatic costs involved in using Honduran or Salvadoran airfields for supply flights. On the other hand, the Sandinista air force's lack of interceptors and still limited radar coverage of the national territory tends to limit the risks involved in an insurgent logistical network centered on air drops, most of which are undertaken at night.

Some insurgent units are self-contained to a large extent, able to carry their own ammunition for months, as they travel on foot between Honduras and the central departments of Boaco and Chontales, a distance of some 600 kilometers.[57] Even at the beginning of the insurgency, and even more so today, large areas of Nicaragua's eastern half were clearly outside Sandinista control, due to lack of roads, difficult terrain, and sparse (often Indian) population. Today, following Sandinista resettlement policies resulting in the forcible removal of some 250,000 peasants from military regions V, VI, I and the Atlantic naval district,[58] even larger parts of Nicaragua are depopulated but still remain safe guerrilla areas. Those areas cover extensive regions of northern and southern Zelaya, Jinotega, and northern Segovia, are heavily forested, and lack passable roads. The only transportation lines between the Pacific coast and the El Bluff and Bluefields ports to the Caribbean are the Rama road and the Rio Grande de Matagalpa, none very reliable and both passing through the type of wild, thickly wooded regions favorable to the guerrillas. In those areas the insurgents had a free hand, and jungle, swamp, and hilly airstrips were used for air drops by CIA planes at low risk; even with the end of such means of supply, in those regions, covering some 60 percent of Nicaragua's territory, the resistance still has the geographic, popular, ethnic, and logistic advantages that should enable it to survive indefinitely, albeit at a far lower level of effectiveness.

## Military Performance and the Evolution of the War

In October 1984 a senior insurgent commander claimed that a 7,000-strong underground operated in cells in the cities of Managua, Masaya, Grenada, Leon, and Chinandega.[59] The following year the Sandinistas themselves claimed to have arrested 159 persons belonging to an insurgent underground group called Sombra in the city of Matagalpa.[60]

By 1987 the economic collapse of the country, the government's unpopular draft, and the continuing conflict with the Catholic Church had resulted in increased urban opposition to the FSLN, manifested in large-scale demonstrations in Managua and violent riots in Masaya. Even more disturbing from the Sandinistas' viewpoint was the first spectacular expression of the trend toward coordination among the various types of opposition, legal and armed, internal and in exile, which occurred in January 1988, when a top-level Coordinadora Democratica delegation,[61] including the leader of the Conservative party, Mario Rappaccioli, and a prominent PSC leader, as well as the editor of the recently reopened opposition paper, *La Prensa*, met with the top contra leadership in Guatemala City. That the domestic opposition might coordinate at least in part its activities with the insurgents and that a broad front similar to that which overthrew Somoza and brought the FSLN into power might again emerge, this time against the government, was a possibility taken seriously in Managua. It explains in part the Sandinistas' willingness to talk to the resistance. There was, however, no follow-up to the Guatemala meeting, and no effective cooperation, let alone coordination between the internal political opposition and the insurgents.

The first and foremost indication of success by any guerrilla organization is its capability to survive over the long term. The fact that the Nicaraguan insurgents have consistently been able to more than offset their casualties by recruiting new fighters is admitted, indirectly at least, by the Sandinistas themselves, who have put the number of insurgents at the vastly understated number of about 6,000, while also admitting a steady and rapid intensification in the number of actions taken over the past few years.

The insurgents' ability to replenish their ranks and to grow in numbers depends on the level of peasant support they receive; for the regime, therefore denying such support is essential if the guerrillas are to be defeated. Thus, by 1985 a large-scale Sandinista campaign to relocate the rural population began, and by the end of 1987 some 250,000 peasants in

Rio San Juan, Chontales, Boaco, Zelaya, Jinotega, and Madriz were forcibly placed in what amounts to strategic villages—*asentamientos*. While such standard anti-insurgency tactics may be relatively successful for the short term, in Nicaragua they tend to exacerbate the problems in the medium and long terms. Although the insurgents may lose valuable recruiting grounds and intelligence support, discontented peasants relocated to unfamiliar areas and living under the conditions of economic crisis may "infect" their new neighbors.[62]

The field performance of the insurgents has from the start been dependent upon their training and resources, and has changed over time, as has their strategy. Initially, the members of the "15th of September Legion," as former guardsmen bent on revenge, engaged primarily in hit-and-run commando attacks close to the relative safety of the Honduran border. Among their targets were bridges and factories, attacked by small groups that had been trained by Argentine officers in Honduras and Guatemala.

The reason for the Argentine role in "retraining" ex-guardsmen and future insurgents in 1981 and 1982 remains unclear but seems to have been largely centered on politics and ambitions rather than actual needs. Prior to the Falklands debacle, the junta in Buenos Aires wanted to extend its influence in Central America and was prepared to provide weapons and funds to do so. Despite their lack of expertise in irregular warfare and rural counterinsurgency, Argentine officers undertook the task of training the Nicaraguans. The urban counterinsurgency experience of the Argentines had little relevance for the intended aims of the Nicaraguan insurgents. The conventional tactics the Argentines favored (but had not mastered, as was proved in the Falklands a short time later) serve to explain the original strategy of the Honduran-based insurgents. Indeed, by November 1982, with new, US-provided equipment, the insurgents, led by ex-Guardia NCO "Suicida" attempted to take the town of Jalapa, but failed.[63]

At about that time it became clear that a more appropriate guerrilla approach was being introduced, and the task forces, vaguely modeled after units with the same name used by the United States in Vietnam, came into being. Highly mobile and flexible, divided into groups made up of commando detachments of some twenty men, the task forces were intended to provide maximum area coverage and relied upon a high degree of tactical autonomy on the part of the officers.[64] By 1987 between 300 and 1,200 regional command, task force, and special units officers and NCOs had been trained by US Special Forces in Panama, Honduras, and the continental United States.[65]

Since 1982 the insurgents have pursued a dual-track strategy: attacks

278    The New Insurgencies

on large objectives, including some small towns, with the specific political purpose of convincing Washington that they are active and strong; and, far more significant in the long run, steady proselytizing and organizing among the rural population, small but increasingly numerous attacks on collective farms, isolated mining operations in Zelaya, power pilons in Esteli and Matagalpa,[66] and roads. With CIA help, in 1984 the Corinto fuel depots were destroyed and a brief mining blockade imposed on the major ports of both coasts. The more spectacular, but ultimately futile actions of old-time showmen like Pastora, which included an air attack on Managua's airport, have been avoided since 1985 in favor of a more traditional, long-term approach to guerrilla warfare. What is essential is that by 1987 the long-term approach was accepted as the only valid one by the rank and file. As one US correspondent noticed, "Younger [insurgent] soldiers often used to say they expected to be marching into Managua within six months. Now the most frequent answer to the question, How long do you think you'll have to fight?, is As long as it takes."[67] That such attitudes are widespread was demonstrated at the end of 1987, when extremely attractive Sandinista promises of amnesty and a return to civilian life to insurgent combatants in the field went unheeded to an extent surprising even to Bermúdez.

On the military level, 1987 was unquestionably the best year of the anti-FSLN insurgency. They made great progress in consolidating peasant support in the northern and central departments, particularly Jinotega, Matagalpa, Nueva Segovia, Boaco, and Chontales, and also succeeded in establishing permanent bases inside Nicaragua and lessening their dependence on safe havens in Honduras. Furthermore, in addition to infiltrating as many as 14,000 fighters into Nicaragua, and increasing the number of contracts with the EPS to almost ten a day, the insurgents repeatedly demonstrated an ability to operate skillfully in large units. Attacks such as those against San José de Bocay in July and the Siuna and La Rosita gold mining installations in December involved hundreds of insurgents, yet they took the army by surprise. This indicates that insurgent intelligence was better than that of the Sandinistas, which in turn reflects the sentiments of the local population. On the other hand, Sandinista infiltrators have been a constant problem for the resistance. In fact, in April 1987, a Sandinista sabotage and espionage network was uncovered in Honduran insurgent camps, particularly Aguacate, even including Aristides Sànchez's driver. It was involved in sabotaging insurgent transport planes and was said to have transmitted intelligence data to the EPS for three years before it was eliminated.[68]

The insurgent capabilities were enhanced by the increased, but still insufficient use of antiaircraft weapons, particularly British- and Soviet-made; according to the insurgents, they destroyed or damaged thirteen helicopters, or a quarter of the EPS's fleet, by June.[69] Perhaps even more significant is the fact that the insurgents succeeded in significantly increasing their numbers in 1987, despite higher casualties resulting from the intensification of the war. The combination of small unit operations over most of the country, including for the first time areas close to or within the Pacific coast strip where the country's population is concentrated, and some major attacks in the northeast for the first time offered the possibility of actually defeating the regime.

By the beginning of 1987 Bermúdez could correctly state that his forces were "perfectly at home in the regions of Chontales, Boaco, central Zelaya, Rio San Juan, the northern and central parts of Jinotega, and the eastern part of Matagalpa."[70] The attacks on the Rama road in 1987 not only placed new strains on the EPS capability to defend crucial areas, but also suggested that the price to be paid by the regime for thwarting the insurgents' strategic goal—the isolation of the Pacific coast from the rest of the country—was increasingly higher.

At the strategic level, the most important development took place in July and August, when the bulk of the insurgent forces in Honduras managed to infiltrate into Nicaragua, eluding the Sandinista army's border defenses.

At the propaganda level, at the beginning of 1987 the RN started a highly effective and popular new radio station, Radio Liberación, which has rapidly become the main source of both news and entertainment for most Nicaraguans.[71]

By forcing the Sandinistas into temporary concessions to freedom of expression, the "Arias Peace Plan" resulted in the reappearance of *La Prensa*, the opposition newspaper, whose editorial line is as anti-FSLN as the insurgents' Radio Liberación and Radio 15 de Septiembre. It also permitted a reorganization and re-mobilization of the internal opposition parties. The advantage these developments offered to the insurgents were manifold. For the short term—that is, as long as the FSLN is prepared to tolerate the new "democratic" situation—their ability to establish contacts and coordinate actions with the urban opposition is enhanced. In the long term, after the FSLN once again cracks down on the internal opposition, the newly invigorated followers of the latter could conceivably become all-out supporters of the resistance in a permanently polarized political arena.

### The Indian Resistance

The ethnically and racially distinct Indian and Creole resistance, which came into being as early as September 1980, was more socially homogeneous than the Spanish-speaking insurgency; they were not, however, spared similarly divisive personality clashes and also had their share of vacillating, weak leaders. The overwhelming majority is not just Indian but largely Miskitu, which explains the prominent role of such Miskitu leaders as Steadman Fagoth Muller, Brooklyn Rivera, and Wycliffe Diego, each of whom attempted to establish his own organization. MISURASATA (Miskitu, Sumo, Rama, Sandinista Asla Takanka — Miskitu, Sumo, Rama, Sandinista All Together) was largely Fagoth's instrument, KISAN (Kus Indian Sut Asla Nicaragua ra — United Indigenous Peoples of Eastern Nicaragua) was Diego's, and MISURA (Miskitu, Sumo, Rama Unity) Rivera's. US and UNO/RN pressures resulted in the formation of YATAMA (Yapti Tasba Masraka Aslika — United Nations of Yapti Tasba — the Sacred Homeland) in 1987, including as its Directorate members all three of the above, plus largely ceremonial members from among the Rama and Sumo Indians and the Creoles.

This proved to be yet another unstable arrangement, with Rivera accusing Fagoth of "human rights" abuses and the latter, more to the point, accusing Rivera of weakness and a propensity for accepting Sandinista terms under any conditions.

Following the Sandinistas' murder of Lyster Athders, the dominant leader of the Miskitu Elders Council in 1980, younger and better-educated Spanish and English leaders rose to the forefront, largely through their "foreign" connections. Sandinista pressure and threats to the ancestral Indian communal lands, Managua's forced relocation of the villages along the Rio Coco, large-scale emigration to Honduras,[72] and the loss of many Moravian clergymen rapidly brought about a probably permanent collapse of the older Indian social, religious, and economic way of life. Young warriors tended to follow newly prominent young leaders who could provide them with weapons, and respect for the elders declined, as did the latter's influence. Not coincidentally, Yatama acknowledged this reality, at least implicitly, and by 1987 the Council of Elders was merely providing advice and performing judicial duties for the Directorate.[73]

Despite only limited US support (a disproportionate share of which was largely wasted on Brooklyn Rivera's minuscule organization), the Indian resistance has played a significant military role in weakening EPS capabilities for coping with the far stronger FDN/ERN forces throughout most of the Zelaya. Not only did the Indians play an important logistical support role for the resistance in general by keeping open large segments of the Honduran border in the northeast, but their intelligence capabilities in that region, combined with their familiarity with the terrain, climate, and targets enhanced the capabilities of the resistance in general. This was particularly true of the Fagoth-Diego activities in northern Zelaya, if less so of Brooklyn Rivera's marginal activities in the largely uninhabited, and certainly non-Miskitu southern Zelaya. On the other hand, Rivera's connections with ex-American Indian Movement leader Russell Means, and through him with such liberal and "progressive" stalwarts as Senator Kennedy, served to further discredit the Managua regime in the United States, particularly with regard to its treatment of ethnic and racial minorities. It also produced further ideological, political, and public relations confusion among the resistance's Washington lobby and its supporters.

Although 1987 was a very good year for the main insurgent groups, it was a bad time for the ethnically based Indian resistance on the Atlantic coast. The Indians failed to reach the same level of political unity as their "contra" counterparts, and their military and political strategies were clearly unsatisfactory.

In January, former MISURASATA leadership member Jimmy Emery Hodgson accepted amnesty and defected to the government's side.[74] Attempts by KISAN/Yatama to establish a southern front largely failed, and the group complained of receiving less US money than it thought it deserved.[75] MISURASATA leader Brooklyn Rivera, while complaining about Sandinista attacks on civilians, "inhuman tortures, psychological intimidation, and . . . constant persecution,"[76] was also the only major insurgent leader to meet with Daniel Ortega in January 1988 in Costa Rica to discuss a political solution.[77] Finally, some Yatama leaders, including the most important, were arrested, threatened, and made ineffective by the Honduran authorities.

The Sandinista policy toward the Indians was predictable. A militia to "repel the contras" was formed in March under the nominal leadership of a former minor KISAN member, Forne Rabonia,[78] and an indoctrination campaign was launched in the region and justified ideologically by Tomás Borge himself.[79] Indeed, after blaming pirates, the British, and US "Imperialism" for the Indians' problems, Borge claimed that "we do not use the term 'nationality' [in regard to the Atlantic coast]. . . . We believe that the past hostilities on the Atlantic Coast were not ethnic strife but a patriotic battle against external aggression."[80]

The main tactical problem facing the ethnic minorities, particularly the Miskitu Indian opposition to the FSLN, is largely one of personality clashes among the top leaders, a difficulty they share with the Spanish-speaking resistance. The most important of those are Wycliffe Diego of Yatama, Steadman Fagoth, the former leader of MISURASATA who still retains a significant following, and Brooklyn Rivera of MISURA, the most ineffective and conciliatory Indian leader.[81]

In addition, neither the blacks nor the Creoles are prepared to accept Miskitu or "Spaniard" RN leadership for long. For the regime, however, such divisions presented not only opportunities but also problems, inasmuch as the most conciliatory Indian leaders are also the weakest in terms of having a following. Practically all Indian fighters, about 600 to 1,000, are under Yatama control and still are strongly committed. When on 4 October 1987 a major local Yatama leader, Uriel Vanegas, signed an agreement with the government and met Tomás Borge in Puerto Cabezas, he could only deliver the surrender of a few dozen guerrillas in exchange for Sandinista support for vaguely defined "Indian rights."[82]

Whether people like Rivera and Vanegas can deliver peace to the Atlantic coast is questionable, and the outcome of talks between the RN, which includes Yatama's main leaders, and the government remains to be seen. The natural and logical conclusion, however, remains that a Nicaraguan "peace settlement" under a Sandinista regime in Managua will eliminate what is left of Indian (and Creole) cultural, linguistic, and religious autonomy. Not only will their cause be weakened by the permanent exile of their most effective leaders, but they would also be portrayed as disloyal and defeated aliens in the "new" Nicaragua.

By the end of 1988 the mostly Indian east coast resistance was practically defunct. On hindsight, the reasons for that failure are clear enough: small numbers, a divided leadership, and a strategic goal — regional independence or at least significant autonomy — that went against the nationalistic grain of the overwhelming majority of Nicaraguans. Indeed, José Santos Zelaya, the Nicaraguan president who annexed the eastern coast and gave his name to the department including it to this day, is a hero for the ERN insurgents as well as for the FSLN. In practical terms, the Zelaya department included almost a third of Nicaragua, most of its mineral resources, and the only access to the Caribbean. It represented a great amount of nationalist pride, all too much for either the resistance or the regime to accept it as an autonomous, let alone separate, region under the control of the Indian and creole minorities.[83]

## Perspectives

On 3 March 1988, the US House of Representatives rejected Speaker Jim Wright's formula for "humanitarian aid" to the Nicaraguan insurgents by a vote of 216 to 208. The vote came after a February defeat for the Reagan administration's own proposal for $36 million in aid, most of which (90 percent) was for nonmilitary assistance. After this, despite renewed nonmilitary aid to the tune of $100 million in early 1989,[84] the resistance entered a period of suspended animation. Funds for weapons and ammunition dried up and the shrinking supplies remaining had to be carefully rationed. Although no major fighting has taken place since the

Sapoá agreements of 24 March 1988 between the resistance and the Managua regime, clashes between the two forces have sporadically continued ever since. What is clearly gone is the ability of the insurgent military command to think in strategic terms, let alone plan a long-term strategy. On the contrary, all the leaders' efforts have to go toward maintaining the discipline and unit cohesiveness of idle troops in the difficult conditions of an uncertain future.

By the end of 1988 the Nicaraguan resistance was reduced to some 10,000–12,000 committed fighters, almost all of them veterans with four or more years of combat experience. Former Strategic Command Assistant for Operations Luis Alfonso Moreno Payan, alias "Mike Lima," one of the two commanders who led the first FDN raid into Nicaragua in 1981 and is still active despite losing an arm in combat, was born in 1959;[85] in terms of age he is typical of the majority of top commanders. As for the troops, most are younger still, with many still in their teens or in their early twenties. Most spent the largest part of their lives fighting the FSLN, have no other skills but fighting, and are united by a hatred for the *piricuacos* ("mad dogs" — the insurgents' name for the Sandinistas) that goes well beyond ideological (Communist vs. democratic) or religious (Christian vs. atheistic) considerations as it is based on the loss of family members, friends, and comrades. The insurgents now live in a largely self-contained spiritual universe, centered not on the past (although congressional actions have certainly strengthened and magnified the historic Nicaraguan distrust of Washington) as much as on the experience of the war. It remains to be seen whether the United States will resume military support to the insurgents and thus enable them to pursue their war to a successful conclusion, but it seems highly unlikely. The insurgency, however, will continue, probably at lower levels of intensity but with the potential for wider political support than ever if, as it seems probable, the Sandinista regime manipulates the promised February 1990 elections and the economic situation does not improve. In any case, the influence of the United States with the insurgents will decline further, as the sense of American betrayal intensifies in the resistance's Honduran camps.

Ultimately, the Nicaraguan resistance fell victim to its own inability to limit its dependence on American financial and political aid, to the growing isolationist instincts of the American body politics, and to its own and its conservative friends' failure to come anywhere close to the massive public relations and media campaign staged by the Managua regime and its American apologists. The American Left has probably provided more aid to the Sandinistas than the US government gave to the insurgents at the same time (1981–1988), but American leftists lobbied for Managua in Washington, defended its case in the International Court of Justice, and openly served as Sandinista advisers during negotiations with the insurgents at Sapoa. They also staged effective propaganda shows in Managua and the United States, had direct access to leaders of the Congress, including former Speaker O'Neill,[86] and had a huge impact on Congress in general.

The peculiarly factionalized and personalistic nature of Nicaraguan politics also prevented the resistance from either unifying its own political leadership or from establishing viable and permanent links with the still legal opposition on the Pacific coast. Politics, especially Washington politics, rather than strategically or tactically sound considerations often led to a waste of resources, higher than necessary casualties, and to exaggerated reliance upon US aid. When those failed, despair and a sense of hopelessness pushed even the most intelligent leaders, like Robelo, into retirement.

In the overall context of contemporary anticommunist insurgencies in the Third World, the Nicaraguan one is clearly, in terms of mentalities and groundless hopes in a foreign Messiah, the closest to the East European attempts to shake communist rule in Poland and Romania during the late 1940s. Like them, and for the same reasons, it seems to have failed.

## Notes

1. The following discussion is drawn in part from Michael Radu, "The Origins and Evolution of the Nicaraguan Insurgencies, 1979-1985," *Orbis,* vol. 29, no. 4 (Winter 1986), pp. 821-840; reprinted as "The Nature of the Insurgency," *The Continuing Crisis,* ed. Mark Falcoff and Robert Royal (Washington, D.C.: University Press of America, 1987), pp. 411-432; and as "Los orígenes y la evolución de la insurrección Nicaraguënse: 1969-1985," *Revista Occidental*, vol. 4, no.1 (1987), pp. 67-92.
2. The sociology of the Guardia Nacional under Somoza remains a prohibitively delicate subject for academic students of Nicaragua. The point to be mentioned here is that the overwhelming majority of the rank and file and NCOs, as well as some officers, were of peasant origin, from such conservative departments as Jinotega, Matagalpa, Chinandega, and areas of northern and southern Zelaya.
3. For details, see Christopher Dickey, *With the Contras. A Reporter in the Wilds of Nicaragua* (New York: Simon & Schuster, 1985). Dickey's is an interesting book, inasmuch as his reporter talent tends to have the best over his liberal instincts, thus resulting into a highly informative account. See also Michael Radu, op.cit., and some of the interviews in Dieter Eich and Carlos Rincón, *The Contras. Interviews with Anti-Sandinistas,* (San Francisco: Synthesis Publications, 1984).
4. The fascinating story of "Suicida" is presented in Christopher Dickey's, *With the Contras.* Dickey provides a highly informative chronicle of the early days

of the insurgency. "Suicida" was tried and executed by the resistance leadership for abuses against fellow fighters and civilians.
5. Dickey, *With the Contras*, pp. 64–66; it seems that Bravo was personally tortured and murdered by Lenin Cerna, now the top official in the Sandinista secret police. Most of the facts in Dickey's account were confirmed confidentially to me by Honduran and Salvadoran officials and citizens closely involved with Salazar's activities between July 1979 and his murder. Like Somoza's murder in Paraguay, Salazar's assassination was part of the Sandinistas' original campaign of international terrorism directed against real and potential leaders of opposition.
6. Unlike Salazar, Bermúdez was not a field commander nor was he highly known, let alone popular, with the exiles of the *guardia*. On the contrary, Bermúdez was a non-participant in the civil war since he was stationed in Washington as Nicaragua's military attaché throughout the war. His main strengths and appeal with them was then, and remains to this day, his commitment to the use of military force for a honorable solution, his professionalism, and his ability to articulate the demands of the rank and file, both politically and ideologically. Bermúdez turned his disadvantages into assets by using his political and diplomatic skills in order to attract foreign (Argentine and US) support for the insurgent cause.
7. Anastasio Somoza García was assassinated in 1956. He was succeeded by his sons, Luis and Anastasio Somoza Debayle; the latter has appointed his eldest son, Anastasio Somoza Portocarrero, "El Chiguïn," as his successor. Today, El Chiguïn" receives no respect from any sector of the Nicaraguan resistance and lives in his comfortable Miami condominium, ignored and often hated or despised by all Nicaraguans, whichever side of the civil war they are supporting.
8. The original name of the organization was the National Liberation Front (FLN); it took a few months for Carlos Fonseca Amador to add the "Sandinista" attribute to the title. See David Nolan, *FSLN. The Ideology of the Sandinistas and the Nicaraguan Revolution* (Coral Gables, Fla.: Institute of Interamerican Studies, 1984), p. 24.
9. For details on the social background of the Sandinista leadership, see Shirley Christian, *Nicaragua. Revolution in the Family* (New York: Random House, 1985); and Michael Radu, "The Nature of the Insurgency," pp. 409–432; The most detailed analysis to date is in US Department of State, *Nicaraguan Biographies. A Resource Book* (Washington, D.C.: GPO), January 1988. See also Manuel Jiron, *Quien es Quien en Nicaragua* (Editorial Amor, San Jose: 1986).
10. Nolan, *FSLN,* p. 22.
11. Ibid. See also Antonio Ybarra-Rojas, "The changing role of revolutionary violence in Nicaragua, 1959–1979", in Michael Radu, ed., *Violence and the Latin American revolutionaries* (New Brunswick, NJ: Transaction Books, 1989), pp. 56–77.
12. Excelsior, June 25, 19, 1988, p. A21.
13. Ibid.
14. Ibid.
15. Ibid.
16. *FBIS*, July 16, 1988, p. I1.
17. The *New York Times*, 29 December 1987.

18. *The Economist*, Foreign Report, 29 January 1987, p. 5.
19. *Los Angeles Times*, 20 September 1987.
20. *Los Angeles Times*, 20 September 1987.
21. *Washington Post*, 5 March 1988.
22. *FBIS-LAM*, 5 July 1988, p. 19.
23. *Central America Report*, 27 October,1988, p. 3.
24. *FBIS-LAM*, 16 December, 1988, p. 30.
25. Ibid.
26. Joint Publications Research Services, *Latin America*, 9 February 1988, p. 21.
27. *Barricada*, 9 February 1987, p. 2.
28. Ibid., 1 November 1986, p. 2.
29. *Izvestia*, 24 June 1987.
30. *El Nuevo Diario*, 4 August 1987 , p. 1.
31. *New York Times*, 4 March 1988.
32. See Douglas Payne, *A Chronicle of the Central American "Peace Process,"* (New York: Freedom House, 1987), p. 17.
33. *The Military Balance, 1987-1988* (London: IISS, 1987), p. 194.
34. Ibid.
35. Ibid.
36. For details on the intricate shifting of attitudes and negotiations between Managua, Moscow, and Havana regarding the MIG planes, see the testimony of high-ranking EPS defector Roger Miranda Bengoechea in George Gedda, "The Making of a Defector," *Foreign Service Journal*, March 1988, pp. 26-27.
37. *General del Pino Speaks* (Washington, D.C.: Cuban-American Foundation, 1987), pp. 27-31.
38. US Department of State, *Nicaraguan Biographies*, p. 18. See, also, the remarks of ex-MININT counter-intelligence officer Miguel Bolanos Hunter in *Hydra of Carnage, International Linkages of Terrorism. The Witnesses Speak,* ed. Uri Ra anan et al. (Lexington, Ky.: Lexington Books, 1986), p. 310.
39. The US government has consistently estimated that the number of Cuban advisers and military personnel in Nicaragua is about 3,000. Roger Miranda estimates the number at only 500 as of late 1987, a decline of over 1,500 from 1980 to 1983. They have participated, and some have died, in counterinsurgency operations. See Gedda, "The Making of a Defector," p. 28. Additional data on the role of the Cubans, Libyans, Bulgarians, and East Germans, as well as Costa Rican leftists, can be found in the testimony of former Interior Ministry Officer Alvaro José Baldizon Aviles, in US Department of State, *Inside the Sandinista Regime: A Special Investigator's Perspective* (Washington, D.C.: GPO, February 1986), pp. 16-17. See also Latin America Regional Reports, Mexico & Central America, 10 January 1986, p. 4.
40. See Michael Radu and Vladimir Tismaneanu, *Revolutionary Organizations in Latin America: A Handbook*, (McLean, VA.: Pergamon Press, 1989).
41. In Nicaragua, as well as more generally along Central America's Caribbean coast, the term "Creole" indicates black Protestant speakers of pidgin English. In Nicaragua they are concentrated largely in and around the port of Bluefields.
42. For some details on this question, see Robert F. Turner, *Nicaragua vs. United States: A Look at the Facts* (Washington, D.C.: Institute for Foreign Policy

Analysis, Pergamon-Brassey's, 1987), pp. 120-123; US Department of State, *Nicaraguan Biographies,* passim; and Michael Radu, "The Nicaraguan Insurgencies: 1979-1985."
43. *Central America Report*, 8 January 1988, p. 2.
44. Tomás Borge claimed in June 1987 that there were 2,095 contras and 2,110 Somozist guardsmen (Semana, Bogota, June 9, 1987) in the jails controlled by his ministry. In September the same year, however, Borge said that the number of prisoners (political or otherwise, a distinction not always easy to make) was 8,000, of whom 3,000 were Somozist guards and over 1,000 contras. (*FBIS*, Latin America, 8 September 1987, p. 11).
45. See US Department of State, *Human Rights in Nicaragua under the Sandinistas* (Washington, D.C.: GPO, December 1986) p. 27.
46. US Department of State, *Nicaraguan Biographies*, pp. 88-91.
47. For a discussion of "El Negro's" present activities, see the *New York Times*, 4 March 1988.
48. See Edgar Chamorro's plaintive pro-FSLN testimony to the International Court of Justice in *The Central American Crisis Reader*, ed. Robert Leiken and Barry Rubin (New York: Summit Books, 1987), pp. 265-270.
49. US Department of State, Nicaraguan Biographies, p. 61.
50. *Christian Science Monitor*, 21 January 1987.
51. A definitive, thorough and well-documented debunking of those claims is to be found in L. Francis Bouchey, J. Michael Waller, and Steve Baldwin, *The Real Secret War. Sandinista Political Warfare and Its Effects on Congress*, Council for Inter-American Security, Washington, D.C., 1987.
52. *Los Angeles Times*, 8 May 1987. The July 1988 resistance meeting in Santo Domingo resulted in the election of Bermúdez as director, while Pedro Joaquin Chamorro lost his seat. Robelo, with all his business and family ties in Costa Rica, was forced by his "friend" Oscar Arias to renounce politics as a price of staying in San José; by the first half of 1989 Ferrey and César returned to Nicaragua, and the only prominent civilians left in the leadership were Sanchez and Calero.
53. US Department of State, *Nicaraguan Biographies,* p. 88.
54. A former medical student, "Aureliano," was apparently murdered by FSLN agents, following the pattern started with the killing after torture of Bravo.
55. Ibid. As of the end of 1988 it was unclear how many of these were still active. It appeared that most of those in the south were largely dismantled, while those in the central and northern departments were reduced in effectiveness and strength but still survived as operational units.
56. *Washington Times*, 22 October 1984.
57. Eich and Rincón, *The Contras*, p. 99. The women among the insurgents seem to be far more resilient in this respect than men.
58. US Department of State, *Nicaraguan Biographies,* p. 6.
59. *Washington Times*, 22 October 1984.
60. FBIS *Latin America*, 25 October 1985, p. 22.
61. The Coordinadora is an umbrella organization including the most important anti-Sandinista parties, independent unions, and business organizations.
62. Even such apologists for the Sandinistas as William I. Robinson and Kent Norsworthy (both of whom receive their salaries from the Managua regime), in their *David and Goliath. The US War against Nicaragua* (New York: Monthly Review Press, 1987), p. 267, admit that there was "peasant resent-

ment" against the *asentamientos*. The consistently anti-contra correspondents of *Newsweek* also admitted that the Sandinistas have forcibly removed "hundreds" of peasants "in order to prevent them from helping the contras." (*Newsweek*, 13 April 1987, p. 31.).
63. See the statement of Jorge Ramirez Zelaya in Eich and Rincón, *The Contras*, pp. 36–37.
64. Ibid., pp. 34–35.
65. *Insight*, 11 May 1987, p. 27.
66. FBIS, *Latin America*, 27 February 1987.
67. *Washington Times*, 13 April 1987.
68. *Washington Post*, 25 January 1987.
69. Ibid., 26 June 1987; similar though somewhat smaller figures appeared in the *Christian Science Monitor*, 23 July 1987.
70. *Le Figaro*, 20 February 1987.
71. *New York Times*, 12 March 1987.
72. According to the State Department, by the summer of 1986 as many as 36,000 Indians, out of a total Nicaraguan Miskitu, Sumo, and Rama population of 110,000 in 1979, were refugees in Honduras. US Department of State, *Dispossessed. The Miskitu Indians in Sandinista Nicaragua* (Washington, D.C.: GPO, June 1986), p. 8.
73. US Department of State, *Nicaraguan Biographies,* p. 41.
74. *El Nuevo Diario*, 23 January 1987, p. 1.
75. *Tico Times*, 23 January 1987, p. 1.
76. FBIS, *Latin America*, 13 February 1987, p. 12.
77. *New York Times*, 17 January 1988.
78. FBIS, *Latin America*, 20 March 1987, p. 18.
79. *El Nuevo Diario*, 30 June 1987, p. 4.
80. *World Marxist Review*, August 1987, pp. 121–22.
81. *Los Angeles Times*, 9 June 1987.
82. *New York Times*, 6 October 1987.
83. Neither the Sandinistas nor the resistance are immune to "racism," as demonstrated by the former's roughshod treatment of the east coast "savages" and the latter's private description of the Indian resistance fighters as lazy, unreliable, and basically alien.
84. In fact, the condition extracted by congressional democrats from President Bush for supporting humanitarian aid was precisely that the resistance will engage in no military activity, at least until the promised elections of February 1990.
85. *Nicaraguan Biographies, US Department of State*, p. 54.
86. O'Neill proudly and openly admitted that his information on Nicaragua and El Salvador came from the Maryknoll brothers and sisters, known for their unflinching and indiscriminate support for the hard Left, an attitude that provoked the Vatican into disciplinary measures against the order. For the amounts of aid delivered by the American (without even mentioning the West European) Left, see *The Miami Herald*, April 25, 1987.

# Selected Bibliography

## General

Beckett, Ian F. W., and John Pimlott. *Armed Forces and Modern Counter-Insurgency*. New York: St. Martin's Press, 1985.

Bernstein, Alvin H. "Insurgents against Moscow." *Policy Review*, Summer 1987.

Bode, William R. "The Reagan Doctrine in Outline." in *Central America and the Reagan Doctrine*, ed. Walter H. Hahn (Lanham, Md.: University Press of America, 1987).

Bouchey, L., M. Waller, and S. Baldwin. *The Real Secret War*. Washington, D.C.: Council for Inter-American Security, 1987.

Cilliers, J. K. *Counter-Insurgency in Rhodesia*. London: Croom Helm, 1985.

Clay, Jason W., and Bonnie K. Holcomb. *Politics and the Ethiopian Famine 1984–1985*. Cambridge, Mass.: Cultural Survival, Inc., 1986.

Daly, Reid, and Peter, Stiff. *Selous Scouts. Top Secret War*. Alberton, South Africa: Galago Publishing, 1982.

Deutscher, Isaac. "Marxism and Primitive Logic." in *The Stalinist Legacy*, Tariq Ali ed. Harmondsworth: Penguin Books, 1984.

"Foggy Bottom Freedom Fighter. Elliott Abrams talks candidly about Reagan Policy in Latin America." *Policy Review*, Winter 1989.

Fossedal, Gregory A. *The Democratic Imperative. Exporting the American Revolution*. New York: Basic Books, 1989.

Fraser, Glenda. "Basmachi – I." *Central Asian Survey* 6, no. 1 (1987).

Fraser, Glenda. "Basmachi – II." *Central Asian Survey* 6, no. 2 (1987).

*Fundamentals of U.S. Foreign Policy*. Washington, D.C.: Department of State, Bureau of Public Affairs, 1988.

*General del Pino Speaks*. Washington, D.C.: The Cuban American Foundation, 1987.

Griffith, Samuel B., trans. and Introduction to *Mao Tse-Tung on Guerrilla Warfare*. New York: Praeger, 1961.

Hawkins, William R. "Reagan Rebellion or National Renewal." *The World & I*, April 1988.

International Security Council. *Central America: A political strategic assessment: 1988*. New York, 1988.

Jones, David R. "Lessons of the Tambov Campaign of 1920." Paper presented at

the Conference on Soviet counterinsurgency experience, University of New Brunswick, Fredericton, NB, 3–4 October 1987.
Krauthammer, Charles. "Guerrilla Warfare, Morality and the Reagan Doctrine." *The New Republic*. 6 September 1986, pp. 17–24.
La Justicia de Pilatos." *Caretas*, 8 February 1988.
Ledeen, Michael A. "Secrets." *The National Interest*, no. 10 (Winter 1987).
McClintock, Michael. *The American Connection*. London: Zed Books, 1985.
McGovern, George. "The 1988 election: U.S. policy at a watershed." *Foreign Affairs. America and the World*, 1987/1988.
*The Military Balance 1985–1986*. London, IISS 1986.
Montaner, Carlos Alberto. *Secret Report on the Cuban Revolution*. trans. by Eduardo Zayas-Bazán. New Brunswick, NJ: Transaction Books, 1982.
Muravchik, Joshua. *The Uncertain Crusade. Jimmy Carter and the Dilemmas of Human Rights Policy*. American Enterprise Institute, Washington, D.C., 1988.
Myrdal, Gunnar. *The Challenge of World Poverty*. New York: Vintage Books, 1970.
Neier, Aryeh. "The Legal Implications of the CIA's Nicaragua Manual." In *Psychological Operations in Guerrilla Warfare*. New York: Vintage Books, 1985.
Paschal, Rod. "Marxist Counter-insurgencies." *Parameters*, 16, no. 2, (1986).
Pastor, Robert A. "The invasion of Grenada: a pre- and post-mortem." In Scott B. MacDonald et al., editors. *The Caribbean after Grenada. Revolution, Conflict, and Democracy*. New York: Praeger 1988.
Ra'anan, Uri et al. *Hydra of Carnage*. Lexington, Mass.: Lexington Books 1985.
Radu, Michael. "Terror, terrorism and insurgency in Latin America. *Orbis*, Spring 1984.
Radu, Michael, ed. *Violence and the Latin American Revolutionaries*. New Brunswick, N.J.: Transaction Books, 1988.
Samuel, Peter. "The Evolving Character of the Philippines Insurgency." *Global Affairs*, Winter 1988.
Sharpe, Kenneth E. "The Real Cause of Irangate." *Foreign Policy*, Fall 1987.
Shtromas, Alexander. "The Baltic States." In *The Last Empire. Nationality and the Soviet Future*. Ed. by Robert Conquest. Stanford: Hoover Institution Press, 1986.
Smith, Frederic. "The War in Lithuania and the Ukraine against Soviet Power." In *Combat in Communist Territory*. Ed. by Charles Moser. Lake Bluff, Ill.: Regnery Gateway, 1985.
Tauras, K. V., *Guerrilla Warfare on the Amber Coast*. New York: Voyage Press, 1962.
Turner, Robert F. *Nicaragua v. United States: A Look at the Facts*. Institute for Foreign Policy Analysis, Pergamon-Brassey's, Washington, D.C., 1987.
Winsor, Curtin. "From Reagan Doctrine to Detente." *Global Affairs*, Winter 1988.

## Eritrea

"Andauernder Krieg in Tigre und Eritrea." *Neue Zuercher Zeitung*, 24 April 1987.
Davidson, Basil, Lionel Cliffe, and Selassie Bereket Kabte, eds. *Behind the War in Eritrea*. Nottingham, UK: Spokesman, 1980.
"Der Vergessene Krieg in Eritrea." *Neue Zuercher Zeitung*, 20 November 1986.
"Eritrea: The Endless War." In *The Washington Quarterly*, 9 no. 2 (Spring 1986).

Selected Bibliography  291

Erlich, Haggai. "The Eritrean Autonomy, 1952-1962: Its Failure and Contribution to Further Escalation." In Yoram Dinstein, ed. *Models of Autonomy.* New Brunswick, NJ: Rutgers University Press, 1981.
Erlich, Haggai. *The Struggle over Eritrea, 1962-1978.* Stanford, CA: Hoover Institution, 1983.
Firebrace, James and Stuart Holland MP, with a Preface by Neil Kinnock, MP. *Never Kneel Down: Drought, Development and Liberation in Eritrea.* Trenton, NJ: Red Sea Press, 1985.
Habte Selassie, Bereket. *Conflict and Intervention in the Horn of Africa.* New York: Monthly Review Press, 1980.
Henze, Paul B. "Getting a Grip on the Horn" in Walter Z. Laqueur, ed., *The Pattern of Soviet Conduct in the Third World.* New York, Praeger, 1983.
Henze, Paul B. *Russians and the Horn: Opportunism and the Long View.* Marina del Rey, CA: European American Institute for Security Research, 1983.
Henze, Paul B. "Arming the Horn, 1960-1980." In *Proceedings of the Seventh International Conference of Ethiopian Studies.* Lund, Sweden, 1982. African Studies Center, Michigan State University, East Lansing, MI, 1984.
Henze, Paul B. *Rebels and Separatists in Ethiopia: Regional Resistance to a Marxist Regime.* RAND/R-3347-USDP, Santa Monica, CA, December 1985.
Henze, Paul B. *Ethiopia's Economic Prospects for the 1990s.* RAND N-2857-USDP, Santa Monica, December 1988.
Kaplan, Robert D. *Surrender or Starve. The Wars Behind the Famine.* Boulder, CO.: Westview Press, 1988.
Keneally, Thomas. "In Eritrea." *New York Times Sunday Magazine,* 27 September 1987.
Korbonski, Andrzej and Francis Fukuyama, eds. *The Soviet Union and the Third World.* Ithaca, NY: Cornell University Press, 1987.
Korn, David A. *Ethiopia, the United States and the Soviet Union.* London: Croom Helm, 1986.
Longrigg, Stephen H. *A Short History of Eritrea.* Oxford Clarendon Press, 1945.
Medhanie Tesfatsion. *Eritrea, Dynamics of a National Question.* Amsterdam, 1986.
Smith, John Edwin. "Eritrea." *Soldier of Fortune,* February 1987.
Suau, Anthony. "Region in Rebellion: Eritrea." *National Geographic,* September 1985.
Trevaskis, G. H. K. *Eritrea, A Colony in Transition, 1941-1952.* London: Oxford University Press, 1960.
US Arms Control and Disarmament Agency. *World Military Expenditures and Arms Transfers, 1986.* Washington, D.C., 1987.
Wolde Mariam, Mesfin. *An Atlas of Ethiopia.* Addis Ababa, 1970.
Wolde, Dawit Giorgis. *Red Tears.* Trenton, NJ: Red Sea Press, 1988.

## Angola

Breytenbach, Cloete. *Savimbi's Angola.* Howard Timmins Publishers, 1980.
Breytenbach, Jan. *Forged in Battle.* Capetown: Saayman & Weber, 1986.
Bridgland, Fred. *Jonas Savimbi. A Key to Africa.* New York: Paragon House, 1987.
Cain, Edward P. "The Agony of Angola." In *Combat on Communist Territory.* Charles Moser, ed., Lake Bluff, Ill.: Regnery Gateway, 1985.

Cintra Torres, Eduardo. "Angola: Um Beco cum Saida?" In Africa num Mundo Multipolar, *Estudios Africanos*, no. 1. Lisbon: IEEL, 1983, pp. 89-106.
Dixon, Glen. *Hostage*. Alberton, South Africa: Galago Books, 1986.
Dohning, W. *UNITA*. Kwacha/ UNITA Press, 1984.
Gabriel, Claude. *Angola: le tournant africain?* Paris: Editions La Brèche, 1978.
Kitchen, Helen, ed. *Angola, Mozambique, and the West*. New York: Praeger, 1987.
Marcum, John A. *The Angolan Revolution*. Vol. 2 of *Exile Politics and Guerrilla Warfare (1962-1976)*. Cambridge Mass. and London: MIT Press, 1978.
Mockler, Anthony. *The New Mercenaries*. London: Sidgwick & Jackson, 1985.
Oliver, B. J. *The Strategic Significance of Angola*. Ad Hoc Publication no. 19. Pretoria: Institute for Strategic Studies, University of Pretoria, 1984.
Ottaway, David and Marina. *Afrocommunism*. New York: Africana Publishing House, 1981.
Rosa, Joao. *Jonas Savimbi, O Homem do Projecto Angolano*.
Rotberg, Robert I. "Angolan Sting." *Christian Science Monitor*, 16 April 1986.
Savimbi, Jonas. *Angola, a resistencia em busca de uma nova nacao*.
"Siege at Cuito Cuanavale." *Soldier of Fortune*, May 1988.
Sommerville, Keith. *Angola. Politics, Economics and Society*. Boulder, Colo. and London: Lynne Rienner Publishers, 1986.
Steenkamp, Willem. *Borderstrike*. Alberton: Galago Publishers, 1983.
Terchinet, Josiane. "Cuba et l'Afrique." *Arès* (1983), pp. 287-308.
UNITA. *The Angola Road to National Recovery*. Jamba, December 1883.
Venter, Al J. *The Zambesi Salient. Conflict in Southern Africa*, Old Greenwich, CT.: Devin-Adair, 1974.
Vinicios, M. *Jonas Savimbi*. Lisbon: 1976.
Wheeler, Douglas, and Rene Pelissier. *Angola*. London: Pall Mall, 1971.
Wolfers, Michael and Jane Bergerol. *Angola in the Front Line*. London: Zed Press, 1983.
Zafiris, Nicos. "The People's Republic of Angola: Soviet-type Economy in the Making." In Peter Wiles, ed. *The New Communist Third World*. New York: St. Martin's Press, 1982, pp. 53-88.

## Mozambique

Behn, Sharon. "Behind Rebel Lines in Mozambique." *The Los Angeles Times*, 20 March 1987.
Bryan, Kindra. "My Three Month Trek Out of Africa." *Washington Post*, 23 August 1987.
Cole, Barbara. *The Elite: The Story of the Rhodesian Special Air Service*. Transkei, South Africa: Three Knights Publishing, 1984.
Flower, K. *Serving Secretly*, Alberton, South Africa: Galago Publishing, 1987.
Gersony, R. *Summary of Mozambican Refugee Accounts of Principally Conflict-Related Experiences in Mozambique*. Washington, D.C.: Government Printing Office, US Department of State, April 1988.
Godwin, Peter. "RENAMO's Hard Men Rule Over the Bush." *London Sunday Times*, 5 April 1987.
Hanlon, J. *Mozambique: The Revolution Under Fire*. London, Zed Books, 1984.
Henriksen, Thomas. *Revolution and Counter-Revolution in Mozambique*. Westport, CT: Greenwood Press, 1983.
Henriksen, Thomas. "The People's Republic of Mozambique." In Dennis L.

Bark, ed. *The Red Orchestra. The case of Africa*. Stanford, CA: Hoover Institution Press, Stanford, 1988.
Legum, Colin, "The MNR." *CSIS Africa Notes*, no. 16, 15 July 1983.
Maier, F. X. *Revolution and Terrorism in Mozambique*. New York: American African Affairs Association, 1974.
Mondlane, Eduardo. *The Struggle for Mozambique*. London: Penguin, 1969.
Moorcraft, Paul. "The Savage, Silent Civil War." *Army*, April 1987.
Rees, David. *Soviet Strategic Penetration of Africa*. London: Institute for the Study of conflict, 1976.
Reid-Daly, Lt. Col. Ron. *Top Secret War*. Alberton, South Africa: Galago Publishing, 1982.
Thomashausen, A. E. "Mozambique: 10 Years' Independence." Lecture, South African Institute of International Relations, Johannesburg, 8 February 1986.
Thomashausen, Andre. "The National Resistance of Mozambique." *African Insight*, February 1983.

## Cambodia

Amnesty International, *Kampuchea. Political Imprisonment and Torture*. London: Amnesty International Publications, 1987.
Carney, Timothy. "Heng Samrin's Armed Forces and the Military Balance in Cambodia." *International Journal of Politics*, 16, no. 3 (Fall 1986), pp. 150–185.
Carney, Timothy. "The Heng Samrin Armed Forces and the Military Balance in Cambodia." In *The Cambodian Agony*. David A. Abling and Marlowe Hood, eds. Armonk and London: M. E. Sharpe Inc., 1987.
Chandra, Nayan. *Brother Enemy*. New York: Harcourt Brace Jovanovitch, 1986.
Chandler, David P. *A History of Cambodia*. Boulder, Colo.: Westview Press, 1983.
Chandler, David P., and B. Kiernan., eds. *Revolution and Its Aftermath in Kampuchea: Eight Essays*. New Haven: Yale University Southeast Asia Studies, 1983.
Chang, Pao-min. "Beijing Verus Hanoi." *Asian Survey*, 23, no. 5 (May 1983), pp. 598–617.
Dassé, M. "Cambodge: la tutelle Vietnamienne." *Défense Nationale*, 39 (April 1983), pp. 95–106.
Eliot, D. W. P. *The Third Indochina Conflict*. Boulder, Colo.: Westview Press, 1981.
Etcheson, Craig. *The Rise and Demise of Democratic Kampuchea*. Boulder, Colo.: Westview Press, 1984.
Kiernan, Ben. "Conflict in the Kampuchean Communist Movement." *Journal of Contemporary Asia*, 10, no. 1 (1980), pp. 7–47.
Kiernan, Ben and Chanthou Boua, eds. *Peasants and Politics in Kampuchea, 1942-1981*. London: Zed Press, 1981.
Monjo, John C. "The Cambodian Issue." *Department of State Bulletin*, May 1987, pp. 29–30.
Mosyakov, D. "National Rebirth of Kampuchea." *Far Eastern Affairs*. Soviet Academy of Sciences, Moscow. no. 2, 1984, pp. 52–63.
People's Republic of Kampuchea, Foreign Ministry. *Undeclared War against the People's Republic of Kampuchea*. Phnom Penh, 5 December 1985. Foreign Broadcast Information Service Reports, Washington, D.C., December 16–17, 1985, pp. H1-H24.

Porter, Gareth. "Vietnam in Kampuchea: Aims and Options." *Indochina Issues* 16 (May 1981), pp. 1–17.
Rosenberger, Leif. "The Soviet-Vietnamese Alliance and Kampuchea." *Survey*. London. Autumn-Winter 1983, pp. 207–231.
Sak Sutsakhan. *The Khmer Republic at War and the Final Collapse*. Washington, D.C., U.S. Army Center for Military History, 1980.
Samphan, Khieu. "Cambodge: l'Union Sacrée," *Politique Internationale* 34 (Winter, 1986–1987), pp. 331–339.
Samrin, Heng. "The Process of Kampuchea's Renaissance Is Irreversible." *World Marxist Review* vol. 29, no. 2 (February 1986), pp. 36–42.
Schier, Peter. "Kampuchea in 1985: Between Crocodiles and Tigres." In *Southeast Asian Affairs, 1986*. (Institute of Southeast Asian Studies, Singapore, 1986). pp. 139–161.
Schier, Peter and Manola Schier-Oum, eds. *Prince Sihanouk of Cambodia. Interviews and Talks*. (Institut fuer Asienkunde, Hamburg, 1980).
Stuart-Fox, Martin. *The Murderous Revolution. Life and Death in Pol Pot's Kampuchea*. Chippendale, NSW: Alternative Publishing Cooperative, 1985.
Tasker, Rodney. "Cambodia—The Reality of Coalition." *Far Eastern Economic Review*, 10 July 1986, pp. 11–12.
Thailand, Government of. *Documents on the Kampuchean Problem 1979-1985*. (Ministry of Foreign Affairs, Bangkok, 1986.
van der Kroef, Justus M. *Dynamics of the Cambodian Conflict*. (Institute for the Study of Conflict, London, 1986).
Vickery, Michael. *Cambodia, 1975-1982*. Boston: South End Press, 1984.
Vickery, Michael. *Kampuchea. Politics, Economics and Society*. Boulder, Colo.: Lynne Riemer, 1986.
Weatherbee, Donald E., ed. *Southeast Asia Divided—The ASEAN-Indochina Crisis*. Boulder, Colo.: Westview Press, 1985.
Yang Mu. "Three Decisions Vital to Anti-Vietnamese War." *Beijing Review*, no. 52, 29 December 1986, pp. 14–15.

## Afghanistan

Amstutz, Bruce J. *Afghanistan: The First Five Years of Soviet Occupation*. Washington: National Defense University Press, 1986.
Arnold, Anthony. *Afghanistan's Two-Party Communism: Parcham and Khalq*. Stanford: Hoover Institution Press, 1983.
Arnold, Anthony. *Afghanistan: The Soviet Invasion in Perspective*. Stanford: Hoover Institution Press, 1985.
Bernstein, Carl. "Arms for Afghanistan." *New Republic*, 18 July 1981.
Bodansky, Yossef. "Soviet Military Involvement in Afghanistan." In *Afghanistan. The Great Game Revisited*. Ed. Rosanne Klass. New York: Freedom House, 1987.
Dupaigne, Bernard. "Les Peuples." In *Afghanistan: La Colonisation Impossible*. Paris: Les Editions du Cerf, 1984.
"Forgotten Refugees: Afghans in Iran." *The Middle East*, August 1986.
Girardet, Edward. *Afghanistan: The Soviet War*. New York: St. Martin's Press, 1985.
Hammond, Thomas T. *Red Flag over Afghanistan*. Boulder, Colo.: Westview Press, 1984.
Kaplan, Robert. "The View from Baluchistan." *American Spectator*, March 1988.

Newell, Nancy Peabody, and Richard S. *The Struggle for Afghanistan*. Ithaca and London: Cornell University Press, 1981.
Roy, Oliver. *Islam and Resistance in Afghanistan*. Cambridge, England: Cambridge University Press, 1986.
Shahrani, Nazif and Robert L. Canfield, eds. *Revolutions and Rebellions in Afghanistan: Anthropological Perspectives*. Berkeley: University of California Press, 1984.
Shansab, Nasir. *Soviet Expansion in the Third World: Afghanistan, a Case Study*. Silver Spring, MD: Bartleby Press, 1986.
US Department of State, Bureau of Public Affairs. *Afghanistan: Seven Years of Occupation*. Special Report no. 155, December 1986, p. 15.
Yusufzai, Rahimullah. "Resistance in Afghanistan: the Panjshir Model." *Regional Studies, Quarterly Journal of the Institute of Regional Studies* (Islamabad) 3, no. 3 (Summer 1985).

## Nicaragua

Christian, Shirley. *Nicaragua. Revolution in the Family*. New York: Random House, 1985.
Dickey, Christopher. *With the Contras. A Reporter in the Wilds of Nicaragua*. New York: Simon & Schuster, 1985.
Eich, Dieter, and Carlos Rincón. *The Contras. Interviews with Anti-Sandinistas*. San Francisco: Synthesis Publications, 1984.
Falcoff, Mark, and Robert Royal, eds. *The Continuing Crisis*. Washington, D.C.: The Ethics and Public Policy Center, University Press of America, 1987.
*Inside the Sandinista Regime: A Special Investigator's Perspective*. (Washington, D.C.: US Department of State, February 1986).
Leiken, Robert, and Barry Rubin, eds. *The Central American Crisis Reader*. New York: Summit Books, 1987.
LeMoyne, James. "Teaching the Contras Leftist Rebel Methods." *New York Times*, 8 March 1987.
Nolan, David. *FSLN. The Ideology of the Sandinistas and the Nicaraguan Revolution*. Coral Gables, Fla.: Institute of Interamerican Studies, 1984.
Robinson, William L., and Kent Norsworthy. *David and Goliath. The U.S. War against Nicaragua*. New York: Monthly Review Press, 1987.
Turner, Robert F. *Nicaragua vs. United States: A Look at the Facts*. Washington, D.C.: Institute for Foreign Policy Analysis, Pergamon-Brassey's, 1987.
US Department of State. *Nicaraguan Biographies. A Resource Book*. Washington, D.C.: GPO, January 1988.
Vaky, Viron. "Positive Containment in Nicaragua." *Foreign Policy*, Fall 1987.

## Periodicals

*Afghanistan Forum*
*Africa Confidential*
*Africa Contemporary Record*
*The American Spectator*
*The Beijing Review*
*Boletim da Republica* (Maputo)
*British Broadcasting Corporation Summary of World Broadcasts*
*Caretas (Lima)*

*Central Asian Survey*
*The Christian Science Monitor*
*Défense Nationale*
*The Ethiopian Herald*
*Far Eastern Affairs* (Moscow)
Far Eastern Economic Review
Financial Times
*Financial Times* (Johannesburg)
*Foreign Affairs*
*Foreign Broadcast Information Service (FBIS)*
*Foreign Policy*
*Frankfurter Allgemeine Zeitung*
*Global Affairs*
*Granma*
*InformAfrica*
*Insight*
*Jane's Defence Weekly*
*The Johannesburg Star*
*Kabul New Times*
*The London Times*
*London Times Spectrum*
*Manchester Guardian Weekly*
*Middle East*
*Mozambique News Agency* (AIM)
*National Geographic*
*The National Interest*
*Neue Zurcher Zeitung*
*The New Republic*
*The New York Times*
*Newsweek*
*Orbis*
*Pakistani Times*
*Parameters*
*Policy Review*
*Pretoria News*
*The Rand Daily Mail* (Johannesburg)
*Regional Studies. Quarterly Journal of the Institute of Regional Studies* (Islamabad)
*The San Francisco Chronicle*
*Scope* (Johannesburg)
*Soldier of Fortune*
*South China Morning Post*
*Sueddeutsche Zeitung*
*Survey*
*Time*
*The Wall Street Journal*
*The Washington Post*
*Washington Quarterly*
*The Washington Times*
*Weekly Compilation of Presidential Documents*
*The World & I*
*World Marxist Review*

# Contributors

ANTHONY ARNOLD served with the CIA in Afghanistan during the early 1970s and is the author of *Afghanistan's Two-Party Communism: Parcham and Khalq* (1983) and *Afghanistan: The Soviet Invasion in Perspective* (1985).

PAUL B. HENZE is resident consultant at the RAND Corporation in Washington, D.C. and has held senior positions with the State and Defense Departments. Among his many publications are *Russians and the Horn* (1983) and *Rebels and Separatists in Ethiopia: Regional Resistance to a Marxist Regime* (1985).

MICHAEL RADU is resident scholar at the Foreign Policy Research Institute in Philadelphia and contributing editor of *Orbis*. Among his edited or authored volumes are *Eastern Europe and the Third World* (1981), *Violence and the Latin American revolutionaries* (1988), and *Latin American Revolutions* (1990).

JUSTUS VAN DER KROEF is Dana Professor and Chairman of the Department of Political Science at the University of Bridgeport, Connecticut. His extensive publications include *Communism in Southeast Asia* (1980), *Kampuchea—The Endless Tug of War* (1982), and *Dynamics of the Cambodian Conflict* (1985).

JACK WHEELER is the director of the Freedom Research Foundation in Washington, D.C., and the author of numerous articles on Third World anticommunist insurgent movements. He has published in *Reason, The Wall Street Journal, Africa Confidential*, and *The Washington Times*. He has also traveled extensively with all the anticommunist groups examined in this volume.

# Index

Abrams, Elliott, 56, 69-70
Acevedo, Manuel Adan Rugama ("Aureliano"), 274
Adamishin, Anatoly, 153
Afghanistan, 8, 38
   analysis of situation in, 250-253
   anti-Soviet resistance in, 235-239
   background of, 233-235
   counter-states within, 30-31
   exile opposition in 1987 in, 239-242
   goals, assets, and strategies of, 245-247
   lessons learned and future of, 253-255
   massive offensives of Soviets in, 39-40
   mujahideen in, 242-245
   tactics, weapons, and outside support in, 48-49, 52, 247-250
*Al Nasr* (Victory), 241
*Aldeamentos*, 51
Altamirano, Jos Fransisco Hernandez "Camilo," 274
Alves, Nito, 134, 144
Alvla, Ras, 98
Amador, Carlos Fonseca, 262
Aman Andom, 108, 109
ANC (African National Congress), 136-137
Andrade, Joaquim Pinto de, 134
Andrade, Mario Pinto de, 134
Angola, 8. *See also* UNITA
   broadcast propaganda in, 24
   counterinsurgent militias in, 48
   cuito cuanauvale and, 148-151
   evolution of conflict in, 127-133
   geography of war in, 145-148
   nature of regime in, 133-139
   organization of UNITA in, 139-145
   and peace in Southwest Africa, 154-156
   politics of insurgency in, 151-154

ANS (Armeé Nationale Sihanoukiste), 209, 211, 212, 217, 220, 221, 225
Antitank weapons, 38
Argentine, 277
Arias, Oscar, 59, 60, 84
Arnold, Anthony, 233
ASEAN (Association of Southeast Asian Nations), 201-203, 206, 211, 226, 227
Asmara, 96-97
Athders, Lyster, 280

Bairu, Tedla, 103
Banti, Teferi, 109
Barrios, Pedro Joaquin Chamorro, 24, 269
*Basmachi* campaign, 35, 36
Bengoechea, Roger Miranda, 264
Bermúdez, Enrique, 14, 261, 273, 274, 278, 279
Bernstein, Alvin, 59
Berry, Jack, 169
Black, Wally, 131
Borge Martenez, Tomás, 281, 282
Botha, Rolof, "Pik," 176, 182
Broadcast propaganda, 23-24
Brzezinski, Zbigniew, 80
Buchan, Charlie, 171
Burlison, John, 174
Burt, Peter, 169
Bush administration, 79-80

Caetano, Jacobo, 134
Calero, Aldolfo, 269, 271, 273
Cambodia
   background of, 197-198
   military performance in, 214-221
   legitimacy to resistance in, 233
   origins and evolution of insurgencies in, 198-214

Cambodia (*continued*)
  politics of conflict in, 221–228
Cardoso, Oscar, 168
Careira, Henrique Teles "Iko," 133, 134, 145
Carter, Jimmy, 71
Castao, Bayardo Arce, 263
Castro, Fidel, 36, 154
Casualty rates, 22–23, 32–33
Catholicism, 8
Centeno, Pedro Pablo Ortiz "Commander Suicida," 261, 273
César, Alfredo, 269, 273
CGDK (Coalition Government of Democratic Kampuchea), 198, 204, 205, 207, 209, 211, 214–218, 220, 221, 223–224, 226, 228
Chagas, Alexandra Xavier, 187
Chamkor Kor camp, 217
Chavarria, Encarnacion Baldivia "Tigrillo," 274
Chaviro, Agosta, 178
Chhut, Chea, 208
China. *See* People's Republic of China
Chipenda, Daniel, 135, 145
Chissano, Joaquim, 178, 187, 188
Christina, Orlando, 167–169, 173, 175
Cold War, 55, 58
Collectivization, 51–52
Colombia, 1
Combined-Arms Reinforced Battalions (CARBs), 38
Committee in Support of the People of El Salvador (CISPES), 61
Communism, 4–5
Communist Party of Angola (PCA), 133
Communist regimes
  guerrilla tactics of, 13–14
  performance of, 54–55
Concentration, 50, 51
Coronel, Edgar Chamorro, 270
Corrales, Renán Montero "Andrés Barahona Lopez," 267–268
Counterinsurgency (COIN)
  casualty rates, 22–23, 32–33
  nature of, 17–19, 21
  role of public relations and media in, 53–54
  rural, 50–53
  secret police's role in, 42–43
  Soviet. *See* Soviet counterinsurgency
  special forces of, 45–47
  special operations of, 43–45
  urban, 48–50
Coutinho, Roas, 128

CPSU (Communist Party of the Soviet Union), 251, 252
Crocker, Chester, 70–71, 78, 176, 182, 187
Crocket, George, 72
Cruz, Arturo, 269, 271
Cruz, Luis Carrin, 262
Cuba
  interest in Ethiopia, 114, 116
  involvement in Angola, 136–138, 148–149, 151
  presence in Nicaragua, 267
Cuban Fifth Army, 136
Cuito Cuanavale, 148–151, 153

Da Costa, Manuel Pinto, 136
Da Cruz, Viriato, 134
Da Fonseca, Artur, 178
Da Silva, Ernesto Gomes, 144
Daoul, Mohammed, 235–238
Davidson, Basil, 134
Debayle, Anastasio Somoza, 261
Decolonization, 56
Del, Dien, 208
Dembo, Antonio, 144
Democracy, 63–65
Derg
  activities of, 105, 108–111
  background of, 95–96, 105
  dominance of, 114–115
Dhlakhama, Afonso Maccacho Marcetta, 66, 166, 168, 172–174, 176, 178, 181, 184, 186–188
Diego, Wycliffe, 280, 281
Diplomacy, 25–28
DK (Democratic Kampuchea), 197–198, 200–208, 210, 211, 220
Dlakhama, Afonso, 30
Do Amaral, Antonio Jacinto, 135
Dos Santos, Marcelino, 162, 163
DRA (Democratic Republic of Afghanistan), 238, 239, 244, 245, 247, 250
Dukakis, Michael, 60, 69
Duvalier, Jean-Claude, 63, 72
Dyke, Lionel, 186

East Germany, 139
Egypt, 101–102
EPS (Ejercito Popular Sandinista), 264, 266, 269–270, 278, 279
Eritrea. *See also* Ethiopia
  future of, 117–121
  geography of, 96–97
  historical background of, 97–99, 112
  people of, 101, 119

political background of, 99–101
terrain of, 11
Eritrean insurgency. *See also* EPLF; Ethiopia
  alliance reversals and, 110–111
  background of, 10–11, 28, 95–96, 101–103
  Derg dominance and, 114–115
  deadlock in, 106–107, 115–117
  and defeat on threshold of victory, 112–114
  and Ethiopean revolution, 108–110
  expansion of, 103–106
  ideology of, 12–13
  national consciousness of, 65–66
  use of militia in, 48
Eritrean Liberation Front (ELF), 102, 106
Eritrean Liberation Front – Popular Liberation Forces (ELF–PLF), 113
Eritrean Liberation Front – Revolutionary Council (ELF–RC), 106, 108–113
Eritrean Liberation Movement (ELM), 102
Eritrean People's Liberation Front (EPLF), 113, 114
EPLF (Eritrean Popular Liberation Forces), 11
  formation and activities of, 106–108, 111–117, 120
  ideology of, 12, 13
ERN (Ejercito de la Resistancia Nicaragüense), 269, 274
ERP (Ejercito Revolucionario del Pueblo), 261
Esteira, Joao Carlos, 187
Ethiopia. *See also* Eritrea
  Muslim-Christian conflict in, 102
  relationship with Israel, 101, 102
  revolution and Eritrean insurgency, 108–110
  size of armed forces, 105
Ethiopian Democratic Union (EDU), 110, 111, 115
Ethiopian People's Revolutionary Party (EPRP), 113
Evaristo, Eduardo, 134

Faise, Albino, 178
FAPLA (Popular Armed Forces for the Liberation of Angola), 131–133, 136, 137, 143, 146–150, 152, 153, 155
FDN (Frente Democratico Nicaragüense), 269
Fernandes, Evo, 173, 175, 186, 187
Ferrey, Azucena, 269, 273

FNLA (Frente Nacional de Libertacao de Angola), 127–130, 145, 151
FNLC (National Front for the Liberation of the Congo), 136
Fonseca, Carlos, 263
Frank, Manuel, 178
Freedom, 64
FRELIMO (Frente de Libertacao de Mocambique). *See also* Mozambique; RENAMO
  assessment of, 185–189
  background and nature of, 161–166
  military capacity and tactics of, 179, 181–183
  and origin of RENAMO, 166–178
  rural insurgency and, 50–51
Frias, Leopoldo Cintra, 138
FSLN (Frente Sandinista de Liberacion Nacional), 259–265, 267–271, 276, 279, 283
FUNCINPEC (National Union Front for an Independent, Neutral, Peaceful and Cooperative Cambodia), 209, 213
FUNK (Khmer United National Front), 209

Gailani, Sayed Ahmad, 240
"Gato," Armindo Lucas, 154
Gerard, Eric, 186
Germany, East, 139
Gersony, Robert, 185–186
Gersony Report, 185–186
*Glasnost*, 251
Gómez, Eden Pastora "Commandante Zero," 260–261, 270, 271
Gonzaga, Mario Luis, 178
Gorbachev, Mikhail, 251–253
Graffiti, 24
Great Britain, 98–99
Greek Communist guerrillas, 82, 83
Guerrilla warfare
  Chinese model of, 180–181
  Soviet model of, 180
  in Third World, 3
Guerrillas
  anticommunist, 14–15
  background of, 3–4
  Communist, 13–14
Gutierrez, Sebastian Flores "Florito," 274
Gwambe, Adelino, 161

Haq, Abdul, 21
*Harakat-e-Enqilab-e-Islami* (Islamic Revolutionary Movement – IRM), 239

*Harakat-e Islami* (Islamic Movement—IM), 242
Hekmatyar, Gulbuddin, 241-242
Henze, Paul B., 95
Herdocia, Victor Sanchez "Licenciado," 274
*Hezb-e-Islami* (Islamic Party—IP), 239, 243
*Hezb-e-Islami/Khales* (Islamic Party/Khales—IP/K), 240, 243
*Hizbullah* (God's Party), 242
Hodgson, Jimmy Emery, 281
Humphrey, Hubert, 57

Icaza, Carlos, 271
Ideology, 12-17
Individualism, 64
Infiltration capabilities, 28-29
Insurgencies. *See also* Counterinsurgency
 adaptability and growth of, 19-22
 area of operations, 23
 casualty rates of, 22-23, 32-33
 counter-states, 29-31
 elements of, 7
 guerrilla diplomacy, 25-28
 ideology of, 12-17
 impact of, 31-33
 intelligence and infiltration capabilities, 28-29
 propaganda, 23-25, 53-54
 role reversal and, 17-19
 U.S. view of, 57
Intelligence capabilities, 28-29
International law, 62-63
Isaac, Antonio, 165
Islam
 as motivation in Afghan resistance, 233-234
 role of insurgencies and, 8
 Soviet encounters with, 36
Israel
 activities in Eritrea, 101, 102
 relationship with Ethiopia, 102, 104, 106-107
Italy, 98, 99, 101
Itihad-e Islami Barave Azadi Afghanistan (Islamic Union for the Liberation of Afghanistan—IULA), 240, 243
Itihad-e Islami Mujahideen Afghanistan (Islamic Unity of Afghanistan Mujahideen—IUAM), 240

Jabha-e-Melli Neiat (National Liberation Front—NLF), 239
Jakarta Informal Meeting (JIM), 226-227
*Jamiat-Islami Afghanistan* (Islamic Society—IS), 28, 239, 243
Jardim, Jorge, 167, 168, 171
Jihads, 234, 235
Jirón, Manuel, 24
JPN (Juventud Patriotica Nicaragunse), 263

Kampuchean Communist Party, 200
Kankhombe, Paulo, 162
Karmal, Babrak, 237, 252
Karn, Sak Suthsa, 207-208
Kashaka, Vakulakuta, 144
Kassa, Ras Asrate, 105
Kaunda, Kenneth, 146
KCP, 205-207
KHAD (State Information Service), 44
Khales, Yunes, 241
Khmer Bleu. *See* Khmer Serei
Khmer Issarak, 199
Khmer People's Revolutionary Party (KPRD), 199
Khmer Rose, 212
Khmer Rouge, 12, 13, 65, 197, 198, 200, 211, 212, 219-220, 223-227
Khmer Serei, 199-202
Kikongo, 143
KISAN (United Indigenous Peoples of Eastern Nicaragua), 280
Kissinger, Henry, 110
KNUFNS (Kampuchean United Front for National Salvation), 201
Koornhof, Peter, 187
KPNLF (Khmer People's National Liberation Front), 202-203, 207-210, 212, 217-221, 225, 228
KPRAF (Khmer People's Republic Armed Forces), 201, 218, 225
Kunthon, Hing, 208
Kusumaatmadja, Mokhtar, 213

Lara, Lucio, 133-135, 145
Latin America, 56-57
Ledeen, Michael, 64
Leven, Horacio, 178
Liberated zones, 29-31
"Lima Mike" (Luis Alfonso Moreno Payan), 283
Linder, Benjamin, 273
Linh, Nguyen Van, 222
Lithuania, 35
Lon Nol, 199, 200, 202
Lopez, Andrés Barahona (Renén Montero Corrales), 267-268
Lopez, Victor Tirado, 267

McGovern, George, 58, 59
Machel, Moises Malangatane, 162
Machel, Samora Moises, 66, 162–164, 169, 172–178
MacKenzie, Bob, 169–173, 187
Magaia, Filipe, 162
*Mahaz-e-Melli Islami* (National Islamic Front—NIF), 239
Mahluza, Fanuel, 161
Malaya, 1
Mao Tse-tung, 180, 181
Marcos, Ferdinand, 63, 72
Marques, Joao, 184
Martínez, Tomás Benitez, 138
Marxism
　adaptation of, 4–6
　in Eritrea, 120
Massawa, 96, 98
Massoud, Ahmad Shah, 14, 30, 243–244, 254, 255
Matola, Lourenco, 162
Matsangaisse, Andre Matadi "Commander Andre," 168–169
May, Rick, 169, 171, 172
Mayorga, Francesco, 265
Mayorga, Silvio, 262–263
Mbundus, 143
Means, Russell, 281
Media, 53–54
Membreno, Diogenes Hernandez, 274
Menelik II, King of Shoa, 98, 117
Mengistu Haile Mariam, President of Ethiopia, 111, 114, 120, 121
Mental decolonization camps, 51
Mikulski, Barbara, 57
Militias, 47–48
MISURA, 280
MISURASATA, 280
Mitan, Yusuf, 227
Mmole, Matthew, 161
Mobutu Sesse, Seko, 132
Mohammedi, Mohammed Nabi, 240–241
Moises, Francisco Mota, 178
Mojadeddi, Sibqatullah, 240
Mondale, Walter, 69, 71
Mondlane, Chivambo, 161–162
Moulinaka (*Mouvement de Liberation Nationale du Kampuchea*), 209
Movimento Popular de Libertacao de Angola (MPLA), 127–130, 132–138, 140, 141, 145, 150–156
Mozambique. *See also* FRELIMO; RENAMO
　broadcast propaganda in, 24
　counterinsurgent militias in, 48
　counter-states within, 30
Mugabe, Robert, 172
*Mujahideen*, 242–245. *See also* Afghanistan
Mulatto, Ernesto, 144
Muller, Steadman Fagoth, 280, 281
Murrial, Agostinho, 162–163
Mushlangu, Lucas "Luke," 171, 173

Najibullah Mohammed, 252
Namibia, 131
Natavidade, Macias, 187
Neier, Aryeh, 68
Neto, Agostinho, 133–135
Nicaragua
　broadcast propaganda in, 24
　counterinsurgency coalition in, 266–268
　diplomacy, 27–28
　Indian resistance in, 279–282
　military performance of, 276–279
　militias, 47–48
　nature of insurgency in, 268–273
　organization and structure of insurgency in, 273–276
　origins of insurgency in, 259–262
　in perspective, 282–284
　regime in, 262–266
　Reagan doctrine and, 69–70
　urban COIN in, 50
Nicaraguan Civil War, 260
Nicaraguan insurgents
　goals of, 15–16
　Reagan's view of, 63, 64, 69
Nimeiry, Gaafar, President of Sudan, 104, 105
Nkomati Accords, 176
Nong Chan camp, 217, 219

O Smach camp, 217
ODP (Organizacao do Defencao Popular), 130–131
Oman, 183
O'Neill, Thomas P. "Tip," 60, 284
Operation Red Sea, 40
Operational areas, 23
Organization of African Unity (OAU), 102, 116, 151–153
Ortega, Daniel, 262–263, 265, 267, 281
Ortega, Humberto, 262–263, 265, 267
Osman Salih Sabbe, 103, 106, 112, 113
Ovimbundo, 143, 144

Pakistan, 252, 253
Pamphlets, 24

Panama, 63
*Pasdaran Jihad Islami* (Islamic Jihad Army—IJA), 242
Payan, Luis Alfonso Moreno "Mike Lima," 283
PDPA (People's Democratic Party of Afghanistan), 235–238, 247, 251, 252, 254
Peang, Abdul Gaffaer, 208
People's Republic of China
 involvement in Cambodia, 201, 203, 214, 227
 relationship with Ethiopia, 105, 106
Philippines, 2
Phiri, Jimo, 175
Phnom Chat camp, 217
Pires, Lucinda, 164
*Piricuacos*, 83
Pol Pot, 200–202, 206, 208, 213, 225
Police, secret, 42–43
Political cooperation, 31–32
Political violence, 10
Popular Liberation Forces (PLF), 103, 104
Portocarrero, Anastasio Somoza "El Chiguin," 260, 262
Portuguese Communist Party (PCP), 133
Prey Moin camp, 217
PRK (People's Republic of Kampuchea), 197, 198, 202–204, 211, 212, 216, 219, 221–223, 225, 226. *See also* Cambodia
Proletarian internationalism, 9, 12–13, 45
Propaganda
 nature of Third World, 23–25
 use of, 53–54
PSN (Partido Socialista Nicaragunse), 263
Puna, Miguel N'Zau, 144

Qaddafy, Muammar, 104
Qian Qichen, 224
Quadrillage technique, 49
Quiroz, Rodolfo Ernesto Ampie "Invisible," 274

Rabbani, Sayed Burhanuddin, 241
Rabonia, Forne, 281
Radio Liberación, 279
Radu, Michael, 127, 259
Rannaridh, Norodom, 207, 209–212, 218
Rappaccioli, Fernando Chamorro "El Negro," 270
Rappaccioli, Mario, 276
Reagan, Ronald, 58, 71, 76, 177
Reagan administration

approach to anticommunist insurgencies, 63
 involvement in Nicaragua, 270, 271
 mixed foreign policy statements of, 76–80
Reagan Doctrine
 defining, 74–80
 justification for, 80–81
 nature of, 68–73
Red Terror, 41
Reid-Daly, Ron, 170
RENAMO (Resistencia Nacional Mocambicana), 19. *See also* FRELIMO; Mozambique
 adaptability of, 20
 assessment of, 185–189
 combat tactics of, 180–182
 communications, logistics, and transport of, 179–180
 diplomacy of, 26
 external support of, 182–183
 ideology and program of, 16, 66, 183–185
 infiltration capabilities of, 28–29
 leadership and command structure of, 178–179
 members of, 13–14
 origins and evolutions of, 166–178
 retraining of, 17
Resettlement
 as rural counterinsurgency tactic, 50–53
 Soviet use of, 36–37
Rhodesia, 168–172
Rivera, Brooklyn, 280–281
RN (Nicaraguan Resistance), 270, 272, 273, 279, 282
Robelo, Alfonso, 269, 273
Roberto, Holden, 13, 129, 130, 144, 151
Rocha, Carlos, 133
Romania, 35–36
Rotberg, Robert, 67
RPK (People's Republic of Kampuchea), 197, 201–204, 207, 211
Rural counterintelligence tactics, 50–53

SADF (South African Defense Force), 129–131, 137, 138, 146, 173, 175, 176, 182
Safe havens, 81
Sakharov, Andrey, 233
Sakun, Ok, 227
Salazar, Pablo Emilio "Comandante Bravo," 260, 261
Salinas, Carlos José Guillén "Gustavo," 274

Index    305

SAMI (South African Military Intelligence), 173, 182, 186
Samphan, Khieu, 199, 203-207, 213, 227
Samrin, Heng, 213, 226
Sànchez, Aristides, 271, 273
Sanchez, Arnaldo Ochoa, 138
Sandinistas. *See also* Nicaragua
  aid to, 283
  nature of regime of, 262-266
  policies of, 259-260, 280, 281
  propaganda, 268-269, 272-273
  Reagan's hostility toward, 69
  Western media and, 53-54
Sann, Son, 202-204, 207-209
Sary, Ieng, 205, 225
SAS (Rhodesian Special Air Service), 169-172
Saudi Arabia, 183
Saur revolution, 239
Savimbi, Jonas Malheiro, 13, 14, 16, 67, 127, 128, 130, 132, 141, 142, 146, 147, 151, 155-156
Sayaf, Abdi-Rab Rasoul, 241
Schaaf, Tom, 187
Secret police, 42-43
Selassie, Haile, 98-102, 105, 108, 118
Sen, Hun, 226, 227
Sen, Son, 225
Serapiao, Luis, 178
Shafie, Ghazali, 204
Shevarnadze, Edvard, 153
Shultz, George, 69, 74-75
Shura-e-Enqilab-Ettefaq-e-Islami (Revolutionary Council of Islamic Unity — RCIU), 242
Siad Barre, 107, 111
Sierra de Escambray guerrillas, 36
Siguake, Jaime, 162
Sihanouk, Norodom, 198-200, 202, 204, 207-214, 217, 226
Simango, Urias, 161
Sithole, Daniel, 165-166
Smith, Ian, 168
SNASP, 165
Soares, Felipe, 178
Socialist Republic of Vietnam (SRV), 198, 203. *See also* Vietnam
Soft states, 5
Solarz, Stephen, 15, 72
Somalia, 110, 111, 114
South Africa
  in Angola, 129-133, 137
  in Mozambique, 182-183
South West Africa People's Organization (SWAPO), 131, 133, 137, 145, 146, 154, 155

South Yemen, 254
Soviet counterinsurgency
  record of, 34-37
  special force operations, 45
  style of, 37-40
Soviet Union
  activities in Ethiopia, 96, 104, 107, 114-116, 119-121
  activities in Mozambique, 175-177
  on Cambodia, 227
  Cold War and, 55
  economic basis of policies of, 84
  history of, 34
  Islam and, 36
  presence in Afghanistan, 234-239, 243-255. *See also* Afghanistan
  presence in Angola, 138, 139, 153-154
  technology used by, 37-39
  training style of, 39-40
Special forces, 45-47
Spetsnaz troops, 45, 46, 249
Stingers, 21, 38, 250
Sudan, 110, 111
Sutsakhan, Sak, 221
SWAPO (South West African People's Organization), 131, 133, 137, 145, 146, 154, 155

Ta Mok, 207, 225
Tambo, Oliver, 187
Tambov revolt, 34-35
Taraki, Nur Mohammed, 237
Tatum camp, 219
Teng Hsiao-ping, 223
Terrorism, 2-3, 44
Tewodros, Emperor of Ethiopia, 97
Thailand, 203, 215, 216, 227, 228
Thanh, Song Ngoc, 199, 200
Third Indochina War, 201, 203
Tigre Popular Liberation Front (TPLF), 110, 111, 113, 115
Tigrean insurgents, 28
Tomassevich, Raúl Menéndez, 36
Turcios, Oscar, 262-263

Ukranian People's Army (UPA), 35
Ululu, Vincente, 178
UNITA (Uniao Nacional para ao Independencia Total de Angola), 8, 17. *See also* Angola
  adaptability of, 19-20
  coalition against, 136-139
  cuito cuanavale and, 148-151
  diplomacy of, 26-27

UNITA (*continued*)
  establishment and conflict within, 127–133
  future of, 154–156
  ideology of, 14
  organization of, 139–145
  politics of insurgency and, 151–154
  strategy of, 145–148
  weapons used by, 21
U.S.S.R. *See* Soviet Union
United States
  foreign policy approach of, 58–60, 62
  involvement in Cambodia, 203, 227–228
  policy regarding Afghanistan, 248
  policy regarding Mozambique, 187–189
  policies toward insurgencies, 61
  relationship with Ethiopia, 104
  role in Eritrea, 100, 101
  role in Nicaragua, 259, 268, 270–272, 274–275, 281–284
University campus organizations, 61
Urban counterinsurgency tactics, 48–50

van der Kroef, Justus M., 197
van Dunem, Jos, 134
van Niekerk, Charles, 173
Vanegas, Uriel, 281
Varela, Enrique Bermúdez, 269
Venter, Al, 128
Vietnam, 199, 200, 201, 205, 210, 214–215, 217–227. *See also* Socialist Republic of Vietnam

Villegas, Harry, 138
Voice of Democratic Kampuchea (VDDK), 206
Voz da Africa Livre (Voice of Free Africa), 168, 172, 173

Weapons
  antitank, 38
  Soviet-bloc made, 37
  understanding of, 21–22
  used in Afghanistan, 247–249
  used in Cambodia, 221
  used in Mozambique, 181–182
  used by UNITA, 139–140
Westhuizen, Pieter van der, 173, 176
Wheeler, Jack, 161
Wolde-Ab Wolde-Mariam, 101, 102, 106, 112
Wolpe, Harold, 72
Wright, Jim, 60–61, 70–72, 84, 282

YATAMA (United Nations of the Sacred Homeland), 280
Young, Andrew, 71

ZANLA guerrillas, 168, 169
Zedong, Mao, 14, 19
Zelaya, José Santos, 282
Zelaya, Lorenzo, 268
Zia, Muhammad, 81
Zimbabwe, 172. *See also* Rhodesia
ZIPRA guerrillas, 168, 169